Educational Dialogues

Educational Dialogues provides a clear, accessible and well-illustrated case for the importance of dialogue and its significance in learning and teaching. The contributors characterize the nature of productive dialogues, to specify the conditions and pedagogic contexts within which such dialogues can most effectively be resourced and promoted. Drawing upon a broad range of theoretical perspectives, this collection examines:

- Theoretical frameworks for understanding teaching and learning dialogues;
- Teacher–student and student–student interaction in the curricular contexts of mathematics, literacy, science, ICT and philosophy;
- The social contexts supporting productive dialogues;
- Implications for pedagogic design and classroom practice.

Bringing together contributions from a wide range of internationally renowned researchers, this book will form essential reading for all those concerned with the use of dialogue in educational contexts.

Karen Littleton is Professor of Psychology in Education at the University of Jyväskylä, Finland.

Christine Howe is Professor of Education at the University of Cambridge, UK.

Educational Dialogues

Understanding and promoting productive interaction

Edited by Karen Littleton
and Christine Howe

Routledge
Taylor & Francis Group

LONDON AND NEW YORK

First published 2010
by Routledge
2 Park Square, Milton Park, Abingdon, Oxon OX14 4RN

Simultaneously published in the USA and Canada
by Routledge
270 Madison Avenue, New York, NY 10016

Routledge is an imprint of the Taylor & Francis Group, an informa business

Typeset in Galliard by
Pindar NZ, Auckland, New Zealand
Printed and bound in Great Britain by
CPI Antony Rowe, Chippenham, Wiltshire

British Library Cataloguing in Publication Data
A catalogue record for this book is available from the British Library

Library of Congress Cataloging in Publication Data
Educational dialogues: understanding and promoting productive
interaction / edited by Karen Littleton and Christine Howe.
    p. cm.
  1. Interaction analysis in education. 2. Communication in
education. I. Littleton, Karen. II. Howe, Christine.
  LB1034.E355 2010
  371.102'2—dc22   2009023876

ISBN10: 0–415–46215–0 (hbk)
ISBN10: 0–415–46216–9 (pbk)
ISBN10: 0–203–86351–8 (ebk)

ISBN13: 978–0–415–46215–0 (hbk)
ISBN13: 978–0–415–46216–7 (pbk)
ISBN13: 978–0–203–86351–0 (ebk)

Contents

Illustrations

Figures

Tables

Contributors

Mikaela Åberg, University of Gothenburg, Sweden.

Jaume Ametller, University of Leeds, UK.

Aleksandar Baucal, University of Belgrade, Serbia.

Christine Chin, National Institute of Education, Singapore.

Jennifer Colwell, University of Brighton, UK.

Barbara Delafield, Leeds Metropolitan University, UK.

Jonathan Emberton, Calder High School, Mytholmroyd, UK.

Kenneth J. Goldman, Washington University in St. Louis, USA.

Margaret Hardman, Leeds Metropolitan University, UK.

Roxy Harris, King's College London, UK.

Rina Hershkowitz, The Weizmann Institute, Israel.

Flora Hernández, National Autonomous University of Mexico, Mexico.

Christine Howe, University of Cambridge, UK.

Kristiina Kumpulainen, University of Helsinki, Finland.

Peter Kutnick, King's College London, UK.

Adam Lefstein, Institute of Education, UK.

Patrick J. Leman, Royal Holloway, University of London, UK.

Lasse Lipponen, University of Helsinki, Finland.

Karen Littleton, University of Jyväskylä, Finland.

Åsa Mäkitalo, University of Gothenburg, Sweden.

Neil Mercer, University of Cambridge, UK.

Eduardo Mortimer, Universidade Federal de Minas Gerais, Brazil.

Jonathan Osborne, Stanford University, USA.

Anne-Nelly Perret-Clermont, University of Neuchâtel, Switzerland.

Naomi Prusak, The Hebrew University, Israel.

Ben Rampton, King's College London, UK.

Sylvia Rojas-Drummond, National Autonomous University of Mexico, Mexico.

Roger Säljö, University of Gothenburg, Sweden.

R. Keith Sawyer, Washington University in St. Louis, USA.

Baruch B. Schwarz, The Hebrew University, Israel.

Phil Scott, University of Leeds, UK.

Valérie Tartas, University of Toulouse, France.

Rupert Wegerif, University of Exeter, UK.

Mariana Zúñiga, National Autonomous University of Mexico, Mexico.

Acknowledgements

This book is based, in part, upon the presentations and discussions that comprised the 'Dialogue and Development' seminar series, funded by an Economic and Social Research Council award to Philip Adey and Rupert Wegerif (RES-451-26-0190). We particularly wish to thank Philip for all his work in respect of the seminar series.

We also wish to thank Bruce Roberts, Sophie Thomson and the team at Routledge for their professional support, and encouragement, during the production process.

Introduction

Dictionary definitions of 'dialogue' typically equate the term with 'conversation', stating for instance that dialogue is 'a conversation between two or more people' (Oxford University Press 2002). Treated as synonymous with conversation, dialogue becomes a highly inclusive concept, encompassing all exchanges (and series of exchanges) where one individual addresses another individual and the second individual replies (Howe 1981). Perhaps the concept is too inclusive, for cutting across the dictionary approach is an alternative, more restrictive perspective upon dialogue. This perspective is a central theme within the writings of the Russian literary analyst Mikhail Bakhtin, for Bakhtin was not thinking of a concept that includes gossip and informal chat when he wrote of the dialogue that appears in novels:

> The importance of struggling with another's discourse, its influence in the history of an individual's coming to ideological consciousness, is enormous. One's own discourse and one's own voice, although born of another or dynamically stimulated by another, will sooner or later liberate themselves from the authority of the other's discourse.
>
> (Bakhtin 1981: 348)

We do not plan to rehearse or weigh up the relative merits of inclusive and exclusive definitions of dialogue. As will become clear, the contributors to this volume take a variety of stances on the issue (and also over what constitutes productive dialogue), and we see little merit in prioritizing one approach over others. For us, the importance of the variability is that it highlights the concerns that have been expressed in respect of the productivity of *educational* dialogues, specifically the nature and quality of classroom talk, for about 40 years. Therefore, it allows us to introduce some of the book's central themes. Talk is obviously a pervasive feature of schooling. Indeed, few scholars would query Flanders' (1970) conclusion that, within classrooms, about two-thirds of the time someone is talking. However, there is widespread suspicion that most classroom talk is non-conversational, that is it does not even comply with the broad, dictionary definition of dialogue. At the same time, many people suspect that when conversation does occur in classrooms, it is relatively superficial and circumspect. In other words, it does not comply either with a deeper, more exclusive conception of dialogue. Whether this conception coincides with Bakhtin's is an open question, although as will become clear as the book proceeds, many scholars see parallels. In any event, concerns about classroom talk have led to research which attempts to understand and chart what actually takes place. As the results of this research provide a useful backcloth to the chapters that follow, we shall begin with a short summary.

Observational studies of classroom talk

The stereotypic image of classroom activity is one where a teacher works with the whole class in a one-to-many relation. However, this is clearly not the only way in which teaching proceeds. Students can be divided into smaller subgroups, with the teacher moving around to work with each group in turn. Small groups can indeed be asked to work collaboratively on a task without direct involvement from the teacher. Moreover, for much of the school day, students work on their own, completing exercises that the teacher has designed. There are cultural differences in preferences for each of these modes of organization. For instance, Alexander (2001) found that small group activity is relatively frequent in England and the United States, rare but detectable in France, and virtually unknown in India and Russia. Osborn, Broadfoot, McNess, Raven, Planel and Triggs (2003) find similar differences between England and France to those that Alexander reports, while suggesting that small group activity is even more frequent in Denmark than it is England.

Within cultures, there is variation in mode of organization as a function of teacher preferences: observations made by Galton and colleagues in English classrooms (Galton, Hargreaves, Comber, Wall and Pell 1999; Galton, Simon and Croll 1980) have led to the identification of 'class enquirers' and 'group instructors', teachers who respectively concentrate activity at the classroom level and make significant use of small groups. Moreover, school subject makes a difference. Research reported by Baines, Blatchford and Kutnick (2003) and covering 378 primary and secondary schools located in many parts of England, indicates that while 28 per cent of primary classes use small groups for science, only 5 per cent do this for mathematics. The equivalent figures at the secondary level were 52 per cent for science and 14 per cent for mathematics. ICT was not specifically targeted in Baines *et al.*'s research, but earlier work suggests that small groups are common in that context too. For instance, surveys by Jackson, Fletcher and Messer (1986) covering 110 English primary schools, and McAteer and Demissie (1991) covering 111 Scottish secondary schools established that between 80 per cent and 97 per cent of ICT usage involves pupils working in small groups. ICT and science both rely on equipment, which is relatively expensive for schools to provide. It seems likely therefore that the heavy use of groups in these contexts is resource driven: most schools simply cannot provide the requisite facilities on a one-to-one basis.

Teacher-led whole-class interaction

As regards the talk that occurs in whatever organizational structures are used, the focus of research has been teacher-led whole-class interaction. This is scarcely surprising, given that this is the one structure that appears to be universal across cultures, teachers and school subjects. Based on observations that they made in English classrooms, Sinclair and Coulthard (1975) indicate that whole-class interaction characteristically follows a three-turn 'initiation-response-feedback' (or IRF) sequence exemplified below. Pupils typically provide responses (R), and teachers offer feedback (F) as well as initiating, usually through the use of questions (I):

TEACHER: So what is the nearest planet to the sun? (I)
PUPIL: Is it Mercury miss? (R)
TEACHER: That's right, very good, Mercury, remember we talked about this yesterday.
    (F)

Subsequent research has sometimes referred to initiation-response-*evaluation* (or IRE) sequences rather than IRF. However, as Cazden (2001) points out, feedback is a broader concept than evaluation, since it includes confirming that knowledge is shared as well as appraising its quality. Therefore, IRF may be preferable. Whatever term is used, there can be little doubt about the pervasiveness of the underlying sequence. Commenting on Sinclair and Coulthard's work in relation to classroom talk recorded at least ten years later, Edwards and Mercer (1987) assert that the IRF sequence is 'once seen, impossible to ignore in any observed classroom talk' (p. 9).

Nowadays, the IRF sequence (with teachers initiating and providing feedback, and pupils responding) is regarded as such a well-established feature of classroom interaction that few researchers examine it specifically. Nevertheless, high frequency of occurrence remains apparent. For instance, IRF sequences are so ubiquitous and embedded in classroom practice in the United States that Cazden (2001) felt comfortable about referring to them as 'traditional' structures. She cites the large-scale investigation of Nystrand and colleagues (e.g. Nystrand, Wu, Gamorgan, Zeiser and Long 2003) as one of several sources of evidence. Alexander (2001) documents IRF sequences during whole-class interactions observed in all five of the countries that he worked in (England, France, India, Russia, and the United States). An article by Pontefract and Hardman (2005) reviews studies of classroom interaction conducted throughout Africa, and also reports observations of 27 teachers working with 5- to 13-year-olds. IRF sequences proved the norm across mathematics, science and English. Finally, a contemporary perspective on IRF interaction has followed from the mass introduction of interactive whiteboards (IWB) into British schools (by 2005, available in 94 per cent of primary schools across England and Wales, with 84 per cent of primary school teachers claiming to use an IWB in at least half of their lessons (Becta 2008)). For instance, Mercer (2007, but see also Gillen, Kleine Staarman, Littleton, Mercer and Twiner 2007) describes the use that four teachers made of the technology while working with 7- to 11-year-olds. He includes associated patterns of social interaction. Despite the potential for revisiting and restructuring that interactive whiteboards afford, the essentially linear IRF style was predominant in the talk that actually occurred.

IRF sequences fit the broad dictionary definition of dialogue with which we started. In other words, one person addresses a remark and an addressee replies. Nevertheless, as characteristically used, the sequences are often thought to result in dialogue of a rather limited kind. This is mainly because of a tendency on the part of teachers to use closed initiatives (e.g. Alexander 2004, 2008; Galton *et al.* 1999; Mercer and Littleton 2007), that is initiatives (typically questions) that permit a single answer, such as 'What is the French for dog?', 'When did Queen Victoria come to the throne?' and 'What was the main industry in Lancashire at the time of the Industrial Revolution?' Closed initiatives do not necessarily constrain contributions to a single student. The whole class could respond in chorus, and choral responses are actually a well-documented feature of contemporary classrooms (e.g. Alexander 2001; Pontefract and Hardman 2005). However, closed initiatives do not facilitate a range of contributions from students, nor do they support the gradual development of an integrated 'story'. Valuable opportunities for productive dialogue therefore can be squandered, for as Hardman (2008, p. 133) has suggested, 'the "recitation script" of closed teacher questions, brief student answers and minimal feedback ... requires students to report someone else's thinking rather than think for themselves, and to be evaluated on their compliance for doing so'. Given, then, that much of the talk teachers invite from pupils is 'presentational', being proffered for display and teacher evaluation, there is a danger of passivity on the part of students (Barnes 2008). Notwithstanding that when it is well managed, the question and answer routine of the IRF can enable a teacher to lead a class through a complex sequence of ideas (Barnes 2008) and can result in developed discussion (Cazden 2001; Alexander 2004), the characteristically restricted usage is one of the main reasons why the prevalence of IRF sequences has occasioned concern.

Recognizing the reservations being raised in relation to teacher-led whole-class interaction, what then of the nature and quality of the talk that occurs during classroom-based small group activities? Do pupils, for example, engage in open, extended discussion and argumentation when they are working with their peers outside the visible control of their teacher?

Small group work

Although less extensively observed than whole-class settings, small group activity has attracted some research attention. The classic investigations are the studies of Galton and colleagues that were referred to above (i.e. Galton *et al.* 1980, 1999). Consistent across the studies was the finding that, just because several children were sitting together at a table (as was common) this did not mean that they were collaborating or working and talking effectively together. Pupils rarely talk to each other when supposedly collaborating. Typically they work in parallel on individual tasks and when they do talk, their conversation is likely to be about non-school topics, for instance gossiping about out-of-school events. In fact, talk during small group activity was nearly three times as likely to be off-task as on-task in the 1980 study. The results from the 1999 study were somewhat more positive, but even there off-task talk was at least as frequent as on-task. Similar findings have been reported in Alexander (2001), Bennett, Desforges, Cockburn and Wilkinson (1984), Boydell (1975) and Galton and Patrick (1990), with Alexander's research of particular interest because, as noted above, it covers several countries. A compelling specific example of the problem emerged in the Spoken Language and New Technology (SLANT) project – see Wegerif and Scrimshaw 1997). The project focused on children working with computers, an important context when, as noted above, a relatively high proportion of classroom activity around computers involves small groups. Detailed analysis of group interaction suggested that the activity was not typically task-focused, productive or equitable. In some groups one child so completely dominated the discussion that the other group members either withdrew from the activity, becoming increasingly quiet and subdued, or else they participated marginally, e.g. as passive scribes of the dominant child's ideas. In other groups, the children seemed to ignore each other altogether, taking turns at the computer, each pursuing their own ideas when 'their turn' came round. Many groups' talk involved them in unproductive, often highly competitive disagreements characterized by disputation and interpersonal conflict. Talk of any educational value was seldom heard.

From the material we have reviewed thus far, be it focused on the nature and quality of educational dialogues in the context of teacher-led whole-class interaction or students' small group work, there appears to be significant grounds for concern. There is certainly a lot of talk going on in classrooms, but seemingly to little effect. There also seems to be a yawning gap between classroom realities and theories of development and learning that underscore the significance and consequence of social interaction.

In brief, scholars have gained from Piaget and Vygotsky (and the researchers who have subsequently extended their work) an affirmation of the importance and value of social interaction for learning and development, be this interaction between learners of similar levels of understanding or people in the position of learner and guide (see Mercer and Littleton 2007). From a Piagetian perspective, the germs of intellectual progress are to be found in the socially motivated resolution of conflicting perspectives arising through discussion between peers (e.g. Piaget 1932). In contrast, it is the *guided* construction of knowledge that is underscored in Vygotskian (e.g. Vygotsky 1978) and neo-Vygotskian accounts. The apparent 'gap' between what theory construes as being of significance, and the apparently bleak picture emerging from actual classroom practice, gives pause for thought. This is because it exposes the limitations of this theorizing when applied to educational contexts.

Consider for example the work of Vygotsky. While his seminal ideas have informed, and continue to inform educational research, there is a significant disjunction between his account of guidance in the Zone of Proximal Development and the kinds of teaching-learning encounter that are feasible in classroom settings (an issue we consider further in the Introduction to Part 1). Moreover, language is written about in very general terms – as a single homogeneous tool or mediating artefact. It is our contention that it is now necessary to move beyond a conception of language as a unitary tool. What is needed are research-based accounts of educational dialogues, and productive interaction, that are sensitive to the variety of forms and functions of language as used in pursuit of teaching and learning in classroom settings. Plurality and complexity are ignored at our peril. If we are to be able to conceptualize, resource and promote productive educational dialogues, then we need a secure research evidence-base from which to develop practical theories of educational dialogues rooted in classroom realities. This book is intended to make a substantive contribution to the development of this evidence-base – with each of the 16 chapters in the book representing a distinctive input.

The structure of the book

The book is organized into four thematic sections, each prefaced by an editorial introduction that orients the reader to the key concerns of specific chapters and identifies cross-cutting themes. The chapters in Part 1 begin the volume's exploration of what constitutes 'productive dialogue'. While there is variability, the authors' accounts clearly cohere around the idea that productive dialogues are those in which students actively construct understanding from the possibilities presented in dialogue – options are not foreclosed. The need for sensitivity to plurality is continually underscored – an issue that assumes prominence in Part 2. In Part 2 the emphasis is on understanding the forms of dialogue that support classroom learning in the specific curricular contexts of science, mathematics, literacy and philosophy. The significance of, for example, argumentation, exploratory talk, co-constructive talk and dialogic teaching are all explored. Whist recognizing the need for situated accounts of educational dialogue, it becomes evident that for these authors productive educational dialogues offer opportunities for engagement with dialogic perspectives such that learners do not simply talk about, for example, science – rather they *do* science through the medium of language.

Part 3 addresses the important issue of socially-mediated variability in educational dialogues, considering, for example, how social goals and social identity impact participation patterns. These contributions raise significant challenges for those interested in fostering and promoting productive educational dialogues. The issue of how to promote productive educational dialogue is the concern of the authors in Part 4. As we have seen, the normative environment for talk in most classrooms is incompatible with students' active and extended engagement in using language to construct knowledge and understanding. Orienting to this, the contributors to this section ask how efficacious forms of dialogue can be learned and resourced such that talk in educational settings becomes a valuable opportunity for learning.

This is a book about multiplicity, plurality and complexity and it is an instantiation of its own thesis concerning the significance and value of dialogue. The scholars who have contributed to this book are engaged in a dynamic process of interthinking and are participating in an ongoing process of dialogue across difference to both advance understandings of educational dialogues and support theoretically informed ways of promoting productive interaction. And now the dialogue continues …

References

Alexander, R. (2001) *Culture and Pedagogy: international comparisons in primary education*, Oxford: Blackwell.

Alexander, R. (2004) *Towards Dialogic Teaching: rethinking classroom talk*, Cambridge: Dialogos.

Alexander, R. (2008) 'Culture dialogue and learning, notes on an emerging pedagogy', in N. Mercer and S. Hodgkinson (eds) *Exploring Talk in School*, London: Sage.

Baines, E., Blatchford, P. and Kutnick, P. (2003) 'Changes in grouping practices over primary and secondary school', *International Journal of Educational Research*, 39:9–34.

Bakhtin, M. (1981) 'Discourse in the novel', in M. M. Bakhtin *The Dialogic Imagination: four essays by M. M. Bakhtin*, Austin, TX: University of Texas Press.

Barnes, D. (2008) 'Exploratory talk for learning', in N. Mercer and S. Hodgkinson (eds) *Exploring Talk in School*, London: Sage.

Bennett, S. N., Desforges, C.W., Cockburn, A. and Wilkinson, B. (1984) *The Quality of Pupil Learning*, Hove, East Sussex: Lawrence Erlbaum.

Boydell, D. (1975) 'Pupil behaviour in junior classrooms', *British Journal of Educational*

Psychology, 45:122–9.

British Educational Communications and Technology Agency (Becta) (2008) *Harnessing Technology Review 2008: the role of technology and its impact on education. Full Report*, Coventry: Becta.

Cazden, C. (2001) *Classroom Discourse: the language of teaching and learning*, Portsmouth, NH: Heinemann.

Edwards, D. and Mercer, N. (1987) *Common Knowledge: the development of understanding in the classroom*, London: Methuen/Routledge.

Flanders, N. A. (1970) *Analyzing Teacher Behavior*, Reading, MA; Addison-Wesley.

Galton, M. and Patrick, H. (1990). *Curriculum Provision in Small Primary Schools*, London: Routledge.

Galton, M., Hargreaves, L., Comber, C., Wall, D. and Pell, A. (1999) *Inside the Primary Classroom: 20 years on*, London: Routledge.

Galton, M., Simon, B. and Croll, P. (1980) *Inside the Primary Classroom (the ORACLE Project)*, London: Routledge and Kegan Paul.

Gillen, J., Kleine Staarman, J., Littleton, K., Mercer, N. and Twiner, A. (2007) 'A "learning revolution"? Investigating pedagogic practice around interactive whiteboards in British primary classrooms', *Learning, Media and Technology*, 32:243–56.

Hardman, F. (2008) 'Teachers use of feedback in whole class and group-based talk', in N. Mercer and S. Hodgkinson (eds) *Exploring Talk in School*, London: Sage.

Howe, C. J. (1981) *Acquiring Language in a Conversational Context*, London: Academic Press.

Jackson, A., Fletcher, B. C. and Messer, D. J. (1986) 'A survey of microcomputer use and provision in primary schools', *Journal of Computer Assisted Learning*, 2:45–55.

McAteer, E., Anderson, T., Orr, M., Demissie, A. and Woherem, E. (1991) 'Computer-assisted learning and groupwork: the design of an evaluation', *Computers and Education*, 17:41–7.

Mercer, N. (2007) *Interactive Whiteboards as Pedagogic Tools in Primary Schools. Full Research Report*. ESRC End of Award Report RES-000-22-1269. Swindon: ESRC.

Mercer, N. and Littleton, K. (2007) *Dialogue and the Development of Children's Thinking: a sociocultural approach*, London: Routledge.

Nystrand, M., Wu, L., Gamorgan, A., Zeiser, S. and Long, D. (2003) 'Questions in time: investigating the structure and dynamics of unfolding classroom discourse', *Discourse Processes*, 35:135–98.

Osborn, M., Broadfoot, P., McNess, E., Raven, R., Planel, C. and Triggs, P. with Cousin, O. and Winther-Jensen, T. (2003) *A World of Difference? Comparing learners across Europe*, Open University Press: McGraw-Hill Education.

Oxford University Press. *Shorter Oxford English Dictionary*, Oxford: Oxford University Press, 5th edition, 2002.

Piaget, J. (1932) *The Moral Judgement of the Child*, London: Routledge.

Pontefract, C. and Hardman, F. (2005) 'Classroom discourse in Kenyan primary schools', *Comparative Education*, 2:87–106.

Sinclair, J. and Coulthard, M. (1975) *Towards an Analysis of Discourse: the English used by teachers and pupils*, Oxford: Oxford University Press.

Vygotsky, L. S. (1978) *Mind in Society: the development of higher psychological processes*, Cambridge, MA: Harvard University Press.

Wegerif, R. and Scrimshaw, P. (eds) (1997) *Computers and Talk in the Primary Classroom*, Clevedon: Multilingual Matters.

Wells, G. (1999) *Dialogic Enquiry: toward a sociocultural practice and theory of education*, Cambridge: Cambridge University Press.

Part I

Productive dialogue

Introduction

The introductory chapter discussed the concept of dialogue and sketched the reasons for the strong (and growing) interest in the concept within educational circles. The chapter also summarized some of the numerous observational studies that have been published over the past 40 years, which describe the form that educational dialogue usually takes. As the studies were reviewed, it became apparent that many authors are uncomfortable with what they observed in classrooms, sensing that educational dialogue is typically less effective than it ought to be. When one study indicates that about 75 per cent of the discussion is usually off-task during group work amongst pupils (Galton *et al.* 1980) it is not difficult to share this pessimism. Nevertheless, recognizing that something is wrong is a far cry from knowing how to remedy it, and it is only recently that research has reached the point of providing the necessary guidance. The present section comprises four cutting-edge examples from this research.

One reason for the relatively slow progress is the all-pervading influence of Vygotsky, for while Vygotsky is undoubtedly the giant upon whose shoulders all later researchers stand, his theorizing is both utopian when applied to educational contexts and also somewhat vague. This is scarcely surprising when the theorizing took place nearly a century ago, and occurred during the Russian revolution, when aspirations for far-reaching change were extremely high. Of particular significance here is Vygotsky's (e.g. 1978) insistence that adults (or more knowledgeable peers) guide children in the creation of social products that surpass what they are capable of individually, and that they subsequently 'internalize'. The utopianism within such claims relates to the guided creation of superior products, for contemporary research suggests that achieving this often depends upon finely tuned adjustments that are challenging for mothers and teachers in one-to-one interaction with children (see, e.g. Wood 1986). They are virtually inconceivable in the one-to-many contexts that typify classrooms. One instance of Vygotsky's vagueness concerns his failure to indicate whether there are alternative forms of guidance, which, while remaining helpful, are feasible in classrooms. A further instance of vagueness (recognized by Vygotsky himself – see Bereiter 1985) relates to the concept of internalization. Is individual knowledge envisaged as a copy of preceding social products, in which case the learning process must be primarily imitative? However, if individual knowledge is indeed a copy, how can it be transferred to new contexts? The purpose of formal education is not, after all, to teach students to solve specific problems, but to extrapolate principles that can be applied in a range of situations.

What is needed, then, are practical theories of educational dialogue, which take classroom realities as their starting place and focus not just on problem solving within the here-and-now but also upon transferable knowledge. It is here that the four chapters, which comprise the present section, make a contribution, for all four are sensitive to the demands of authentic educational settings and associated curriculum goals. The chapters report research conducted in four countries, with contrasting educational traditions. Theoretical assumptions differ across the chapters, as do research designs. In some cases, the research is exclusively qualitative; in other cases, it mixes qualitative and quantitative methods. Sometimes, learning outcomes are formally assessed, for instance through comparing performance on pre-tests prior to some form of intervention with performance on post-tests once the intervention is complete; in other cases, there is no formal assessment, and perhaps even a theory-driven rejection of what assessment implies. Nevertheless, despite the differences, all chapters recognize that transferable knowledge depends upon students actively constructing understanding from the possibilities presented in dialogue. Thus, productive dialogue does not foreclose options, but structures these in a fashion that permits optimum co-ordination by the students themselves. At the same time, the chapters also indicate variability in the mechanisms through which students achieve co-ordination, and practitioners need to be sensitive to this in the strategies that they use to promote productive dialogue.

The dialogic options pinpointed in Chapter 1 from Mikaela Åberg, Åsa Mäkitalo and Roger Säljö are those that arise during classroom project work, the key point being that anticipated future use in dialogue exerts a powerful influence upon how present material is prioritized. The chapter focuses upon the dialogue that was observed while 15- to 16-year-old students worked on a project relating to 'resources and industries'. Within the first phase of the project, the students, operating in pairs, researched the issue from the perspective of specific countries, e.g. Bangladesh, Russia, Sweden, with each pair taking a different country. Subsequently, the students represented their country during a debate with representatives of the other countries. The students' own (largely 'environmentalist') values influenced how they interpreted the material that they unearthed during the research phase, but of equal importance was the rhetorical demands of the anticipated debate. Because debate is itself dialogic, the implication is that by adolescence students have framed their experiences along communicative lines, perhaps differentiating amongst parent-child, friend-friend, teacher-pupil, examiner-candidate, and doctor-patient (and many more). Such framing is reminiscent of the classic cognitive psychological notion of 'scripts' (Schank and Abelson 1977), although it is not clear whether Åberg and colleagues would find this association helpful. Whatever the case, the researchers are subtly re-defining the concept of knowledge transfer, by indicating that the anticipated activity organized as a high-stake event in the form of a public debate structures the learning of students. Thus, the students organize their learning in anticipation of a particular situation, but they also have to respond to the arguments and claims made by others in a flexible manner. In the particular communicative genre of a debate one is held accountable both for what one knows and for how one can respond *in situ* to the contributions of others. In this sense, a debate is a specific rhetorical genre in which knowledge is presented but also challenged. This may be what Åberg and colleagues are referring to when, in their chapter's concluding paragraph, they claim to have provided 'a glimpse of a complex and extended socialization process in which the students are familiarized with how to craft descriptions and arguments in a world characterized by a multitude of potentially relevant sources of knowledge' and how they learn to defend them in the particular genre of communication which is a debate. The point certainly needs to be borne in mind when developing strategies for shaping classroom dialogue.

Åberg, Mäkitalo and Säljö's research is with relatively senior students, whose dialogic scripts and ability to look ahead will be relatively well developed. At younger ages, understanding of scripts will be in embryonic form, and awareness of future use may be relatively limited. In Chapter 2, Christine Howe outlines research relating to dialogue and learning during middle childhood. Some of the conclusions that she draws seem attributable to limitations in the capacities that Åberg and colleagues justifiably take for granted at older age levels. Howe's interest is in small group activity, where students work together without direct supervision from teachers, and her chapter starts by considering studies that demonstrate the value of opinion exchange during such activity. In other words, there is copious evidence from studies of group work to confirm the emphasis placed above upon students constructing understanding from possibilities expressed in dialogue. Drawing upon her own research conducted in Scotland with 8- to 12-year-olds working on science tasks, Howe then shows that differences of opinion at this age level are seldom resolved at the time they are expressed. Rather, differences trigger a protracted period of (essentially private) post-group activity, dependent upon dialogue during group work but perhaps also upon subsequent events. This suggests internalization of social products in a rather different sense than the one envisaged by Vygotsky, and signals a relation that is the reverse of the one indicated by Åberg, Mäkitalo and Säljö. For Åberg and colleagues, future events shape present use of dialogue; for Howe, present dialogue shapes the use of future events. More precisely, for Howe, present dialogue shapes future usage in middle childhood. In the second half of her chapter, Howe summarizes research that suggests developmental changes in the processes through which students learn from dialogue. Importantly, she sees these changes as part and parcel of growing ability to co-ordinate information within and across tasks.

Amongst many other things, Chapter 3 from Kristiina Kumpulainen and Lasse Lipponen provides what may be the missing link between its two predecessors, insights into how classroom dialogue can support relatively young children in making connections across place and time. The chapter's empirical focus is recordings made in a Finnish classroom, where 9- to 10-year-old students worked with their teacher to build upon information obtained during out-of-school visits (to a forest, science centre and technology museum). Kumpulainen and Lipponen show how the classroom teacher skilfully scaffolds connections between lesson content and experiences in other contexts, allowing the students to achieve what is termed 'situated agency', i.e. the ability to act authoritatively and accountably in one situation and to extend knowledge and skills to further settings. One of Kumpulainen and Lipponen's main points is that such connectedness was only possible because the classroom ethos was that of a community of dialogically based enquiry. In other words, it cannot be achieved 'out of the blue', but rather depends on traditions that value talk, and specifically the exchange of views. It seems likely that many students in Kumpulainen and Lipponen's classroom progressed via processes that are very different from the ones outlined for the equivalent age group in Howe's chapter. Nevertheless, it is not necessarily the case that all students did this.

Kumpulainen and Lipponen describe one student who flatly refused to accept the lesson 'message' that money can be made from wool, and another who was adamant that he had learned nothing from a trip to the forest. It would be interesting to revisit such students a few weeks after the relevant lesson to see whether their positions had changed. Following from Howe's work, the discussions held during the lesson might have stimulated subsequent post-lesson processing, and the outcome might have been delayed learning gain.

As signalled already, one message for practitioners from the chapters reviewed so far is the need to be sensitive to multiple learning processes. The processes that students employ probably vary within and across age groups. Such variation (and the need for sensitivity within teaching situations) is underlined in the section's concluding contribution, Chapter 4 from Valérie Tartas, Aleksandar Baucal, and Anne-Nelly Perret-Clermont. Drawing upon a range of theoretical perspectives, Tartas, Baucal and Perret-Clermont summarize studies, conducted in Switzerland, where children were first trained to solve problems in one-to-one sessions with adults, and subsequently worked with fellow students to solve the same problems. They focus on one study in particular, which used a Kohs Cubes task as the problem to be solved. In this study, the adults followed a training strategy of encouraging the children to complete the task themselves, only offering guidance when this was requested or otherwise clearly needed. In other words, the children's agency was respected. Tartas, Baucal and Perret-Clermont found that the strategy was generally successful. The children learned from the training, typically demonstrating performances on subsequent post-tests that exceeded those demonstrated by control children. Moreover, skills acquired during training proved transferable: the outcomes of interaction between trained children and peers were generally positive. Nevertheless, two case studies discussed in the second half of the chapter illustrate differences in the depth of understanding that the trained children achieved. Some children merely appropriated the adults' discourse practices. Other children appropriated discourse practices but also understood their meaning. The latter children usually demonstrated the greatest level of progress on the subsequent post-tests, but interestingly they did not necessarily make the most effective partners when working with peers. This aside, the key point is the variability across children in how they responded to adult instruction; for, as with all of the other chapters, the need for sensitivity to plurality is amply demonstrated.

References

Bereiter, C. (1985) 'Toward a solution of the learning paradox', *Review of Educational Research*, 55:201–26.

Galton, M., Simon, B. and Croll, P. (1980) *Inside the Primary Classroom (the ORACLE Project)*, London: Routledge and Kegan Paul.

Schank, R. C. and Abelson, R. P. (1977) *Scripts, Plans, Goals, and Understanding: an inquiry into human knowledge structures*, Hillsdale, NJ: Lawrence Erlbaum.

Vygotsky, L. S. (1978) *Mind in Society: the development of higher psychological processes*, Cambridge, MA: Harvard University Press.

Wood, D. (1986) 'Aspects of teaching and learning', in M. Richards and P. Light (eds) *Children of Social Worlds*, Cambridge: Polity Press.

Chapter 1

Knowing and arguing in a panel debate

Speaker roles and responsivity to others

Mikaela Åberg, Åsa Mäkitalo and Roger Säljö
University of Gothenburg

Introduction

In current debates on issues of learning and schooling, a rationalist and instrumental perspective on knowledge and skills dominates. The underlying assumption is that learning can be described in quantitative terms as a matter of individuals acquiring 'more' of some defined and clearly delimited body of knowledge or academic subject. Analogously, the development of cognitive skills is conceived in a rather unidimensional manner as the abstract training of the mind to master given intellectual techniques. The dominant metaphor implies that knowledge resides within the individual, and the point of schooling is to master the skills that make it possible for the learner to answer questions referring to the predefined body of knowledge, while, for instance, the ability to formulate interesting questions has seldom been a prominent goal of schooling.

The general background of the research reported below is an interest in how people accommodate to the demands and affordances of the communicative ecologies of present day society. In particular, we are interested in how they learn to use the resources available when finding out what is interesting to know about a particular issue, what they need to know to be informed and, in addition, how to present problems and argue with others. Thus, our ambition is to address issues of how young people develop the communicative and literacy skills necessary to engage in discussions with others about significant social problems. The challenges encountered in such situations have to do with a range of issues such as judging how different stakeholders define a problem, how they account for it and act upon it. What do people need to learn in order to navigate in the modern media world, how do they need to inform themselves so that they can exert agency in such settings?

Currently, many attempts are made to organize teaching and learning activities with a view to developing these kinds of generic skills among students. In the Swedish context, many teachers perceive some kind of project work as one such approach to teaching and learning. Project work is held to be conducive to preparing students for dealing with complex, 'real world' issues, while at the same time it allows them to engage in more scientific types of knowledge seeking (Driver, Newton and Osborne 2000; Kolstø 2001). Such project work typically includes activities such as: a) independent search for relevant information (in books, journals and digital resources including the Internet); b) analysis and synthesis of information and the evaluation of its relevance; and c) the production of an essay or some other form of documentation that clarifies the issue and expresses an informed point of view (Nagel 2001).

One element of such learning practices is to promote skills of engaging in what Michaels, O'Connor and Resnick (2008) refer to as accountable talk in classroom dialogue. Such talk is characterized by accountability to the learning community in which the activity takes place, i.e. it responds to and develops what others in the group have said (Mercer and Littleton 2007; Mercer and Wegerif 1999). Furthermore, such talk is characterized by accountability to accepted standards of reasoning in specific disciplines, i.e. it uses evidence and arguments in ways appropriate to the discipline, such as for instance proofs in mathematics and documentary sources in history (Bazerman 1988, 1994). It is also characterized by accountability to knowledge – or to put it differently – such talk implies assuming epistemic responsibility, i.e. the argumentation presents and builds on knowledge that is accurate and relevant to the issue under discussion (see also Resnick 1999). Thus, the widespread use of project work can per se be seen as an interesting response to the challenges posed by media society. Even though pedagogical approaches of this kind have support in research and normative pedagogical ideologies, they, to a large extent, represent a grass-roots response to the changing conditions of teaching and learning. This at least seems to be the case among teachers working in a tradition where there is considerable academic freedom when it comes to organizing classroom work to reach politically formulated educational goals.

In the present case, the idea of project work is also related to the ambition of preparing students for articulating their knowing and values in the particular communicative format of a panel debate. Thus, the goal of the activities in the project we have followed is for students to be able to present their case, and defend and argue for it, in a public setting where concerns of different kinds are at stake. In this sense, the panel debate, and the preparation for it, serve as a context for learning how to argue and discuss socio-political issues in a democratic society. In a debate, where several concerns need to be considered, it is not sufficient to ground arguments in disciplinary forms of evidence and argumentation. In addition to the dimensions that characterize accountable talk as described above, such face-to-face activities also imply that participants are responsive to others and flexible with respect to the multiplicity of concerns potentially displayed by the parties in an ongoing debate.

So-called socio-scientific issues are frequently addressed through project work. Such issues concern complex and multidisciplinary problems such as global warming or genetic modification of food (Kolstø 2001), and in society they are interpreted and discussed in partially conflicting, partially overlapping, discourses (Mäkitalo, Jakobsson and Säljö 2009). An interesting problem is to explore what learning, knowing and arguing mean in such practices. We will refer to the issue of learning how to argue in this particular setting as the *in situ* production of *accountable knowing.*

In this chapter we draw on an authentic case of project work in a Grade 9 class (students aged 15 to 16) on topics that concern environmental issues. The issue attended to in the debate is climate change, and we will analyse sequences of interaction before and during the panel debate. Our analytical interest concerns how students construe accountable knowledge and what they consider to be acceptable arguments. We are also interested in the issue of how students show epistemic responsibility, i.e. to what extent and in what manner students take responsibility for the arguments they introduce in this kind of activity. An interesting difference, which emerges in our empirical material, is that in some cases the students ground their arguments in relevant literature or other sources, while in other cases they introduce arguments that fit the situation as a debate, but for which they have no substantive evidence. This raises the issue of what it means to be knowledgeable as a participant in these kinds of educational arrangements, and, more generally, in debates and discussions on controversial issues.

A dialogical approach to the analysis of classroom interaction and argumentation

During the last decades, argumentative skills of students have been highlighted as an important area of research on learning, and several ways of training and assessing students' argumentation skills have been developed. A large part of the studies on class-room argumentation have used Toulmin's (1958) well-known model of argumentation skills as an analytical tool for investigating classroom interaction (e.g. Aufschnaiter, Erduran, Osborne and Simon 2008; Driver *et al.* 2000; Erduran, Simon and Osborne 2004; Jiménez-Alexaindre, Bugallo Rodríguez and Duschl 2000; Osborne, Erduran and Simon 2004; Simon, Erduran and Osborne 2006). Toulmin's model has also served as an inspiration for attempts to design computer-supported learning environ-ments intended to train argumentation skills (Baker, Quignard, Lund and Séjourné 2003; Cho and Jonassen 2002; Clark and Sampson 2008). These studies are, among other things, interested in the quality of scientific argumentation and how students' argumentative skills can be enhanced. In most of these studies, learning is viewed as a cognitive process and students' knowledge and argumentation skills are assessed by means of pre- and post-tests. When using Toulmin's argumentation model, or similar models and frameworks, researchers often end up with a comparison where students' performances are compared to, or measured against, a particular norm or model of how they ideally should argue.

In a socio-cultural and dialogical perspective, however, learning how to argue can-not be viewed solely as a matter of acquiring and following a model, which per se will produce an internally consistent form of argumentation. Rather, argumentation must be viewed as a creative practice, which involves a capacity to articulate ideas and argu-ments in contextually relevant manners. From a research point of view, this implies that one cannot analyse the activities of the students solely against the standards of a pre-formulated model of what it implies to argue. Instead one needs to ground the understanding of argumentative practices as *accountable knowing* in a dialogic perspec-tive in which issues of what Bahktin (1986) refers to as responsive understanding are central. From such a perspective, any utterance or claim is shaped by, and crafted in response to, other utterances:

> From the very beginning the utterance is constructed while taking into account possible responsive reactions, for whose sake, in essence, it is actually created [...] The speaker expects a response from them, an active responsive understanding. The entire utterance is constructed as it were in anticipation of encountering this response.
>
> (Bakhtin 1986: 94)

Claims to knowledge, then, are always dependent on, and produced in response to, the alternative perspectives and argumentative positions that are anticipated (Billig 1996). The force of a claim is, accordingly, normatively assessed 'both in the contexts of *in situ* interaction and within the socio-cultural practices established over long traditions of indulging in such interactions' (Linell 1998: 54) within a particular activity system. The meaning and relevance of argumentation as an activity, as well as the interpretation of the specific issue addressed, are thus locally negotiated through communicative formats established in a particular institutional setting. Classroom dialogues, for instance, inevitably 'reflect the values and social practices of schools as cultural institutions' (Mercer 2004: 139). Success or failure in argumentation, in other words, is relative to the normative expectations at work within such institutions of what are productive types of contributions (Bergqvist and Säljö 2004; Edwards and Mercer 1987; Furberg and Ludvigsen 2008).

The challenges of collaborative project work are considerable for students – not only do they imply searching, finding and scrutinizing relevant information, they also challenge participants' abilities to frame problems and to produce adequate descriptions of what is at stake. As Potter (1996) points out, descriptions of events per se represent a decisive discursive move:

> On the one hand a description will be oriented to action (i.e. it will be used to accomplish an action, and it can be analysed to see how it is constructed so as to accomplish that action). On the other, a description will build its own status as a factual version. For the most part, the concern is to produce descriptions which will be treated as *mere* descriptions, reports which *tell how it is.*
>
> (Potter 1996: 108)

The narrative organization of descriptions can, for instance, be made to make a specific version of events credible (Potter 1996). From our analytical perspective, the adoption of a neutral stance in producing descriptions is as much an accomplishment as taking an overtly evaluative one. Descriptions may thus be seen as elements in the accomplishment of specific types of social action; they are made to achieve something in the particular social activity of which they are part (in our case a panel debate).

The stance, which a speaker takes towards what she claims, can be discussed in terms of epistemic responsibility. An important feature of the particular kind of activity we have been studying is the participants' identification with the speaker roles they are assigned. Does for instance a speaker mention that she speaks from a certain standpoint – as a citizen, a student or as an assigned representative of an institution? Being assigned a role in a panel debate implies work to be done in terms of constructing a speaker role (Potter 1996). For instance, one has to realize what the category obligations and entitlements are, and what is at stake for the partners involved in the debate.

Empirical case: the panel debate as a project work assignment

The theme of the project work we followed during 7 weeks in the winter of 2007–8, was 'Resources and industries', and it involved grappling with issues of uses of energy sources and the global environmental consequences. It was planned by two homeroom teachers for a class in Grade 9 (ages 15–16 years). In curricular terms it covered several school subjects, including language (Swedish), science, civics and technology. The students had considerable experience of project work. The project, as a whole, was divided into six sections of different assignments and examinations. The pedagogical goal of the activity, which must be seen as ambitious since the skills to be acquired are rather advanced, implied that students should:

- Investigate and understand historical and current societal relations and contexts, be able to reflect over them and consider implications for the future.
- Develop their ability to use different sources of information and develop a critical attitude to these.
- Develop the ability to see the consequences of their own and others' views and actions.
- Develop insights into, and a responsible attitude towards, the use of natural resources.

After a few weeks of project work, a panel debate followed. The debate was intended to take about two hours, and the students had four to six lessons to prepare. The teachers gave instructions on how to behave in a panel debate (e.g. you do not scream, you listen to what the others have to say, you raise your hand if you want to speak, you must be polite even if disagreeing).

The students worked in pairs (boy/girl). Each pair was assigned a country, continent or the European Union to represent. The countries and regions were chosen by the teachers to offer a wide spectrum of different energy sources and environmental problems. The students were told that they should discuss issues of climate change from the perspective of the country assigned. To find information, the students were encouraged to use different resources: internet sources, the school library, textbooks and newspaper articles. The students organized the preparatory part of the work, and the teachers supported them by answering questions and by giving advice. In the panel debate, students were expected to be able to use what they had learned in terms of contents but also to show that they had learned how to engage in a panel debate. That is, the contents and the interactional format were equally important to consider for the students.

Data production, transcription and analytic procedures

The data were produced through ethnographic fieldwork over the whole project period of 7 weeks. Along with field notes, approximately 50 hours of video were recorded. Written instructions and student essays were collected. For this particular study, we have analysed 7 hours of video recordings. Methodologically we subscribe to the position taken by Jordan and Henderson (1995) when they argue for the complementarity of fieldwork and video documentation. Thus, ethnography 'furnishes the background against which video analysis is carried out, and the detailed understanding provided by the microanalysis of interaction, in turn, informs our general ethnographic understanding' (1995: 43). Video data give access to the rich details of participants' activities and features, such as how they use artefacts, how they move around and co-ordinate with each other; details which are often impossible to document in full through ethnographic records (cf. Heath and Hindmarsh 2002).

For this particular study, we followed a pair of students, Annie and Benny. The data were collected during the preparation phase (5 hours of video data) and during the debate (2 hours). The conversations were transcribed verbatim (see attached transcript legend), and non-verbal interaction significant for the analysis was added as comments in the transcriptions. The transcripts were used along with the video recordings when analysing the material. The analysis was done using the notion of dialogicality also at the level of utterances (Linell 1998), i.e. we analysed consequences of utterances as responsive social actions. An utterance needs to be crafted to fit the unique circumstances of its performance. It responds to a previous utterance, and in that capacity it shapes the situated sense of what was said, simultaneously it anticipates a response in return, and in that capacity it establishes some conditions for the next verbal act.

We have approached the activity as *a participant's project and concern*, and then asked ourselves what (dialogically and rhetorically) seemed necessary to get the task done. In the empirical analysis of the interaction, the analytical questions concerned the following:

1 What stance do the students take to the information they have collected about their country, i.e. what kind of version do they produce (factual, aligning with, or distancing)?
2 How do they position themselves as speakers in relation to this information (i.e. as assigned representatives of their specific country and/or as students)?
3 How do they respond to potential critique and arguments from their opponents, i.e. how do they rhetorically incorporate such potential critique in their own argumentation?

Results

By means of selected episodes, we will first follow Annie and Benny as they prepare for the panel debate. Then we will follow them during the debate. They are aware that they will have to respond to questions posed by the other students about the country they represent and about environmental issues. They also know that their performance in the debate will be assessed by the teachers.

Accounting for 'facts': stance and engagement with the task

Annie and Benny represent Russia in the debate. As we enter their preparatory work, they have searched for information about industries and natural and economic resources in Russia on the Internet, and they have printed some of these pages. The information they have found concerns the uses of energy, and they use this information to formulate arguments in anticipation of the upcoming debate on climate change. Annie, who is writing in a notepad, pauses and looks up at Benny while commenting on her own writing about the Russian government having signed the Kyoto protocol:

Excerpt 1

101. ANNIE: we're lucky to at least having signed the Kyoto protocol that's something good ((keeps on writing))
102. BENNY: yes
103. ((Benny changes paper))
104. ANNIE: ((writes and reads out loud)) °*the Kyoto protocol*°
105. (4 s)
106. ANNIE: ((reads out loud))*signed the Kyoto protocol* (1 s) ((writes and reads out loud)) *since we* ((inaudible))
107. (8 s)
108. BENNY: ((stops reading and looks at Annie)) we do have a lot– or we have one fifth of u:hm (.) water power stations as well did we write that?
109. ANNIE: yea (.) re– so now we have started to realize how eh important it is (.) ((writes and reads out loud))*how important it is* (.) for the environment ((finishes the sentence in writing)) ((reads out loud)) *started to realize how important it is with the environment* and– wait ((orients towards the printouts and reads))
110. ANNIE: how important it is with the environment and uhm (3 s) ((contentedly)) our future hm

Starting with the information collected about Russia, Annie points out that at least one thing is positive: 'we're lucky to at least having signed the Kyoto protocol' (utterance 101). Benny agrees (102) and continues to read the printouts. Annie then starts formulating a sentence in writing (104) about this piece of information, and she reads it aloud (106). Benny looks up and interrupts Annie in order to make sure that she has noted another positive 'fact' about water power that he has found while reading (108). Annie confirms that she has seen this and continues formulating a description of Russia as having realized the importance of environmental issues by signing the Kyoto protocol. She reads it out loud to Benny (109) and then finishes the sentence contentedly (110).

This fragment of interaction is interesting for illustrating how the students handle the task. They are, on the one hand, doing typical project schoolwork: they find, read, evaluate and write down what they understand as relevant facts. But another dimension of their work, which is visibly present here, is that they do this in anticipation of an upcoming debate where they will be held accountable. It is obvious that they prepare themselves to speak as representatives of Russia, since they use the pronoun *we* when anticipating what they will be accountable for in the debate. However, Annie and Benny also take an evaluative stance to the information they have collected about Russia and distance themselves from their assigned speaker role. Annie's point about 'we're lucky to at least having signed the Kyoto protocol that's something good' (101) testifies to this evaluative stance, and the expression 'at least' indicates that she does not align with the speaker role she has been given. To represent a country such as Russia may become a problem for Annie and Benny, since they will be assessed as students in terms of their insights into justifiable uses of natural resources. The students initially deal with this particular dilemma by making a description based on a selection of what they regard as positive facts (signing the Kyoto protocol and pointing out that 'we have one fifth

Figure 1.1 Benny and Annie are reading from the printed papers.

of u:hm (.) water power stations as well' (108). This mode of making a description contains elements of alignment and distancing.

However, information speaking in favour of, as well as against, Russia is available to their future opponents as well, and this needs to be attended to in their argumentative strategies. For example, in their description they anticipate critique of Russia as not being environmentally concerned by pointing out that they are starting 'to realize how important it is with the environment' (109). As we shall see in the following, the students – qua students – are careful not to align with or lend their voice to a country that uses what they consider to be destructive energy sources, and that is not prepared to take action for the future.

Narrative organization of the description: producing credibility as speakers

Representing Russia is, for reasons we have already alluded to, not an easy task for Annie and Benny. They have trouble finding what they see as positive information about the country. Instead, they have to deal with what they perceive as a set of negative circumstances. Looking through the printouts, Benny notices aspects of Russia's energy consumption that he finds disturbing:

Excerpt 2

201. BENNY: this is not particularly good ((points to a printout)) really (.) that we have uhm (.) a lot of oil and that it's like (1 s)
202. ANNIE: n[o:: but uhm]
203. BENNY: [one of our most impor]tant sources of income
204. ANNIE: uh(h)m nope (.) uhm ((reads her notes)) (2 s) but I have written like this ((reads out loud from her notes)) *over the years we have unfortunately built up a large nuclear* and oil indust- (.) nuclear a- and oil industry or something like that
205. BENNY: yes
206. ANNIE: nuclear ((hesitates and puts down the pencil)) and ((takes a rubber in her hand)) oil industry ((erases something in her notes)) nuclear ((takes the pencil and writes)) *power and o[il]*
207. BENNY: [we] can say that we will raise the prices like uhm: the prices on it then fewer will buy [it]
208. ANNIE: [mm] (1 s) ((reads out loud)) *this is not something we are proud of and we will of concern for the environment from now on try to* (.) *cut down on that* ((marks in her notes where to insert Benny's proposal)) uhm: we- we're going to raise ((starts to write))

Benny draws attention to the Russian oil and nuclear industry (utterance 201), and Annie agrees that this is a problem (202). Benny then adds an even more aggravating circumstance: that oil is one of Russia's most important sources of income (203). Annie confirms this by responding with faint laughter in her voice (204). She then turns back to her notes and reads out loud how she has taken this into consideration when describing Russia. Benny is positive about Annie's description (205), and she continues to write (206). Benny then contributes to the version they are co-producing by adding a made up, but potentially useful, argument about raising the price of oil to reduce consumption (207). Agreeing with Benny that this is a useful argument, Annie continues to elaborate her own formulations and then adds Benny's contribution to their notes (208).

In this excerpt, Russia's dependence on oil and nuclear energy is addressed as a problem – both in its own right (since both are considered problematic energy sources and since the Russian economy is dependent on oil) and rhetorically for them to defend during the upcoming debate. The faint laughter by Annie (204), as she responds to Benny's concerns, is a sign of acknowledging that they face a dilemma. The description Annie and Benny produce contains relevant and problematic information about Russian energy production, and simultaneously makes Russia appear as a country that is *aware of environmental issues* and willing to take action *for the future*. In our interpretation, this construction responds to the dilemma of the double accountability as representatives of Russia and of appearing as environmentally concerned and informed students.

The narrative organization functions to respond to the students' concerns. In the narrative, the negative information is described as a thing of the past. The formulation 'over the years we have unfortunately built up a large nuclear and oil industry' (204) reports the history in such a manner that it makes it possible for the students to distance themselves from what has evolved. A complementary way of displaying their evaluative stance as students is to prepare formulations about the future claiming that Russia 'will of concern for the environment from now on try to cut down' its dependence on nuclear power and oil (208). By organizing the narrative of past events and future action in this way, they are able to display their environmental understanding as students while at the same accounting for Russian energy production and use.

Making claims: anticipating and incorporating critique in the production of arguments

Annie and Benny then try several different ways of constructing their arguments. Annie reads out loud what she has written, and together they test possible formulations. While the final sentence in this part of their work (utterance 301) is formulated aloud by Benny and finished in writing by Annie, she picks up an additional problem that they need to address:

Excerpt 3

301. BENNY: so that fewer uhm countries or fewer people or what to say fewer=
302. ANNIE: =but we'll still be needing them but uhm ((reads out loud from her notes)) *we are going to raise the prices on oil and the gas so that* uhm
303. BENNY: but they'll continue to buy from us and so we'll still make a profit on it so (.) there surely will be fewer buyers
304. ANNIE: but if it is as many buyers
305. BENNY: mm
306. ANNIE: then we still will get more mo- money
307. BENNY: mm
308. ANNIE: and that money could go to research within like
309. BENNY: new uhm fuel
310. ANNIE: yeah to new [uhm]
311. BENNY: [yeah] yeah we can write that
312. ANNIE: yes or like to- yeah research on electric cars or some[thing]
313. BENNY: [yeah] something like that
314. ANNIE: yeah

Annie objects to Benny's suggestion (302) about having fewer buyers as a sufficient argument for how Russia should act in the future. Benny argues that there will be enough buyers even if prices are raised (303). However, there is nothing in this argument that demonstrates environmental concerns on the part of Russia. The idea Annie comes up with in response to this potential argumentative dilemma is that the increased margin from higher prices could be used for funding research on environmental issues (306 and 308). Benny contributes by saying that research could produce 'new […] fuel' (309). Annie agrees (310) and Benny asks her to write down what they have agreed upon (311). Annie adds another concrete example of electric cars (312).

By preparing this kind of formulation the students will be able to more firmly ground their forthcoming argumentation in a specific normative environmental discourse. If the issue of economic stake for Russia appears in the debate, they now have formulated a counter-argument. This hypothetical line of reasoning allows them to display their own understanding of environmental issues. They are, in other words, well prepared to succeed as being knowledgeable of facts about Russia, while simultaneously displaying their understanding of and concern for environmental issues.

Put to the test: the panel debate as a discursive activity

Above we illustrated parts of the preparatory work that Annie and Benny engaged in. Below we will present parts of the panel debate activity. The debate took place in the assembly hall of the school. A podium with spotlights was used as a stage (see Figure 1.2). The students who were not on stage served as audience. Before they started the activity, the teachers repeated some rules: members of the audience were not to ask questions during the debate, the debaters should speak in a loud voice, they should raise their hand to get the floor and only one person should speak at a time. The students were allowed to have written notes as support, but each party in the debate was given only five minutes to speak. One of the teachers timed all verbal activity. Immediately before starting the debate, one of the teachers told the students to address how they were going to reduce the greenhouse effect. Then the students could start asking each other questions.

The excerpts below are taken from the beginning of the debate activity. The parties represented on stage are Russia (Annie and Benny), Bangladesh (Daniel and Peter), Sweden (Ellie) and China (Jacob and Frida). This is the first and only time during the debate that Russia's environmental measures were questioned. As we enter the debate, Daniel representing Bangladesh has raised his hand. The teacher gives him the floor:

Excerpt 4

401. TEACHER: Daniel
402. DANIEL: yes Russia uhm you have quite many nuclear power stations and uhm the safety is considered poor (.) what are you going to do about that?
403. ANNIE: safety? ((clears her throat))
404. DANIEL: yes
405. ANNIE: well u:hm well we concentrate on improving safety
406. (1 s)
406. BENNY: and [reduce] nuclear power
407. ANNIE: [but we] (1 s) yeah uhm first of all we'll try to reduce it (.) and then uhm (.) it won't go- it will not be done in a year that we get (.) it- it will take- it will take time but we concentrate on making more environment friendly (.) yeah
408. PETER: ((raises his hand)) uhu so what were you thinking would replace nuclear power then?
409. BENNY: water power- uhm stations and wind power turbines is what we have thought of
410. ANNIE: yep

Figure 1.2 The students have taken their place at the stage.

Daniel opens the debate. He points out that Russia has a lot of nuclear power and that there are safety problems. He asks Russia how they are going to solve this alleged problem (402). This question was probably unexpected, as Annie's first response seems to be a request for clarification: 'safety?' (403). The interpretation that she is taken by surprise is supported by her hesitation when answering (405). As she responds that they 'are concentrating on improving the safety' (405), she simultaneously accepts the claim Daniel has made. Thus, as a participant in a debate speaking on behalf of Russia she is obliged to answer. Denying that there are issues of safety would be speaking against what they should know from the information provided. It would also risk making her appear ignorant of the significance of these kinds of problems. In 407 and 408, Annie and Benny continue along the line of argumentation they have prepared about how to improve the situation.

In dealing with this dilemma about the safety problems, they invoke claims for which they have no substantive evidence. In their preparations they have not considered if Russian *policy* is in the direction they suggest. Their response displays their own evaluative stance – as students – about what is the expected argument. In other words, they improvise and create claims that follow the logic of debate but which are not grounded in arguments they have formulated. This illustrates the complexity of the project work and the debate format. In their preparations, and in their argumentation, Annie and Benny are researching and describing Russia's energy sources and they account for these sources in a factual manner. They are in a preparatory phase, however, not attending to Russian policy or developmental plans and problems. As can be seen, the questions they receive are primarily about Russian policy and not about their energy production per se.

The answers Annie and Benny give are, for the time being, accepted. Peter then raises his hand and the teacher gives him the floor. Peter continues with another question (409) pointing out that Russia cannot abandon one energy source without substituting it for a different one. In line with their preparations, Annie and Benny respond to this with the claim that they will replace nuclear power with water power and wind power. One interesting aspect of this particular activity is that none of the other students objects to or questions Annie and Benny's construction of the alleged Russian position. It is unclear whether this kind of questioning was not considered as part of the task or if the strict time limits or the rules of the debate were perceived as preventing such scrutiny.

What is striking about the panel debate is that all students, when discussing environmental issues, seem to identify with a similar stance to such concerns, even though the choice of countries to represent has been done in order for different types of arguments to surface in the debate. One example of this is the evaluative stance they take as they discuss nuclear energy. For instance, Russia could have used the argument that nuclear power is an acceptable energy source at present, because it is *not* contributing to the 'greenhouse effect'. This argument, however, is not used; nuclear energy is considered a problem throughout.

After Annie and Benny have answered the questions about the alleged Russian position towards nuclear power, Ellie (representing Sweden) raises her hand to get the floor. Ellie points out that oil production is Russia's primary source of income. By framing the issue in economic discourse, she implicitly challenges the credibility of Russia as being environmentally responsible. However, this is a challenge for which Annie and Benny have prepared (see Excerpt 3), and they respond within the same discursive framing:

Excerpt 5

501. ELLIE: uhm Russia since your principal uhm source of income is export of gas and oil how will you: change cause it's it's from there you get your economy?
502. ANNIE: mm u:hm we will raise- we will of course raise- ((turns and points to Benny)) °and then you can°=
503. BENNY: =yes we will raise the price on oil gas and uhm (.) if they buy as much the money will go to (.) environment- environment friendly fuels and (.) green energies
504. (9 s)
505. TEACHER: mm?
506. JACOB: mm ((reluctantly raises his hand)) I'll say something then
507. TEACHER: mm Jacob
508. JACOB: that uhm Russia discharge uhm (.) or what will you do to not let- or you discharge most (.) tons of carbon dioxide per person of these countries (.) what will you do (.) for this not to continue like that?
509. BENNY: yeah we are doing research on more environment friendly cars and things like that- (.) yea=
510. ANNIE: =mm you see in the future we concentrate on uhm what's it called (.) to- reduce the discharge of carbon dioxide (.) we do (.) we make an effort with more environment fri(h)endly methods

Annie starts responding to the issue of having an oil dependent economy but hesitates and lets Benny take over (utterance 502). Benny presents the line of argument for which they have prepared but have no evidence. The solution is that they 'will raise the prices on oil gas'. Benny continues by saying that if there is still a profit the money should go to 'environment friendly fuels and (.) green energies' (503). Their argumentation effectively closes the discussion on this topic. After a pause of 9 seconds, one of the teachers encourages the students to continue by saying: 'mm?' (505). Jacob responds and, rather reluctantly, raises his hand (506). He seems to struggle somewhat with the formulations about what to do with Russia's discharge of carbon dioxide (508). Benny introduces an argument they have prepared about how Russia is handling this problem (509). Again, Benny is making a claim for which they have no evidence. Annie contentedly contributes by pointing out that they will reduce the discharge of carbon dioxide, and she reassures the panel that they are investing in more environment friendly methods (510).

All questions that the students ask are grounded in information about Russia that they have read. They are not challenging Annie and Benny's arguments or directly testing the grounds on which they are making their claims. Instead they all seem to respond to the situated task given by the teachers to discuss how they are going to reduce the greenhouse effect. Students' knowledge about this issue, and their knowledge about how to respond in the debate format, determine the logic of the argumentation. Thus, the speaker position of Russia disappears in favour of responding to the issue of climate change in their capacity as students demonstrating their insight into the normatively expected discourse.

Discussion

The basic interest of this study is how students learn to argue and how they prepare themselves for engaging in such activities. Our argument has been that learning to argue is more than mastering a given intellectual technique and the ability to use disciplinary forms of knowledge in accountable manners. What we have referred to as accountable knowing, in addition, stresses responsiveness to the perspectives of others and *in situ* rhetorical flexibility in argumentation. Thus, in relation to complex 'real world' issues, the conception of what it means to be accountable also incorporates issues of responsiveness to the perspectives of others.

In the classroom we have followed, the particular communicative activities of preparing for and engaging in a panel debate are introduced for pedagogical purposes. This implies that the activity is situated in an activity system with specific communicative traditions and with a specific speaker role for students. The activity differs in several respects from traditional instructional formats. Students are not just accountable for responding to questions about facts. Rather, they have a broad set of obligations including activities such as searching, selecting and evaluating information in terms of its relevance and validity for the issue to be addressed. They have to organize the information in writing so that it expresses an informed and well-argued point of view. In the present case, students also have to perspectivize the information and the issues in terms of the participant role assigned to them in the debate as representatives of a country or a political body and, as we have shown, throughout their discussion there is tension over which speaker roles to adopt.

The complexity of the task is illustrated, for instance, by the observation that Annie and Benny in their preparatory work concentrate on how to account for 'facts' about the use and production of energy in Russia. They do not inquire into Russian *policy* on energy and environmental issues. This is a kind of category mistake, which forces them to invent arguments and make claims about future initiatives and measures. In the debate, and when responding to challenges about policy (regarding nuclear safety and having an oil-dependent economy), they improvise by invoking arguments from the normatively preferred discourse about energy use (e.g. reducing dependence on oil) they know as students. As in many debates, it is the policy issues that are primarily focused on; causes and consequences are more interesting than mere descriptions of states of affair, and maybe this is what Annie and Benny are learning as part of this exercise.

The debate element of the project represents a communicative format that presents specific challenges both in the preparations and in the *in situ* performance. The format implies presenting accountable knowing, but it also requires considerable creativity and rhetorical flexibility. Like all face-to-face interaction, debates are dynamic and unpredictable in terms of how they evolve, and the students in their preparations have to anticipate what arguments and claims they may face on the podium. However, in a debate one also has to be able to respond to the unexpected and to improvise, as we saw in Excerpt 4 when Annie faces the question about safety in the context of nuclear energy. But even such improvising has to be done in a relevant and accountable manner. Responsiveness is a prominent feature of how the students organize their work, and how they contribute to the debate. What is obvious is that they engage in producing descriptions that are relevant and at the same time rhetorically convincing in the sense that they may successfully defend a position or win a debate against adversaries. What is at stake in this context is thus not just knowing but to some extent also winning or losing.

In terms of learning, the panel debate generates activities that touch the core of citizenship and knowing in a democratic society. The students are expected to recognize what are valid arguments and substantiated claims, while at the same time they need to show rhetorical flexibility and accommodate to the dynamics of debating. From an analytical perspective, introducing this communicative format in this particular field with a range of disciplinary perspectives and highly contested views represents a considerable challenge. From a historical point of view, the type of literacy skills required to deal successfully with such tasks go far beyond the conventional expectations of what it means to read, interpret and produce texts in the school setting. In their work, the students are accountable for producing contextually relevant and appropriate versions of an issue, where there are many possible positions and conflictual perspectives. Thus, what they say and write must be accepted as a valid description fitting the occasion in a highly complex field.

Debates represent a specific communicative format in contemporary society. There is a normative order when it comes to entitlements and obligations on the part of the participants. This format is what is introduced into the educational setting, and the instructions students receive specify how to act and behave in the situation. But, even within such a format students are still primarily accountable as students. They respond to several situated forms of accountability. They have to give voice *to* their assigned country, while at the same time they are expected to show their awareness of the environmental problems *of* their assigned country, and this is a dilemma for them.

In this educational context, there is a recognizable and normatively preferred environmental discourse that the students are aware of and feel obliged to follow in their role as competent students. When approaching the task, for instance, they make a clear distinction between what are considered as 'positive' and 'negative' facts to be accounted for. This normative discourse frames how they make the description of Russia in terms of past events and future actions. When describing the past, and Russia's dependence on oil and nuclear energy, they show that they are knowledgeable about Russia's energy production: they account for 'facts'. In order to account for their own evaluative stance as students, they invent supporting arguments by formulating future policies of raising prices and investing in research.

The results show that the debate format has clear implications for how the students engage in the project theme. There are many signs of this orientation during their work. Even when discussing with each other, they anticipate their position in the upcoming debate. When organizing teaching and learning practices in this manner, students have to respond to the complexities of producing knowing relevant to a situation; a process that includes a range of discursive and evaluative activities that traditional pedagogy has often kept out of view. What we have seen is a glimpse of a complex and extended socialization process in which the students are familiarized with how to craft descriptions and arguments in a world characterized by a multitude of potentially relevant sources of knowledge. To what extent this will empower students and make it possible for them to exert agency in media society is an empirical question. What is intended as regards pedagogical practice is to provide students with opportunities to engage in tasks that give them some ownership of the process of producing knowing in contemporary society. This is an obligation for schooling and such complex socialization is hard to achieve without productive support from teachers and schools.

Acknowledgements

The research reported here has been funded by the Knut and Alice Wallenberg Foundation, the Bank of Sweden Tercentenary Foundation and the Swedish Research Council. The authors are members of LinCS, the Linnaeus Centre for Research on Learning, Interaction and Mediated Communication in Contemporary Society funded by the Swedish Research Council. This chapter was written while the third author was a Finland Distinguished Professor at the Centre for Learning Research, University of Turku.

References

Aufschnaiter, C., Erduran, S., Osborne, J. and Simon, S. (2008) 'Arguing to learn and learning to argue: case studies of how students argumentation relates to their scientific knowledge', *Journal of Research in Science Education*, 45:101–31.

Baker, M.J., Quignard, M., Lund, K. and Séjourné, A. (2003) 'Computer-supported collaborative learning in the space of debate', in B. Wasson, S. Ludvigsen and U. Hoppe (eds) *Designing for Change in Networked Learning Environments: proceedings of the International Conference on Computer Support for Collaborative Learning 2003*, Dordrecht, The Netherlands: Kluwer.

Bakhtin, M. M. (1986) *Speech Genres and Other Late Essays*, Austin, TX: University of Texas Press.

Bazerman, C. (1988) *Shaping Written Knowledge: the genre and activity of the experimental article in science*, Madison, WI: University of Wisconsin Press.

Bazerman, C. (1994) *Constructing Experience*, Carbondale and Edwardsville: Southern Illinois University Press.

Bergqvist, K. and Säljö, R. (2004) 'Learning to plan: a study of reflexivity and discipline in modern pedagogy', in J. L. van der Linden and P. Renshaw (eds) *Dialogic Learning: shifting perspectives to learning, instruction, and teaching*, New York, NY: Kluwer.

Billig, M. (1996) *Arguing and Thinking: a rhetorical approach to social psychology* (2nd edn), Cambridge: Cambridge University Press.

Cho, K. L. and Jonassen, D. H. (2002) 'The effects of argumentation scaffolds on argumentation and problem solving', *Educational Technology Research and Development*, 50:5–22.

Clark, D. and Sampson, V. (2008) 'Assessing dialogic argumentation in online environments to relate structure, grounds, and conceptual quality', *Journal of Research in Science Education*, 45:293–321.

Driver, R., Newton, P. and Osborne, J. (2000) 'Establishing the norms of scientific argumentation in classrooms', *Science Education*, 84:287–312.

Edwards, D. and Mercer, N. (1987) *Common Knowledge: the development of understanding in the classroom*, London: Methuen.

Erduran, S., Simon, S. and Osborne, J. (2004) 'TAPping into argumentation: developments in the application of Toulmin's Argument Pattern for studying science discourse', *Science Education*, 88:915–33.

Furberg, A. and Ludvigsen, S. (2008) 'Students' meaning making of socioscientific issues in computer mediated settings: exploring learning through interaction trajectories', *International Journal of Science Education*, 30:1775–99.

Heath, C. and Hindmarsh, J. (2002) 'Analysing interaction: video, ethnography and situated conduct', in T. May (ed.) *Qualitative Research in Practice*, London: Sage.

Jiménez-Aleixandre, M. P., Bugallo Rodríguez, A. and Duschl, R. A. (2000) '"Doing the lesson" or "doing science": argument in high school genetics', *Science Education*, 84:757–92.

Jordan, B. and Henderson, A. (1995) 'Interaction analysis: foundations and practice', *The Journal of the Learning Sciences*, 4:39–103.

Kolstø, S. D. (2001) 'Scientific literacy for citizenship: tools for dealing with the science dimension of controversial socioscientific issues', *Science Education*, 85:291–310.

Linell, P. (1998) *Approaching Dialogue: talk, interaction and contexts in dialogical perspectives*, Amsterdam: John Benjamins.

Mäkitalo, Å., Jakobsson, A. and Säljö, R. (2009) 'Learning to reason in the context of socioscientific problems: exploring the demands on students in "new" classroom activites', in K. Kumpulainen, C. Hmelo-Silver and M. Cesar (eds) *Investigating Classroom Interaction: methodologies in action*, London: Sense Publishers.

Mercer, N. (2004) 'Sociocultural discourse analysis: analysing classroom talk as a social mode of thinking', *Journal of Applied Linguistics*, 1:137–68.

Mercer, N. and Littleton, K. (2007) *Dialogue and the Development of Children's Thinking: a sociocultural approach*, London: Routledge.

Mercer, N. and Wegerif, R. (1999) 'Is "exploratory talk" productive talk?', in K. Littleton and P. Light (eds) *Learning with Computers: analysing productive interaction*, London: Routledge.

Michaels, S., O'Connor, C. and Resnick, L. (2008) 'Deliberative discourse idealized and realized: accountable talk in the classroom and in civic life', *Studies in Philosophy and Education*, 27:283–97.

Nagel, N. (2001) *Learning through Real-World Problem Solving: the power of integrative teaching*, Thousand Oaks, CA: Corwin Press.

Osborne, J., Erduran, S. and Simon, S. (2004) 'Enhancing the quality of argumentation in school science', *Journal of Research in Science Teaching*, 41:994–1020.

Potter, J. (1996) *Representing Reality: discourse, rhetoric and social construction*, London: Sage.

Resnick, L. (1999) 'Making America smarter', *Education Week Century Series*, 18:38–40. Available online at: http://ifl.lrdc.pitt.edu/ifl/media/pdf/MakingAmericaSmarter.pdf (accessed 17 February 2009).

Simon, S., Erduran, S. and Osborne, J. (2006) 'Learning to teach argumentation: research and development in the science classroom', *International Journal of Science Education*, 28:235–60.

Toulmin, S. (1958) *The Uses of Argument*, Cambridge: Cambridge University Press.

Appendix

Transcription legend

(.)	Shows just noticeable pauses (micro pauses).
(1 s)	Shows pauses over 1 second.
((text))	Gives a description of an activity or something that is hard to phonetically write out in words e.g. laugher.
° text °	Shows when the speech is noticeably quieter.
text	Shows when a person is reading out loud or when a person writes and reads out loud what is being written.
tex:t	Shows that it is a stretched sound.
text-	A sharp cut-off.
[text]	Shows co-occuring talk where the square brackets indicate where the
[text]	overlap starts and ends.
Te(h)xt	Talk with a laughing tone.
text=	Shows that there is no pause between speakers turns.
=text	

Chapter 2

Peer dialogue and cognitive development

A two-way relationship?

Christine Howe
University of Cambridge

Introduction

Over 75 years ago, two books authored by the then young scholar, Jean Piaget, were published in English. One of these books (Piaget 1932) emphasized the role that dialogue between children can play in fostering cognitive growth, with children's conceptions of morality used for illustration. The other book (Piaget 1926) stressed how the form of children's dialogue when interacting with peers, particularly their skills of argumentation, is dependent upon their ability to reason. Jointly, in other words, the books promulgate a two-way relation between peer dialogue and cognitive growth: dialogue can promote growth, but as cognition develops, it shapes the form that dialogue takes and, by implication, the manner in which dialogue promotes subsequent growth. Over the past 30 years, a significant body of research has been published that relates peer dialogue to cognitive development. A sample is summarized in the early part of this chapter. As will become clear, much of the research has been directly or indirectly influenced by the work of Piaget. However, the influence is typically from only one of the two strands within Piaget's writings, the strand concerned with the role of peer dialogue in triggering growth. The converse relation, as developed in Piaget (1926), is overlooked, and as the chapter proceeds, evidence is presented to suggest that this may be a mistake. Thus, the overall conclusion is that even if the focus is dialogic influences upon cognitive growth (as is the case throughout the present volume), the picture is likely to be impoverished unless the two-way relationship highlighted so many years ago is also acknowledged.

In detail, the first of the following sections outlines literature underpinning what is probably the most certain finding as regards peer dialogue and cognitive growth: the value of interactions where children express contrasting opinions in the pursuit of joint goals.[1] It is a finding that is not simply supported by the studies that are summarized below, but also re-iterated in many of the other chapters that comprise this volume. For example, it is enshrined in the concept of 'exploratory talk' discussed by Littleton and Mercer, and it is implicit in Scott, Ametller, Mortimer and Emberton's elaboration of Bakhtin's (1981) dialogic function. However, discussing contrasting opinions cannot be sufficient to guarantee growth. Children must also resolve their differences in a progressive direction, and resolution becomes the focus of the chapter's second section. Research is presented that suggests, in middle childhood at least, children seldom achieve resolution during the relevant dialogue itself. Rather resolution takes place subsequently, sometimes many weeks after the dialogue's completion. Although the literature does not currently allow for definite conclusions, there are indications that such 'delayed resolution' may reflect developmental constraints, and this possibility is discussed in the chapter's third section. It is suggested that, with development, there may be increasing potential for 'dialogic resolution'; that is, resolution of differences at the point they occur. However, if this is the case, research does not merely support the two-way relationship between dialogue and development that Piaget acknowledged; it also suggests a reversal of Vygotsky's (1978: 57) famous claim that 'every function in the child's cultural development appears twice: first, on the social level, and later, on the individual level'. As regards peer dialogue, the capacity to create functions at the individual level is, in one sense at least, available long before it can be used in social interaction.

Contrasting opinions and common goals

The emphasis that Piaget (1926, 1932) placed upon dialogue between peers is, in some respects, unique among the theorists whose work underpins the present volume. Vygotsky (1962, 1978) highlighted the role of dialogue in cognitive development, and drew attention to the contribution made by peers, for instance in his definition of the 'zone of proximal development' as 'the distance between the actual developmental level as determined by independent problem solving and the level of potential development as determined through problem solving under adult guidance or *in collaboration with more capable peers*' (Vygotsky 1978: 86, emphasis added). However, Vygotsky's own focus was adult guidance, and this has been the case with most subsequent research in the Vygotskian tradition (for example Wertsch 1979; Wood 1989). The cognitive benefits of peer collaboration have, furthermore, been addressed from perspectives other than the one adopted by Piaget, for instance within the co-operative learning tradition (Johnson and Johnson 2000; Slavin 1995) or following the peer tutoring approach (Goodlad and Hirst 1989; Topping and Ehly 1998). However, the co-operative learning tradition usually emphasizes the goals that children pursue together, rather than the dialogic processes through which joint goals are realized. Peer tutoring typically focuses upon the outcomes of exchanges where one child instructs another, rather than the exchanges themselves. Thus, it is the Piagetian approach, beyond all others, that highlights peer dialogue per se, and this is apparent in how the literature has developed.

For instance, many of the earliest studies used Piaget's own research tasks, with conservation and spatial transformation (that is the famous 'three mountains' problem) being particular favourites. Some of these studies (for instance, Doise, Mugny and Perret-Clermont 1975) compared children who worked on the tasks in groups with children who worked on them individually. Although these studies document greater progress in the 'grouped' children (as ascertained from pre-tests administered before the tasks to post-tests administered afterwards), the positive results do not necessarily stem from dialogue. Perhaps the mere fact of being part of a group was sufficient to stimulate progress. Further studies (for example, Ames and Murray 1982; Bearison, Magzamen and Filardo 1986; Doise and Mugny 1979; Mugny and Doise 1978) focused upon dialogue, albeit not invariably to the extent of studying it directly. For instance, some studies formulated groups such that varying dialogic styles can be virtually taken for granted, a favoured manipulation being groups where children hold differing views about the topic and groups where children hold similar views. With task held constant, contrasting patterns of pre- to post-test growth can be attributed, with a modicum of confidence at least, to dialogic differences, with dialogue not actually being analysed. Other studies, by contrast, included attempts to categorize dialogue, and to relate category frequencies directly to pre- to post-test growth. Because the categories, like the tasks, were often influenced by Piaget's research, particularly the emphasis in Piaget (1926) upon argumentation, contrasting opinions became a strong focus. Results endorsed the focus: children were found to benefit when they discussed differences of opinion around common goals.

Similar conclusions emerged from slightly later research, which used social tasks rather than conservation and spatial transformation problems. For instance, Damon and Killen (1982) and Kruger (1992) considered the relevance of dialogue to children's reasoning about 'distributive justice', as exemplified in a scenario where four children were described as receiving ten candy bars for making bracelets and the task was to divide the bars fairly, bearing in mind factors like one child making more bracelets and another child being poorer. Leman and Duveen (1999) recorded pairs of children working on the moral reasoning task that was originally reported in Piaget (1932). The task requires judgments of who is naughtier, a boy who breaks a large number of cups accidentally, or a boy who breaks a small number while engaging in forbidden behaviour. Using a specially designed board game entitled 'Conviction', Roy and Howe (1990) examined 9- to 11-year-olds' reasoning and dialogue about legal transgressions of both a trivial nature (for example, parking on a double yellow line) and a serious nature (for example, stealing from an elderly person). In all of these studies, evidence was provided for the value of exchanging opinions in the pursuit of shared goals, with such exchanges sometimes termed 'transactive dialogue' (see also Berkowitz and Gibbs 1983; Berkowitz, Gibbs and Broughton 1980).

Even more recently, peer dialogue has been examined with standard school subjects, with results once more indicating the significance of exchanging views. Literacy and the arts have been examined (for example, Miell and Littleton 2004; Miell and MacDonald 2000; Pontecorvo, Paoletti and Orsolini 1989), but the focus has undoubtedly been upon mathematics and science. With mathematics, support for an emphasis upon difference has been obtained in research on rational number (for example, Damon and Phelps 1989; Schwarz, Neuman and Biezuner 2000) and matrices (Blaye 1990). With science, my own research with 8- to 12-year-olds can be cited as supportive. This research involved small groups working on tasks relevant to elementary concepts, for example the properties of objects that determine whether they float or sink (Howe, Rodgers and Tolmie 1990; Tolmie, Howe, Mackenzie and Greer 1993), the relative speeds of toy vehicles as they roll down slopes (Howe, Tolmie and Rodgers 1992b), and the characteristics of containers that determine the rate at which hot water cools (Howe and Tolmie 2003; Howe, Tolmie, Greer and Mackenzie 1995a). Group tasks comprised series of items where the outcomes of relevant events had to be predicted, observed, and interpreted. Task instructions pressed groups to discuss their predictions and interpretations, and reach agreement. Participating children were individually tested before and after the group tasks, using items that also required the prediction and interpretation of outcomes. Some of my studies compared pre- to post-test change after groups where children were known, from pre-test responses, to have differing views with change after groups where they were known to have similar views. Other studies considered peer dialogue directly, relating pre- to post-test change to dialogue category frequencies. Regardless of method, results confirm the power of differing opinions regarding shared goals.

Among the studies that I have contributed to, the most telling perhaps is work reported in Howe, Tolmie, Thurston, Topping, Christie, Livingston, Jessiman and Donaldson (2007), which involved recording the dialogue of 10- to 12-year-olds, while they worked through extended (3+ weeks) programmes of teaching on first evaporation and condensation and then force and motion. The programmes made extensive use of group work, employing tasks that were modelled on the tasks used in the work summarized above (and not just the predict-test-interpret format, but also the emphasis upon discussion and agreement). However, unlike my earlier work, the programmes were fully embedded in routine classroom practice. Teachers rather than researchers delivered the programmes, in contrast not just with my other studies but also with most of the other research discussed so far. Moreover, whole-class teaching and practical demonstration were used in addition to group work, as is normally the case in classrooms. Yet the expression of contrasting opinions during group work with peers turned out to be the single most important predictor of learning gain. Furthermore, this was gain that was not simply detected between pre-tests prior to the programmes and post-tests a few weeks later, but also found to be sustained on further post-tests held after an 18-month interval (Tolmie, Christie, Howe, Thurston, Topping, Donaldson, Jessiman and Livingston 2007).

Resolution and contradiction

Given the volume and variety of relevant research, the conclusion heralded earlier does appear warranted: as regards peer dialogue and cognitive growth, there is value in interactions where children express contrasting opinions in pursuit of joint goals. Nevertheless, as also signalled earlier, the expression of contrasting opinions cannot be sufficient to precipitate growth. Progress in most of the topic areas discussed above is not conventionally regarded as inhabiting some post-modern universe where a multitude of perspectives is the ultimate goal. Rather progress means moving towards the specific knowledge and understanding that constitute 'received wisdom', and this is how pre- and post-test responses were evaluated throughout the work considered so far. The implication is that, in addition to exchanging views, children must also resolve differences in a productive fashion. Recognizing this, many studies have included resolution during peer dialogue among their coding categories. Strangely though, few have obtained evidence that what might be termed 'dialogic resolution' plays a critical role, at least during the period of middle childhood. During this period, differences of opinion are seldom resolved during the course of peer dialogue, no matter whether they occur in the context of formal group work (Hartup, French, Laursen, Johnston and Ogawa 1993) or unstructured play (Howe and McWilliam 2001, 2006). As noted already, my studies of group work in science placed considerable emphasis upon discussion and agreement. Yet even here groups typically either by-passed the agreement stage altogether, or restricted their agreement to superficial features. For instance, groups might converge on predictions (such as that particular objects will float in water), but not on the factors that justify predictions (hollowness, woodenness, lightness, etc.) or that explain outcomes once predictions are tested. Moreover, in my work and in the work of others, dialogic resolution in middle childhood seldom emerges as a determinant of cognitive growth on the rare occasions that it is observed (for evidence and further discussion, see Howe *et al.* 2007).

If progress depends upon differences being resolved but resolution during peer dialogue makes a limited contribution, there must be 'post-dialogic' activity that includes resolution. Although seldom contemplated explicitly, evidence already exists that such activity occurs. The ideas that children produce during post-tests a few weeks after group work with peers have sometimes been found to be superior to the ideas produced during group work itself (Howe *et al.* 1992b; Mugny and Doise 1978). Yet post-test performance was predicted by differences of opinion during group discussion. The ideas produced at post-tests 11 weeks after group work with peers have been found to be superior to the ideas produced at post-tests only four weeks after (Tolmie *et al.* 1993), despite the fact that progress was again predicted by within-group differences. Intrigued by such results, my colleagues and I have recently attempted to explain them via research that considers both group dialogue *and* post-group experiences (Howe, McWilliam and Cross 2005). Our main conclusion is that what might be termed 'delayed resolution' stems from the productive use of post-group events, such use being 'primed' by peer dialogue. Specifically, our research involved: a) pre-testing children aged 9 to 12 years to ascertain their initial understanding of floating and sinking; b) grouping them into foursomes to work on tasks where they formulated joint predictions about floating and sinking, tested these predictions and interpreted outcomes, with their dialogue recorded throughout; c) providing relevant demonstrations without instruction (or even discussion) 2, 4 and 6 weeks after the group task, for example evidence that all other things being equal, big things are more likely to float than small things; d) post-testing the children 2 weeks after the final demonstration. The children were more receptive to the demonstrations than control children who witnessed the demonstrations without experiencing the group tasks (and the associated dialogue), and they also performed better at post-test. Moreover, their pre- to post-test progress also surpassed children who completed the group task without experiencing the demonstrations, and children who experienced neither the group task nor the demonstrations.

With evidence for priming, we also considered what it is about peer dialogue that allows this to happen, bearing in mind the established relation between the expression of differences and cognitive growth. We noted that difference can sometimes amount to contradiction, for instance 'Big things float' and 'Small things float' are different ideas and also contradictory. Difference does not necessarily involve contradiction. 'Big things float' and 'Light things float' are different, but not contradictory. However to the extent that contradiction occurs (and is not resolved), basic memory processes (detailed in Howe *et al.* 2005) guarantee that the incompatibility will remain 'activated' for some considerable period. Recognizing this, we hypothesized that unresolved contradiction during peer dialogue plays a role in triggering the post-group processes that, ultimately, result in delayed resolution. We also provided some (albeit limited) evidence to support this hypothesis: groups that expressed contradictory ideas about the contribution of object size to floating and sinking progressed about ten times as much from pre-test to post-test as groups who did not discuss object size. Even more recent work (Howe 2009) has attempted to supplement this evidence by examining the associations between unresolved contradiction and pre- to post-test progress through new analyses of data obtained for three further (and already published) studies: a) Howe *et al.* (1992b) on motion down an inclined plane (the source of what below are called the 'motion data'); b) Howe *et al.* (1995a) on the cooling of warm liquids (the source of what are termed the 'cooling data'; c) another study reported in Howe *et al.* (2005) and also on floating and sinking (the source of the so-called 'flotation data'). The remainder of this section will summarize the methods that were used in the studies, the new analyses that were conducted, and the relevant results.[2]

All three of the selected studies were conducted in primary schools, and involved 8- to 12-year-old children (motion data, cooling data) or 9- to 12-year-old children (flotation data). They all began with individual pre-tests covering the relevant area of science to establish base-line knowledge. The pre-tests used items where: a) the results of manipulating apparatus had to be predicted and explained, for instance whether (and why) the water inside containers that vary in thickness, material, surface area or colour cools down quickly or slowly; b) the described outcomes of real-world scenarios had to be interpreted, for example why boats float on the sea. The pre-tests were administered in one-to-one interviews with responses noted by the interviewer (motion data, cooling data) or via whole-class presentation with responses written in answer books (flotation data). Pre-tested children were assigned to foursomes for purposes of group work, although absence from school on the relevant day meant that some groups operated as triads. Groups were all same-age, but since gender was not taken into consideration during group assignment, groups varied in gender composition. Groups came one-by-one to private rooms in their schools to undertake tasks, which were completed in single sessions. The tasks deployed the predict-test-interpret format that has been discussed already, specifically they revolved around series of items where outcomes had to be jointly predicted through discussion within the group, agreed predictions had to be tested, and test results had to be jointly interpreted. For instance, the distances that toy vehicles of varying weight and starting position roll off slopes of varying angle and friction had to be predicted, observed through testing, and interpreted. Groups were guided through the tasks via workbooks, with a researcher on hand in the early stages to offer procedural advice. Group interaction was recorded on videotape (motion data, cooling data) or audiotape (flotation data). Group participants were post-tested following procedures that were equivalent to those used at pre-test. The Howe *et al.* (1992b) study from which the motion data were derived involved two post-tests, an immediate post-test within half a day of the group task (to a 25 per cent sample, that is one randomly chosen child from each group), and a delayed post-test about 4 weeks later (to all group participants). The Howe *et al.* (1995a) study that generated the cooling data involved a single delayed post-test held between three and eight weeks after the group task. The study from Howe *et al.* (2005) that produced the flotation data involved an immediate post-test within half a day of the group task, and a delayed post-test about 8 weeks later. All group participants completed both post-tests.

The motion data amount to a 50 per cent sample of the data collected for the Howe *et al.* (1992b) study, that is all data relating to the 12 groups (48 children) who comprised the more productive of what can be regarded as two experimental conditions. The cooling data derive from a 25 per cent sample of the groups that were involved in the Howe *et al.* (1995a) research, that is the six groups (23 children) who constituted the simpler of two relatively productive conditions. The flotation data were a 50 per cent sample of the data obtained during the original study, that is all data relating to the nine groups (30 children) who comprised the simpler of two equally productive conditions. Group dialogue was transcribed and, with each dataset, dialogue around four key factors was analysed: a) angle of incline, height of starting position, surface friction of slope, and weight of rolling vehicle with the motion data; b) container thickness, container material, container surface area, and container colour with the cooling data; c) object weight, object size, fluid weight, and fluid volume with the flotation data. Across the datasets, the factors were referred to on 1,887 occasions in total, but on only three occasions did references signal that previous uses were being contradicted. All three are presented below in (1), where it can be seen that only the third goes beyond merely highlighting contradiction and attempts resolution:

(1) A: No, slippy will go much further.
B: I thought you said the surface doesn't matter.
A: I never said the surface doesn't matter.

C: We all thought that one would go faster.
D: Because here she, that has some kind of bumps. The grass, there could be a stone in it.
C: Last time you said surface doesn't matter.
D: And then be quiet now will you. It has kind of bumps and her bike goes like this and when a stone comes she'll stop and put her bike.

E: The weight slows it down.
F: Aha, but he [Child G] was saying that's what pushes it.
E: When it's on the hill, it will just go down 'cos it will just push it right down, but on a surface it will slow it down 'cos it's stuck.

Thus, to the extent that contradiction occurred, it can be safely assumed that it was unresolved, this of course constituting further evidence for the rarity of dialogic resolution as discussed already. Accepting that unresolved contradiction was the norm, its frequency within each group interaction was quantified using two variables. The first variable was restricted to contradiction between adjacent utterances, as when one child said 'I thought heavy things would go further' and another child responded with 'I think light things will go further'. This variable was referred to as *successive contradiction*, and it was found to occur on 106 occasions across the 27 groups. The second variable covered *total contradiction* across the whole interaction, even if the incompatible claims were displaced in time. To appreciate its derivation, it is important to note that every time a factor was referred to, its operation could be clear (for example 'Cooling is faster from wide containers') or unclear ('It's the width'). Clear uses could be in either of two directions (for example 'Cooling is faster from wide containers' or 'Cooling is faster from narrow containers'), or they could deny the factor's relevance (for example 'Width makes no difference'). To quantify total contradiction, the number of times that the *most frequent* use occurred (which happened to be 'Cooling is faster from wide containers' in the cooling data) was divided by the total number of clear uses (for example 'Faster from wide + Faster from narrow + Width makes no difference', but excluding 'Directionality unclear'), and transformed to a percentage. In reality, the variable underestimates the amount of contradiction, for it ignores contradiction between the second and third most frequent uses. This was regarded as justified, in the interests of simplicity, when the least frequent use averaged only 3 per cent of total clear uses across the 12 factors.

Averaging the values for total contradiction across groups on a factor-by-factor basis produced mean percentages for each factor that ranged from 52 per cent to 95 per cent ($M = 79$ per cent across the 12 factors). Within this range, lower percentages indicate more contradiction. Therefore, *negative* correlations between total contradiction and pre- to post-test change indicate positive associations between unresolved contradiction and progress. With successive contradiction, higher values indicate more contradiction (since this variable depends simply on frequency). Therefore here, *positive* correlations with pre- to post-test change suggest positive associations between unresolved contradiction and progress. Correlations were computed using pre- and post-test scores that were either the ones awarded in the original studies or straightforwardly derived from the original scores. With the motion data, this meant scores from '1' to '4' for each of the items that addressed each factor, with '1' indicating no understanding and '4' indicating full understanding. Factor totals for the pre- and post-tests were obtained for each child by totalling across relevant items. A similar approach was taken for each factor in the cooling data and the flotation data, except that the scales ran respectively from '0' to '3' and '0' to '4'. In all cases, change scores were obtained through subtracting pre-test scores from post-test scores, and correcting for pre-test scores. Correlations were computed between pre- to immediate post-test change and total contradiction with four motion factors ($N = 12$ children) and four flotation factors ($N = 30$ children), and between pre- to delayed post-test change and total contradiction with four motion factors ($N = 48$ children), four cooling factors ($N = 23$ children) and four flotation factors ($N = 30$ children). Essentially the same approach was taken with successive contradiction, but its non-occurrence with fluid volume (flotation data) and container thickness (cooling data) meant that it was only computed with three flotation factors and three cooling factors. Correlations were computed for each factor separately, and then average correlations (un-weighted and weighted for sample size) were calculated following guidelines provided in Rosenthal and DiMatteo (2001). Averages were computed first across all pre-test to immediate post-test factors and then across all pre-test to delayed post-test factors.

Neither total nor successive contradiction was associated with pre- to immediate post-test growth. Only three of the correlations between total contradiction and pre- to immediate post-test change were in the negative direction that, with this variable, imply associations with progress. All three correlations were small, and statistically non-significant ($r = -.07$ to $-.24$). In fact the only values to approach statistical significance ($r = .46$ with surface friction and $r = .51$ with vehicle weight, both motion data) were positive. In other words, the *less* the children contradicted each other over these factors, the more progress they made from pre- to immediate post-test. Successive contradiction was positively correlated with pre- to immediate post-test change with four factors and negatively correlated with three. In all cases, the values were too small to achieve statistical significance ($r = -.10$ to $.28$). Overall, the un-weighted and weighted average correlations involving the immediate post-test data were non-significant with both indices of contradiction (for total contradiction, un-weighted $r = .13$, weighted $r = .08$; for successive contradiction, both un-weighted and weighted $r = .10$). With the delayed post-test data by contrast, there was strong evidence for associations between unresolved contradiction and progress. Ten of the 12 correlations between total contradiction and pre- to post-test change were in the (encouraging) negative direction ($r = -.01$ to $-.91$). Four of the values were statistically significant ($p < .05$ to $< .001$). All ten of the correlations involving successive contradiction were positive ($r = .06$ to $.46$), and four values were statistically significant ($p < .05$). With both variables, the un-weighted and weighted averages were also highly significant (for total contradiction, un-weighted $r = -.32$, $p < .001$, weighted $r = -.25$, $p < .001$; for successive contradiction, un-weighted $r = .25$, $p < .001$, weighted $r = .24$, $p < .001$) .

From delayed resolution to dialogic resolution

The analyses reported in Howe (2009) are correlational, and therefore no causal relation can be inferred between unresolved contradiction and knowledge growth. Nevertheless, the pattern of relationships is exactly what would be expected if Howe *et al.*'s (2005) proposal is correct, and the unresolved contradiction that may occur when differing opinions are expressed triggers post-dialogic processes that can result in productive but delayed resolution. In other words, there was no relation between unresolved contradiction and immediate post-test performance, but unresolved contradiction was strongly and consistently related to delayed post-test performance. Therefore, the analyses should set the scene for the design of the controlled investigations that could, in principle at least, provide compelling evidence. Suppose, though, that such investigations proved confirmatory, the question would be raised of *why* delayed resolution occurs, rather than the seemingly more efficient dialogic resolution. One answer lies with the reasoning demands that dialogic resolution imposes. Specifically, in the context of tasks like those discussed above, dialogic resolution requires that one participant (at least) evaluates the competing ideas in a principled fashion, and by virtue of doing this produces a superior account. This might involve rejecting both ideas and looking for an alternative, rejecting one idea and asserting the other, or combining both ideas into a superior construction. Whatever the case, it would require what Inhelder and Piaget (1958) termed 'co-ordination of co-ordinations' or 'formal operations'. Inhelder and Piaget's evidence for the challenge that this form of reasoning poses, in adolescence and beyond, has been replicated on many subsequent occasions (for example, Howe, Tolmie and Sofroniou 1999; Kuhn, Garcia-Mila, Zohar and Andersen 1995; Schauble 1990). It is little wonder, then, that dialogic resolution was challenging in the period of middle childhood that was the focus above.

However, while the form of reasoning discussed by Inhelder and Piaget (1958) and others may be challenging, it is also thought to become more accessible as development proceeds. Therefore, if it does have something to do with the absence of dialogic resolution during middle childhood, there should be signs of increasing capacity for dialogic resolution at later stages. The results of two further studies with older students may be indicative of precisely this capacity. Specifically, one study with undergraduate students studying arts, science and social science at university could be interpreted as implicating dialogic resolution. A second study with 12- to 15-year-olds could signify transition during adolescence between delayed and dialogic resolution. Starting then with the former study (Howe, Tolmie, Anderson and Mackenzie 1992a; Howe and Tolmie 1998), the task presented to the students involved watching two trains move across a computer screen, one at constant speed and one at varying speed. Working in pairs, the students were asked to judge, using a 'Help' facility that included distance-time information if they wished, at which of three points, the trains' speed would have been identical. To produce problems of varying difficulty, the trains sometimes started together, and sometimes started successively. They sometimes started from the same side of the screen, and sometimes started from opposite sides. Sometimes, the students were asked to adopt the perspective of an observer seated on a moving third train that appeared on a track between the other two. Whatever the problem, the students were required to compare judgments of speed that they had made independently, resolve differences, input their agreed judgment to the computer and receive feedback on its accuracy (for example 'Sorry, that's the wrong answer'), and jointly interpret any discrepancies between agreed judgment and feedback.

Pairs were formulated to work on the task using pre-test responses such that some pairs contained students with similar views, and others contained students with differing views. The superiority of students from the latter pairs as regards pre- to post-test change, together with the elements of dialogue that were predictive of change, provided yet more evidence for the power of difference in the pursuit of shared goals. In addition, though, differences over initial judgments or discrepancies between judgment and feedback typically triggered references to conceptual material, sometimes material derived from earlier problems. On occasion, such references led to the construction of superior conceptual frameworks as in (2) below. When this happened, on-task performance improved, and improvements were sustained to post-test. When this did not happen, on-task and post-test performance were poorer. Because the conceptual framework illustrated in (2) seems a clear-cut instance of dialogic resolution, the implication is that in this undergraduate sample, dialogic resolution was critical to effecting growth. When it occurred, the students progressed. In its absence, they did not fall back upon delayed resolution, but simply failed to progress.

(2) A: When they get to X, they're moving almost beside each other, and then the top one overtakes it.
B: So what does that tell us?
A: Well, because they're not moving relative to each other, they must be doing the same speed.
B: I'm not sure.
A: Let's put a graph up. That's the distance travelled in the time. At X, the spaces are about the same size. By the time it gets to Z, they're bigger.

B: I'll go for X. [Inserts answer – correct]
A: Let's put the graph up like before.
B: Yes, if we can work out that it's definitely right by using the graph, we should do
    that. [Accesses distance/time display]
B: So we need somewhere where the spaces are the same.
A: Yes, looks like Y. [Inserts answer – correct]
B: This is easy, isn't it?

Moving now to the study with 12- to 15-year-olds (Howe and Tolmie 1998; Howe, Tolmie and Mackenzie 1995b; Tolmie and Howe 1993), the task here was also computer-presented, and completed in pairs. Once more, some pairs comprised students with similar views, and others comprised students with differing views. The positive contribution of differing views was confirmed through comparison of pre- to post-test change in the two types of pair, and through analysis of dialogue. However, in contrast to the undergraduates, the 12- to 15-year-olds were required to plot the paths traced by objects as they fall after horizontal, pendular or circular motion. Thus, the problems included a golf ball rolling off a cliff, a swinging conker falling from a string, and sparks flying off a Catherine wheel, with paths to be plotted by clicking on-screen. As with the undergraduates working on the train task, references to conceptual material were stimulated by difference, this time the discovery of differences between the paths that individual students drew prior to working together and/or between agreed paths plotted on-screen and the feedback on accuracy that the computer provided. However, in this study, there was no evidence of conceptual material being drawn together into a superior framework, let alone of this framework being instrumental in subsequent growth.

   With some pairs, references to conceptual material influenced the quality of the paths that the students drew together, and when this happened, the quality of the paths predicted pre- to post-test change. However, there were no signs of explicit, shared frameworks emerging at the conceptual level. The relationship was between conceptual references and paths, not between conceptual references themselves. With other pairs, references to conceptual material triggered references to earlier problems, and jointly the extent of these references predicted pre- to post-test change. However, once more this does not constitute co-ordination at the conceptual level; it simply means co-ordination between current concepts and previous solutions. Nevertheless, although there was no evidence for shared conceptual frameworks in either response style, the students must have realized that progress rested on relating conceptions to something else. With some pairs, it was typically the present paths; with others it was typically previous solutions. In making these linkages on-task, the students were clearly achieving something that the younger children discussed in the previous section did not manage. This is what suggests that the 12- to 15-year-olds may have been transitional between the delayed resolution observed with the younger children, and the dialogic resolution aspired to (and sometimes achieved) by the undergraduates.

Conclusions

The literature surveyed in this chapter leads to four conclusions, which can be drawn with varying degrees of confidence. The first conclusion is that there is value in peer dialogue that involves the exchange of differing opinions in the service of joint goals. Evidence to support this conclusion has been drawn from a wide variety of topic areas, and as the chapter has progressed, a broadening age range. It is therefore as close to a certainty as it is possible to achieve. The second conclusion is that, although differing opinions must be productively resolved if progress is to occur, resolution does not always happen at the time differences are expressed. It can take place on a subsequent occasion. This conclusion is also well supported. Consistent evidence has been available (albeit overlooked) for some considerable period, and this evidence has now been supplemented via the new research of Howe (2009). The third conclusion is that delayed resolution may depend upon contradictory views being expressed during peer dialogue, and the contradiction not being addressed. This conclusion is less certain, for despite the support provided in Howe *et al.* (2005) and Howe (2009), definitive research has yet to be conducted. The correlational nature of the analyses does not, for instance, preclude the trigger from being an *associate* of unresolved contradiction, rather than unresolved contradiction itself. The final conclusion is the least certain, and it is that there may be developmental progression from delayed resolution to dialogic resolution. The conclusion is consistent with data that have been presented here. Indeed, it would be difficult to use anything but a 'developmental transition' account to explain the relations between dialogue and progress that were observed with the 12- to 15-year-olds working on the object fall task. Nevertheless, the account is *post hoc*, and there are many differences in addition to participant age between the studies with 12- to 15-year-olds and undergraduates and the studies with younger groups. Computer versus workbook presentation is one such difference, as is the use of pairs versus large groups.[3] Task content varied across the studies, when consistency would be preferable.

Thus, the chapter contributes to literature (also developed elsewhere in this volume) indicating that peer dialogue can promote cognitive growth, but in addition tentatively endorses the possibility, raised over 75 years ago by Piaget, that the relation may not be unidirectional. This said, it is important to stress that, even if a two-way relationship does eventually become established, this should not be interpreted as meaning that the 'development', which shapes dialogue, is independent of dialogue itself. Towards the beginning of the chapter, research was summarized that demonstrates the relevance of group work and/or peer dialogue to performance on Piaget's conservation and spatial transformation tasks (i.e. Ames and Murray 1982; Bearison *et al.* 1986; Doise and Mugny 1979; Doise *et al.* 1975; Mugny and Doise 1978). Within Piaget's theory and also within most modern approaches to cognitive development, the cognitive structures that underpin success on these tasks are regarded as necessary, but insufficient, conditions for the 'co-ordinations of co-ordinations' (or 'formal operations') that earlier were seen as underpinning dialogic resolution. The implication is that dialogically triggered development becomes consolidated and abstracted, creating structures that influence future dialogically triggered development. In other words, the relation between peer dialogue and cognitive growth is *interactive*, which is of course how Piaget construed the situation in his two early books. Indeed, despite the incompatibility, noted earlier, with specific claims made in Vygotsky (1978), the relation is entirely consistent with the broader thrust of Vygotskian thinking.

The possibility of an interactive relation between dialogue and development stems from the identification of two forms of resolution, delayed and dialogic, and the existence of these two forms needs to be taken into consideration regardless of developmental progression. In particular, researchers and teachers need to be wary of presuming dialogic resolution (and measuring success solely with reference to on-task progress) when key changes may occur subsequently. Teachers need, in addition, to recognize the implications of delayed resolution for classroom support. Perhaps delayed resolution can be supported through follow-up activities, via wall-charts, internet resources or visits to museums. Perhaps it can be undermined through inadvertent attempts to achieve premature closure. Results obtained by Howe *et al.* (2007) in the study that was discussed earlier make this latter possibility only too plausible, for these results indicate significant *negative* relations between teachers' efforts to shape group outcomes and the amount that children learned. Recent research summarized in Webb (2009) suggests that teachers should employ 'softly-softly' strategies when consolidating group work, hinting and coaxing rather than evaluating and correcting. The reason why such strategies are successful may be their greater compatibility with delayed resolution. Thus, it is possible already to derive significant implications for research and practice from the distinction between delayed and dialogic resolution. As more is learned about the contexts in which the two forms apply, it ought to be feasible to sharpen these implications into precise models. The enterprise is challenging, but hopefully the present chapter has made a start by highlighting developmental change as one key dimension for future research.

Notes

1 The summary presented in the first section appears in similar form as part of Howe and Mercer (2007).
2 The research was supported by the British Academy, whose contribution is gratefully acknowledged.
3 The variation over group size was, in fact, a *consequence* of the variation over mode of presentation. There is evidence that pairs are the normal classroom group size for computer-based work, while larger groups are typically used in non-computer environments (for details, see Howe *et al.* 1995; Howe and Tolmie 1998). It was a desire to mimic routine practices that led to the use of pairs with computer-based tasks in my research, and the use of large groups with workbook-based tasks.

References

Ames, G. J. and Murray, F. B. (1982) 'When two wrongs make a right: promoting cognitive change by social conflict', *Developmental Psychology*, 18:894–7.
Bakhtin, M. M. (1981) *The Dialogic Imagination: four essays*, Austin, TX: University of Texas Press.
Bearison, D. J., Magzamen, S. and Filardo, E. K. (1986) 'Socio-cognitive conflict and cognitive growth in young children', *Merrill-Palmer Quarterly*, 32:51–72.
Berkowitz, M. W. and Gibbs, J. C. (1983) 'Measuring the developmental features of moral discussion', *Merrill-Palmer Quarterly*, 29:399–410.
Berkowitz, M. W., Gibbs, J. C. and Broughton, J. M. (1980) 'The relation of moral judgement stage disparity to developmental effects of peer dialogues', *Merrill-Palmer Quarterly*, 26:341–57.

Blaye, A. (1990) 'Peer interaction in solving a binary matrix problem: possible mechanisms causing individual progress', *Learning and Instruction*, 2:45–56.

Damon, W. and Killen, M. (1982) 'Peer interaction and the process of change in children's moral reasoning', *Merrill-Palmer Quarterly*, 28:347–67.

Damon, W. and Phelps, E. (1989) 'Critical distinctions among three approaches to peer education', *International Journal of Educational Research*, 5:9–19.

Doise, W. and Mugny, G. (1979) 'Individual and collective conflicts of centrations in cognitive development', *European Journal of Psychology*, 9:105–8.

Doise, W., Mugny, G. and Perret-Clermont, A.-N. (1975) 'Social interaction and the development of cognitive operations', *European Journal of Social Psychology*, 5:367–83.

Goodlad, S. and Hirst, B. (1989) *Peer Tutoring: a guide to learning by teaching*, New York: Nichols.

Hartup, W. W., French, D. C., Laursen, B., Johnston, M. K. and Ogawa, J. R. (1993) 'Conflict and friendship relations in middle childhood: behavior in a closed-field situation', *Child Development*, 64:445–54.

Howe, C. and McWilliam, D. (2001) 'Peer argument in educational settings: variation due to socioeconomic status, gender, and activity context', *Journal of Language and Social Psychology*, 20:61–80.

Howe, C., McWilliam, D. and Cross, G. (2005) 'Chance favours only the prepared mind: incubation and the delayed effects of peer collaboration', *British Journal of Psychology*, 96:67–93.

Howe, C. and Mercer, N. (2007) 'Children's social development: peer interaction and classroom learning', *The Primary Review*, Research Survey, 2/1b.

Howe, C., Rodgers, C. and Tolmie, A. (1990) 'Physics in the primary school: peer interaction and the understanding of floating and sinking', *European Journal of Psychology of Education*, V: 459–75.

Howe, C., Tolmie, A., Greer, K. and Mackenzie, M. (1995a) 'Peer collaboration and conceptual growth in physics: task influences on children's understanding of heating and cooling', *Cognition and Instruction*, 13:483–503.

Howe, C., Tolmie, A. and Mackenzie, M. (1995b) 'Computer support for the collaborative learning of physics concepts', in C. O'Malley (ed.) *Computer-Supported Collaborative Learning*, Berlin: Springer.

Howe, C., Tolmie, A. and Rodgers, C. (1992b) 'The acquisition of conceptual knowledge in science by primary school children: group interaction and the understanding of motion down an incline', *British Journal of Developmental Psychology*, 10:113–30.

Howe, C., Tolmie, A., Thurston, A., Topping, K., Christie, D., Livingston, K., Jessiman, E., and Donaldson, C. (2007) 'Group work in elementary science: Towards organizational principles for supporting pupil learning', *Learning and Instruction*, 17:549–63.

Howe, C. and Tolmie, A. (1998) 'Productive interaction in the context of computer-supported collaborative learning in science', in K. Littleton and P. Light (eds), *Learning with Computers: analysing productive interaction*, London: Routledge.

Howe, C. J. (2009) 'Collaborative group work in middle childhood: joint construction, unresolved contradiction and the growth of knowledge', *Human Development*, 39: 71–94.

Howe, C. J. and McWilliam, D. (2006) 'Opposition in social interaction amongst children: why intellectual benefits do not mean social costs', *Social Development*, 15:205–31.

Howe, C. J. and Tolmie, A. (2003) 'Group work in primary school science: discussion, consensus and guidance from experts', *International Journal of Educational Research*, 39:51–72.

Howe, C. J., Tolmie, A., Anderson, A. and Mackenzie, M. (1992a) 'Conceptual knowledge in physics: the role of group interaction in computer-supported teaching', *Learning and Instruction*, 2:161–83.

Howe, C. J., Tolmie, A. and Sofroniou, N. (1999) 'Experimental appraisal of personal beliefs in science: constraints on performance in the 9 to 14 age group', *British Journal of Educational Psychology*, 69:243–74.

Inhelder, B. and Piaget, J. (1958) *The Growth of Logical Thinking*, New York: Basic Books.

Johnson, D. W. and Johnson, F. P. (2000) *Joining Together: group theory and group Skills* (7th edn), Boston: Allyn and Bacon.

Kruger, A. C. (1992) 'The effect of peer and adult-child transactive discussions on moral reasoning', *Merrill-Palmer Quarterly*, 38:191–211.

Kuhn, D., Garcia-Mila, M., Zohar, A. and Andersen, C. (1995) 'Strategies in knowledge acquisition', *Monographs of the Society for Research in Child Development*, 60, Serial No. 245.

Leman, P. L. and Duveen, G. (1999) 'Representations of authority and children's moral reasoning', *European Journal of Social Psychology*, 29:557–75.

Miell, D. and Littleton, K. (2004) *Collaborative Creativity*, London: Free Association Books.

Miell, D. and MacDonald, R. (2000) 'Children's creative collaborations: the importance of friendship when working together on a musical composition', *Social Development*, 9:348–69.

Mugny, G. and Doise, W. (1978) 'Socio-cognitive conflict and structure of individual and collective performances', *European Journal of Social Psychology*, 8:181–92.

Piaget, J. (1926) *The Language and Thought of the Child*, London: Routledge and Kegan Paul.

Piaget, J. (1932) *The Moral Judgment of the Child*, London: Routledge and Kegan Paul.

Pontecorvo, C., Paoletti, G. and Orsolini, M. (1989) 'Use of the computer and social interaction in a language curriculum', *Golem*, 5:12–14.

Rosenthal, R. and DiMatteo, M. R. (2001) 'Meta-analysis: recent developments in quantitative methods for literature reviews', *American Review of Psychology*, 52:59–82.

Roy, A. W. N. and Howe, C. J. (1990) 'Effects of cognitive conflict, socio-cognitive conflict and imitation on children's socio-legal thinking', *European Journal of Social Psychology*, 20:241–52.

Schauble, L. (1990) 'Belief revision in children: the role of prior knowledge and strategies for generating evidence', *Journal of Experimental Child Psychology*, 49:31–57.

Schwartz, B. B., Newman, Y. and Biezuner, S. (2000) 'Two wrongs may make a right ... if they argue together!', *Cognition and Instruction*, 18:461–94.

Slavin, R. E. (1995) *Co-operative Learning: theory, research and practice* (2nd edn), Boston: Allyn and Bacon.

Tolmie, A. and Howe, C. J. (1993) 'Gender and dialogue in secondary school physics', *Gender and Education*, 5:191–209.

Tolmie, A., Christie, D., Howe, C., Thurston, A., Topping, K., Donaldson, C., Jessiman, E. and Livingston, K. (2007) 'Classroom relations and collaborative groupwork in varying social contexts: lessons from Scotland', paper presented at the Annual Meeting of the American Educational Research Association, Chicago.

Tolmie, A., Howe, C. J., Mackenzie, M. and Greer, K. (1993) 'Task design as an influence on dialogue and learning: primary school group work with object flotation', *Social Development*, 2:183–201.

Topping, K. and Ehly, S. (1998) *Peer Assisted Learning*, Mahwah, NJ: Lawrence Erlbaum.

Vygotsky, L. S. (1962) *Thought and Language*, Cambridge, MA: MIT Press.

Vygotsky, L. S. (1978) *Mind in Society: the development of higher psychological processes*, Cambridge, MA: Harvard University Press.

Webb, N. M. (2009) 'The teacher's role in promoting collaborative dialogue in the class-room', *British Journal of Educational Psychology*, 79:1–28.

Wertsch, J. V. (1979) 'From social interaction to higher psychological processes: a clarification and application of Vygotsky's theory', *Human Development*, 22:1–22.

Wood, D. (1989) 'Social interaction as tutoring', in M. H. Bornstein and J. S. Bruner (eds) *Interaction in Human Development*, Hillsdale, NJ: Lawrence Erlbaum.

Chapter 3

Productive interaction as agentic participation in dialogic enquiry

Kristiina Kumpulainen and Lasse Lipponen
University of Helsinki

Introduction

Over the years, many critical voices have surrounded formal education and its pedagogical practices (Hubbard, Mehan and Stein 2006; Resnick 1987; Sarason 1993; Tyack and Cuban 1997). One of the major criticisms posed is that formal education rarely manages to harness those experiences and agency that learners bring to school from other contexts, such as from their homes, playgrounds, after-school clubs, libraries, science centres and museums. Formal education is argued to fail in exploiting the cultural resources, i.e. funds of knowledge (Gonzáles, Moll and Amanti 2005) of learners and the communities they are part of – their expertise, knowledge, and artefacts. This has encouraged school learning to stay disconnected from learners' other worlds.

There is clearly a need for the development of pedagogical approaches that allow learners to make connections between formal and informal settings of learning (Bransford, Vye, Stevens, Kuhl, Schwartz, Bell, Meltzoff, Barron, Pea, Reeves, Roschelle and Sabelli 2006). The funds of knowledge that learners have developed in one setting should become resources in the other. This is likely to increase learners' agency and active engagement in learning that stretches beyond settings and contexts. It is in these pedagogical settings where interaction and learning at school can become productive for learners and their lives, and not only for the schooling itself.

In this chapter, we shall investigate 'dialogic inquiry' as a potential pedagogical approach for productive classroom interaction that promotes learner agency and active participation by harnessing learners' funds of knowledge embedded in diverse settings across time and space. We shall draw upon empirical case study data from one Finnish classroom community whose formal learning spaces were extended to more informal settings of learning, namely to a technology museum, science centre and a forest. The pedagogical learning culture of this classroom community is embedded in the dialogic inquiry approach with a heavy emphasis on the development of students' communication and collaboration skills. In particular, the classroom teacher has systematically promoted students' engagement in exploratory talk and its ground rules (Dawes, Mercer and Wegerif 2004; Mercer and Littleton 2007).

Dialogic inquiry

The proponents of the idea of teaching and learning as dialogic inquiry have been motivated by attempts to convert the culture of formal education into authentic 'communities of practice' (Lave and Wenger 1991) where meanings are jointly explored and negotiated (Mercer and Littleton 2007; Wells 1999). Here, teaching and learning practices are conceptualized as collective, reciprocal, supportive, cumulative and purposeful (Alexander 2006). Stress is placed on multiple positions of authority and identity, promoting negotiation and dialogue for the social construction of knowledge and understanding (Kaartinen and Kumpulainen 2001; Kovalainen and Kumpulainen 2005, 2007). An essential component of dialogic inquiry is that classroom members build openly and freely on each other's knowledge and experiences, and in doing so, further extend their collective thinking about the issues in question (Mercer and Littleton 2007).

Although there is widespread interest in enhancing dialogic inquiry in contemporary classrooms as a medium for participatory pedagogy, several studies have suggested that fostering genuine student engagement in productive interactions is a highly demanding task (Engle and Conant 2002; Lipponen 2000; Polman and Pea 2001; Scott, Mortimer and Aquiar 2006). The multidimensional nature and the flow of classroom interaction require specific sensitivity as well as practical pedagogical know-how from the teacher to follow and respond to various lines of inquiry (Nathan and Knuth 2003; Scott *et al.* 2006). Further, the potentiality of dialogic inquiry practices, in supporting students' active and productive engagement in classroom interactions that extend beyond spaces and places of learning, requires further exploration.

The analytic focus of our chapter is on the culture of a specific classroom and the situated agency and discourse of the students whose dialogic inquiry practices are described and analysed. We have conceptualized the culture of the classroom in terms of patterns of engagement in everyday tasks and activities, accepted ways of talking and interacting with others, and selective deployment of symbolic, technical and concrete tools. By agency we refer to a conception of learning that entails acting authoritatively and accountably, together with the ability to transfer knowledge and skills across contexts (Greeno 2006). Identity (who am I, who do I want to be), we hypothesize, is continually negotiated and re-negotiated in the processes of participation, and is closely related to the development of agency.

In our chapter, we are interested in exploring the potentiality of the dialogic inquiry approach to support learners' agency, and active engagement in learning as they transit and participate in formal and more informal settings of learning as a part of their educational program/curriculum activities.

Dialogic inquiry as participation and positioning

In this study, we define participation in classroom interaction as a socially constructed phenomenon. The participatory positions constructed by and for each individual in the classroom community are made visible in the interactions and actions members take, what they orient to, what they hold each other accountable for, how they respond to each other, and how they engage with, interpret and construct meaning from ongoing interactions (Castanheira, Crawford, Dixon and Green 2001; Stevens and Hall 1998). The participatory positioning of the students cannot be viewed as stable and fixed, in the sense of being identifiable across different social contexts. Rather, the nature of participation in classroom interaction is a dynamic and locally established process that is being constructed and reconstructed within the community. Being a legitimate member of a classroom community, then, means understanding and engaging in joint interactions in ways that mark membership in the community (Castanheira, Green and Dixon 2009). In this process, individuals may also display actions that indicate their membership with other social groups they are part of (Bloome and Egan-Robertson 1993; Wertsch 1991). Thus, when talking about participation in the interactions of the classroom community it is important to recognize the flexibility and possibility of changing one's position even within the same community or social group.

To conceptualize participation in classroom interaction as socially constructed is to understand that the participatory positions of classroom members are both a product of, and a tool for, the community. That is, the interactive practices constructed and made available to members constitute participation as a situated process. Moreover, the participatory practices of the classroom and the position individuals take during the practices develop and change at the same time as the community develops itself. Thus, the participation opportunities and possibilities can be regarded as serving both collective and the individual needs (Lima 1995). Classroom members are afforded and sometimes also denied access to particular interactions within the community. The development of the individual's repertoire of participatory skills in classroom interactions is, consequently, dependent on the kinds of opportunities she or he has access to and which opportunities he or she takes up during the joint activities of the classroom (Alton-Lee and Nuthall 1992; Castanheira *et al.* 2001; Floriani 1993; Heras 1993).

According to Greeno (2006), the competence to function in multiple contexts is developed while students are positioned in activity systems where they are framed as authors of their own learning. It is hypothesized that this strengthens students' agency; in other words, it gives them the possibility to learn to act authoritatively and accountably (problematizing and solving issues), and to build a strong participatory identity and ownership of learning. Children do not merely react and repeat given practices, but intentionally transform and refine their social and material worlds as they confront particular challenges (Emirbayer and Mische 1998).

Dialogic inquiry in the socio-cultural framework

Theoretically, our research work is grounded on the socio-cultural tradition. From this theoretical framework human activities are socially mediated and, thus, learning is seen as a matter of participation in a social process of knowledge construction rather than as an individual endeavour (Vygotsky 1978). Knowledge emerges through the network of interactions and is distributed among those (humans and tools) interacting. As stated by Lave and Wenger (1991), learning is a process that takes place in a participation framework, not in an individual mind. By emphasizing both the processes of enculturation *and* transformation, we are positing an agentic learner whose capacities are afforded and constrained by the cultural tools they can *access* within their social setting. Culture itself has been theorized as a shared way of living within communities that is continuously being re-constituted through the use (invention and reinvention) of cultural tools, technologies, artefacts and concepts (Gonzáles *et al.* 2005). In the socio-cultural framework, learning is not just a matter of epistemology, but also a matter of ontology, the development of identity and *agency* (Packer and Goicoechea 2000).

The conceptual framework of our research work is embedded within the socio-cultural, as well as ethnographic and socio-linguistic (i.e. interactional socio-linguistics) perspectives that all view the context of learning as a cultural site of meaning, in which norms, values, rules, roles and relationships are socially constructed into being in the local interactions of the community (Bowers, Cobb and McClain 1999; Castanheira *et al.* 2001; Cole 1996). The socially established cultural practices of the learning environment become evident and are continuously re-constructed in the social life of the classroom community, reflected in the legitimate ways of participation and communication (Wells 1999; Wenger 1998). The local, moment-by-moment classroom interactions thus signal what counts as learning, participating and communicating. The commonly shared and patterned ways of interacting in the classroom community can be regarded as both providing and also limiting the access of classroom members to particular opportunities for learning (Castanheira *et al.* 2001; Kantor, Green, Bradley and Lin 1992; Nathan and Knuth 2003).

Classroom community

The empirical study we draw upon in our chapter has been carried out in a comprehensive school setting in the metropolitan area of Helsinki. The participants were 18 third-grade students from a Finnish elementary class, and their teacher. Of the 18 students, nine were boys and nine were girls, aged from 9 to 10 years. The students were a representative sample of children in Finnish society in terms of socio-economic background. Unique to this classroom was, however, the practice of working and acting as a community of dialogic inquirers (Wells 1999) as evidenced by the pre-study observations of the classroom community in different subject domains as well as interview data and informal discussions with the classroom teacher. Distinctive of this classroom community was also that its learning spaces were extended by the classroom teacher to more informal settings of learning, namely to a technology museum, science centre and a forest.

The classroom teacher could be described as an expert teacher who has continually developed his professional competence by studying and researching educational sciences. The teacher's pedagogical thinking has been influenced by the socio-cultural approach, namely the Thinking Together project (Dawes *et al.* 2004; Mercer and Littleton 2007), which he has actively applied in his classroom to provide students with greater opportunities to communicate, collaborate and learn. The instructional activities applied by the teacher while working with the students on academic tasks are mostly collective discussions and small group activities. In sum, in this classroom a heavy emphasis was placed upon social interaction and discourse as tools for learning and thinking.

Chronotopic analysis of dialogic inquiry practices

In our study, we are interested in exploring the potentiality of the dialogic inquiry approach to operate as a form of productive interaction that promotes students' agentic participation in learning within the formal context of schooling. In our analysis we are focusing on learner agency and how it manifests itself in classroom interaction. Our investigation is based on a chronotopic analysis (Brown and Renshaw 2006), which functions as a conceptual and analytic tool to locate evidence of learner agency and active engagement in dialogic inquiry.

The chronotopic analysis makes visible students' participation in different settings of learning, mediated by the interaction of past experiences, ongoing involvement and goals that are intended to be accomplished (Brown and Renshaw 2006). The analysis illuminates learners' agency as they collectively explore and negotiate their experiences, understandings and relationships embedded in different settings. In viewing the processes of learning as relational and transformative, chronotopes can be defined as creative spaces in which students' agency and identities are negotiated. It is these time-space relationships and students' agency that we are interested in exploring as the classroom community moves both physically and psychologically to different spaces and timescales in their interactions.

The concept of chronotope can be traced back to the work of Bakhtin (1981) who defines the spatiotemporal matrix as being produced, shaped and reshaped by the discourses of the participants as they relate to spaces and times beyond here and now (Brown and Renshaw 2006; Hirst 2004). In his work, Bakhtin captures the temporal and spatial situatedness of human actions. Specific chronotopes are said to correspond to particular genres, or relatively stable ways of speaking, which themselves represent particular worldviews and ideologies. To this extent, a chronotope can be regarded as both a cognitive concept and a narrative feature of language. The distinctiveness of chronotopic analysis, in comparison to most other uses of time and space in language analysis, stems from the fact neither time nor space is privileged by Bakhtin; they are utterly interdependent and they should be studied in this manner.

Conducting the analysis

The empirical data on which we draw were collected during a 5-month period (January–May) in the classroom community. The classes were observed and video recorded. Field notes were made to help create transcripts from the videotaped lessons. Interviews with the teacher were also conducted, audio recorded, and transcribed. In addition, classroom artefacts, such as student work, were available.

Our data analysis is grounded on an ethnographic logic of inquiry (Castanheira, Green, Dixon and Yaeger 2007; Castanheira *et al.* 2009). This approach to data analysis proceeds as a series of cycles during which questions are posed, data are represented – in our case in the form of video recordings, transcriptions and students' artefacts – and significant events are analysed. Our analytic approach is, thus, not linear. Central to our analysis is a *multi-step, multi-phase recursive analysis process.* In following the suggestions of Erickson (2007) we considered the videotapes as data sources, from which we constructed the core data. Firstly, we took a rough preview of all the videos, and made content logs, that is, a time-indexed list of topics taking place during sessions (Jordan and Henderson 1995). We observed the videos several times in order to learn more, and engaged in, what Engle, Conant and Greeno (2007) call progressive refinement of hypotheses, for providing more specific focuses for our analysis. We have also applied contrastive analysis in order to validate our interpretations through triangulating perspectives.

Via our multi-step and multi-phase recursive analysis, we have identified anchors, or key events in the interaction data that are relevant to our chronotopic analysis. Through our analysis we created what Mitchell (1984) calls a *telling case*. Mitchell argues that ethnographically described events can be presented to make logical inferences or generalizations that will serve to illuminate obscure aspects of general theory. Selection and analysis of telling cases is informed by the researcher's knowledge of the connections between the telling case and the contexts informing the researcher and the participants constituting a telling case. Therefore, in using chronotopes as a tracer unit, we are able to explore students' agency and its manifestation.

Locating learner agency in dialogic inquiry: telling cases

Below, we share and discuss five transcripts of students' dialogic inquiry practices. Our examples, i.e. 'telling cases', illuminate the ways in which learners' agency manifested itself as the classroom community collectively explored and negotiated their experiences, understandings and relationships embedded in different settings.

Learners positioning themselves as accountable authors

Our first telling case highlights the ways in which the classroom community collectively explores a statement that one of the students, Roope, had taken up from their visit to the museum of technology. The guide in the museum had informed the classroom that money is made from wool and not from paper. Roope found it important that this piece of information be collectively discussed back in the classroom. The teacher valued Roope's initiation and he gave Roope a space to realize and lead a collective discussion on the matter. In doing so, the teacher appears to leave his expert's role, and shares the authority with the students. Especially, Roope's position is expanded by receiving the rights and duties of a chairman. This distribution of rights and duties puts him in a position where he has an increased possibility to learn to act authoritatively and accountably (Greeno 2006). But the possibility of acting accountably, is not just Roope's privilege. In fact, in this episode, students are being positioned as active agents in the classroom discussion with the role of contributing to shared inquiry and knowledge construction. As pointed out by Boaler and Greeno (2000), students are framed in a position where they are mutually accountable for constructing shared understanding. How you can function in a situation depends on how you are positioned or how you position yourself. Positioning students as accountable authors appeared to set up a lively and multi-voiced discussion and to open up opportunities for new purposes and modes of discursive action. To become an agent one must be treated as if one can do something of one's own volition. Thus, agency, for its realization depends upon and is constrained by social relations. It is, to the core, a social phenomenon; a potential, a capacity, which must be develop through social activities (Ratner 2000).

What is notable also in this extract is the way in which a student, Saara, contests the claim of money being made from wool. She also convincingly justifies her argument by referring to her experiences at home. In all, this episode demonstrates reasoning and argumentation by the students evidencing their active engagement and agency.

Excerpt 1

ROOPE: well there, when we were at the museum of technology, the guide said that they don't make money from paper, but from wool

TEACHER: Roope is the chairman now, does anyone want to comment on this

SAARA: I don't believe that

TEACHER: put your hand up, and Roope will give you your turn

ROOPE: Saara

SAARA: I can say that, even if it is scientific, I don't believe that

TEACHER: ok, does anyone else want to comment

ROOPE: Kimmo

KIMMO: yes, it can be true, if they put it into some kind of machine, and the machine makes them

ROOPE: exactly, you can see, if you look really closely, you can see some of it

KIMMO: exactly, just that

ROOPE: Aaro

AARO: well, I think they make it, well, maybe out of wool, I'm not sure

SAARA: I don't believe it, whoever the guide is

ROOPE: Kimmo

KIMMO: some kind of machine makes it, just like they make money with machines, too

ROOPE: yes, it's the same, in a way, made of wool completely, it's not paper

TEACHER: I have something to say on this topic

ROOPE: teacher

TEACHER: yes, relating to this, could someone tell me why they might make it out of wool instead of paper, even though it might be easier just to make it out of paper, with a photocopier

KIMMO: Roope, you are the chairman

ROOPE: I know, it lasts longer, from what I hear, because money circulates a long time, so if you buy something from the store, pay with money, then it circulates, they give cash back to someone who buys something else with it. So it needs to be durable.

ROOPE: Pauliina

PAULIINA: yeah, it's probably also because it's more durable, because if it was just paper, anybody could just take the money and put it into a copying machine, and they could just make copies very easily, because it was just paper, and you copy it. It would be very easy that way. (unclear)

ROOPE: Saara

SAARA: well I have two things now, can I say both

TEACHER: do they have anything to do with this topic

SAARA: yes. I don't understand how they could make it out of wool, I once cut one of those foreign notes, which was useless, I cut it in half. Or then, I've cut a Finnish note, too, once, when mum said I can cut just the one, so I cut it and it wasn't durable at all, and I tore it and it wasn't durable at all.

ROOPE: well it isn't that durable in that sense, but from what I've heard, paper is weaker, so should they make money out of some metal, so that you need some kind of cutters to break it

SAARA: and I don't have to believe that

TEACHER: no you don't have to believe it. If you get a good explanation, then maybe you can change your mind.

Taking on different positions

This short episode highlights another out-of-school visit in which the class participated in collaboration with the first and third graders. Here, the students flexibly change positions as teachers and students, helping and guiding one another when needed; using the support of others, and recognizing others' need for support. This is what Edwards and D'Arcy (2004; Edwards 2007) refer to as relational agency. Relational agency is a matter of adjusting what one does with the strengths and needs of other members in the community. Relational agency is therefore based on the notion of the ZPD (Zone of Proximal Development), and gains its strength from collaborating with other people.

Excerpt 2

KIMMO: Otto, did you get it, yeah and, let's ask something, how do you tell the difference between these two trees? (waits for an answer) I don't mean you have to say these (points to the exhibition texts), but just in general, how do you tell them apart, Otto (unclear)

OTTO: and those have smaller those things

OLIVER: and look at what colour they are

OTTO: yeah, from that you can tell, too

KIMMO: and from the colour you can tell, too (unclear)

OLIVER: and from that, how you can tell a pine, do you see there, a pine is like, it has lots of these

AARO: Oliver this is a birch

OLIVER: Yeah. No a fir … no, a birch, yeah. It has lots of this stuff.

The interplay of time and place in dialogic inquiry

In our third telling case the classroom community is collectively exploring stones as a part of their curriculum activities. In addition to school-based activities, the project on stones has involved visits to a forest, science centre and a technology museum. The role of the teacher as a guide in helping students to navigate in the past, present and future (Emirbayer and Mische 1998) is powerfully demonstrated here. The teacher initiates the episode by asking students to recall their experiences of the science centre and their stone laboratory. In doing so, he refers to the shared history of the learning community. A student, Jimi, responds to the teacher's invitation and shares his investigations at the countryside about the weight of different types of stones. The teacher builds his next turn on Jimi's contribution. By referring to Jimi's idea, 'now this is interesting', the teacher is crediting Jimi's authority by recognizing his contribution as valuable for the learning community. Then the teacher visits the future with the classroom in encouraging the students to use their knowledge later on (in the future); to investigate and measure stones in a similar manner in the forthcoming visit to the museum of technology. The excerpt shows that while responding to the demands of dialogic inquiry, students must reconstruct their view of the past in order to create future oriented actions of inquiry.

Excerpt 3

TEACHER: Hey, how do you recognize a lodestone, well, there are probably lots of ways, *remember when you were at the museum*, you studied stones, and there you did, you studied conduction of electricity, does this ring a bell? Then there was, Jimi, do you want to say something, about this topic directly?
JIMI: (unclear) for example a lodestone is heavier
TEACHER: okay
JIMI: for example, I've in the countryside, limonite, if you have a limonite the size of a fist, then it probably weighs the same as a regular stone three times that size, you can tell by the weight
TEACHER: *now this was interesting*, because *when you go the the museum of technology*, you can try, there's three different kinds of stones, one of which is lodestone, they're the same size, and you have a scale, so you can test *if it's true what Jimi says, we'll see there*, that might be one way.

Revisiting past experiences as a learning potentiality

In this episode the classroom community is reflecting on experiences and learning gains from the visit to the museum of technology. Beforehand, the students had constructed questions for reflection under the guidance of the teacher and now each child in the classroom community was engaged in answering the questions. The teacher engaged in reflective discussions with some of the students while they were working on their texts. The extract highlights the challenges the students faced in reflecting on their learning experiences. Moreover, it demonstrates the complexities in pedagogical design of learning activities in and out of school. These are related to the design of reflection activities as well as learning and teaching practices in more informal settings of learning. Out-of school activities do not automatically guarantee more meaningful learning than activities constructed into being within the physical premises of the school.

Excerpt 4

TEACHER: okay, let's stop for a moment, the others can help. What for example could you write on question number one …
PEKKA: I learn … I learnt how to move around in the forest (whispering)
TEACHER: yes, let's think about number one at first, Pekka
PEKKA: I learnt how to move around in the forest and take care
TEACHER: you learnt how to take care of children, take care of children, younger kids, pupils, Anni

ANNI: well Pekka, you're supposed to put there what you learnt about forest as a topic, and not what you learnt in general. So did you learn how to take care of kids with forest as a topic

PEKKA: yeah, I learnt the forest

TEACHER: should we expand the question then, to what I learnt on the trip, so that you can put there whatever

MAJORITY OF PUPILS: no, oh, aah (complaining voices)

JARI: Teacher, how can you write two sentences if you didn't learn anything

TEACHER: well, then one sentence is enough

JARI: I'm just going to write that [I learnt] nothing

TEACHER: okay

SAMI: I know, you can do …

TEACHER: good

JARI: I didn't learn anything on the forest trip

TEACHER: don't talk over me, it could be, that you didn't learn anything, this time around, then we'll think, what we could do, that we'll learn about the topic

JARI: this number two is pretty difficult

TEACHER: has anyone learnt anything or what have you written on number one

JARI: nothing

MARI: I haven't made it that far yet

TEACHER: are there any examples

JARI: no

TEACHER: okay, has anyone thought, that you could answer how I could have learnt

MARI: but not that either, it's pretty impossible to answer

JARI: I just put down nothing

TEACHER: for example … well okay, for example the options that come to my mind, that if you had found an interesting thing there, or if the forest would have been different, or if I had had more time to go where I wanted to go … or if I had received more teaching

JARI: is it ok if I put down, if the forest would have been more interesting

TEACHER: if the forest would have been more interesting, that's one possible answer for sure

JARI: okay

TEACHER: you need to think carefully what

JARI: if the forest would have been more interesting, that's just one sentence

TEACHER: okay, let's agree that one sentence is enough, if you can't think of anything else, but, if all answer sheets say that I learnt nothing, then … I … it's enough, but I'll be a bit disappointed, in that case

JARI: we agreed, on numbers one and two, that [I learnt] nothing

TEACHER: so please try to think about number three still

JARI: on three I put down (unclear)

JARI: I can never see there, I want to go closer

TEACHER: maybe you should check your eyesight

JARI: no (commotion)

JARI: no, no

TEACHER: okay, we'll work on this for another three minutes in complete silence and then

Negotiating ground rules for collective participation

As noted above, some of the outdoor visits to the forest were realized in collaboration with other classroom communities from the school. The following extract involves a first-grade classroom community and the pedagogical idea behind their involvement was to encourage peer tutoring and guidance between older and younger students. The shared visit challenged existing ground rules in the classroom community, resulting in frustration among the older students. The older students appeared to blame the younger ones for not acting as intentional and responsible members of the learning community. For them, the younger students did not follow expected practices and ground rules for participation, i.e. what it is to engage in collaborative inquiry in a forest setting. What is also notable, is that some of the older boys appear to take an agentive activity by slightly questioning and resisting the teachers' authority. The extract below highlights an interaction episode that took place after the visit to the forest. Here, the two teachers of the classroom communities participate in the dialogue with the first and third graders when the students reflect upon their feelings and experiences. This episode powerfully highlights the importance of a shared culture of participation, communication and learning.

Excerpt 5

KIMMO: Afterwards he is complaining to us about it

TEACHER 1: I wasn't complaining to you, I understand that it was challenging for you to be with the first graders, but you were acting up a bit, too, Jimi come to your group Teemu and Ville, come with your groups, Erkki with your group, go

TEACHER 2: I understand, boys, that you had a challenging task, it was really difficult for you, too, it wasn't easy

TEACHER 1: the main thing is you did your best, even I couldn't do what you tried. You tried really hard, this was only the first time. You can't succeed at once.

AARO: well it wasn't with me

TEACHER 1: really good, the first graders have never worked with third graders before

TEACHER 2: And you took Tuukka into consideration really well, you waited for him, even if it was a little bit frustrating for you, but we'll have other times, so you ...

TEEMU: and we waited a bit for Ville as well

KIMMO: well not just a bit. We waited for him during the whole trip.

TEACHER 1: Can you hear now, Tuukka, the boys are a bit upset that you didn't go with them, even when they went with you first, and you were being slow

KIMMO: Yeah, well we ran everywhere, when you went on the ice, we had to run after you on the ice, and when you stopped to look at a cone, we had to stop and look at the cone.

TEACHER 1: But then you didn't go after them to look at what the older boys wanted to look.

KIMMO: Yeah, you just wanted to go on the ice, when we wanted to climb the rock. We wanted to be there first, and all of a sudden we're there last.

TEACHER 2: Now we'll try to learn that everyone, everyone, you too listen a little to the bigger boys. And you big boys, I bet you, or did you tell Tuukka that now you are irritated, that you want to go and look at something else

KIMMO: well we told him

TEACHER 2: Yes, so Tuukka, you must listen more carefully next time

KIMMO: he just carried on

TEACHER 2: okay, but hey

KIMMO: he was interested in everything that was in the forest

TEACHER 2: well in a way that

KIMMO: everything, even the rug

AARO: he could go there after school

TEACHER 2: your interests are a bit different now, but

KIMMO: maybe it might interest you the first time around, but even I wasn't that interested the first time, I just looked around and jumped on the rocks

TEACHER 2: yeah, boys, but it doesn't sound very nice to me, that you, you can't say on behalf of someone else, what they're interested in, every person is interested in different things.

These discursive practices of the classroom community can be viewed as descriptions of socially established and taken-as-shared ways of reasoning, i.e. norms of a community (Bowers *et al.* 1999). While participating in classroom interactions both the teacher and students apply the structures of the material and social world to align their activities with a cultural system (Cole 1996). Thus, practices define the legitimate interactional and physical moves within a given context. Full participation in a practice requires that one is oriented toward certain aspects of experience, that one frames one's activity in particular ways, and that one interacts with the physical and social environment in appropriate ways (Stevens and Hall 1998).

Promoting productive interaction in dialogic inquiry

Often learners of all ages are left to navigate in spaces and places of learning without adequate support or tools. In this study we have explored and discussed the potentiality of a dialogic inquiry approach for providing students with opportunities to participate in productive interactions characterized by learner agency and active engagement. In our study, we were able to identify discursive practices that gave evidence of the students' active engagement and agency in learning. We were able to identify the students' negotiation of time-space relationships, contesting knowledge and authority, negotiating the ground rules for participation, taking on different roles, revisiting past experiences as a learning potential as well as weaving experiences and worlds together during their collective discussions. In all, the results of our study suggest that a dialogic inquiry approach to teaching and learning has potential to provide students with opportunities to participate meaningfully and powerfully in learning spaces beyond the classroom.

Whereas in many traditional classrooms, the pedagogical strategies of the teacher have mainly comprised lecturing, explaining and questioning factual knowledge (cf. Tharp and Gallimore 1988), in dialogic inquiry the learners were provided with spaces and tools to participate in social negotiations as legitimized and authorized individuals (Brown 1994; Brown and Renshaw 2006; Mercer and Littleton 2007; Wells 1999; Wenger 1998). The learners in this classroom community were afforded the stance of being active initiators in collective discussions who negotiate, challenge, reason, justify and provide feedback to the ideas presented by other members of the learning community. Significance was placed here on the learners' personal experiences, natural curiosity and authority in learning (Goos, Galbraith and Renshaw 1999).

In this classroom community, the teacher was not identified to act as a passive classroom member during dialogic inquiry. Learner initiation, agency and horizontal information flow was not found to limit teacher participation in classroom interactions (Nathan and Knuth 2003). Rather, as an expert member of the learning community, the teacher's role was to support learners' meaningful engagement in joint negotiations (Tharp and Gallimore 1988). The teacher's pedagogical activities during dialogic inquiry included evoking ideas and views, scaffolding problem solving, monitoring and modelling reasoning processes, re-voicing questions and interpretations, promoting collective responsibility, as well as pacing the tempo of interaction according to the needs of the participants (Kovalainen, Kumpulainen and Vasama 2001).

The task of creating and enacting social practices that support dialogic inquiry in the classroom community clearly reconfigures the role of the teacher and students, as well as spaces and places of learning. Here, the students have agency in meaning-making and knowledge creation. In this classroom community, the students clearly took charge of the cognitive work, whereas the teacher's responsibility was more directed to the management of the interaction.

The study demonstrates the value and importance of researching the interactional micro-moments of the classroom and how teachers' participation in those interactions is pivotal in shaping students' identity-building processes. Micro-level, contextual insights into classroom practices in dialogic inquiry classrooms are valuable not only for evaluation purposes but also for future design and realization of such practices. Furthermore, they provide a powerful resource for professional development activities (Nathan and Knuth 2003).

Conclusions

The design of classroom pedagogies that encourage active student participation and meaningful engagement in knowledge building; transform traditional student and teacher roles; and reconfigure spaces and places of learning has been of interest to many educators and researchers in different parts of the world (e.g. Brown 1994; Renshaw and Brown 1997; Roth 1995; Walker and Nocon 2007; Wells 1999). Understanding and supporting the development of learners' multiple worlds, identity work and active agency is vital in a world where barriers continue to block understanding and obstruct attempts to develop and implement policies to ensure the success of all learners in today's schools and society. Learners' competence in moving between settings and having an active role in meaning making has significant implications for the quality of their lives and their chances of participating in schooling as a grounding to life-long learning, and a meaningful life. Our study is an attempt to explore and develop models and best practices of participatory pedagogy for schools and for non-school institutions to bridge the gap between contexts and funds of knowledge. Moreover, we take seriously the student's own learning experiences, and their endeavours in organizing their own learning in these transitions. Via our research and development work we are beginning to see the possibilities dialogic inquiry can offer for creating educational practices that make sense.

Research questions that we find worthwhile to explore in more depth include (a) how working in different contexts creates possibilities for identity and agency development (identity and agency trajectories); (b) what kind of tools and forms of participation students create in order to increase their agency; (c) how students learn to transfer knowledge and skills across contexts (act authoritatively and accountably); and finally (d) how students promote collective agency and in what kind of situations, and how, it manifests itself.

References

Alexander, A. (2006) *Towards Dialogic Teaching: rethinking classroom talk*, Cambridge: Dialogos.

Alton-Lee, A. and Nuthall, G. (1992) 'Children's learning in classrooms: challenges in developing a methodology to explain "opportunity to learn"', *Journal of Classroom Interaction*, 27:1–8.

Bakhtin, M. M. (1981) *The Dialogic Imagination: four essays by M. M. Bakhtin* (trans. C. Emerson and M. Holquist), Austin, TX: University of Texas Press.

Bloome, D. and Egan-Robertson, A. (1993) 'The social construction of intertextuality in classroom reading and writing lessons', *Reading Research Quarterly*, 28:305–33.

Boaler, J. and Greeno J. (2000) 'Identity, agency and knowing in mathematics worlds', in J. Boaler (ed.) *Multiple Perspectives on Mathematics Teaching and Learning*, Westport, CT: Ablex Publishing.

Bowers, J., Cobb, P. and McClain, K. (1999) 'The evolution of mathematical practices: a case study', *Cognition and Instruction*, 17:25–64.

Bransford. J, Vye, N., Stevens, R., Kuhl, P., Schwartz, D., Bell, P., Meltzoff, A., Barron, B., Pea, R., Reeves, B., Roschelle, J. and Sabelli, N. (2006) 'Learning theories and education: toward a decade of synergy', in P. Alexander and P. Winne (eds) *Handbook of Educational Psychology*, Mahwah, NJ: Lawrence Erlbaum Associates.

Brown, A. (1994) 'The advancement of learning', *Educational Researcher*, 23:4–12.

Brown, R. and Renshaw, P. (2006) 'Positioning students as actors and authors: a chronotopic analysis of collaborative learning activities', *Mind, Culture and Activity*, 13:247–59.

Castanheira, M. L., Crawford, T., Dixon, C. and Green, J. (2001) 'Interactional ethnography: an approach to studying the social construction of literate practices', *Linguistics and Education*, 11:353–400.

Castanheira, M. L., Green, J., Dixon, C. and Yaeger, B. (2007) '(Re)formulating identities in the face of fluid modernity: an interactional ethnographic approach', *International Journal of Educational Research*, 46: 172–89.

Castanheira, M. L., Green, J. and Dixon, C. (2009) 'Investigating inclusive practices: an interactional ethnographic approach', in K. Kumpulainen, C. Hmelo-Silver and M. César (eds) *Investigating Classroom Interaction: methodologies in action*, Rotterdam: Sense Publishers.

Cole, M. (1996) *Culture in Mind*, Cambridge, MA: Harvard University Press.

Dawes, L., Mercer, N. and Wegerif, R. (2004) *Thinking Together: a programme of activities for developing speaking, listening and thinking skills* (2nd edn), Birmingham: Imaginative Minds Ltd.

Edwards, A. (2007) 'Relational agency in professional practice: a CHAT analysis', *Actio: An International Journal of Human Activity Theory*, 1:1–17.

Edwards, A. and D'Arcy, C. (2004) 'Relational agency and disposition in sociocultural accounts of learning to teach', *Educational Review*, 56:147–55.

Emirbayer, M. and Mische, A. (1998) 'What is agency?', *American Journal of Sociology*, 103:962–1023.

Engle, R. A. and Conant, F. R. (2002) 'Guiding principles for fostering productive disciplinary engagement: explaining an emergent argument in a community of learners classroom', *Cognition and Instruction*, 20:339–483.

Engle, R. A., Conant, F. R. and Greeno, J. G. (2007) 'Progressive refinement of hypotheses in video-supported research', in R. Goldman, R. Pea, B. Barron and S. J. Derry (eds) *Video Research in the Learning Sciences*, Mahwah, NJ: Lawrence Erlbaum.

Erickson, F. (2007) 'Ways of seeing video: toward a phenomenology of viewing minimally edited footage', in R. Goldman, R. Pea, B. Barron and S. J. Derry (eds) *Video Research in the Learning Sciences*, Mahwah, NJ: Lawrence Erlbaum.

Floriani, A. (1993) 'Negotiating what counts: roles and relationships, content and meaning, texts and context', *Linguistics and Education*, 5:241–74.

Gonzáles, N., Moll, L. C. and Amanti, C. (2005) *Funds of Knowledge: theorizing practices in households, communities, and classroom*, Mahwah, NJ: Lawrence Erlbaum.

Goos, M., Galbraith, P. and Renshaw, P. D. (1999) 'Establishing a community of practice in a secondary mathematics classroom', in L. Burton (ed.) *Learning Mathematics from Hierarchies to Networks: studies in mathematics education, Series 13*, London: Falmer Press.

Greeno, J. G. (2006) 'Authoritative, accountable positioning and connected, general knowing: progressive themes in understanding transfer', *The Journal of the Learning Sciences*, 15:537–47.

Heras, A. I. (1993) 'The construction of understanding in a sixth grade bilingual classroom', *Linguistics and Education*, 5:275–99.

Hirst, E. W. (2004) 'The diverse social contexts of a second language classroom and the construction of identity', in K. M. Leander and M. Sheehy (eds) *Space Matters: assertions of space in literacy practice and research*, New York: Peter Lang.

Hubbard, L., Mehan, H. and Stein, M. K. (2006) *Reform as Learning: school reform, organizational culture, and community politics in San Diego*, New York: Routledge.

Jordan, B. and Henderson, A. (1995) 'Interaction analysis: foundations and practice', *The Journal of the Learning Sciences*, 4:39–103.

Kaartinen, S. and Kumpulainen, K. (2001) 'Negotiating meaning in science classroom communities: cases across age levels', *Journal of Classroom Interaction*, 36:4–16.

Kantor, R., Green, J., Bradley, M. and Lin, L. (1992) 'The construction of schooled discourse repertoires: an interactional sociolinguistic perspective on learning to talk in preschool', *Linguistics and Education*, 4:131–72.

Kovalainen, M. and Kumpulainen, K. (2005) 'The discursive practice of participation in an elementary classroom community', *Instructional Science*, 33:213–50.

Kovalainen, M., and Kumpulainen, K. (2007) 'The social construction of participation in elementary classroom community', *International Journal of Educational Research*, 46:141–58.

Kovalainen, M., Kumpulainen, K. and Vasama, S. (2001) 'Orchestrating classroom interaction in a community of inquiry', *Journal of Classroom Interaction*, 36:17–28.

Lave, J. and Wenger, E. (1991) *Situated Learning: legitimate peripheral participation*, Cambridge: Cambridge University Press.

Lima, E. S. (1995) 'Culture revisited: Vygotsky's ideas in Brazil', *Anthropology and Education Quarterly*, 26:443–57.

Lipponen, L. (2000) 'Towards knowledge building discourse: from facts to explanations in primary students' computer mediated discourse', *Learning Environments Research*, 3:179–99.

Mercer, N. and Littleton, K. (2007) *Dialogue and the Development of Children's Thinking: a sociocultural approach*, London: Routledge.

Mitchell, C. J. (1984) 'Typicality and the case study', in R. F. Ellens (ed.) *Ethnographic Research: a guide to general conduct*, New York: Academic Press.

Nathan, M. J. and Knuth, E. J. (2003) 'A study of whole classroom mathematical discourse and teacher change', *Cognition and Instruction*, 22:431–66.

Packer, M. and Goicoechea, J. (2000) 'Sociocultural and constructivist theories of learning: ontology, not just epistemology', *Educational Psychologist*, 35:227–41.

Polman, J. L. and Pea, R. D. (2001) 'Transformative communication as a cultural tool for guiding inquiry science', *Science Education*, 85:w–62.

Ratner, C. (2000) 'Agency and culture', *Journal for the Theory of Social Behavior*, 30:413–34.

Renshaw, P. and Brown, R. (1997) 'Learning partnerships: the role of teachers in a community of learners', in I. Logan and J. Sachs (eds) *Meeting the Challenges of Primary Schools*, London: Routledge.

Resnick, L. B. (1987) 'Learning in school and out', *Educational Researcher*, 16:13–20.

Roth, W-M. (1995) *Authentic School Science: knowing and learning in open-inquiry science laboratories*, Dordrecht, The Netherlands: Kluwer.

Sarason, S. (1993) *The Predictable Failure of Educational Reform: can we change course before it's too late?*, San Francisco: Jossey Bass.

Scott, P. H., Mortimer, E. F. and Aquiar, O. G. (2006) 'The tension between authoritative and dialogic discourse: a fundamental characteristic of meaning making interaction in high school science lessons', *Science Education*, 90:579–766.

Stevens, R. and Hall, R. (1998) 'Disciplined perception: learning to see in technoscience', in M. Lampert and M. Blink (eds) *Talking Mathematics in School: studies of teaching and learning*, New York: Cambridge University Press.

Tharp, R. and Gallimore, R. (1988) *Rousing Minds to Life: teaching, learning and schooling in social context*, New York: Cambridge University Press.

Tyack, D. and Cuban, L. (1997) *Tinkering Toward Utopia: a century of public school reform*, Cambridge: Harvard University Press.

Vygotsky, L. S. (1978) *Mind in Society: the development of higher mental processes*, Cambridge, MA: Harvard University Press.

Walker, D. and Nocon, H. (2007) 'Boundary-crossing competence: theoretical considerations and educational design', *Mind, Culture and Activity*, 14:178–95.

Wells, G. (1999) *Dialogic Inquiry: towards a sociocultural practice and theory of education*, New York: Cambridge University Press.

Wenger, E. (1998) *Communities of Practice: learning, meaning and identity*, Cambridge: Cambridge University Press.

Wertsch, J. (1991) *Voices of the Mind: a sociocultural approach to mediated action*, Cambridge, MA: Harvard University Press.

Chapter 4

Can you think with me?

The social and cognitive conditions and the fruits of learning

Valérie Tartas, University of Toulouse
Aleksandar Baucal, University of Belgrade
and Anne-Nelly Perret-Clermont, University of Neuchâtel

Introduction

Since Piagetian and Vygotskian times, co-operation, social interactions, language, learning and cognitive development have been considered in their interdependencies along different lines of research that are contributing to the ever more complex and rich image of what thinking is. Recent advances have drawn specific attention to the dialogical dimension of thinking and to a reconsideration of context as the social matrix of the development of thinking skills. But neither thinking nor context is a static reality: each affects the other via its authors' and participants' initiatives and interpretations. Joint actions and thought sharing (via language and semiotic mediations) are dynamical processes and these are more or less likely to be productive for knowledge creation and learning in individuals and groups. In this chapter, we would like to contribute to the description of the way in which socio-cognitive processes and their productions are transformed during dialogues and other interactions. A specific hypothesis is the red thread of our research: since learning is socially embedded, the nature of what is being learned and the capacity to transfer this learning and re-use it should be observed to be dependent on the socio-cognitive contexts of both its acquisition and its re-use. We will, in particular, pay special attention to the role of social asymmetries in knowledge appropriation. We will also illustrate our concern via a study of children solving a kind of open puzzle (Kohs cubes) individually and collectively. This task makes visible to a large extent the participants' actions and operations.

Origins of the focus on verbal interactions and collaboration in learning

'Please, listen ...!' We can easily imagine that from the dawn of humanity, mothers and fathers have hoped that their children would pay attention to what they were saying and thereby learn from them. In most formal teaching situations in the world, students are supposed to acquire knowledge via close (and often silent) attention paid to experts' displays of language and semiotic tools intended to convey knowledge. But only in the last century have psychologists managed to describe under which conditions (developmental conditions, as Howe shows in her chapter in this volume) this reliance on language can favour the development of higher psychological functions. This has drawn attention to the important role of the learners themselves in this process: silence, attention, concentration, memorization and internalization are not the only processes at stake; learners are co-authors of their development via their own initiatives in action and discourse, accommodating to what they try to assimilate, learning to use socially provided tools and language, giving meaning to the situation, trusting or distrusting the information sources, elaborating solutions to solve the problems they meet, and relying for that on some appropriation of other people's experience and knowledge. This is not a lonely activity, but a socially embedded one, in formal and informal settings, in which the learner's identity is at stake: accepting that to relate to – or even identify with – a caretaker or teacher will confirm or modify the learner's status, conformity with the cultural norms, future perspectives, narratives, and social image. In particular, especially in social settings (such as schools) designed with the intention of fostering learning, the participants' 'competencies' as part of their identity, will become a matter of attention and social validation.

Piaget's very first studies of children were concerned with a developmental approach to the role of language (Piaget 1959). Attention was paid to the development of children's capacity to interact verbally with others in a non-egocentric way. But language, as such, was not to remain Piaget's central object of study. His model progressively started to grant primacy to reciprocal adaptation and equilibration (of action and operations, interactions and co-operation), as the processes permitting the growth of reflection and meta-reflection and thereby the development of mental structures (Piaget 1950; 1977). If Piaget then does not contribute much to the understanding of the role of language in learning, he does make important points for our concern: since birth, children learn a lot (including language) by being active in their social and physical environment; taking another person's perspective is not easy, and collaboration is a capacity that develops; what is said cannot be understood if the cognitive prerequisites are not present in the learner; and cognitive conflicts disturb ('disequilibrate', in Piagetian terms) present understanding, inducing the individual into mental reconfigurations that can be developmentally productive. Piaget also made an important point in a time of authoritarian interpersonal and social relationships in society and in education: asymmetrical relationships may disturb learning processes because authority is not a developmental source of rationality (Perret-Clermont 2008). Piaget introduced here a distinction between, on the one hand, the transmission of opinions and social conformity that takes place in asymmetrical relationships and, on the other hand, true learning that requires autonomy in checking the validity of the assertions and their backings. This constructive process of cognitive challenging is favoured by the reciprocal relations between equal peers (Piaget 1995). But these hypotheses have remained relatively unexplored in Piaget's empirical research. Vygotsky, who had published an early translation of Piaget (1923) in Russian, considered in much more depth the role of language in development. For our concern here, we would like to retain the advances Vygotsky (1962; 1978) made in alerting psychologists and educationalists to the role of semiotic mediations not only in behaviour but also in thinking itself. Pointing to a common reference is important for joint action. Signs and semiotic resources are even more important because they allow for dialogues and thus become instruments for thinking. Vygotsky contrasted everyday learning and formal settings where academic concepts could be taught. Contrary to Piaget, Vygotsky was particularly interested in describing the asymmetrical relationships by which experts help learners in their zone of proximal development.

Wood, Bruner and Ross (1976) extended this approach with the concept of scaffolding, which adults use in order to offer novices occasions to learn and develop new competencies. These scaffoldings can also be described as joint activities, for instance, when Wertsch (1979) observes mothers and children playing with a puzzle and depicted learning. The way in which semiotic mediations are used in joint activities in 'communities of practice' (Lave 1988), creates discourse genres (including academic concepts) that are learned in order to deal with specific categories of problems and instruments. From this perspective, as we will suggest later in this chapter, scaffolding is not just a matter of an expert scaffolding a novice, but of a whole situation of activity (with its tools, semiotic resources and genres, tasks, goals and partners) scaffolding novices' learning. We are interested in this approach to learning also because it allows us to encompass not only the case of novices learning already established knowledge, but also the case of experts' advancements in knowledge creation. In both situations, through social interactions, active individuals develop a new understanding – new to them and/ or new to the group or even to society. This is in line with Piaget's initial scope, which was to identify processes that can account both for learning and knowledge creation. Another consequence of this approach, when trying to understand if an individual or a group is learning, or when trying to foster learning, is that it requires considering not only a single joint activity but also a sequence of activities.

From effects to processes in the study of collaboration in learning

During the preceding decades, in line with the debates mentioned above, and in different fields (for example, psychology of learning: Carugati 1999; Gilly, Roux and Trognon 1999; Howe and Tolmie 1999; Joiner, Littleton, Faulkner and Miell 2000; Light and Littleton 1999; anthropology: Lave 1988; education: Forman and Cazden 1985; Mercer 2000; Mercer and Littleton 2007; Pontecorvo, Ajello and Zuccchermaglio 1991; Tolmie, Christie, Howe, Thurston, Topping, Donaldson, Jessiman and Livingstone 2007; vocational training: Perret and Perret-Clermont 2004; social psychology: Darnon, Butera and Mugny 2008; Perret-Clermont, Pontecorvo, Resnick, Zittoun and Burge 2004), research has paid attention to the central role of social interaction in learning. Among the questions raised are the following: Can the benefits of learning via social interaction be measured in post-tests at the individual level (Ames and Murray 1982; Doise and Mugny 1984; Gilly 1984; Perret-Clermont 1980; Roy and Howe 1990; Schwarz, Neuman and Biezuner 2000; and others)? Are the benefits predicted by the form the interaction took (Davenport and Howe 1999) or by the affective relations or gender representations between the partners (Psaltis and Duveen 2007; Sorsana 1997)? Are the learning gains related to the verbal activities in the interactions (Teasley 1995)? Under which conditions is the collectively co-constructed knowledge simply internalized (a superficial and static form of learning) by the individuals or interiorized in such a way as to become available in a new situation (Psaltis, Duveen and Perret-Clermont submitted)?

Progressively, the focus of attention has moved from the impact of social interactions on subsequent learning gains to the processes that mediate these cognitive progressions. As a result, researchers are not now looking for 'variables' or 'factors' that have a direct causal effect on the participant's thinking, but are becoming interested in the processes that mediate learning. These processes do not take place in a social vacuum but in living persons who are attributing meaning to their environment (and to its predetermined characteristics in the case of experiments in the laboratory) and, as a consequence, modifying it through thoughts or acts. In order to study these mediating processes, researchers have opened the 'social black box' and looked in detail at the socio-cognitive processes at work during the interactions. We will see that the learning situation does not appear anymore as a fixed learning context but as a dynamical encounter that modifies its characteristics and context as the conversation unfolds (Grossen 2001; Wegerif in this volume).

Socio-cognitive processes involved in learning: towards the rediscovery of verbal interactions

A repeated result is that cognitive progress is made by individuals after having interacted with others on a given task, although, of course, not in every circumstance. Beyond classical studies on imitation and social learning, socio-cultural approaches have described how knowledge is co-constructed during the interaction phase, when an adult scaffolds children and passes on to them their expertise (e.g. Rogoff 1990; Wertsch and Hickmann 1987). But it is known that confrontation with the correct solution during these interactions cannot be the only source of learning: studies on socio-cognitive conflict have reported cognitive gains even when both are novices, demonstrating thereby that the asymmetry of expertise is not necessary but that 'two heads are better than one' (Azmitia 1988; Perret-Clermont 1980; Schwarz *et al.* 2000). Non-competent partners can become competent after having been exposed to another way of solving a task, even if they did not reach the solution together during the interaction. Why?

It seems that being confronted with different answers from someone else creates a discrepancy between the learner's initial understanding and the necessity to grasp a new perspective: the learner then enters into a reflexive stance that may lead to the restructuring of his or her own thinking (Muller-Mirza and Perret-Clermont 2009). Evidence also shows that under some conditions collaboration may lead to regression (Tudge 1989, 1992). What are the specific features of the social relationship and verbal interaction that open the way for cognitive gains in the interlocutors? The fact that more competent partners verbalize their reasoning and less advanced partners accept it may lead to productive collaborative interactions (Tudge 1992). Transactive discussions (where a participant acts on the reasoning of the interlocutor through language) have repeatedly been observed to promote cognitive growth (Azmitia and Montgomery 1993; Howe and Tolmie 1998; Kruger and Tomasello 1986; Williams and Tolmie 2000). These transactive dialogues may be self-oriented (justifying one's own reasoning) or other-oriented (building on the partner's reasoning), as shown by Kruger (1992). In these studies, students involved in such a dialogue entered into a reflective attitude that was beneficial for learning. Following these findings, some researchers then raised the pedagogical question: Can training for some form of talk contribute to more positive effects of collaboration on thinking?

Effect of language-based training for productive forms of collaboration

Fawcett and Garton (2005) have shown that children who were instructed to talk during collaboration were subsequently able to perform better on post-tests compared to those children in dyads where talk was minimal. They concluded from their study that training children in interactive skills (such as providing explanations, being sensitive to others' needs) may be a prerequisite for successful peer collaboration.

Mercer and his colleagues (Mercer 1995, 2006; Wegerif, Mercer and Dawes 1999) identified a specific educational dialogue called 'exploratory talk' in which all the members of the group were invited to contribute to the discussion, learn to make their information and reasoning clear, and to try to reach agreement before making a decision or acting. These authors have shown that teaching children this kind of explicit dialogue helps them develop social and cognitive skills that can be transferred to other situations (for instance, solving together the Raven's Progressive Matrices test). It seems that active participation in the task and in verbal exchanges, as well as being confronted with different point of view, promotes the children's re-examination of their own understanding. In this line of research, it became clear that learning, beyond being a matter of acquiring cognitive skills and following social rules (e.g. 'wait for your turn to talk'), requires what we would like to call a co-construction of shared meanings within a 'thinking space' that is respectful and emotionally secure enough to confront alternative perspectives and manage them together (Perret-Clermont 2001; Perret-Clermont and Iannaccone 2005). It is not only language and social skills that these educational programmes promote, but also the possibility of experiencing long sequences of individual and collective thinking and reflecting upon them along different cognitive, social, and argumentative dimensions. The whole design of the pedagogical sequence plays a fundamental role. Every element matters: task, goal, teacher's interventions, students' epistemic agency, interpersonal relationships, language, production of artefacts, time spent consolidating the sharing of meaning etc. Now, if children can develop in such a carefully designed supportive and challenging environment, can they demonstrate their advancement elsewhere and transfer their learning to other social settings that might be less supportive or simply different? Mercer's answer to these questions, given his research results on post-tests, is yes. Such transfers are not often reported in the literature; transfer has been observed but is dependent on the participants' understandings not only of the cognitive, but also of the social demands of the new situation and task (Beach 1999; Carraher and Schliemann 2002; Howe, Tolmie, Greer and Mackenzie 1995; Tuomi-Gröhn and Engström 2003). We will consider now if laboratory investigations of the socio-cognitive processes that mediate transfer can contribute to the understanding of 'transferability' of collaborative learning. The quality of talk depends on the interlocutors' capacity to participate in such talk. We will then expect the quality of thinking to be related to the partner's mode of thinking during the collaborative activity.

Learning and transmitting new skills in collaborative activities: some puzzling findings in successive activities

Elbers (1991) describes the learning situation as an introduction to socio-cultural ways of thinking and not as a situation of knowledge transmission. Then, what is it that is learned and how is it re-used later in other situations that might afford a different 'socio-cultural way'? Novices always develop cognitive and social competencies within a specific social situation with a specific set of tasks. Is it the case that the specificity of this social situation affects the possibility of further developing in other successive situations?

These questions require the rethinking of experimental designs in order to take into account all the phases (pre-test, intervention, post-test) as a succession of activities through which the participants construct their understanding of the micro-history that they are experiencing, both intellectually and socially, and establishing (or not) links between the different phases (Perret-Clermont and Schubauer-Leoni 1981). These activities are joint activities: in the pre-test and post-test, experimenter and child communicate, trying to succeed at establishing a common response; in the intervention phase, the activity is either individual or collective but, even when it is supposedly individual, there is still an adult who has set the task for the participant and expects to see it done in a certain way. These activities afford different opportunities for the partners to co-construct some degree of intersubjectivity and common cultural artefacts such as a common language, signs, and shared meanings (Grossen 1988, 1999; Zittoun, Gillepsie, Cornish and Psaltis 2007). How do these cultural artefacts circulate from one interaction to another?

In a four-phase experiment (pre-test, training, peer-interaction, post-test), Nicolet (1995) examined the acquisition of expertise in two different training conditions (joint activity with a more advanced peer on a balance-beam task (not knowing that the peer is more advanced), or predictions confronted by feedback received from demonstrations of the balance beam operated by an adult); and then looked at how the freshly acquired knowledge was used in a new social context (interaction with a less advanced peer). In all cases, the participants did not know whether they or their partner was a novice or an expert. The adult was careful to give to the participant, via feedback, the same cognitive information as that received by the matched participant in the other experimental condition. Nicolet chose the balance-beam task because once weights are set and brakes removed, the balance gives direct 'physical' feedback. The traditional conservation or moral judgment tasks do not offer such feedback from reality. The general hypothesis was that the socio-cognitive contexts in which novices learn may have an impact on their task-related skills and social roles during the following peer session. Horizontal peer-to-peer joint activity was expected to be more productive than 'physical' demonstration embedded in an asymmetrical adult-child relationship. Nicolet found that the novices who had gained their knowledge with the adult's demonstration promoted less learning in their novice partners than their counterparts who had become experts via horizontal problem-solving activity with a peer.

Grossen replicated Nicolet's four-phase design but with Kohs cubes, a puzzle-like task (Grossen, Liengme Bessire, Iannaccone and Perret-Clermont 1993). The task was chosen because it is well documented in the literature and because it gives participants direct feedback at every step of the action. It also allows for direct observation by the experimenter of the procedures (strategies) used by the participants without requiring them to make their thoughts and judgments explicit via an experimenter-led dialogue. Grossen *et al.* (1993) slightly modified Nicolet's two experimental conditions in order to give the adult the opportunity to transmit her knowledge explicitly (and not 'hide' behind the display of 'physical' feedback from the task): in one condition the children had to jointly construct the puzzle with an expert peer (but not known to them as an expert); in the other experimental condition, the adult taught strategies to the novices by demonstrating and verbalizing them. Precautions were taken to match the two groups of participants to the level of expertise reached after this training. The results show that participants who had learned with the adult and then interacted with novices shared their knowledge efficiently but notably regressed on the post-test. The novices who had interacted with these participants progressed the most. Conversely and quite surprisingly, many of the adult-trained children regressed in the post-test as if they had 'given away' their knowledge to the novices and remained somehow disrupted by the interaction.

This larger progression of the novices who interacted with the trained participants raised interesting questions. How could these adult-trained children have been able to scaffold their novice partners to develop more advanced thinking strategies during their collaboration without being able to apply these strategies themselves in the post-test? They seemed to be able to re-use these strategies given by the adult during the training session, but did they understand them? This finding could be taken as an indication that through demonstration and modelling, trained experts acquire relatively isolated academic concepts, but are not able to relate them to spontaneous ones. Is it due to their relatively passive position during the adult demonstration? Is it surface imitation of the adult with only internalization of words and gestures and no construction of an understanding? An important unanswered question thus remains: How is it possible that a trained expert with such 'shallow' academic concepts can successfully support the development of another peer, as the results of this experiment revealed? From a neo-Piagetian perspective, it could be that the novices were confronted with a point of view different from their own (the trained child's knowledge) with a sufficiently horizontal relationship to be able to work out their own reconstruction of what was at stake. Previous observations of Schubauer-Leoni (1986), Grossen (1988) and Nicolet (1995) also allow for the hypothesis that the adult-trained children felt insecure about their recently and passively acquired knowledge and more concerned with maintaining their status as 'experts' than co-constructing a shared understanding of the situation with their partner. Yet, from a post-Vygotskian perspective, the results of the training with the adult are uncomfortable and require further investigation. This was done in the following study led by Tartas[2] in which an experimenter diversely trained the novices in order to maximize the chances that they would learn to link their spontaneous knowledge and the academic concepts they are offered (Tartas *et al.* 2004).

Child-centred adult support and peer interaction: an empirical investigation

Tartas *et al.* (2004) designed the study with two aims: to explore in more depth an unresolved issue from the study of Grossen *et al.* (1993), i.e. the apparent failure of adult training to generate progress in the post-test of adult-trained children; and to explore further, in the joint activity of Phase III, to what extent the modality of knowledge acquisition affected the social ability to share the new knowledge with partners and to benefit from interacting with them.

The design was the same as Grossen *et al.* (1993): 100 children took part, 46 of whom formed the control condition (they only participated in pre- and post-test sessions of Phases I and IV). The experiment consisted of three conditions: a control condition (Phases I and IV only) and two experimental conditions. Some novices (defined as such on the basis of the pre-test results in Phase I) were assigned to *condition 1*. Some experts and some novices, as identified in the pre-test were assigned to *condition 2*.

In *condition 1*, the novices went through Phases I (pre-test), II (adult training), III (joint activity) and IV (post-test). During Phase III they were asked to perform a joint activity with a novice (not knowing that their partner was a novice). Phase IV was a post-test similar to the pre-test of Phase I. In *condition 2*, children were not trained by the adult. They only went through Phases I (pre-test), III (joint activity) and IV (post-test). In the joint activity, the dyads always comprised a novice and an expert. The expert could either be an expert diagnosed as such on the pre-test (*condition 2*), or a child who has become an expert via adult training (*condition 1*).

In Phase II, a third of the novices were trained by an adult in a way that put them in an active position with opportunities to externalize their spontaneous thinking. The adult adjusted to the child when bringing academic concepts into the conversation and suggesting more advanced strategies. The intention was to enable the child to appropriate a specific kind of talk about Kohs cubes. Contrary to Grossen *et al.* (1993), Tartas *et al.*(2004) wanted the adult to be focused on the child who was trying to solve the task, giving help only when the child needed it, granting agency to the learner, trying to adjust the support to the specificity of the problems encountered in doing the task, and grounding the explanations in the child's activity. For example, if the child stopped because of not knowing how to proceed further, the adult intervened with some valuable thinking mediation tools in order to help define a further strategy. Consequently, it was expected that the trained participants, having had more opportunities to relate the academic concepts offered to their spontaneous knowledge, would develop a better understanding. As a consequence, in a subsequent interaction, they should be as productive or even better partners for their novice peers' progress as in Grossen *et al.* (1993), but without regressing after having interacted with them. Since their understanding was better constructed, they should not be destabilized through the interaction with their novice partners and hence not show regressions in Phase IV.

The results of the study are interesting. As expected, the children who were guided by a supportive adult, one who offered them scaffolding without depriving them of their agency, did not regress in Phase IV. The training in this study was resistant to the potentially disruptive impact of the peer interaction observed in Grossen *et al.*'s (1993) study. It also favoured the growth of the novice partner in Phase III. Another major result is that, confirming the 1993 study, the novices who interacted with a spontaneous expert also progressed. Novices in both experimental conditions progressed as well. From a cognitive point of view, we see that social interaction with a more advanced peer was as efficient as a sequence consisting of child-centred adult training followed by interaction with a novice peer. From a social point of view we observed that the horizontal relationship between peers offered the novices opportunities for progress. The asymmetrical teaching relationship with an adult helped circulate academic concepts to the benefit of the novice partners in Phase III of both studies. But only in Tartas *et al.*'s (2004) study was it to the benefit of the trained child also. If such was the case in this study, we then wondered why, on the post-tests, the children who had benefited from adult training and peer interaction were not seen to be out-performing those who had only experienced peer interaction. Was the traditional scoring method of the Kohs cubes that we were using, sufficiently precise? We decided to turn to the Rasch model (Baucal and Bond 2004; Baucal and Jovanović 2007; Bond and Fox 2007) to reanalyse the data.

In the following part of this chapter, we will present this new analysis. We will also try to understand better what happened in Phase III and why, with Tartas *et al.*'s (2004) study, the trained children did not lose their knowledge when using it in a joint activity with a novice. We will open the 'social black boxes' of the adult-child and child-child interactions. This required transcribing the transactions of the dyads (or at least of typical dyads) in Phase IV and the training sequences in Phase III, and then relating what was observed happening across the two phases.

The socio-cognitive micro-history of two trained experts

The Rasch model was chosen in order to obtain a more refined measurement of the children's improvement on the Kohs cubes between pre-test and post-test, separating the development of new competencies from the simple improved use of existing competencies. The Rasch model enables this separation by placing participants and items in the same set, and empirically ranking both items and participants by creating a scalogram with as few errors as possible. Different levels of competence then became clear so that improvement could be described not only in quantitative terms (whether the child solves more items in the post-test), but also in qualitative terms (whether the child changes levels of competence).

Applying the Rasch analysis to the data revealed that items from the Kohs cubes form a one-dimensional scale. It also allowed the identification of three levels of competence and what counts as a major improvement. The results show that there were significant differences across dyads related to their improvement between pre-test and post-test. There were no major differences across the experimental and control conditions, except for the adult-trained children: they changed level significantly more than other groups. This was not evident in the former analysis based on classical scores.

Two cases were then selected for qualitative analysis: Isidor (adult-trained) and his novice partner, Francis; and Henry (adult-trained) and his novice partner Michael. Isidor was the child who progressed the most across the whole study, from the first level in Phase I to the third level in Phase IV. However, his novice partner, Francis, remained at level 1. In other words, this four-phase sequence offered Isidor opportunities to develop advanced understanding of Kohs cubes but, as a partner in a joint activity, he did not provide Francis with appropriate learning opportunities. (We will remember this case as exemplifying the Latin proverb '*Discendo docebis, docendo disces*' ('By learning you will teach; by teaching you will learn'), even if Isidor, of course, was not explicitly asked to teach Francis anything.)

Henry and Michael were selected because the novice child, Michael, made very significant progress between pre-test and post-test, from level 1 to level 3. He surpassed Henry, the adult-trained partner, who also made progress from level 1, but without fully reaching level 3. Again, the four-phase sequence sustained the child's progress, but was not as productive for him as the two-phase experiences for his novice partner. (We will remember this dyad as an illustration of another saying about teaching: 'The good teacher is the one whose student surpasses him', even if we ask the reader to recall that the relationship had not been established as a teaching one.)

Case I. Isidor and Francis: 'Discendo docebis, docendo disces'

Isidor was given the standard instruction that when he finds it too difficult to complete the construction on his own he can rely on the adult's help. Subsequently, he spontaneously began to speak aloud, explaining to the adult what he was doing. Isidor seemed to want to make his strategies apparent and encouraged the adult to correct him before he acted. The discourse used by Isidor was both individual and social. As the following excerpt will illustrate, his discourse (and its academic concepts) seems to function as a mediation tool, directing Isidor's own action as well as explaining it to the expert adult for a check.

Isidor: excerpt from the beginning of Phase II (adult training)

ADULT 1: Now let's begin with this figure. (*On commence avec cette figure. Vas-y*)

ISIDOR 2 : There is a blue cube here (*Il y a un cube bleu ici*)

ADULT 3 : Yes (*Oui*)

ISIDOR 4 : It is completely blue, hence I put a blue one (*C'est complètement bleu, donc je mets un cube bleu*)

ADULT 5 : Yes (*Oui*)

ISIDOR 6 : Here there is blue and yellow, so I put a blue and yellow one (*Ici il y a du bleu et du jaune, donc je mets un cube bleu et jaune*)

ADULT 7: Ok, have you then seen that the yellow is toward the outside and the blue toward the inside? (*D'accord, as-tu alors vu que le jaune est vers l'extérieur et le bleu vers l'intérieur?*)

ISIDOR 8: Yes ... heum ... here it's alike, the blue is inside and the yellow ... (places the cube without finishing his sentence) (*Oui ... heum ... ici c'est pareil, le bleu est à l'intérieur et le jaune ...*)

ADULT 9: Ok (*Ok*)

ISIDOR 10: (now finishing the sentence) the yellow is toward the outside (*le jaune est vers l'extérieur*)

ADULT 11: I agree, so now don't forget to check a final time. (*D'accord, maintenant n'oublie pas de vérifier une dernière fois.*)

ISIDOR 12: It's fine! (*C'est bon!*)

The fact that Isidor spoke aloud before (or during) the construction of the figures (for instance saying: 'I did this thing here') seems to have induced the adult into teaching him the specific names of the geometrical forms, describing them by pointing at the model. The adult prompted him: 'Ok, would you like to begin with this triangle here?', 'This diagonal there?' At the beginning of the training, Isidor used the word 'things' to designate the forms; but progressively, he started to use the conceptual terms. This example shows that the difference between the adult's discourse and the child's was an opportunity for development. Because of the training, Isidor gained the ability to correct himself step by step without any adult intervention. He learned to locate the position of the cubes on the model and to adjust his own construction; to locate specific geometrical forms on the model and to use them as markers; and to recognize and name triangles, diagonals, etc.

During the first part of the interaction with Francis (Phase III), Isidor took charge of the building and constructed the three first items alone. But then, as shown in the excerpt below, Francis reminded him of the adult's instruction: 'Aren't we supposed to work together?'

Isidor and Francis: excerpt from their interaction in Phase III

ISIDOR 1 : Here, there is some white and some red ... eh look on which side the white is, eh look the red is here on the top, it is like that; in the bottom like that (places the cube in the right direction); look it is a triangle. (*Ici, il y a du blanc et du rouge ... euh regarde de quel côté est le blanc, eh regarde le rouge est ici en haut, c'est comme ça; regarde c'est un triangle.*)

FRANCIS 2: Where? Here? (*Où? Ici?*)

ISIDOR 3: Then there is some red. (*Ensuite il y a du rouge.*)

FRANCIS 4: Here (places a cube next to Isidor's construction) (*Ici*)

ISIDOR 5: Look if it's correct, if we get a line (points on the model and on his construction) (*Regarde si c'est correct, si on forme bien une ligne*) (...)

FRANCIS 10: Aren't we supposed to work together? (*On ne doit pas travailler ensemble?*) (...)

After Francis's reminder, the dyad conformed to this social demand by entering into a very systematic division of labour: they alternated, with each child in turn placing a cube or two. Only on limited occasions did they negotiate a move. Isidor kept to the same rules and routines that he had developed with the adult, but talked aloud less often (he might have kept using inner speech, talking to himself in the way he had been trained). He sometimes controlled his partner's construction by saying: 'It's wrong'. Only during the last item did Francis show signs of starting to learn something, but for such a short amount of time that he would not re-use it later during Phase III or during the post-test, demonstrating no learning. Isidor progressed: Phase III seems to have been an opportunity for him to better interiorize the knowledge gained from the adult.

Case 2. Henry and Michael: 'A good teacher is the one whose student surpasses him'

At the beginning of the training in Phase II, Henry managed to solve the first items using four cubes. But when the items involved nine and 16 cubes, he had serious difficulties dividing the model into cubes and orienting them. The adult's interventions started there, when Henry showed hesitations or stopped himself, as in the example below.

The adult's first intervention in Henry's training (Phase II)

ADULT 22: Where have you decided to begin? (*Où as-tu décidé de commencer?*)

HENRY 23: There (he is pointing at the top of the model) (*Là*)

ADULT 24: Ok (*D'accord*)

ADULT 25: And afterwards then, what are you going to do? (the adult asks this question because the child had stopped his construction) (*Et ensuite, alors que vas-tu faire?*)

HENRY 26: I am not sure … (*Je ne suis pas sûr …*)

ADULT 27: You are not sure, so what I can tell you is that we can imagine this cube here (the child agrees); you can check by putting it just next to the model in order to check the direction of the diagonal. We are in this direction, the yellow is outside and the blue is inside, and we know by the model that it is next to a blue cube. In addition, you can use the grid of the model, it corresponds exactly to the cubes. So, now try to place this one. (*Tu n'es pas sûr, alors ce que je peux te dire c'est qu'on peut imaginer ce cube là, tu peux vérifier en le mettant juste à côté du modèle pour vérifier dans quel sens est la diagonale. On est dans cette direction, le jaune est à l'extérieur et le bleu à l'intérieur, et on sait qu'avec le modèle il est à côté d'un cube bleu. En plus tu peux utiliser la grille du modèle, ça correspond exactement aux cubes. Donc maintenant essaie de placer celui-là.*)

Henry performs the placement.

ADULT 28: How do you check? (*Comment tu vérifies?*)

HENRY 29: I look at the blue here. It's finished. (*Je regarde le bleu ici. C'est fini.*)

ADULT 30: Very well. (*Très bien.*) (…)

In this excerpt, the adult explains to Henry how to place his cubes, for instance using the grid on the model in order to check the orientation of the cubes. With the next items, Henry continues to spontaneously ask for help when he does not know how to proceed. Henry progressively uses the same vocabulary and strategies as the adult, for instance, saying prior to his action: 'Now I start this line, and the colour of the first cube is red and white'; and 'I have to check on the model the direction of the diagonal.'

During the first part of Henry and Michael's interaction, Henry directed the construction by explaining procedures to his partner ('we have to begin with the corner'; 'we must do the line'; 'next we must do the other line like that'). Henry imitated the adult in asking questions and giving explanations. During the first item, Michael was rather passive: only on two occasions did he try to signal an error or place cubes but these cubes were immediately taken away by Henry. At the beginning of the second item, Henry declared that he had been doing everything and that now it should be Michael's turn. But he kept acting on his own. Michael managed nevertheless to construct some parts. The interaction continued and progressively Michael started to take more responsibility. Finally, it was Michael who reminded Henry of the procedures that he had suggested following and with which he was not complying.

Even if Henry had given his partner vocabulary and strategies to solve the task, he was not always able to use them properly. In the brief excerpt below (beginning with the third item), we can see Henry using the same words as the adult. In fact, it is probably only on the surface that these words look like the adult's: they do not seem to have the same meaning.

Interaction phase between Henry and Michael

(...) MICHAEL 3: Wait, wait, we will do ... (*Attends, attends, nous allons faire ...*)

HENRY 4: this side (*ce côté-là*)

MICHAEL 5: We begin with this line at the top (*On commence avec cette ligne là-haut*)

HENRY 6: No, this line, this line! Ooh, you are doing the top?! (*Non cette ligne, cette ligne! Ah tu fais le haut?!*)

MICHAEL 7: No, I am doing this side (*Non, je fais ce côté*)

HENRY 8: A white one! (*Un blanc!*)

MICHAEL 9: Wait! (*Attends!*)

HENRY 10: I prefer you to complete the triangle, this triangle (he gives Michael two cubes for this triangle) (*Je préfère que tu complètes le triangle, ce triangle*)

MICHAEL 11: Which triangle? (*Quel triangle?*)

HENRY 12: This one! (*Celui-là!*)

MICHAEL 13: I have already done all the top (*J'ai déjà fait tout le haut*)

HENRY 14: The top? (*Le haut?*)

MICHAEL 15: Yes! (*Oui!*)

HENRY 16: Yes (checks Michael's construction) (*Oui*) (...)

It seems that there is a gap between what Henry was saying and what he was able to do. All through the interaction, Henry can be observed mentioning everything that the adult had told him in Phase II. On the post-test, Henry was not quite able to use it, but Michael did this with success.

General discussion

It is very interesting to compare the micro-history of Isidor and Henry and that of Francis and Michael in their four-phase learning sequence and to connect it with the kind of learning (surface or deep) that they accomplish. Equally novice on the pre-test, they have been invited to participate in pre-determined experimental conditions being trained by an adult before meeting a novice for a joint activity. The general results of the study presented earlier had shown that this experimental condition was the most productive one, but that the second was also a rich occasion for learning. In looking into details of their cases, it becomes obvious that an experimental condition is not a fixed context but a dynamic encounter in which the participants interpret differently their roles and focus differently on the social, linguistic or cognitive aspects of the task. Hence they engage in learning activities of different natures allowing for simple internalization of the semiotic means offered (as in the case of Henry) or for more profound learning with interiorization and thinking at a higher level (Isidor and Michael).

In the cases analysed here, this more productive learning was not directly dependent on the (a)symmetry of the relationship. Isidor benefited from an asymmetrical relationship with a caring adult in order to ask questions and enrich his thinking. It is interesting to note that in the next phase, when Isidor was in a new social situation in which he had to do a similar task with a peer, he did not manage to establish a cognitively collaborative relationship: first he acted and went thinking on his own in a sort of monologue and then he shared the work in a 'bureaucratic' way with Francis. As for Michael, he benefited from a horizontal relationship: his partner Henry was confused but verbalized useful academic concepts that he had learned previously from the adult. Indeed, Henry does not seem to have really interiorized at a deep level the adult's contributions in spite of her scaffolding help: he did not succeed in using them efficiently in Phases II and IV. Because of this, Henry left an open thinking space for Michael, who, seeing that his partner was sometimes wrong, progressively started to discuss his actions and to share the responsibility for the construction.

Isidor is seen acquiring a discourse that he will be able to re-use in a different social situation but he gives Francis no social opportunity to share the discourse. Henry is ready to imitate the adult (and hence her discourse) and as a consequence, Michael has a chance to practise it too. But perhaps this imitative role deprives Henry of a more autonomous attitude, which would have allowed him to think on his own and really listen to his partner.

These children diversely interpreted the social role in which the experimenter placed them. Isidor was doing things his own way, autonomous but not very social. He had a limited understanding of what the experimenter meant by 'working together'. By contrast, Henry seemed to understand that he was to learn to behave as the adult did and then reproduce this in front of his peer, placing him in the role of an observer – but he placed himself in the position of an unqualified observer, not of the qualified observer and helper that the adult was. Both Francis and Michael joined in the activity and tried to find their place in it. Michael was luckier than Francis with his partner. In fact, to share in the activity, Francis had to rely on the authority of the adult's instruction that 'frames' (Perret-Clermont 2001) the interaction: 'Aren't we supposed to work together?' But the argument of authority is not sufficient to invite his peer to join in a cognitive co-construction.

The relationship to the peer was also diversely understood. Isidor did not display any particular attention to his partner's point of view. He limited himself to expressing his own point of view. In fact, it is interesting to note that the experimenter in Grossen et al.'s (1993) research had acted in the same way when demonstrating the 'official' discourse and strategies that she intended to teach. As a consequence, her participants did not show much interiorized learning. Isidor's partner did not progress either. Henry behaved differently: he looked at Michael's productions and commented on them. Michael is then participating in a real dialogue and not facing a monologue. From this interactive experience, he starts gaining resources that he is given a chance to try out immediately during the activity. Finally, he will master them and re-use them successfully in Phase IV.

Conclusion

The instructions given by the adult were the same but the 'thinking spaces' that the children developed in Phase III were quite different, most probably because the attention of the adult was focused on the cognitive task and not on the social relationship that the children established, nor on the social skills and capacities of decentration that Howe (in this volume) has shown important. The adult was focused on the transmission of semiotic mediations to the child and not on the social management of each person's place, space and point of view.

Further research could study the scaffolding procedures of the adult along several dimensions. First, by exploring how the child-centred help offered by the adult contributes not only to making resources available that sustain the child's thinking, but also to shaping the social relationship in a way that does not always sustain the child's autonomy. Second, by analysing in more detail, as in Schwarz, Perret-Clermont, Trognon and Marro (2008), how peers, when they enter into a real dialogue, scaffold each other along the way. You do not need to be an expert to sustain the other's thinking. Third, by enlarging the concept of 'learning' in order to more clearly differentiate 'shallow' learning of academic concepts from the development of higher thinking resistant to social pressure.

Learning and thinking will then appear more clearly as the collaborative result of autonomous minds confronting viewpoints and cultural artefacts (tools, semiotic mediations, tasks, division of roles, etc.) and trying to manage differences, feedback and conflicts to pursue their activities. Moving from one activity to another, from one social space to another, individuals and groups have to reorganize their understanding, their language, and the organization of their social interactions. Transfer of learning is not only a cognitive matter. If experimenters or teachers expect transfer, they will have to learn to design not only scaffolding actions but whole sequences of joint activities (between experts and novices, between novices, with and without an awareness of the other's expertise) in which the learners will experience epistemic agency in discovering and appropriating different semiotic resources. These sequences of joint activities will need to be emotionally secure enough to grant the learners a thinking space in which to confront others' assertions so as not just to imitate what is said but also to critically reconstruct or deconstruct cultural assertions and develop new ones. In the next phase, the fruits of these joint actions and discursive collaborations will have to become objects of reflection. Something is learned only when it is socially recognized as 'learned'. Only then, it becomes a shared piece of knowledge in accordance with social and epistemic criteria that also need to be learned and developed.

Notes

1   The preparation of this article was supported by the project 'Psychological problems in the context of social changes' implemented by the Institute of Psychology, University of Belgrade, which was financed by the Ministry of Science and Environment of the Republic of Serbia (No. 149018).

2   Study conducted by Valérie Tartas with the collaboration of Raffaella Rosciano and Aleksandar Baucal. (For more detailed results see Tartas, Perret-Clermont, Marro and Grossen 2004; Tartas and Perret-Clermont 2008.)

References

Ames, G. J. and Murray, F. B. (1982) 'When two wrongs make a right: promoting cognitive change by social conflict', *Developmental Psychology*, 18:894–7.

Azmitia, M. (1988) 'Peer interaction and problem solving: when are two heads better than one?', *Child Development*, 59:86–7.

Azmitia, M. and Montgomery, R. (1993) 'Friendship, transactive dialogues and the development of scientific reasoning', *Social Development*, 2:202–21.

Baucal, A. and Bond, T. G. (2004) 'Rasch measurement: zone of proximal development of the measurement of the ZPD', paper presented at IOMW XII, Cairns, Australia, 28 June–2 July.

Baucal, A. and Jovanović, V. (2007) 'Critical role of the Rasch measurement in studying construction and co-construction of new cognitive competencies', paper presented at the EARLI Conference, Budapest.

Beach, K. (1999) 'Consequential transitions: a sociocultural expedition beyond transfer in education', *Review of Research in Education*, 24:101–39.

Bond, T. G. and Fox, C. M. (2007) *Applying the Rasch Model: fundamental measurement in the human sciences* (2nd edn), Mahwah, NJ: Lawrence Erlbaum.

Carraher, D. and Schliemann, A. D. (2002) 'The transfer dilemma', *The Journal of the Learning Sciences*, 11:1–24.

Carugati, F. (1999) 'From Piaget and Vygotsky to learning activities: a long journey and an inescapable issue', in M. Hedegaard and J. Lompscher (eds) *Learning Activity and Development*, Aarhus: Aarhus University Press.

Darnon, C., Butera, F. and Mugny, G. (2008) *Des Conflits pour Apprendre*, Grenoble: Presses Universitaires de Grenoble.

Davenport, P. and Howe, C. (1999) 'Conceptual gain and successful problem-solving in primary school mathematics', *Educational Studies*, 25:55–78.

Doise, W. and Mugny, G. (1984) *The Social Development of the Intellect*, Oxford: Oxford University Press.

Elbers, E. (1991) 'The development of competence and its social context', *Educational Psychology Review*, 3:73–94.

Fawcett, L. and Garton, A. (2005) 'The effect of peer collaboration on children's problem-solving ability', *British Journal of Educational Psychology*, 75:157–69.

Forman, E. A. and Cazden, C. B. (1985) 'Exploring Vygotskyian perspectives in education: the cognitive value of peer education', in J. V. Wertsch (ed.), *Culture, Communication and Cognition: Vygotskian perspectives*, Cambridge: Cambridge University Press.

Gilly, M. (1984) 'Psychologie de l'éducation' [The psychology of education], in S. Moscovici (ed.), *Psychologie Sociale*, Paris: PUF.

Gilly, M., Roux, J. P. and Trognon, A. (eds) (1999) *Apprendre dans l'Interaction: analyse des médiations sémiotiques* [Learning through interaction: an analysis of semiotic mediations], Nancy: Presses Universitaires, Publications de l'Université de Provence.

Grossen, M. (1988) *L'intersubjectivité en situation de test* [Intersubjectivity in a test situation], Cousset (Fribourg): DelVal. Available online at: http://doc.rero.ch/record/9685?ln=fr (accessed January 2009).

Grossen, M. (1999) 'Approche dialogique des processus de transmission-acquisition de savoirs. Une brève introduction' [A dialogical approach to the process of transmitting and acquiring knowledge. A brief introduction], *Actualités Psychologiques*, 7:1–32.

Grossen, M. (2001) 'La notion de contexte: quelle définition pour quelle psychologie?' [The notion of context: which definition for which psychology?], in J. P. Bernié (ed.) *Apprentissage, Développement et Significations*, Pessac: Presses Universitaires de Bordeaux.

Grossen, M., Liengme Bessire, M-J., Iannaccone, A. and Perret-Clermont, A.-N. (1993) 'Modes d'acquisition de l'expertise et interactions sociales entre enfants' [Modes of acquiring expertise and social interaction among children], *Rapports et documents de recherche du projet 'Perception de l'expertise et interactions sociales chez l'enfant.* [Reports and documents from the research project 'Perception of expertise and social interaction among children'], Institut de Psychologie de l'Université de Neuchâtel, n° 2.

Howe, C. and Tolmie, A. (1998) 'Computer support for learning in collaborative context: prompted hypothesis testing in physics', *Computers and Education*, 30:223–35.

Howe, C. and Tolmie, A. (1999) 'Productive interaction in the context of computer-supported collaborative learning in science', in K. Littleton and P. Light (eds), *Learning with Computers: analysing productive interaction*, London and New York: Routledge.

Howe, C., Tolmie, A., Greer, K. and Mackenzie, M. (1995) 'Peer collaboration and conceptual growth in physics: task influence on children's understanding of heating and cooling', *Cognition and Instruction*, 13:483–503.

Joiner, R., Littleton, K., Faulkner, D. and Miell, D. (eds) (2000) *Rethinking Collaborative Learning*, London: Free Association Books.

Kruger, A. C. (1992) 'The effect of peer and adult-child transactive discussions on moral reasoning, *Merrill-Palmer Quarterly*, 38:191–211.

Kruger, A. C. and Tomasello, M. (1986) 'Transactive discussions between peers and adults', *Developmental Psychology*, 22:681–5.

Lave, J. (1988) *Cognition in Practice*, Cambridge: Harvard University Press.

Light, P. and Littleton, K. (eds) (1999) *Social Processes in Children's Learning*, Cambridge: Cambridge University Press.

Mercer, N. (1995) *The Guided Construction of Knowledge*, London: Multilingual Matters.

Mercer, N. (2000) *Words and Minds: how we use language to think together*, London: Routledge.

Mercer, N. (2006) 'Developing dialogues', in G. Wells and G. Claxton (eds), *Learning for Life in the 21st Century*, Oxford: Blackwell.

Mercer, N. and Littleton, K. (2007) *Dialogue and the Development of Children's Thinking: a sociocultural approach*, London: Routledge.

Muller-Mirza, N. and Perret-Clermont, A.-N. (eds) (2009) *Argumentation and Education*, New York: Springer.

Nicolet, M. (1995) *Dynamiques Relationnelles et Processus Cognitifs: étude du marquage social chez des enfants de 5 à 9 ans* [Relational dynamics and cognitive processes: a study of social marking among children 5 to 9 years old], Lausanne, Paris: Delachaux et Niestlé.

Perret, J. F. and Perret-Clermont, A.-N. (2004) *Apprendre un Métier Technique* [Learning a technical trade], Paris : L'Harmattan.

Perret-Clermont, A.-N. (1980) *Social Interaction and Cognitive Development in Children*, London: Academic Press.

Perret-Clermont, A.-N. (2001) 'Psychologie sociale de la construction de l'espace de pensée', in J. J. Ducret (ed.), *Actes du Colloque Constructivisme: usages et perspectives en éducation*,Vol. I, Genève: Département de l'Instruction Publique: Service de la recherche en éducation. [The social psychology of constructing a thinking space. Symposium proceedings. Constructivism: Uses and perspectives in education.]

Perret-Clermont, A.-N. (2008) 'Epilogue: Piaget, his elders and his peers', in A.-N. Perret-Clermont and J.-M. Barrelet (eds), *Jean Piaget and Neuchâtel*, Hove, East Sussex: Psychology Press.

Perret-Clermont, A.-N. and Iannaccone, A. (2005) 'Le tensioni delle trasmissioni culturali: c'è spazio per il pensiero nei luoghi instituzionali dove si apprende?' [The tensions of cultural transmission: is there space for thinking in the teaching institutions?], in T. Mannarini, A. Perucca and S. Salvatore (eds), *Quale Psicologia per la Scuola del Futuro?*, Roma: Edizioni Carlo Amore.

Perret-Clermont, A.-N., Pontecorvo, C., Resnick, L. B., Zittoun, T. and Burge, B. (eds), (2004) *Joining Society. Social Interaction and Learning in Adolescence and Youth*, Cambridge: Cambridge University Press.

Perret-Clermont, A.-N. and Schubauer-Leoni, M.-L. (1981) 'Conflict and cooperation as opportunities for learning', in P. Robinson (ed.) *Communication in Development*, London: Academic Press.

Piaget, J. (1950) *The Psychology of Intelligence*, London: Routledge and Kegan Paul. First published in 1947 as *La Psychologie de l'Intelligence*, Paris: Alcan.

Piaget, J. (1959) *The Language and Thought of the Child* (London: Routledge and Kegan Paul). First published in 1929 as *Le Langage et la Pensée chez l'Enfant*, Paris, Neuchâtel: Delachaux and Niestlé.

Piaget, J. (1977) *The Origin of Intelligence in the Child*, Harmondsworth: Penguin Books. First published in 1936 as *La Naissance de l'Intelligence chez l'Enfant*, Neuchâtel and Paris: Delachaux and Niestlé.

Piaget, J. (1995) *Sociological Studies*, London: Routledge. First published in 1965 as *Etudes Sociologiques*, Genève: Droz.

Pontecorvo, C., Ajello, A. M. and Zucchermaglio, C. (1991) *Discutendo Si Impara* [Discussing how you learn], Roma: La Nuova Italia Scientifica.

Psaltis, C. and Duveen, G. (2007) 'Conservation and conversation types: forms of recognition and cognitive development', *British Journal of Developmental Psychology*, 25:79–102.

Psaltis, C., Duveen, G. and Perret-Clermont, A.-N. (submitted) 'The social and the psychological: structure and context in intellectual development'.

Rogoff, B. (1990) *Apprenticeship in Thinking*, New York and Oxford: Oxford University Press.

Roy, A. W. N. and Howe, C. J. (1990) 'Effects of cognitive, socio-cognitive conflict and imitation on children's socio-legal thinking', *European Journal of Social Psychology*, 20:241–52.

Schubauer-Leoni, M.-L. (1986) *Maître-élève-savoir: analyse psychosociale du jeu et des enjeux de relation didactique* [Teacher-student-knowledge: a psychosocial analysis of the game and the stakes of the teaching relationship], unpublished doctoral dissertation, Faculté de Psychologie et des Sciences de l'Education, Université de Genève.

Schwarz, B. B., Neuman, Y. and Biezuner, S (2000) 'Two wrongs may make a right ... if they argue together!', *Cognition and Instruction*, 18:461–94.

Schwarz, B. B., Perret-Clermont, A.-N., Trognon, A. and Marro, P. (2008) 'Emergent learning in successive activities: learning in interaction in a laboratory context, *Pragmatics and Cognition*, 16:57–87.

Sorsana, C. (1997) 'Affinités enfantines et co-résolution de la tour de Hanoï' [Children's affinities and the co-resolution of the Hanoi Tower], *Revue Internationale de Psychologie Sociale*, 1:51–74.

Tartas, V. and Perret-Clermont, A.-N. (2008) 'Socio-cognitive dynamics in dyadic interaction: how do you work together to solve Kohs cubes?', *European Journal of Developmental Psychology*, 5:561–84.

Tartas, V., Perret-Clermont, A.-N., Marro, P. and Grossen, M. (2004) 'Interactions sociales et appropriation de stratégies par l'enfant pour résoudre un problème : quelles méthodes?' [Social interactions and children's appropriation of strategies to solve problems: which methods?], *Bulletin de Psychologie*, 57:111–15.

Teasley, S. D. (1995) 'The role of talk in children's peer collaborations', *Developmental Psychology*, 31:207–20.

Tolmie, A., Christie, D., Howe, C., Thurston, A., Topping, K., Donaldson, C., Jessiman, E. and Livingston, K. (2007) 'Classroom relations and collaborative groupwork in varying social contexts: lessons from Scotland', paper presented at the American Educational Research Association Annual Meeting, Chicago.

Tudge, J. (1989) 'When collaboration leads to regression: some negative effects of socio-cognitive conflict', *European Journal of Social Psychology*, 19:123–38.

Tudge, J. (1992) 'Processes and consequences of peer collaboration: a Vygotskian analysis', *Child Development*, 63:1364–79.

Tuomi-Gröhn, T. and Engström, Y. (eds) (2003) *Between School and Work: new perspectives on transfer and boundary-crossing*, Amsterdam: Pergamon.

Vygotsky, L. S. (1962) *Thought and Language*, Cambridge, MA: MIT Press. First published in 1934.

Vygotsky, L. S. (1978) *Mind in Society*, Cambridge, MA: Harvard University Press.

Wegerif, R., Mercer, N. and Dawes, L. (1999) 'From social interaction to individual reasoning: an empirical investigation of a possible socio-cultural model of cognitive development', *Learning and Instruction*, 9:493–51.

Werstch, J. (1979) 'From social interaction to higher psychological processes', *Human Development*, 22:1–22.

Werstch, J. and Hickman, M. (1987) 'Problem solving in social interaction: a microgenetic analysis', in M. Hickman (ed.), *Social and Functional Approaches to Language and Thought*, San Diego: Academic Press.

Williams, J. M. and Tolmie, A. C. (2000) 'Conceptual change in biology: group interaction and the concept of inheritance', *British Journal of Developmental Psychology*, 18:625–49.

Wood, D. J., Bruner, J. S. and Ross, G. (1976) 'The role of tutoring in problem solving', *Journal of Child Psychiatry and Psychology*, 17:89–100.

Zittoun, T., Gillepsie, A., Cornish, F. and Psaltis, C. (2007) 'The metaphor of the triangle in theories of human development', *Human Development*, 50:208–29.

Part II

Understanding productive interaction in specific curricular contexts

Introduction

In Part 2, the focus is on clarifying the forms of dialogue that support classroom learning in the curricular contexts of science, mathematics, literacy and philosophy. The chapters in this part of the book thus develop the consideration of the properties of productive educational dialogues that began in Part 1. As will be seen, the key message to emerge from this section concerns the need for pluralism in conceptions of productive educational dialogue: with analyses pointing to the need for contextually sensitive, situated accounts. In this respect the contributors to Part 2 also endorse the plea for sensitivity to plurality articulated by the authors in Part 1. In contrast to some linguistic studies of classroom discourse, where analyses and findings may be reported solely in terms of patterns of interaction, a central argument that emerges from the contributions in this section is that the actual content of what is being taught and what is being learned matters and is of significance and consequence.

The section opens with contributions from Jonathan Osborne and Christine Chin and from Baruch Schwarz, Rina Hershkowitz and Naomi Prusak. These chapters point to the substantial contemporary evidence-base highlighting the value and significance of *argumentation* for learning in the disciplinary contexts of science and mathematics. Traditionally, especially at school level, the subject pedagogy in these fields has been seen as involving the presentation of a body of consensually agreed, well-established knowledge, with school mathematics in particular being dedicated to 'drill and practice' or the routine processes of problem solving. In contrast, however, these contributions make a compelling case that argumentation is important for learners – this being the way in which meaning-making and understanding develop in classroom discussions. While arguing for the value of argumentation, both contributions orient to what are perceived to be salient gaps in our understanding of the nature and significance of argumentation for learning.

Recognizing the body of work that points to the value and significance of argumentation for the learning of science, in Chapter 5 Osborne and Chin suggest that research in this field will only develop when there are *explanatory models* of how argumentative discourse achieves the positive effects that have been observed in the science education literature. In the chapter the authors venture one such tentative model. Their model is designed to explain what might 'trigger' productive argumentation in science – specifically how students' questions may initiate and sustain argumentation during group discourse. The strength of the model lies in the way it highlights the multiplicity of learning pathways implicated in dialogic discourse – as it describes a number of possible pathways that involve self-explanations and peer explanations (mediated by questions posed to oneself or others). The model also offers explanations for how conflict and co-operation might mediate the process of knowledge construction and affords an account for both the personal and social construction of knowledge via questioning and argumentation. Although elegant in its conception, the model is articulated in quite broad terms and there are therefore a number of crucial mediators of group activity and argumentative dialogue, that are not captured in this instantiation. These include task structure, interactional rules and student grouping, among others. Factors such as these pose a considerable challenge (as Osborne and Chin note) for researchers interested in understanding and promoting productive educational dialogues as they underscore how contextually and situationally sensitive the facilitation, or inhibition, of learning is when it occurs within and through dialogue. Relatively subtle changes in the conditions and circumstances for learning can be of crucial significance and recognition of this reality pervades Chapter 6 by Schwarz and colleagues.

Focusing on mathematics and argumentation, Schwarz and colleagues suggest that it is the lack of *specificity* that makes argumentation a difficult object for study. The implication is that not only do we need to know how to identify argumentation, and its types, but we also need to understand the specific cases in which it succeeds and where and when it fails. Seen from this perspective, argumentation is not an educational panacea and, if it is to be harnessed in support of students' learning, what is called for are secure, contextually sensitive and situationally specific understandings of what impacts upon its efficacy. In the context of mathematics education (which, as noted, is the concern of this chapter), such understandings would need to be situated in respect of key mathematical practices and activities – such as those of 'enquiring', 'proving' and 'inscribing proofs'. The analyses of paired dialogue presented in the chapter are thus intended to begin the process of developing situated understandings of argumentation in the domain of mathematics, exploring, for example, how argumentation can serve as an important bridge between the mathematical activities of enquiring and proving. The analyses also reveal that as situated understandings of productive argumentation are developed they will need to engage with the complexities of multimodal argumentation. Particularly while involved in the enquiry processes of sense-making and conjecturing, mathematics students often explore difficult, abstract mathematical ideas through argumentation in which gestures, computer representations, metaphors and drawings are implicated. For Schwarz and colleagues, this all underscores both the difficulty and the necessity of designing activities for productive argumentation in mathematics: 'It necessitates taking into consideration the students' knowledge, the way to arrange them in groups, the tools to provide them for raising or checking hypotheses, and possibly the strategies the teacher should enact to structure discussions.' In pointing to the complexities of designing for argumentation the authors foreshadow the issue of promoting productive educational dialogues that is discussed further in Part 4.

The need for situationally sensitive accounts of productive educational dialogues expounded by Schwarz and colleagues also emerges as a key theme in Chapter 7 by Sylvia Rojas-Drummond, Karen Littleton, Flora Hernández and Mariana Zuñiga. These authors report work undertaken as part of the educational programme *Learning Together* (influenced, in part, by the UK-based *Thinking Together* programme – see

Littleton and Mercer – Chapter 13), which was designed to develop the dialogic and literacy repertoires of Mexican school children. Previously Rojas-Drummond and her colleagues have offered a characterization of productive educational dialogue that stresses the importance of fostering a form of talk known as 'Exploratory Talk' and assessing the associated evidence of children's ability to explicitly reason-in-talk. However, the analyses of children's group work presented in this chapter, which derive from recent research investigating the processes of children's collaborative writing, imply that 'what counts' as educationally efficacious dialogue is inextricably linked to the *nature of the task*. On the basis of the qualitative analyses presented, it would appear that 'convergent tasks' (closed) may require somewhat different dialogic styles to 'divergent tasks' (open). Whereas for convergent tasks Exploratory Talk is likely to be productive, for divergent tasks it seems that 'co-constructive talk', in which children integrate, elaborate and/or reformulate each other's contributions to negotiate meaning, is effective. This suggests then that while an emphasis on argumentation and explicit reasoning-in-talk takes us someway towards understanding what constitutes productive educational dialogues, this is not the only way in which we can, or should, conceptualize effective dialogue. This call for plurality in respect of conceptualizing productive educational dialogues is reminiscent of the calls for more complex models of productive and creative peer collaboration and educational dialogues that have arisen in the context of work on collaborative creativity. Vass (2004), for example, in investigating children's joint creative writing, points to the need to study the function-specific affordances of particular discursive forms. Vass's work has indicated that the collective processes of content generation were typically supported by the uncritical accumulation and sharing of ideas, with joint content generation being characterized by cumulative and disputational features (see also Mercer and Littleton 2007) and a lack of explicit argumentation and reasoning. Reflective phases, for instance involving the evaluation of the 'appropriateness' of a suggestion, were, however, resourced by detached perspective-taking and explicit argumentation. So for Vass, the notion of productive educational dialogue emerges in the shifts across and the interplay between these different forms of dialogue – drawing attention to the significance of the patterning of dialogue over time.

The final contribution in this section, Chapter 8 from Margaret Hardman and Barbara Delafield, picks up the issues raised by Osborne and Chin and Schwarz, Hershkowitz and Prusak by highlighting the value and significance of argumentation and questioning – and the selection of 'good' questions to explore – as an integral part of the *Philosophy for Children* programme. With the aim of improving children's critical, caring and creative thinking, this programme has at its core the development of a 'community of philosophical enquiry' in which thinking is stimulated by means of philosophical questions and dialogue, with children critically discussing and debating concepts and ideas in which they have a personal interest. In the supportive context of this teacher-guided community of enquiry, children are said to be prompted to think about the world when their knowledge is revealed to them as ambiguous, equivocal and otherwise open to question. Hardman and Delafield describe the specific characteristics of the *Philosophy for Children* programme, the process of dialogic teaching involved, its impact on dialogue and implications for practice. There are here some clear links between this and the more recent *Thinking Together* approach (see Chapter

13 by Littleton and Mercer) and the *Learning Together* programme reviewed by Rojas-Drummond and colleagues (Chapter 7) in terms of the development of a community of enquiry and similarities between the types of talk described as dialogical critical thinking, Socratic dialogue and 'Exploratory Talk'.

Dialogue in any socially defined setting is nested within a wider socio-cultural context and while it is valuable to focus research efforts on micro-genetic analyses of sessions of classroom-based talk and joint activity, as the first three chapters in this section have done, we must be careful not to neglect the ways in which learners' interactions are framed by, and therefore need to be understood within, the context of particular institutional structures and settings. This highlights still further complexities, in respect of conceptualizing and promoting productive educational dialogues, as observable interactions are likely to have unobservable determinants in the histories of individuals, groups – and crucially, *institutions*. Hardman and Delafield also explore the ways in which the wider institutional and socio-cultural context impacts, and is reflected in, classroom dialogue, when the *Philosophy for Children* programme is instantiated in two school settings. Making the case that *Philosophy for Children* could be considered a form of dialogic teaching, their analyses (which deploy Critical Discourse Analysis) indicate how forms of Magistral, Socratic and Menippean dialogue play out across the sessions. Crucially, however, the analyses also highlight the significance of the institutional role of the teacher, the school curriculum and materials used and how these are drawn on as the 'authoritative' third voice in the dialogue. This in turn raises questions concerning how successful the initiative is as a dialogic teaching programme. It also reminds us how the established culture of learning and teaching impact significantly on the nature of and prospects for any new developments designed to foster productive educational dialogues.

While we have suggested that there is a need for 'situated accounts' of educational dialogue, it is also important to recognize the crucial points of commonality evident in the work of the contributors. Thus, confirming the message from Part 1, there is 'variability within limits' in the accounts of productive educational dialogue emerging from the chapters in this section. Across the work presented, that draws on diverse curriculum contexts, it is clear that productive educational dialogues engage learners actively in processes of constructing and negotiating meaning and understandings such that options are not foreclosed. Productive educational dialogues offer opportunities for agentic, dialogic engagement with multiple perspectives, such that learners do not just talk about mathematics, science, literacy and philosophy, but rather they *do* mathematics, science, literacy and philosophy through the medium of language.

References

Mercer, N. and Littleton, K. (2007) *Dialogue and the Development of Children's Thinking: a sociocultural approach*, London: Routledge.

Vass, E. (2004) 'Understanding collaborative creativity: young children's classroom-based shared creative writing', in D. Miell and K. Littleton (eds) *Collaborative Creativity*, London: Free Association Books.

Chapter 5

The role of discourse in learning science

Jonathan Osborne, Stanford University and Christine Chin, National Institute of Education, Singapore

Introduction

This chapter explores the role of discourse in science and in the learning of science. While the community of practising scientists is distinct from that of science educators, they share a common disciplinary foundation and discourse plays a vital role in both. We begin by contrasting the nature of the form of discourse to be found in science and science education before moving to explore the role of language and discourse in science education. A specific focus of interest is the role of argumentation, which is a research programme that has been predominant in the field of science education for the past decade (Ford and Forman 2007; Lee, Wu and Tsai 2008). Here we review the body of evidence and argument that has accumulated about the value and significance of argumentation to the learning of science. Research in this field will only develop, however, when there are better explanatory models of how argumentative discourse achieves the effects that have been observed to date. To this end, a tentative model emerging from our research to date is presented and examined.

This chapter is based on two premises. First, that ideas in science must be seen as the product of the process of constructing models and representations of reality, which are then tested against empirical observations of the material world. That is, that they are outcome of an iterative process of evaluating evidence and refining our ideas about the world. Second, that language is a core element to this process. In short, that language is not some adjunct to science but rather an essential feature without which science would not exist. The chapter seeks to explore these issues in the context of school science while recognizing that they are not unique to science.

Science, school science and discursive practices

Discursive practices and, in particular argumentation, are core to science (as they are to many other disciplines – see also Schwarz, Hershkowitz and Prusak, this volume) as:

> Science is a social practice and scientific knowledge the product of a community. New knowledge does not become public knowledge in science until it has been checked through the various institutions of science. Papers are reviewed by peers before being published in journals. Claims made in published papers are scrutinized and criticized by the wider community of scientists; sometimes experiments are

repeated, checked, and alternative interpretations are put forward. In this process of critical scrutiny argument plays a central role.

(Driver, Newton and Osborne 2000: 298)

Argumentation is used, for instance, to establish how to interpret ambiguous data sets; to decide on the best method of testing an experimental hypothesis; to derive predictions about the possible outcomes of an experiment; or to develop new models of a given phenomenon. Given that it is core to the social practice of science, a normative expectation of any education in science should be that it attempts to offer some insight into the role of this discursive practice.

However, in common with many other school subjects, school science (science-as-it-is-taught) has traditionally been seen (and we would argue still is) as the presentation of a body of consensually agreed, well-established knowledge – what Latour and Woolgar (1986) called a set of 'taken-for-granted facts' that are only of note to those outside the scientific community. From this perspective the teaching of science is too often reduced to presenting science as a 'rhetoric of conclusions' (Schwab 1962) where scientific knowledge seems common sense, straightforward and unequivocal. Duschl (1990) has called this 'final form' science. To most students, presented in this manner, scientific knowledge appears to be both authoritative and non-negotiable, and limited solely to the context of justification. The context of the discovery of scientific ideas, which would necessarily include some elaboration of both the social context and the intellectual achievement it represents, is simply excised or judged irrelevant.

Neither is any time given to the context of its application – that is what the implications might be for society or individuals. Rather, science is presented as a body of disembodied and value-free knowledge and all opportunities for any subjective interpretation or exploration are often curtailed or denied (Osborne and Collins 2001). Such features are captured most eloquently by the following student response from an extensive focus-group study of 16-year-old students' views of their experience of school science (Osborne and Collins 2001):

ROSI: But still like this morning we were talking about genetic engineering ... She didn't want to know our opinions and I don't reckon that the curriculum lets them, lets us discuss it further. I mean science, okay you can accept the facts, but is it right, are we allowed to do this to human beings?

Sustaining a hermetic seal between the school science laboratory and society isolates school science from the wider society it serves. The subject pedagogy is dominated by a view that sees science as a body of knowledge or 'facts' to be established in students' minds. The result is pedagogical practices that are framed by the conduit metaphor, which perceives knowledge as a commodity to be 'got across' or implanted in students' minds (Reddy 1979) rather than an understanding the individual has to construct dialogically, both with themselves and others. The lack of discursive exploration was a major finding of Nystrand's study of the teaching of language arts in American classrooms (Nystrand, Gamoran, Kachur and Prendegarst 1997). Alexander similarly has bemoaned the failure to develop a more dialogic approach to teaching in English primary classrooms (Alexander 2005).

When the emphasis is on transmission of a body of knowledge, children are too often perceived as 'tabula rasa' and little credence or recognition is given to any pre-existing ideas that students might have gained from their prior experiences (Driver 1983). Moreover, from this perspective learning is very much an individual process rather than a social process where the motivation to learn is often extrinsic with teaching directed towards facilitating the ability to demonstrate the reproduction of such knowledge – what Dweck (2000) characterizes as 'performance learning' – rather than directing learning towards developing a deep understanding or 'mastery learning'. While such an approach might be functionally effective at producing students who are knowledgeable of the basic foundational elements of the subject, its affective outcome is increasingly to produce a body of students who are alienated from the subject and its future study (Ogura 2006; Osborne, Simon and Collins 2003).

More fundamentally, what students lack from this form of education is an informed understanding of the epistemic basis of the subject – that is, *how we know what we know* and, specifically in the case of science, the cultural achievement that it represents (Driver, Leach, Millar and Scott 1996; Kang, Scharmann and Noh 2005; Lederman 1992). Rather, evidence suggests that the failure to teach explicitly about the nature of science leaves many with simplistic or naive ideas about that subject (Driver *et al.* 1996). Moreover, in a society where science increasingly permeates the daily discourse, some understanding of its underlying epistemic values, methods, and institutional practices is essential if young people, as future citizens, are to engage with the issues confronting contemporary society and make informed judgments of reports about new scientific discoveries and their application. Understanding science as a process in which theories are evaluated against the evidence is, perhaps, the defining contribution of science to our culture and contemporary milieu. It was the Enlightenment after all, initiated by the study of science, that transformed the basis of belief from accepting the ideas propounded by the accredited agents of tradition (often the priesthood) to one where ideas were held to be true because they offered the best explanation of the available evidence – a perspective that sees science as a process of evaluating theories against empirical evidence and demonstrates that it is the theoretical ideas of science that are its crowning glory (Harré 1984).

Such a view is rarely promulgated in the school science classroom, however. Rather, the daily diet places an emphasis on atomized elements of scientific knowledge – what Cohen (1952) aptly termed a miscellany of scientific facts and whose individual significance, in the greater scheme of things, is hard to perceive. The resultant outcome for most students is that any school subject presented in this manner remains just that – a miscellany of facts and not a set of powerful explanatory theories. Taught in this manner, mathematics is perceived as a set of algorithms and numerical skills rather than a coherent way of investigating and representing a major feature of human life; history becomes a collection of information about the past rather than a study of human society and the social forces that affect its development; and in science there is a failure to grasp the creative and intellectual achievement of ideas such as Pasteur's concept of microbes to explain the transmission of diseases, Darwin's theory of natural selection to explain the evolution of the species, or Einstein's theory of relativity to explain the invariance of the speed of light.

The role of language in school science

How might an emphasis on discourse and dialogue assist? As the focus of this chapter is on the role of discourse in the teaching of science, we must turn to the role of language in this subject and examine what is known not only about the language of science but also about the language of the science classroom. Firstly, the two are not one and the same. The goal of science is the construction of new knowledge, and hence its language commonly consists of speculations or conjectures, or discussion of the circumstances affecting their limits of their validity (Latour and Woolgar 1986). Such language is commonly found in research papers, at conference presentations or in private conversations. In contrast, the goal of science education is to develop an understanding both of a body of well-established knowledge and how explanatory accounts of the material world have been constructed. However, the language of science education, most notably in textbooks, advances claims about the world in the universal present tense where any mention of competing theoretical accounts have simply been excised, removing any sense of how this understanding came to be, what an intellectual achievement its development represents or why alternative accounts might be wrong.

Nor does the common discourse within the classroom assist. School science is dominated by a form of triadic discourse (Sinclair and Coulthard 1975), which the teacher initiates by asking a closed question, where the student responds commonly with a phrase-like or short utterance, and the teacher then offers evaluative feedback (Lemke 1990). While such language, which Mortimer and Scott (2003) term interactive-authoritative, does have the function of making knowledge public and common to all, the predominant cognitive requirement it makes is the least demanding one of recall. Requests that students reason publicly or explain are rare and the common discourse of the science classroom offers little potential to expose the kind of epistemic reasoning that is at the heart of science (Driver *et al*. 2000).

Moreover, language is key to communicating ideas in science. Or rather, it would be more accurate to say that a plural set of languages are key to communicating science as science, more than most other subjects, is a multi-semiotic form of communication (Lemke 1998; Wellington and Osborne 2001). Ideas in science are communicated through the medium of words, diagrams, symbols, mathematics and charts and graphs. These forms of communication are wholly interdependent and making meaning requires an understanding of each. The meaning of a concept 'does not arise simply from each of these [semiotic modes of expression] added to, or in parallel with, the others: it arises from the combination of each of these integrated with and multiplied by each of the others' (Lemke 1998). Being literate in science in its most fundamental sense requires the ability not simply to decode all of these semiotic forms but the ability to construct meaning from them in their entirety (Norris and Phillips 2001; Osborne 2002). And, given that reading is a constructive process, this requires that the teacher of science recognize, first and foremost, that they are a teacher of a language – indeed, several languages – and that students must be helped to decode the languages of science and to make meaning from the text. Literacy from this perspective is not an adjunct for the storage and transmission of information. Rather, as Norris and Phillips (2003) argue, literacy becomes *constitutive of science itself*. For just as there can be no houses without roofs or walls, there can be no science without reading, talking and writing.

The role of argumentation in science

Our contention is that developing an understanding of the ideas and concepts of science means that pupils need to spend 'more time interacting with ideas and less time interacting with apparatus' (Hodson 1990: 34). More importantly, it means that if we wish to place an emphasis on being able to read, write and talk science, then it is important to develop pupils' knowledge and understanding of the standard stylistic conventions of scientific language. Here we need to recognize Lemke's simple but salient point that:

> Talking science does not simply mean talking *about* science. It means *doing* science through the medium of language. "Talking science" means observing, hypothesizing, describing, comparing, classifying, analyzing.
>
> (Lemke 1990: 1)

All of these processes make linguistic and cognitive demands but only if students are given the opportunity to discursively engage in such processes. Drawing on a long standing distinction that has been made between declarative and procedural knowledge made originally by Ryle (1949), Ohlsson (1996) distinguishes these two principal forms of learning as learning to do and learning to understand. Learning to understand requires engagement in a variety of discourse acts, which he defines as follows (Table 5.1):

As Ohlsson argues:

> this tentative taxonomy of epistemically relevant activities is short but surprisingly complete. Whatever else do we ever do when we talk or write, over and above describe, explain, predict, argue, explicate and define. Although there are many other types of speech acts (e.g. to promise, request and threaten) no epistemically relevant extensions to the taxonomy comes to mind.
>
> (Ohlsson 1996: 51)

All of these actions are facilitated by asking students to engage in discursive argumentation and a dialogic process or interaction between student and student (as opposed to the more common interaction between student and teacher). Argumentation is used here in the sense offered by van Eemeren and Grootendorst (2004: 1) where argumentation is defined as a:

> verbal, social and rational activity aimed at convincing a reasonable critic of the acceptability of a standpoint by putting forward a constellation of propositions justifying or refuting the proposition expressed in the standpoint.

Not unreasonably, teachers may choose to use the word 'debate' or 'discussion' asking students to justify their reasoning to avoid any possible confrontational and negative connotations associated with the word 'argument' or 'argumentation' (Cohen 1995).

Ohlsson's analysis then offers an explanation for Lemke's (1990: 1) dictum that 'the one single change in science education that could do more than any other to improve

Table 5.1 List of epistemic discourse activities

Describing	To describe is to fashion a discourse referring to an object or an event such that a person who partakes of that discourse acquires an accurate conception of that object or event.
Explaining	In the canonical explanation task, the explainer is faced with an event of some sort (e.g. the sinking of the Titanic, the demise of the dinosaurs) and fashions a discourse such that a person who partakes of that discourse understands why that event happened.
Predicting	To make a prediction is to fashion a discourse such that a person who partakes of that discourse becomes convinced that such and such an event will happen (under such and such circumstances).
Arguing	To argue is to state reasons for (or against) a particular position on some issue, thereby increasing (or decreasing) the recipient's confidence that the position is right.
Critiquing (evaluating)	To critique a cultural product is to fashion a discourse such that a person who partakes of that discourse becomes aware of the good and bad points of that product.
Explicating	To explicate a concept is to fashion a discourse such that the person who partakes of that discourse acquires a clearer understanding of its meaning.
Defining	To define a term is to propose a usage for it. When the term already exists in the language, the boundary between defining and explicating is blurred.

Source: Ohlssson (1996: 51).

student's ability to use the language of science is to give them more actual practice using it', as engaging in argumentation demands and develops the facility to listen, to think critically and to generate explanations and justification. It is the use of these skills that has been shown to improve student understanding. For instance, Hynd and Alvermann (1986) found that if students were given texts that not only explained why the right answer was right *but also explained why the wrong answer was wrong*, and students were provided with an opportunity to deliberate about the merits of the competing explanations, then students' conceptual learning, compared to a control group, was enhanced. Likewise, Howe, Rodgers and Tolmie (1990) and Howe, Tolmie and Rodgers (1992) found, in studies based on a comparison of the learning of groups that held differing preconceptions compared with those who held similar preconceptions, that the groups consisting of those who held different ideas consistently made greater progress while those who worked in groups who held similar ideas made no progress whatsoever.

   Chi, Bassok, Lewis, Reimann and Glaser (1989) undertook a study where eight college students were asked to explain to another what they understood from reading statements from three examples taken from a physics text. The four students who were more successful at solving problems at the end of the chapter (averaging 82 per cent correct in the post-test) were the ones who had spontaneously generated a greater number of self-explanations (15.3 explanations per example) while studying the chosen examples. In contrast, the four students who were less successful achieved only 46 per cent on the post-test and had generated only 2.8 explanations per example. Similar findings emerged from a later study with 14 eighth-grade students where the focus this time was on declarative knowledge of the functioning of the valves in the heart (Chi, de Leeuw, Chiu and LaVancher 1994). Notably, the improvement for the students required to generate explanations was more significant in the more complex questions used to test understanding. Chi *et al.* (1994) postulate the reason such explanation is effective is that, having articulated an incorrect explanation, further reading of ensuing sentences (which always present the correct information) will ultimately lead to the generation of a contradiction that will generate conflict. The outcome of such conflict will require metacognitive reflection and self-repair by the student if resolution is to occur.

The exercises that Chi *et al.* conducted were essentially a decontextualized psychological experiment and not a process that lends itself easily to the classroom. Small group work and argumentation, however, do provide a naturalistic context in which self-explanation is both required and challenged – the very activities that Chi *et al.* have found to be so effective at enhancing student learning. Evidence that this is so comes from a review conducted by Webb (1989) of 19 published studies on learning mathematics and computer science. Her finding was that the level of elaboration of students' interaction with other students was related to achievement: those that gave high-level elaboration to other members of the group achieved more highly whereas offering only low-level explanations had no effect. Her explanation for this effect was that:

> In the process of clarifying and reorganizing the material, the helper may discover gaps in his or her own understanding or discrepancies with others' work or previous work. To resolve those discrepancies, the helper may search for new information and subsequently resolve those inconsistencies, thereby learning the material better than before ... Furthermore, when an explanation given to a team-mate is not successful, the helper is forced to formulate the explanation in new or different ways.
>
> (Webb 1989: 29)

Another important insight into the value of argumentation comes from the work of Hatano and Inagaki (1991). Drawing on data from many experimental studies of small groups working collaboratively on problems led them to draw three conclusions. First, that students often produce knowledge that can seldom be acquired without such interaction – a point that was recognized by the headmaster of Eton, a leading English public school when he stated that 'we have always recognised two principles in education, which are first that young people teach each other more than adults think they teach them, and, secondly, that at least as much learning goes on outside the classroom as within it' (Eyres 2008). Their second finding was that the nature of the knowledge acquired by the majority of the participants is very context-specific to the group, even when the structure and nature of the activity are very similar. That is that the variance between groups is large. Finally, they also found that the knowledge acquired within the groups by individual members differed considerably – that is that the intra-group variance is large. What this suggests is that the nature of the group dynamics has a considerable effect on the potential outcomes of any small-group discussions or argumentation.

Evidence from studies conducted in the context of school science provides a mounting body of empirical evidence that engaging in argumentation does have significant effects on student learning. There is, for instance, a set of laboratory-based studies with small groups of primary children conducted by Howe, Tolmie and others (2000; 1992) mentioned previously – all of which have shown significant effects on student learning. In the primary classroom, Mercer, Dawes, Wegerif and Sams (2004) have used an experimental programme aimed at teaching young people (age 9–10) to talk and reason with a sample of 90 children and a slightly larger control group. Over the period of the study, 23 weeks, their analysis of children's talk found, compared with the control group, significant increases in: their use of key words indicative of reasoning e.g. 'because', 'I think', 'would'; the number of student utterances of more than 100 characters; their scores on a concept-mapping exercise; and their scores on Raven's matrices, which are a measure of non-verbal reasoning or general intelligence.

Likewise, Zohar and Nemet (2002), working with two classes of 16–17-year-old students studying genetics, required the teacher to permit students opportunities to engage in argumentative discourse about the appropriate answer to specific problems. Comparing the outcomes with similar control classes three statistically significant findings emerged: first, the frequency of the students who did not consider biological knowledge was higher in the comparison group as compared with the experimental group (30.4 per cent versus 11.3 per cent, respectively); second, the frequency of students who used false considerations of biological knowledge was higher in the comparison group as compared with the experimental group (16.1 per cent versus 4.8 pre cent, respectively); and, finally, the frequency of students who correctly considered specific biological knowledge was higher in the experimental group as compared with the comparison group (53.2 per cent versus 8.9 per cent, respectively). More evidence comes from the work of Osborne, Erduran and Simon (2004), who worked with six teachers of secondary science using an intervention programme of activities over the course of a year with their 14-year-old students aimed at enhancing the quality of their argumentation. They found that, compared with the control, there was a notable improvement in students' ability to construct better arguments. However, this was not significant.

What all these studies point to is that engaging in discursive argumentation makes higher-order cognitive demands. Language is not so much a product of thought but the means by which thought is enacted (Vygotsky 1962). And as Billig (1996: 141) points out, thought is essentially dialogical – a private dialogue between inner thoughts and thus 'it is not so much that humans converse because they have inner thoughts to express, but they have thoughts because they are able to converse'. Hence, learning to argue serves an important function of arguing to learn (Andriessen, Baker and Suthers 2003) or – to put it another way – 'from a developmental point of view, learning to argue may be a crucial phase in learning to think' (Billig 1996: 141). Asking students to argue, therefore, is asking students to think.

An explanatory model for argumentation – the role of questions

Jermann and Dillenbourg (2003) point to the fact that there remain two main challenges for the research community interested in developing our understanding of argumentation and its application in educational contexts. These are: a) What are the features of learning environments that 'trigger productive argumentation among students?'; and b) understanding how argumentation produces learning – that is which 'cognitive mechanisms, triggered by argumentative interactions, generate knowledge and in which conditions'.

Considerable work has been undertaken in the past decade by the Computer Supported Collaborative Learning (CSCL) community to address the first of these challenges. In short, they have developed software tools that either enable the visualization of argument, e.g. Belvedere and Digalo, or that scaffold argument by making critical epistemic requests for evidence or deliberation while engaged in the process of enquiry, e.g. WISE. These tools have served to make students thinking visible and have made significant contributions to the study of argumentation, e.g. (Baker 2003; Linn and Bell 2000). Suthers (2003: 31) argues that their role is to:

- initiate negotiations of meaning as any shared representation requires the consent of the group and negotiations of meaning;
- serve as a proxy for the purpose of gestural deixis as the representation offers an easy means to refer to the idea 'on the table' and thus facilitate negotiation and argumentation and, in so doing, increasing 'the conceptual complexity that can be handled by the group';
- provide a foundation for implicitly shared awareness as the representation serves as a 'group memory, reminding the group of previous ideas' and an agenda for further work.

In our recent work, we (Chin and Osborne, submitted) have focused rather on the role of questions as a heuristic for initiating productive argumentation arguing that, when students pose questions about things that they want to know, they become more cognizant of what they do not know or are puzzled about. Posing questions, either to themselves or to their peers, may then scaffold their thinking by acting as a 'thought-starter' and metacognitive or epistemic tool. Such a process has the potential to broaden: a) the 'argumentation space' (Osborne *et al.* 2004) in terms of both the nature and frequency of argumentation patterns; b) the 'questioning space' in terms of the types, depth, range, and frequency of questions; and c) the 'negotiation space' in terms of the multiple perspectives and range of arguments used. To explore these arguments empirically, we gave students a set of question stems and question prompts to ask about the phenomenon of interest – in this case what happens to the temperature of a lump of ice as it is heated. Our interest lay in whether it would initiate argumentative discussion and our findings suggest that a focus on generating salient questions does have these effects.

To explain these outcomes we have developed a model – called the Questioning and Argumentation (QA) model that attempts to explain how students' questions may initiate and sustain argumentation during group discourse (Figure 5.1).

It is based on patterns observed that were grounded in their data and describes a number of possible pathways involving self-explanations (Chi *et al.* 1994) and peer explanations that are mediated by questions posed to the self or to others. The model is based, in part, on the idea that one of the mechanisms responsible for the generation

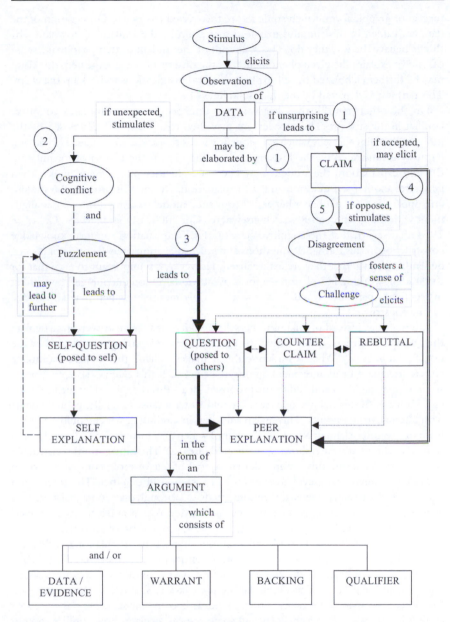

Figure 5.1 The Questioning and Argumentation model.

of questions stems from a need to correct declarative knowledge deficits (Graesser, Person and Huber 1992).

In the QA model, a stimulus presented to students serves as a source of data. The stimulus could be in the form of a demonstration, a discrepant event, or a problem in textual or graphic form, which students are then asked to discuss. Observation of the data embedded in this stimulus may lead to a claim by the student of how and why things behave the way they do. This is a result of the student's attempt to make sense of, and to explain, the given phenomenon. If the observation is as expected, this claim may be further elaborated by self-explanations and justifications to back up the claim. This pathway is depicted by the thin, solid lines (1).

On the other hand, if the observation is unexpected, this stimulates cognitive conflict in the student. This puzzlement may then elicit a *self-question* posed by the individual to him/herself, which subsequently leads to a *self-explanation*. This second pathway is illustrated by the broken, dashed line (2). In the course of formulating this self-explanation, the student may encounter further puzzlement, which then generates another self-question and self-explanation. During this process, the student attempts to reconstruct his or her activated mental model to bring it into closer alignment with the given data. Research elsewhere (Chi 2000; Chi *et al.* 1989; Chi *et al.* 1994) has shown that the cognitive activity of self-explanation supports knowledge construction in this form. Self-questions and self-explanations may be overt or covert, depending on whether they are externalized. However, it is important to note that for the student working in isolation – a form of individualization encouraged by a direct instruction – pathways 1 and 2 represent the only means by which new knowledge can be constructed.

Alternatively, instead of talking to herself, a student may instead verbally articulate the question to others, which would then elicit a *peer explanation*, as indicated by the bold, solid lines (3). When a student publicly makes a claim, this may also stimulate either agreement or disagreement among their peers. If this claim is accepted, other students may build on and add to the proposed idea – this is depicted by the thick line (4). However, if this claim is opposed, it could foster a sense of challenge in students with alternative viewpoints. This may result then in a rebuttal, which could be in the form of a counter-claim or a question, either of which may further elicit a peer explanation. This latter pathway is shown using dotted lines (5). The explanations constructed by the students during this group talk may consist of one or more components of an argument, namely, data, evidence, warrant, backing, and qualifier. The interaction between the social and personal dimensions, mediated through questions, challenge, and explanations, reflects the movement between inter-psychological and intra-psychological planes promoting reflexivity, integration, and the appropriation of knowledge.

The QA model shows how students' questions support the articulation of evidence-based arguments in that questions are the essential pre-cursors of conflict. While pathways 2 and 5 illustrate the role that conflict plays in argumentation and reasoning through the process of accommodation, pathways 1, 3, and 4 are based more on the concept of assimilation where students' ideas become increasingly elaborated by adding to pre-existing concepts. This, in some respect, explains how conflict and co-operation mediate the knowledge construction process. Furthermore, while pathway 2 depicts the role of cognitive conflict as an individual construct, pathway 5 shows how public discursive conflict may be resolved dialogically. Thus, the model offers an account for both the personal and social construction of knowledge via questioning and argumentation.

More fundamentally, what the model offers is some insight into the limitations of direct instruction. Such pedagogy restricts students' opportunities to develop their knowledge and understanding to pathways 1 and 2. Providing students the opportunity to engage in dialogic interaction about their ideas, either with their teacher or with their peers, increases the number of potential pathways through which conceptual understanding might be achieved. Our hypothesis, therefore, is that the use of such methods would enhance the pedagogic effectiveness explaining the results obtained by Zohar and Nemet (2002) and Mercer *et al.* (2004) – all of whom found that the use of a more discursive and argumentative pedagogy led to enhanced conceptual understanding. It would also explain why a knowledge of why the wrong answer is wrong leads to a more secure understanding of why the right answer is right (Hynd and Alvermann 1986). Students who lack such knowledge suffer cognitive conflict (pathway 2) but often cannot generate self-explanations to refute what might appear the common-sense logic of informal scientific thinking. Students who have engaged in argumentation or questioning have had access to the conceptual resources of the community (pathways 3, 4 and 5) and the construction of a peer explanation, which has then to be internalized as a self-explanation – an explanation that not only justifies the scientific view but which has assimilated the means of refuting alternative erroneous theories.

Critically, what the model also shows is how encouraging questioning is central to argumentation that leads to learning. Questions posed to others are a self-recognition of puzzlement or uncertainty, the means of accessing the cognitive capital of the group or the teacher, and the initiator of counter-claims and peer explanations that ultimately lead to enhanced self-explanation. Offering students the opportunity to engage in such a process themselves has three major benefits. First, it exposes students to an epistemic discourse that is more akin to that of the scientific community and, in so doing, may develop an enhanced understanding of the nature of science. Second, it requires critical thought and engagement and helps them to recognize that beliefs are justified by evaluating them against the available evidence – that is, it may advance their personal epistemology beyond a naive realism or a simplistic relativism that holds all ideas to be of equal value. Finally, as we have shown, it provides more pathways to developing a conceptual understanding of science, promoting the use of self-explanation, which is a foundation of mastery learning and intrinsic motivation. What little evidence there is, suggests it is also more engaging as a form of learning (Nolen 2003).

Conclusions

As Alexander (2005), Nystrand (1997) and others have shown, the question-and-answer recitation script is a form of discourse that dominates pedagogy not only in science but in all subjects. What argumentation offers not only school science but all subjects is a chance to transform the common discourse of the classroom – in the case of science to show science as a creative, intellectually challenging subject where ideas are not the product of simple common sense but rather rooted in a careful and rigorous analysis of competing theoretical accounts. In short, that the scientific understanding we hold today has been hard won.

What the insights and model presented in this chapter offer are hopefully some tentative explanatory insight into how argumentation works, addressing one of Jermann and Dillenbourg's (2003) questions and the features that might 'trigger productive argumentation'. However, in offering a possible explanatory model of how argumentation supports collaborative learning we have attempted to answer their second question about how such argumentative interactions might generate knowledge and the conditions that foster their use. Its greatest value lies in explaining how engaging in dialogic discourse facilitates more learning pathways. Nevertheless the task structure, the rules of interaction and student groupings are clearly variables that are significant in enabling access to such discourse. Advancing the use of dialogic discourse in all school subjects requires further exploration and how these factors can facilitate or inhibit student learning remains a challenge for the field.

References

Alexander, R. (2005) *Towards Dialogic Teaching*, York: Dialogos.

Andriessen, J., Baker, M. and Suthers, D. (eds) (2003) *Arguing to Learn: confronting cognitions in computer-supported collaborative learning environments*, Dordrecht, The Netherlands: Kluwer.

Baker, M. (2003) 'Computer mediated argumentative interactions for the co-elaboration of scientific notions', in J. Andriessen, M. Baker and D. Suthers (eds) *Arguing to Learn: confronting cognitions in computer-supported collaborative learning environments*, Dordrecht, The Netherlands: Kluwer.

Billig, M. (1996) *Arguing and Thinking* (2nd edn), Cambridge: Cambridge University Press.

Chi, M., Bassok, M., Lewis, M. W., Reimann, P. and Glaser, R. (1989) 'Self-explanations: how students study and use examples in learning to solve problems', *Cognitive Science*, 13:145–82.

Chi, M., de Leeuw, N., Chiu, M. H. and LaVancher, C. (1994) 'Eliciting self-explanations improves understanding', *Cognitive Science*, 18:439–77.

Chi, M. T. H. (2000) 'Self-explaining expository texts: the dual process of generating inferences and repairing mental models. In R. Glaser (ed.) *Advances in Instructional Psychology*, Mahwah, NJ: Lawrence Erlbaum.

Chin, C. and Osborne, J. (submitted) 'Supporting argumentation through students questions: case studies in science classrooms'.

Cohen, D. (1995) 'Argument is war ... and war is hell: philosophy, education and metaphors for argumentation', *Informal Logic*, 17:177–87.

Cohen, I. B. (1952) 'The education of the public in science', *Impact of Science on Society*, 3:67–101.

Driver, R. (1983) *The Pupil as Scientist?*, Milton Keynes: Open University Press.

Driver, R., Leach, J., Millar, R. and Scott, P. (1996) *Young People's Images of Science*, Buckingham: Open University Press.

Driver, R., Newton, P. and Osborne, J. F. (2000) 'Establishing the norms of scientific argumentation in classrooms', *Science Education*, 84:287–312.

Duschl, R. A. (1990) *Restructuring Science Education*, New York: Teachers College Press.

Dweck, C. (2000) *Self-theories: Their Role in Motivation, Personality, and Development (Essays in Social Psychology)*, Philadelphia, PA: Psychology Press.

Eyres, H. (2008, 23 May) 'Bold Etonians', *Financial Times*, Weekend Section p. 1.

Ford, M. J. and Forman, E. A. (2007) 'Redefining disciplinary learning in classroom contexts', *Review of Research in Education*, 30:1–32.

Graesser, A. C., Person, N. K. and Huber, J. D. (1992) 'Mechanisms that generate questions', in T. Lauer, E. Peacock and A. C. Graesser (eds) *Questions and Information Systems*, Hillsdale, NJ: Lawrence Erlbaum.

Harré, R. (1984) *The Philosophies of Science: an introductory survey* (2nd edn), Oxford: Oxford University Press.

Hatano, G. and Inagaki, K. (1991) 'Sharing cognition through collective comprehension activity', in L. Resnick, J. M. Levine and S. D. Teasley (eds) *Perspectives on Socially Shared Cognition*, Washington: American Psychological Association.

Hodson, D. (1990) 'A critical look at practical work in school science', *School Science Review*, 70:33–40.

Howe, C., Rodgers, C. and Tolmie, T. (1990) 'Physics in the primary school: peer interaction and understanding of floating and sinking', *European Journal of Psychology of Education*, 5:459–75

Howe, C., Tolmie, A., Duchak-Tanner, V. and Rattray, C. (2000) 'Hypothesis testing in science: group consensus and the acquisition of conceptual and procedural knowledge', *Learning and Instruction*, 10:361–91.

Howe, C. J., Tolmie, A. and Rodgers, C. (1992) 'The acquisition of conceptual knowledge in science by primary school children: group interaction and the understanding of motion down an inclined plane', *British Journal of Developmental Psychology*, 10:113–30.

Hynd, C. and Alvermann, D. E. (1986) 'The role of refutation text in overcoming difficulty with science concepts', *Journal of Reading*, 29:440–6.

Jermann, P. and Dillenbourg, P. (2003) 'Elaborating new arguments through a CSCL script', in J. Andriessen, M. Baker and D. Suthers (eds) *Arguing to Learn: confronting cognitions in computer-supported collaborative learning environments*, Dordrecht, The Netherlands: Kluwer.

Kang, S., Scharmann, L. C. and Noh, T. (2005) 'Examining students' views on the nature of science: results from Korean 6th, 8th, and 10th graders', *Science Education*, 89:314–34.

Latour, B. and Woolgar, S. (1986) *Laboratory Life: the construction of scientific facts* (2nd edn), Princeton, NJ: Princeton University Press.

Lederman, N. G. (1992) 'Students' and teachers' conceptions of the nature of science: a review of the research', *Journal of Research in Science Teaching*, 29:331–59.

Lee, M-H., Wu, Y-T., & Tsai, C.-C. (2009). Research Trends in Science Education from 2003 to 2007: A content analysis of publications in selected journals. *International Journal of Science Education*, 31(15), 1999–2020.

Lemke, J. (1990) *Talking Science: language, learning and values*, Norwood, NJ: Ablex Publishing.

Lemke, J. (1998) 'Teaching all the languages of science: words, symbols, images and actions'. Available online at: http://academic.brooklyn.cuny.edu/education/jlemke/papers/barcelon.htm (accessed July 29, 2009).

Linn, M. and Bell, P. (2000) 'Designing the knowledge integration environment', *International Journal of Science Education*, 22:781–96.

Mercer, N., Dawes, L., Wegerif, R. and Sams, C. (2004) 'Reasoning as a scientist: ways of helping children to use language to learn science', *British Education Research Journal*, 30:359–77.

Mortimer, E. and Scott, P. (2003) *Meaning Making in Secondary Science Classrooms*, Maidenhead: Open University Press.

Nolen, S. B. (2003) 'Learning environment, motivation and achievement in high school science', *Journal of Research in Science Teaching*, 40:347–68.

Norris, S. and Phillips, L. (2001) 'How literacy in its fundamental sense is central to scientific literacy', paper presented at the Annual Conference of the National Association for Research in Science Teaching, St. Louis.

Norris, S. and Phillips, L. (2003) 'How literacy in its fundamental sense is central to scientific literacy', *Science Education*, 87:224–40.

Nystrand, M., Gamoran, A., Kachur, R. and Prendegarst, C. (1997) *Opening Dialogue: understanding the dynamics of language and learning in the English classroom*, New York: Teachers College Press.

Ogura, Y. (2006) 'Graph of student attitude v student attainment', Tokyo: National Institute for Educational Research. Based on data from M. O. Martin *et al.* (2000) *TIMSS 1999 International Science Report: Findings from IEA's Repeat of the Third International Mathematics and Science Study at the Eighth Grade*, Chestnut Hill, MA: Boston College.

Ohlsson, S. (1996) 'Learning to do and learning to understand? A lesson and a challenge for cognitive modelling', in P. Reimann and H. Spada (eds) *Learning in Humans and Machines*, Oxford: Elsevier.

Osborne, J. F. (2002) 'Science without literacy: a ship without a sail?', *Cambridge Journal of Education*, 32:203–15.

Osborne, J. F., and Collins, S. (2001) 'Pupils' views of the role and value of the science curriculum: a focus-group study', *International Journal of Science Education*, 23:441–68.

Osborne, J. F., Erduran, S. and Simon, S. (2004) 'Enhancing the quality of argument in school science', *Journal of Research in Science Teaching*, 41:994–1020.

Osborne, J. F., Simon, S. and Collins, S. (2003) 'Attitudes towards science: a review of the literature and its implications', *International Journal of Science Education*, 25:1049–79.

Reddy, M. (1979) 'The conduit metaphor', in A. Ortony (ed.) *Metaphor and Thought*, New York: Cambridge University Press.

Ryle, G. (1949) *The Concept of Mind*, London: Hutchinson.

Schwab, J. J. (1962) *The Teaching of Science as Enquiry*, Cambridge, MA: Harvard University Press.

Sinclair, J. and Coulthard, R. M. (1975) *Towards an Analysis of Discourse: the English used by teachers and pupils*, Oxford: Oxford University Press.

Suthers, D. (2003) 'Representational guidance for collaborative inquiry', in J. Andriessen, M. Baker and D. Suthers (eds) *Arguing to Learn: confronting cognitions in computer-supported collaborative learning environments*, Dordrecht, The Netherlands: Kluwer.

van Eemeren, F. H., and Grootendorst, R. (2004) *A Systematic Theory of Argumentation: the pragma-dialetical approach*, Cambridge: Cambridge University Press.

Vygotsky, L. (1962) *Thought and Language*, Cambridge, Massachusetts: MIT Press.

Webb, N. M. (1989) 'Peer interaction and learning in small groups', *International Journal of Education Research*, 13:21–39.

Wellington, J. and Osborne, J. F. (2001) *Language and Literacy in Science Education*, Buckingham: Open University Press.

Zohar, A. and Nemet, F. (2002) 'Fostering students' knowledge and argumentation skills through dilemmas in human genetics', *Journal of Research in Science Teaching*, 39:35–62.

Chapter 6

Argumentation and mathematics

Baruch B. Schwarz and Naomi Prusak,
The Hebrew University and
Rina Hershkowitz,
The Weizmann Institute

Introduction

When Stephen Toulmin published *The Uses of Argument* (1958), logicians fiercely opposed his views since he challenged the view accepted at the time that all sorts of arguments should be evaluated according to laws of logic. He advocated a dynamic and informal, rather than a formal, notion of validity for arguments. Logic was superseded by what resembled a judicial procedure. His model of the 'layout of arguments' (conclusions driven from data supported by warrants and possibly justified by backing, refutation, etc.) is certainly a landmark in Argumentation Theory. Although it seems very general, Toulmin convincingly showed that this layout is governed by distinctive norms in each domain – that they are *field-dependent* norms according to which arguments are to be judged differently in every domain. Also, Toulmin insisted that his model is not applicable in mathematics and that in pure mathematics, arguments could be judged according to laws of logic. The fact that nowadays mathematical educators use his model in their teaching and that researchers use it to model the object of mathematical activity in classroom discussions suggests that Toulmin's revolution went farther than he himself originally thought.

The present chapter 'completes' in some way *The Uses of Argument*, by focusing on the particular case of mathematics – which was considered by Toulmin as outside the scope of the observation of the emergence of arguments. We will claim that, as with any kind of other activity, mathematical activity in the streets or in classrooms should involve *substantial* in addition to *analytic* arguments. We will also claim, however, that mathematics is a unique domain in which logical necessity should lead the judgment of arguments. Finally we will present the argument claimed by many that this logical necessity is required to be expressed explicitly by mathematical formal means. The first requirement is ubiquitous; the second is ubiquitous among mathematicians, but is not among educators although many of them see it as desirable. The need for the third – expressing logical necessity by formal means, is the object of an unending controversy among educators. The first two requirements, as will be shown later, confer to argumentation in mathematics a very special character.

In this chapter, we analyse argumentation both among professional mathematicians and among people concerned with mathematics education: designers, researchers, teachers and children who learn mathematics in classrooms. One of our foci is to analyse the relations between 'arguing' and 'proving' in mathematics. These relations have always been tense: as shown further on, among mathematicians, they generated creative ideas; among children they generated difficulties and gaps. We show how design efforts, especially with certain technological tools, have succeeded in bridging gaps. Our scope, though, goes beyond the particular perspective of the link between arguing and proving to focus on the role of argumentation in general in constructing mathematical knowledge.

Of course, we should first be clear about what we mean by argumentation. Argumentation is a multifaceted term with different meanings (for a general definition and discussion of argumentation and its historical and cultural development, see Schwarz 2009). It is natural to adopt a definition that fits classroom situations. The most relevant and also widely accepted definition of argumentation has been given by van Eemeren and colleagues (1996: 5):

> Argumentation is a verbal and social activity of reason aimed at increasing (or decreasing) the acceptability of a controversial standpoint for the listener or reader, by putting forward a constellation of propositions intended to justify (or refute) the standpoint before a 'rational judge'.

This definition positions argumentation in a social space and excludes a monological activity to favour a collective one. It fits a classroom context of students engaged in a discussion (with or without the presence of a teacher). Some educational researchers, like Baker (2003: 48), have added a *meaning-making* dimension:

> We see argumentative interaction fundamentally as a type of dialogical or dialectical game that is played upon and arises from the terrain of collaborative problem solving and that is associated with collaborative meaning-making.

Van Eemeren, as well as Baker, stresses the dialectical character of argumentation, the fact that competing ideas are considered, or that, alternatively, a single idea is considered critically. This is what Baker calls *transforming the epistemic status of solutions*. These two definitions also demarcate argumentative from explanatory activities: in explanatory activities, ideas are clarified, *explained*, but not put into questions.

One may ask, why write a chapter on argumentation and mathematics? After all, the term 'argumentation' has seldom been used in relation to mathematics until the nineties. Could it be that application of argumentation to so many contexts, as is done today, is only a passing fashion? And would it be more reasonable to leave mathematics out of the realm of argumentation, as Toulmin thought? We will see that professional mathematicians have struggled with this issue for a long time and still struggle with it. In domains such as science and history, professionals have already reported on the importance of argumentation in their practice. Such recognition has impinged on educational practices to be implemented (see for example Driver, Newman and Osborne 2000 or Osborne and Chin, this volume, for science and Goldberg, Schwarz and Porat 2008 for history). As will be shown in the next section, the case of mathematics is very special and raises exciting controversies among mathematicians. Hearing their voices is crucial for those who design and observe educational practices in mathematics classrooms.

Do mathematicians leave room for argumentation?

Focusing on professional mathematicians is important not only of and in itself, but because observing them may have an impact on what educators would expect from students in their classes. Mathematicians are influential in establishing the norms to be instilled in classes, and their voice should be heard. We also have another reason to hear them: what they themselves say about argumentation puts the final nail in the coffin of formal logic being the only relevant tool for evaluating arguments produced in real-life activities. One could have thought that professional mathematicians use high standards that are not used by 'common mortals' because of their intellectual imperfections.[1] To understand the nature of mathematical practice in mathematicians, we should turn to philosophers of mathematics. In an influential paper entitled 'Why do we prove theorems?', Rav (1999), a philosopher of mathematics, analyses the functions that proofs play for professional mathematicians. Rav rejects the popular belief that proofs check the truth of solutions. *Derivations* – formalizations of proofs – serve as ways to show consistency in mathematical knowledge but are generally not a focus for most mathematicians (except for formal logicians). This is its most uninteresting function. Rather, proving is a creative activity that consists of inventing tools, strategies and concepts for solving problems. Consequently, it often happened in the history of mathematics that the problems to solve were quite insignificant and almost futile but the aim of proving a hypothesized conjecture led to spectacular developments. For example, the Goldbach conjecture (any odd number is the sum of two prime numbers) remains unsolved but has been a catalyst for elaborating powerful modern tools in number theory. Fermat's Last Theorem (the fact that the Diophantine equation $x^n + y^n = z^n$ has no solution when $n > 2$), which remained a conjecture until 1993, catalyzed theoretical bonds between elliptic curves and Diophantine equations. One could even say that finding a counter-example to the Goldbach conjecture would not tarnish the remarkable developments that the efforts to prove it have entailed. For Rav, proofs are the sites of mathematical knowledge, not theorems. Proofs are the roads, the ways, and theorems are the bus-stops, no more.[2]

At the end of the nineteenth century and at the beginning of the twentieth century, mathematicians expected to capture human reasoning from formal derivations. This was what Hilbert thought. However, Gödel showed that for any formal system that formalizes any piece of mathematics, there are statements that are mathematically meaningful but are not provable (these statements are also called 'undecidable'). This theoretical finding raised a strong anti-formalistic criticism. At the beginning, this criticism was moderate. In his *How to Solve It*, Pólya (1948), showed that mathematical activity is based on heuristics – general strategies for problem solving that may or may not help in specific cases; in *Mathematics and Plausible Reasoning*, Pólya models mathematical activity under uncertainty. In his influential book *Proofs and Refutations*, Lakatos (1976) built on Pólya's ideas to show that the development of mathematics does not consist (as conventional philosophy of mathematics tells us it does) in the steady accumulation of eternal truths. Mathematics develops, according to Lakatos, in a much more dramatic and exciting way – by a process of conjecture, followed by attempts to 'prove' the conjecture (i.e. to reduce it to other conjectures), followed by criticism via attempts to produce counter-examples both to the conjectured theorem and to the various steps in the proof. But this attractive approach to mathematical activity conceals dangers. Little by little, any kind of formalism is prohibited to favour mathematical activity as a quasi-experimental enterprise. The thrust of computing tools added vigour to the criticisms concerning the changes to the very nature of mathematical adventure. For example, while discussing the influence of technologies in mathematics, Hanna (1996) entitled one of her papers 'The ongoing value of proof' in which she referred to Zeilberger (1993) who predicted that mathematicians will use proofs that are less complete but cheaper, and that 'mathematicians as a whole will come to accept such semi-rigor as a legitimate form of mathematics validation'. In a detailed description, Arzarello (2008) convincingly shows that most of the critiques raised by the anti-formalists can be answered. His argument can be understood by splitting the activity of proving into two distinct activities: the first activity consists of making sense and of enquiry during which mathematicians raise conjectures and use all tools possible to establish their conjectures. The second activity of proving consists of developing a chain of logical consequences. During this activity, tools such as computational tools or visualization cannot serve as evidence. They can suggest ideas, or metaphors that can be used in the elaboration of logical consequences. The first activity of enquiry is argumentative in nature but the argumentation in this case is more than oral and capitalizes on visual and computational tools (Arzarello 2008).

Ernest (1994), another philosopher of mathematics, has concentrated on the inscription of proofs rather than on their generation. Although proofs are expressed through propositions and theorems with implications of the form A → B, such inscriptions pertain to informal logic, so for a reader to understand the written proof she needs to undertake extrapolations according to her own knowledge of the form A → C → D → E → B and these extrapolations may be different for different readers. Coherence is then not attained through checking logical integrity of derivation, but by *communicating among mathematicians*. As stated by Rav (1999: 36), 'the social process of reciprocal crosschecks seems to be the only way to weed out errors and guarantee the overall coherence and stability of knowledge among the community of mathematicians'. Rav continues:

> The social process is not something that makes it *less* objective or true: rather the social process *enhances* the reliability of mathematics, through important checks and balances (Thurston 1994). We eschew the pitfalls of social relativism because there are *objective criteria* for judging the correctness of an argument. An individual mathematician may overlook or make an unwarranted assertion, but consensus is eventually reached once the error is pointed out.

Therefore, inscriptions of proofs are important for mathematicians to understand each other; they help in constructing logical consequences to communicate or understand proofs.

Our review of what and how mathematicians report on their own activity includes, then, an activity during which they make sense of problems and raise conjectures, another activity of proving, mainly of establishing logical consequences, and a last activity of inscribing proofs in a formal way either to communicate ideas to their community or to check consistencies (through derivations). There is no direct observation of the full range of such activities in mathematicians though. In recent studies some researchers have traced quite locally the activities of university students in mathematics.

It is reasonable to think that such activities resemble the activities of accomplished mathematicians. For example, Douek (2008) observed how undergraduates solved a problem in number theory. She showed that students who elaborated a proof were those who first conjectured and then made up their minds about possible solutions to the problem at hand. This study showed then two related activities, conjecturing and proving – conjecturing being necessary to undertaking successfully the activity of proving. She also showed that conjecturing was a highly argumentative kind of activity. Inglis, Mejia-Ramos and Simpson (2007) asked talented post-graduates in mathematics a challenging problem in number theory. The researchers showed that in their mono-logical talk it was possible to identify the layout of arguments in a Toulminian sense: participants used modal qualifiers that express doubt, reasonableness or high certainty; they also used inductive warrant-type arguments in addition to their deductive warrant-type arguments. In contrast with the mathematical activity observed by Douek, which lasted several sessions, the activity observed by Inglis and colleagues lasted one session of 1 hour during which participants exclusively engaged in an argumentative activity without feeling that they needed to prove anything. Their argumentation was a legitimate activity in itself. In this study, as in the Douek study, we are very far from logically valid proofs, and even from the act of proving. Argumentation in graduate students in mathematics is dialectical – participants consider alternatives. We suggest that these insights have a general character and that dialectical argumentation is a central activity for professional mathematicians. Of course, further research is necessary to confirm and better understand this phenomenon in accomplished mathematicians.

Our analysis of what is told by professional mathematicians and observed in 'near-to-mathematicians' has then delineated three different activities:

1 *Enquiring*. At this stage, a central action concerns *conjecturing* solutions. But other preliminary actions for making sense of the problem are necessary.
2 *Proving*. This activity essentially concerns finding *logical consequences* to possibly turn conjectures into proofs.
3 *Inscribing proofs*. This activity demands rendering the proof as a chain of logical consequences in a formal way. It is a logical organizer. Another distinct activity concerns the elaboration of a derivation.

Since satisfactory reports on these activities are missing, it is difficult to say more on the specific actions that constitute mathematical practice. However, the enquiry stage seems argumentative par excellence. It resembles scientific enquiry as described by Osborne and Chin in this volume. As a quest for logical consequences, proving seems, a priori, to mainly involve explanatory/refinement processes. However, the circumvolutions mathematicians have undergone in proving (and very often failing to prove) what seemed to them plausible, suggests that for challenging problems, proving hugely involves informal reasoning and argumentation. A priori, inscribing proofs seems more straightforward. It concerns translation of the result of the activity of proving into an artefact with a communicative function for the scientific community. Among mathematicians, the three activities are different but intimately related. Some mathematicians, the anti-formalists, try to almost suppress the third activity and to prune from the proving activity any formal character, and in so doing turn mathematical activity into an experimental activity. Detractors of this perspective keep the experimental flavour instilled by the use of various technological tools to characterize the enquiry phase to preserve the heart of proving, seeking logical consequences. For both camps, argumentation is central. We will see that this fierce controversy among mathematicians has adepts from both sides in mathematics education. If anti-formalists among mathematicians have been 'defeated' thus far, the situation among their respective adepts in mathematics education is more balanced.

Argumentation and mathematics education

Argumentation in education in general and not only in mathematics education has excellent press nowadays for several reasons. First, psychology is moving in a discursive direction, and researchers aiming to observe learning in mathematics do so by analysing (mathematical) talk among people in classrooms or 'in the streets'. Secondly, cognitive psychologists (who do not necessarily adopt the tenets of discursive psychology) have recognized the benefits of argumentation for learning. The process of generating an argument, individually or collectively, involves seeking an explanation/justification for a claim (idea, conclusion, verification, etc.). As such, argumentation encourages self-explanation and learning (Chi, Bassok, Lewis, Reiman and Glaser 1989; Schwarz and Asterhan in press). Also, argumentation constructed in order to refute a position, a claim, etc. in a discussion *deepens understanding* of the problem space (Baker 2003; Hershkowitz and Schwarz 1999). The unique characteristics of the argumentation discourse that interweaves premises, conclusions, limitations, rebuttals and so forth, is considered as encouraging the improvement of the *organization of knowledge* (Means and Voss 1996). In addition, argumentative formats of reasoning are likely to significantly reduce some of the extensive cognitive load that is involved in learning, especially in tasks that involve cognitive conflict techniques (Schwarz 2009). Finally, Baker (2003) suggests that when discussants raise different views, adopting one (integrated) view on a rational basis leads discussants to consider this view as objective. In Baker's words:

> Instead of having to represent the different views in one's mind and to elaborate, evaluate and integrate them, an argumentative group discussion enables the objectification of perspectives and their representation by actual persons defending them.
> (2003: 48)

Argumentation is then important for learners. It is well known that for a long time school mathematics has been dedicated to 'drill and practice', or to routine processes of problem solving. Nowadays the main objective of mathematics educators is to foster mathematical reasoning and understanding. Although Pedemonte (2007) correctly argues that there is no common definition for the concept of *argumentation* in the field of mathematics education, the implicit definition is compatible with the quest for collective meaning-making expressed by Baker in the introduction to this chapter.

For many influential researchers in mathematics education, argumentation is seen as the way meaning-making and understanding develop in classroom discussions. For those researchers, argumentation is important inasmuch as it is a way to clarify what it means to teach/learn mathematics for understanding. For example, Krummheuer

(1995) deals with what he calls 'the ethnography of argumentation'. He is interested in 'collective argumentation' where the argumentation process is constructed by two or more individuals in the classroom. Krummheuer considers argumentation as a 'social phenomenon; when the cooperating individuals tried to adjust their intentions and interpretations by verbally presenting the rationale of their actions' (1995: 229). This loose definition is somehow artificially linked to a more classical view of argumentation by using the Toulmin model to represent the arguments children agree upon in teacher-led discussions.

If taken as a way to map the goal of the teacher during discussions she leads, the Toulmin model somehow helps. For example, Yackel (2002) used the theoretical framework of argumentation developed by Krummheuer to describe the teacher role in the mathematical classrooms. She discovered the following kinds of roles: a) initiating the negotiations of classroom norms; b) fostering argumentation as the core of students' mathematical activity; c) providing support for students interacting with their peers to develop a collective argument; d) providing argumentative supports such as data, warrants and backing to enrich the argumentations' processes. As argued by Krummheuer and Yackel (1990), in spite of the recognized importance of small group activities for creating productive opportunities for learning, small group activities are very often the place for routine practices.

For others, argumentation is one of the necessary theoretical components for describing classroom interactions in their vividness, as a way to express the 'problematique' of interweaving the social and the psychological elements together in core socio-cultural theories of learning (Cobb and Bauersfeld 1995). Their position concerning learning mathematics surprisingly resembles Thurston's characterization of social processes among mathematicians mentioned above! This position is now adopted by many researchers (e.g. Cobb, Yackel and Wood 1989; Hershkowitz, Hadas, Dreyfus and Schwarz 2007; Yackel, Cobb, Wood, Wheatley and Merkel 1990; Yackel, Rasmussen and King 2000) to develop interpretive frameworks for analysing classrooms' practices and students' constructing of knowledge.

Without doubt, Cobb and his colleagues have succeeded in distinguishing the different components through which mathematics learning can be understood according to a social-constructivist stance, argumentation being central in this understanding: *social norms* in the classroom culture can be identified through the kinds of explanations, justifications and *argumentation*. The 'sociomathematical norms' (Yackel and Cobb 1996) can be detected through the ways students agree that solutions are considered as acceptable, different or convincing. These norms are also important for clarifying the teacher's role in the mathematics classroom's community. As stated by Yackel and Cobb (1996: 475):

> The analysis of sociomathematical norms indicates that the teacher plays a central role in establishing the mathematical quality of the classroom environment … as a representative of the mathematical community.

In their paper, Yackel and Cobb illustrate how these 'sociomathematical norms' regulate mathematical argumentation and impinge on learning opportunities for the students and the teachers as well.

In spite of the tremendous theoretical contribution of Cobb and his colleagues by their instilling of socio-cultural constructivism through analytic tools that support the observation of mathematical activity in classrooms, argumentation as the vehicle of social and socio-mathematical norms is too general and unspecified. For example, one can wonder whether teacher-led talk in which the teacher initiates questions to invite students to justify answers is really argumentative, or whether it should at least be distinguished from autonomous dialectical discussions within a small group of students. This lack of specificity makes argumentation a difficult object for study. One should know how to identify argumentation, its types, and in which cases it fails or succeeds. In the following we present two activities of enquiry in which argumentation fuelled conceptual change (first example) and a metacognitive strategy (the second).

First example: an enquiry activity for learning the concept of decimal fraction

Students' consistent use of incorrect rules or strategies has been identified for several mathematical concepts. The incorrect rules make sense to those who evoke them and as such are called 'conceptual bugs'. Sackur-Grivard and Leonard (1985) found that children use consistently three incorrect rules to compare decimal fractions:

1 *WN-rule: the number with more decimal digits is the larger.* For example, 4.8 < 4.68 (because 68 is bigger than 8).
2 *F-rule: the number with fewer decimal digits is the larger.* For example, 4.4502 < 4.45. The decimal part .4502 is less than .45 because the whole is divided into more parts that are hence smaller.
3 *Z-rule: if a decimal fraction contains a zero in its decimal part, taking off the '0' does not change the value of the number. Otherwise, the number with more decimal places is the larger (WN conceptual bug).* For example, 4.7 < 4.08 (because 4.08 = 4.8). Also, 4.4502 > 4.45 (because 4.4502 = 4.452 ['0' does not change the value of a number and 4.452 has more decimal places than 4.45]).

In a pre-test in which individuals compared a series of pairs of decimal numbers, Schwarz, Neuman and Biezuner (2000) confirmed what Sackur-Grivard and Leonard had already demonstrated – the fact that students consistently use the same rules (WN-, F- and Z-rules) in their comparisons. They then designed what they called the *six-card task* to encourage argumentation among peers solving, which would hopefully lead to conceptual learning. Six cards, on which the five digits 0, 0, 5, 8, 4 and one period appear, are presented to dyads. The goal is to use all cards to construct: a) the biggest number, b) the smallest number, c) the number closest to 1, and the number closest to 0.5. A calculator is at the disposal of the pairs. The digits on the cards are chosen to create conflicts resulting from different conceptual bugs. For example, WN-students should answer 0.8540 for the third question of the task, whereas F-students should answer 0.0458. In an experimental study, individuals were first given a series of pairs of decimal numbers and asked to compare decimal numbers for each pair. This individual task enabled the diagnosing of individual conceptual bugs. Then students with different conceptual bugs were paired to solve the six cards problem. Finally individuals compared again the same series of pairs of numbers they were given before solving of the six cards task. The comparison between individual performances before and after the six cards task served to identify conceptual learning from interaction. Sixty-four fifth-grade students participated. Schwarz, Neuman and Biezuner (2000) showed that the six cards task was a learning task that helped 'wrong' students (with initial conceptual bugs) to become 'right' students. Also, 'wrong-wrong' dyads led to more gains than 'wrong-right' dyads in 'wrong' students. We present here the dyad Da-Re in which both students were 'wrongs' and turned to 'rights'.

Da is a Z-student and Re is an F-student. We present here an excerpt of the third subtask (to find the closest number to 1). In this subtask, Re has chosen 0.8540 as the closest number to 1:

Excerpt 1

DA23: If we pass your last zero to the beginning, the number will be closer.

RE24: I think that you are right. Let's check [Re computes 1 - 0.8540 and 1 - 00.854 on the calculator]. It's the same, it does not make change

DA25: So, it's possible to take off the two zeros. Let's see [Da computes 1 - .854].

RE26: At the end they make change!

DA27: They don't. See, we took them off from the beginning and we got the same result. At the end or at the beginning before the dot, they do not make change

DA28: [computes 0.0854 - 0.00854 and obtains a positive number]. Why it's not zero?

RE29: Because the zeros in the middle do make change. For example, .85004 is bigger than .80054 because eighty five thousands and four is more than eighty thousands and fifty four.

DA30: And if we'll do .85040?

RE31: It's bigger because it's eighty five thousands and forty

DA32: So let's change to .85400

RE33: This was what we did at the beginning. I don't know

DA34: Let's check again on the computer. [Da enters .85040 - .85400 and obtains a negative number].

RE35: But it's possible to erase the zeros at the end [she enters .8504 – .854 and obtains the same result]

RE36: So the closest number to 1 is .85400, or it's possible to write it .854

DA37: That is [pause]. One moment, I want to put some order [pause]. When the zeros are at the end of the number or at the beginning before the dot, they do not make any change, but if there are other zeros or before them numbers to the right of the dot, they make change

RE38: And something else, more there are zeros one besides the other, smaller the number is. For example, 0.0085 is smaller than 0.085

Schwarz and colleagues focused on the disappearance of the conceptual bugs F and Z. The protocol shows that this task presents a conflict for Re. On the one hand, for her as an F-student, numbers with more digits are smaller (Re states this rule clearly in previous utterances). On the other hand, the manipulations that Re undertakes on the calculator show her that taking off zeros at the end of the number does not change the number. The conflict is visible in Re24 (in which Re thinks that transferring a zero from the end of a number to its beginning – before the dot – makes the number closer to 1), in Re26, and in Re33 (The 'I don't know' expresses Re's perplexity subsequent to her manipulations on the calculator that show that deleting zeros from the end does not change the value of a number). The conflict is resolved through the use of the calculator for evaluating an argument (in Re24 and Re35), and for constructing an argument (in Da28) and through argumentative moves (challenging in Re26, refuting in Da27 and Re29, counter-challenge in Da30). A central finding is that the repair of the two conceptual bugs is collaboratively inferred in Da37 and Re38: Da begins by inferring a rule that repairs the Z conceptual bug, and Re completes Da's utterance by a rule that is correct but which does not violate her Z conceptual bug.

In conclusion, the interactions in the pair Da-Re showed that change was mediated by disagreement (triggered by the pairing of two students with different conceptual bugs and the design of the task, which affords different answers in students with different initial conceptual bugs), and argumentation. The calculator functioned as a hypothesis-testing device to trigger the construction and evaluation of arguments. The change for Re, a Z-student, seemingly originated from the design of the task and led him to experience a conflict and then to resolve it in collaboration with the F-student. The protocols show that the peers engage in an enquiry activity through argumentation and that they raise conjectures and test them with a calculator. We did not show why in certain cases, both wrongs remained wrongs or only one of them turned to right. We should only say that features of the talk, such as dominance of one peer, could explain the lack of learning gains.

Second example: an enquiry activity to foster hypothesizing

A broader context to this example is described by Hershkowitz and Schwarz (1999). Their study concerns argumentation in a group of four ninth-grade girls (around 15 years old) who solve a problem while using a graphical calculator. The example, the 'Overseas' activity, was given towards the end of the year. Students had already investigated various problem situations during the year. Students were first given the following homework assignment:

> The freight company "Overseas Inc." uses containers to ship goods by sea from country to country. The containers are big boxes made of wood. Their base needs to be square and their volume 2.25 m³ [see Figure 6.1]. The containers are open at the top. Find two examples of such containers.
>   Construct two suitable paper models (1 m container = 5 cm on paper).
>   Calculate the wood area needed to construct each of the two containers.

Students brought their models to the class and were then given the following worksheet:

> As wood is expensive, the company is interested in designing ideal containers with as little wood as possible.

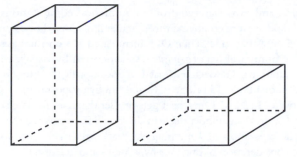

Figure 6.1 Two containers in the 'Overseas' activity.

Try to make hypotheses about the dimensions of the "ideal container" and explain your steps.

Can you help the company find the dimensions of the "ideal container"?

The students were invited to work in groups of four, each of them being equipped with their (eight = 4 × 2) models and two graphic calculators (Phase 1, 40 minutes). In parallel, each group was asked to write a report concerning their ideas and steps (Phase 2). The activity ended in a teacher-led collective reflection (Phase 3). We focus here on one group in the class (Mi, Li, Os and Ha) during Phase 1.

The declared aim of the developers in the problem-solving phase included both fostering hypothesizing and finding the dimensions of the ideal container. Hypothesizing became a central concern for some groups, whereas other groups moved on quickly 'to solve' the problem. The four girls in the observed group were actively engaged in generating and confronting hypotheses. They tried first to extend the limits of what could be guessed or hypothesized, before drawing the graph with the tool and reading the minimum by 'walking' on the graph. The solution was only a way to check the quality of their hypotheses. In the following we explore the four girls' work.

First they computed the surfaces of the models they brought from home with the help of their graphical calculators. Then, they relied on the size and shape of the models to start hypothesizing: Os raised the first hypothesis (H1) and justified it by intuitive considerations: 'Because the height of the container is multiplied by four, the minimum surface is when the height is the smallest possible' (*argument 1*, supported by intuition). From this point on, the four girls generated hypotheses that matched more and more data. Ha hypothesized H2: 'The smaller the height, the bigger the surface', which she derived from two model surfaces (*argument 2*, supported by data from two model examples).

While H2 matches two models, it contradicts others and the girls found themselves in their first situation of conflict. Os expressed this conflict by showing that the computations of the dimensions of the container: S (0.5 [side], 9 [height], 18.25 [overall surface]) and S (3, 0.25, 12) contradict H2 (*argument 3*, supported by a contradiction with some data). Li proposed a new local hypothesis, H3, based on different data: 'Let us go in the opposite direction. When the container is lower the surface is smaller' (*argument 4*, based on new data).

In an argumentative process in which all four girls participated, the two local hypotheses (H2 and H3) were confronted, numerical computations were used as evidence, and models were compared through manipulations. For example, Ha rolled a 'long' model on a 'flat' one. Then Os reformulated H2 on the basis of a different combination of numerical data (*argument 5*, supported by visualization, numerical data and computation). Ha declared that H2 does not fit the models and proposed the construction of a table. Li bridged H2 and H3 by proposing H4: 'There must be a segment between 1/2 and 1, maybe it gets smaller there, as if it's not constant, it has to be like that [Li drew a parabola shape in the air].' Ha completed the formulation of H4: 'Perhaps it's a parabola or something like that' (*argument 6*, supported by logical verification of consideration of previous hypotheses and gestures).

The dialectic process did not end with H4 and *argument 6*, but the girls constructed an organized table of values. Mi then raised H5: 'The smaller the side, the bigger the surface', which is a regression from H4 back to fit a partial fit with the data (*argument 7*, supported by some data). Os even returned to 'her' H1 (the same kind of argument as *argument 7*). The group confronted H1 with data and refuted it. They then confronted H4 with data and interpreted the behaviour of the function. At this point, the students jointly turned to the solution with the calculator to initiate a dialectic process whose starting point was the elaboration of hypotheses before a confrontation with data or with previous hypotheses.

We see then that hypothesizing is embedded in argumentative moves. For example, Li's initiation of H4 follows Ha and Os showing a conflict between H2 and H3, and leads to H4 as a new argument bridging between the previous. H4 ('There must be a segment between 1/2 and 1, maybe it gets smaller there ...') does not eradicate H2 or H3, but unifies them. Li constructs H4 as a result of reflecting on outcomes of previous actions.

The argumentative process we just described was dialectic in the sense that it consisted of raising hypotheses and refuting them or bridging between them. The hypotheses were formulated on the basis of arguments whose nature varied along the chain of actions: from intuitive arguments, based on visual considerations of the models, to arguments based either on data, or on conflicts with data, through arguments based on conflicts between hypotheses that stemmed from focus on local data, to an argument based on logical considerations through integration of local hypotheses while encompassing a broad range of data. The final argument was agreed upon by the girls only when all of them felt convinced.

Argumentation, proving, and proofs in schools

While proving is the *raison d'être* of mathematical activity in professionals, its place in education is the object of vivid controversial debates. These debates have led to a fruitful demarcation between the activity of proving, the role of argumentation in this activity and proofs as their objects/outcomes. For generations, proofs were considered as tools for verifying mathematical statements and showing their universality. Hanna (1990) mentions Leibniz who believed that 'A mathematical proof is a universal symbolic script which allows one to distinguish clearly between fact and fiction, truth and falsity' (1990: 6).

According to this approach, the two classical roles of teaching proofs were first to teach deductive reasoning as part of human culture and second to teach deductive reasoning as a vehicle for verifying and showing the universality of geometric statements. Studies in mathematics education have shown that this traditional approach to the teaching of proofs has failed (Balacheff 1988). Only 30 per cent of the students in full-year geometry courses that teach proofs in the US reach 75 per cent mastery in proving (Senk 1985). Students who successfully function in the ritual of proving are generally not aware of its meaning, and rarely see the point of proving, especially when what needs to be proved is revealed to them (Balacheff 1991). High school students do not realize that formal proofs confer universal validity; many check additional examples for this purpose (Fischbein and Kedem 1982). Students are satisfied with experimental reasoning for confirming the truth of a claim (Chazan 1993) and cannot distinguish between evidence and proofs (see also Schoenfeld 1986, for similar results). They produce proofs because the teacher demands them, not because they recognize their necessity (Balacheff 1988). Balacheff (1991) concludes that if students do not engage in proving processes, it is because a) only the teacher is responsible for the legitimacy and epistemological validity of the constructions and students do not have real access to the 'problématique' of truth; b) most of the tasks are clearly true, and students cannot understand why they should prove something that is 'so obvious'. As claimed by Boero (2008), old models for teaching proofs for unsurprising questions do not fit the new ideas about the meaning of learning and teaching mathematics.

The controversy raised by the anti-formalists among mathematicians mentioned above may have led researchers and educators to rethink the role of proofs in education. Hanna (1990) distinguishes between two kinds of proof: a) proofs that show that a theorem is true, by providing evidential reasons only; b) proofs that explain *why* the theorem is true, by providing a set of reasons that derive from the phenomenon itself. Hanna (1995) asserted that the main function of proof in the classroom should be to *promote understanding*, and therefore students need to deal with proofs that explain. According to Hanna (1996: 31):

> A proof is a transparent argument, in which all the information used and all the rules of reasoning are clearly displayed and open to criticism. It is the very nature of proof that the validity of the conclusion flows from the proof itself.

Researchers such as de Villiers (1998) considerably extended the functions of proving in the mathematical classroom to include not only cognitive roles (explaining, verifying) but social roles (communicating, convincing) and epistemological ones (systematizing). Most of the researchers in mathematics education stress the explanatory/rhetorical/ convincing role of proving to help make mathematics meaningful and understandable. Argumentation is then brought into the proof arena. In order to succeed, students must learn how to prove meaningfully: 'An argument presented with sufficient rigor will enlighten and convince more students, who in turn may convince their peers' (Hanna 2008: 22).

This choice, however, brings tensions with the traditional practices of proving in classrooms, which are close to the activity of inscribing proofs. In this context, Duval (1991: 245) makes a contrast between argumentation and proving:

Deductive thinking does not work like argumentation. However these two kinds of reasoning use very similar linguistic forms and prepositional connectives. This is one of the main reasons why most of the students do not understand the requirements of mathematical proofs.

According to Duval there is a structural gap between the two, even if (and in some cases because) they use very similar linguistic forms. This gap may lead to the conclusion that the use of argumentation as a vehicle to learning to prove is risky – as Balacheff (1999: 5) argues:

> In my eyes it would even be an error of epistemological character to let students believe, by a sort of Jourdain effect, that they are capable of producing a mathematical proof when all they have done is argue.

We interpret the gap Duval and Balacheff discerned as a gap between enquiring or proving and a formal inscription of proofs. Proving can be argumentative even if no formal proof is inscribed. The gap at which Duval pointed is extremely difficult to bridge. Another difficulty is mentioned in the mathematics education research literature on proofs. It consists of the act of proving. The difficulty comes from a shortcoming in design: if students cannot enquire of the problem, use their intuitions and all possible resources to raise conjectures, they will not feel the need to prove. Our identification of enquiring and proving activities makes clear Douek's finding on the need for a *conjecture* phase for the *construction of the proof*. In the enquiring phase, argumentation is particularly vivid and naturally leads to proving. This is what Boero Garuti and Mariotti (1996) called *cognitive unity* between the construction of a conjecture and the construction of the proof. The hypothesis of *cognitive unity* is that when argumentation is rich, enquiry might lead to constructing a proof (see also Pedemonte 2007).

Some researchers have suggested that this cognitive unity can be attained by integrating different channels of communication. Inspired by Nemirovsky's studies (2003) in perceptuo-motor multimodal ways of constructing knowledge (bodily actions, gestures, manipulation of materials or artefacts, drawing, etc.). Arzarello (2008) and Lemke (2002) used the idea of a semiotic system to analyse how mathematics can best be learned or thought. According to Lemke, mathematics can only be learned and taught in natural language, but a single semiotic unified system is central for *sense-making*. Arzarello (2008) found that different modalities such as using paper and pencil or 'dragging' with Dynamic Geometry[3] (DG) software are crucial for triggering a productive shift from what we would call an enquiring to a proving activity through rich and multimodal argumentative processes.

The following two additional examples of activities/episodes demonstrate such a shift from enquiring to proving activities. The third example shows how cognitive unity can be attained; it leads students to adopt a deductive approach as a way to fulfil their need to explain a surprising phenomenon. The fourth example shows how a multimodal semiotic system created proper ground for proving.

Third example: an enquiring and proving activity to foster deductive reasoning

This example is taken from a research conducted by Hadas, Hershkowitz and Schwarz (2002). The aim of the research was to investigate high school students' actions, conjectures and explanations while they coped with a geometrical activity that was designed to create contradictions between the students' assumptions and the outcomes in the DG software environment. The researchers hypothesized that in this situation, as in those described above, students would be encouraged to generate deductive explanations. The activity students were asked to solve appears in Figure 6.2.

We will analyse here some excerpts from Shiri and Tammy, who worked on this activity in the presence of an interviewer (I). Like the majority of the students, Shiri and Tammy had the intuition that the angles would always be the same. After, both students expressed their intuitive answer, the interviewer provided them with a DG tool and asked:

I: Try, if you can, to find situations where the 3 angles are equal and characterize these situations.

The girls changed the triangle by dragging one of the vertices and watched the change of the angles visually as well as numerically.

SHIRI: There is a situation where all of them are equal.
TAMMY: When A and C [the vertices] are moving away, the middle angle takes all the angles [she means degrees] from the other two [see Figure 6.3a]
I: What will happen if you will drag only A?
TAMMY: Then the outside angle [<ABD] will become very small and will not be equal to the other two. Maybe when <B will be very small the angles will be equal [she

Divide the side AC of a dynamic triangle ABC into three equal segments.

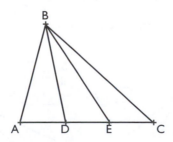

Investigate the relationships between the sizes of the 3 angles (<ABD, <DBE and <EBC). Explain!

Figure 6.2 A task that invites mathematical enquiry through argumentation.

dragged B until the triangle shrunk to a segment]. Oh, but it is not a triangle anymore [see Figure 6.3b]

Tammy, who relates consistently to the process of the *visual change* she creates, accompanies all her claims by *hand movements*. Shiri, who was observing Tammy's actions quietly, interferes: 'The three triangles can't be congruent.'

I: Why?

SHIRI: Let's take an example where the two angles are equal [points at <ABD and <DBE]. Then BD is the bisector angle as well as the median, and ΔABE is isosceles. If the two other angles are equal, then ΔDBC is also isosceles, and the three triangles are congruent. In this situation we will have 6 equal angles [the angles are marked in Figure 6.4] ... but, we saw before that the base angles in isosceles triangles are always less than 90°, and here the two are adjacent angles. Therefore this situation is impossible.

The two girls then discuss together and Shiri explains again her claims to Tammy and writes down her explanation.

In summary, the students needed *to be convinced* by an explanation that would satisfy their curiosity. Hence, they went through various warrants to support their arguments. Their surprise gradually grew as the DG software did not yield any situation in which the angles would be equal. The fact that, even with the DG software, it is impossible to check all cases led the students to *feel the need* for general considerations about whether there is a situation with three equal angles, and if not, to find the reason *why*

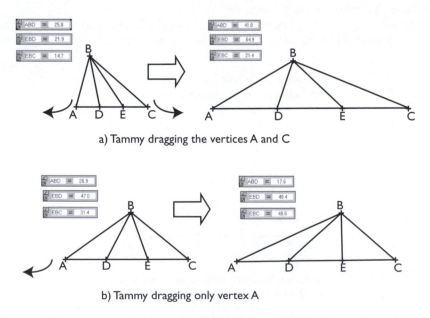

a) Tammy dragging the vertices A and C

b) Tammy dragging only vertex A

Figure 6.3 Tammy drags drawings with DG that do not confirm her conjecture.

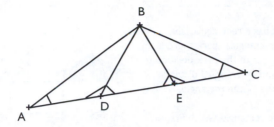

Figure 6.4 Traces of informal deductive reasoning on a geometrical figure as outcomes of an argumentative process.

it is so. Tammy tried to use the dynamic tool to *visualize* extreme cases. When both girls saw that they could not reach a final conclusion by working with the software only, Shiri, the silent but very involved partner, took over and began to propose *deductive arguments*. She capitalized on all geometrical transformations to ground her deductive explanations. The students were fully convinced only by a deductive process that emerged from a rich argumentative process, and that provided what represented for the students a valid proof.

Fourth example: multimodal argumentation for enquiry and proving activities

This example was elaborated by Prusak (2007) to trace argumentation processes in dyads of math pre-service teachers, engaging in an activity in geometry. The activity includes tasks encouraging intuition through visualization, geometric constructions and measurements to progressively foster deduction. The activity consists of finding the best location for selling tickets in a park (see Figure 6.5). Two math pre-service teachers are invited to collaboratively solve the activity. This activity is designed to invite the participants to rely on their intuitions. The intuitions help in Task 1 but naturally lead to a wrong solution for the two other tasks. Like in the third example, a DG tool is at their disposal and helps to showing that intuitive considerations are not sufficient. As we will see here, the task leads the participants to engage in enquiry (to hypothesize and check hypotheses) and then in proving through rich argumentation.

The two students, Anna and Boaz, started to work separately, demonstrating quite different approaches. Anna immediately claimed that they should draw diagonals, and so she did so on her worksheet. She did not feel any necessity to check her solution by measuring, but backed her claim with a theorem – diagonals in a rectangle are equal and intersect in their middle points. Boaz drew the diagonals on his worksheet as well, but then decided to fold the rectangle twice at the middle points of the opposite sides and found the intersection of the two lines. He noticed that it was the same point as the intersection of the diagonals. This gave him the feeling that both solution paths were correct. Yet he checked his solution by measuring the distances from the intersection point to the vertices with a ruler (see Figure 6.6).

Boaz and Anna were then invited to check their solution with a DG software:

BOAZ: I cut in half the rectangle on its length and on its width as well [folds the paper,

Task 1:
A recreational park has a rectangular shape. At each vertex of the rectangular park there is an attraction. The manager of the park decided to locate the ticket booth at an equal distance from the four vertices of the rectangle.

Find the point in the rectangle, which fits for the ticket booth.

Task 2:
Another park has the shape of an equilateral triangle. At each vertex of this triangular park there is an attractive facility. The manager decided to locate the ticket booth at an equal distance from the three vertices of the triangle.

Find the point in the triangle that would satisfy the requirements.

Task 3:
What if the recreational park has the shape of a scalene triangle?
Find the point (if any) in this triangle that would satisfy the requirements.

Figure 6.5 A series of tasks for triggering a proving activity through peer argumentation.

see Figure 6.6]. I found two segments: one from the middle of the length and the other from the middle of the rectangle's width, let's see if the intersection point will be in the middle and the same [the same as the intersection point of the diagonals he drew before] ... This is the point!

ANNA: It has to be in the middle because here [she points at the isosceles triangles created by the diagonals in Boaz's solution (see Figure 6.7)] it is an isosceles triangle and these are the heights of an isosceles triangle so it must be the same point [points at one of the heights of the triangles created by Boaz's perpendiculars].

BOAZ: Could you repeat your explanation?

ANNA: I said that the segment must meet at the middle point because four isosceles triangles are created and these are actually the heights of these triangles [see Figure 6.7].

We can see that Anna argued that the point Boaz found is identical to the point she found. She explained that the segments Boaz drew are the heights of isosceles triangles created by the diagonals. And when he used the DG software to check the solution, Boaz followed Anna's explanation as he drew the diagonals: 'We have the intersection point E, now let's measure whether all distances are equal.'

In summary, although Boaz seems convinced by Anna's explanation, he still performs measurements. Anna's reasoning is based on theorems, while Boaz uses concrete

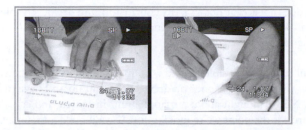

Figure 6.6 Boaz folds and measures to check that his argument is right.

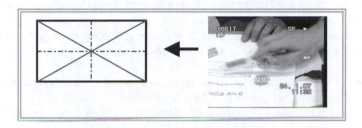

Figure 6.7 Anna relies on logical necessity to justify her solution.

methods. We do not detail how Anna and Boaz solved the same task for the equilateral triangle. They adopted a common intuitive-visual approach, agreed that for equilateral triangles all intersection points coincide, but conjectured that for other triangles the solution should be different. They used the DG software to check conjectures and dragged the vertices to check the invariance of their solution. As foreseen by the designers, the students thought the solution to be the intersection of medians (for Boaz), of heights (for Anna) or of angle bisectors (for both with the DG). Such conjectures helped create a conflict in Task 3, which involved a park whose shape was a scalene triangle.

Anna and Boaz began enquiring together, working out a solution for the scalene triangle. Anna immediately proposed the intersection of the medians. Boaz used visual considerations to rule out the heights and checked bisectors to realize that this solution was wrong too. He then concluded that the medians were the only remaining possibility. He also admitted that one cannot rely solely on visual considerations, but asserted that they serve as counter-examples to refute conjectures. Then Anna and Boaz checked their conjectures with the DG software by constructing medians and measuring distances from the intersection of the medians to the vertices.

BOAZ: There is an intersection point but the distances are not equal. It's a problem, it means that …

ANNA: Does it mean that it is true only for an equilateral triangle?

BOAZ: In a scalene triangle it's impossible to find a point which is in the same distance from all the vertices. This is the conclusion!

ANNA: What?

Boaz is ready to claim that the task does not have any solution, and does not try other points. Anna does not accept Boaz's hasty conclusion, and decides to continue to look for a solution. Boaz's drawing vaguely reminds Anna of some relationships between an obtuse triangle and its circum-circle:

ANNA: I think that it is possible to find a point equidistant from the vertices. Let's imagine a triangle like the one you drew – the point doesn't have to be inside the triangle. Now I thought about a triangle built in a circle and actually the center of this circle is the point we're looking for. If we'll build a triangle inscribed in a circle, then the point ...

Boaz tries to understand the new idea Anna expresses by sketching a drawing in which he marks the centre of a circle (see Figure 6.8).

Anna continues analysing the problem logically, and draws a triangle inscribed in a circle (see Figure 6.9) to start an abductive argumentation:

ANNA: Let's assume that we found the point, so we need ... these segments [pointing on the radiuses, see Figure 6.9] have to be equal
BOAZ: Yes, but how can we find this point? You marked a point that looks like the center.
ANNA: Yes, we have to find the point.
BOAZ: We made a long journey but we're again at the beginning [Anna marked the 'equal segments' on her drawing].
ANNA: This is what we must build. These segments have to be equal! Maybe these triangles should be isosceles ... yeah! All these triangles must be isosceles.
BOAZ: O.K., nice, it means that we have to consider each side of the [scalene] triangle as the base of an isosceles triangle. What we need is to find the point which is the middle of the side [of the scalene triangle] and to build a perpendicular segment which will be the altitude of the isosceles triangle.

This utterance is a clear transition to *deductive thinking*: Boaz realizes that constructing the solution means an accurate step-by-step planning based on logical necessity. Boaz draws a sketch (see Figure 6.10) to convince Anna. By doing so, Boaz reinforces his *deduction* by *visual means*.

Anna and Boaz finally decided to use DG to construct their solution, and by measuring equidistance, to check their solution. Boaz asked Anna to drag the vertices and the invariance led him to admit that his conclusion about the non-existence of a solution was hasty.

Concluding remarks

The four examples we have described show the substantial place that argumentation takes in mathematics learning nowadays. It fosters sense-making and conjecturing (in all examples), leads to substantial learning gains (conceptual change in the first example, acquisition of a strategy in the second example), and integrates a rich semiotic system (especially in the fourth example but not only in this one). It opens opportunities for cognitive unity and by doing so naturally leads from enquiry to proving activity (in the third and fourth examples). If argumentation is so successful, one may ask a trivial

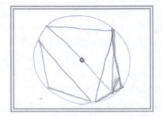

Figure 6.8 Boaz sketches a geometrical figure while listening to Anna.

Figure 6.9 Anna's drawing to support abductive argumentation.

question: Why not design more activities for productive argumentation? This question, however, is not trivial at all. *Argumentative design* – decisions taken to trigger productive argumentation – is indeed a very difficult task. It necessitates taking into consideration the students' knowledge, the different ways to arrange them in groups, the tools to provide them with for raising or checking hypotheses and, possibly, the strategies the teacher should enact to structure discussions. Without taking into account all these considerations, argumentation may not ensue or be sterile (Andriessen and Schwarz 2009; Schwarz and Linchevski 2007). Articulating principles for argumentative design in mathematics is beyond the scope of this chapter. Let us say only that for each of the four examples we described, the decisions that led to the elaboration of the tasks were complex and took into consideration research findings on the specific concepts, strategies or ideas the tasks were designed to afford.

Overall, our examples illustrated the claim that *it is possible to bridge mathematical enquiry and proving through proper argumentation*. When the bridge is constructed,

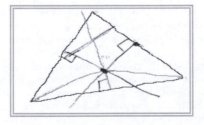

Figure 6.10 Boaz draws a last drawing to convince Anna that his deductions are correct.

proving becomes an exciting adventure during which logical necessity stems from intuitions, data collected and hypotheses confirmed or refuted through the use of devices for hypothesis testing. This logical necessity is attained in critical discussions in which various argumentative moves are initiated by discussants: challenges, explanations, counter-challenges, elaborations, etc.

The examples we presented did not include the activity of inscribing proofs. This absence echoes Duval's claim that there is an incommensurable gap between argumentation and proof inscription. We suggest that another factor distances argumentation from inscribing proofs: it is difficult for most students to see the necessity for inscribing proofs governed by a strict syntax. Argumentation, on the other hand, can develop only when a clear goal is embraced by all discussants.

Was Toulmin right when he claimed that argumentation in mathematics is special inasmuch as it is based on logic? This chapter has shown that his visionary claim was partly right: the hard core of mathematical activity – proving – involves establishing logical consequences. However, as was shown several times, establishing logical consequences generally cannot be expressed through the laws of formal logic. On the other hand, we have seen that argumentation involved in enquiry not only focuses on sense-making and conjecturing but is also enriched by computer representations and accompanied by gestures, metaphors, drawings, etc. This kind of argumentation is multimodal. Such richness is not characteristic to mathematics. However, since mathematics is very often about abstract entities, people have difficulties grasping them and making sense of them through multimodal argumentation. In the stage of sense-making and conjecturing, argumentation in mathematics is absolutely crucial and is multimodal. This situation is quite paradoxical since such a multimodal argumentation is utterly different from formal logic. It brings to the mathematician or to the learners tools for arousing intuitions and for stimulating creativity. It does not impair the goal of mathematical activity – finding logical consequences through proving – but brings to this goal a world of images, metaphors and conjectures that tools, gestures, and exploratory talk brought to the surface. So, Toulmin was right when he claimed that mathematical argumentation is very special, but not in the way he originally thought: some forms of argumentation are close to logic but not to a formal kind of logic, and other forms are multimodal, and are even less formal than informal conversations.

Notes

1 This argument was common in the Vienna circle at the beginning of the twentieth century. The Vienna circle's world-conception was *empiricist* – knowledge originates from experience – but is marked by the application of *logical analysis*. Logical analysis is the method of clarification of philosophical problems; it makes an extensive use of symbolic logic (Sarkar 1996).

2 It is interesting that Erdős, one of the greatest mathematicians of the twentieth century, used to present to the mathematical community an interesting bid. He listed several unproved theorems and offered prizes for their solvers. The amount of the prizes reflected Erdős's estimated difficulty to prove the theorem. It appeared that his intuitions were remarkably correct. This is probably because what remains of the activity of proving is often no more than a formal inscription, and because theorems for Erdős include their conjecture.

3 Dynamic Geometry refers to a class of software affording actions on drawings (e.g. dragging points, segments and angles and changing their measures). Such actions unveil invariants of the associated geometrical figure, which are its defining attributes: each of the (almost!) infinite number of drawings generated by the above DG actions refers to the same figure.

References

Andriessen, J. E. B. and Schwarz, B. B. (2009) 'Argumentative design', in A.-N. Perret-Clermont and N. Muller-Mirza (eds) *Argumentation and Education: theoretical foundations and practices*, New York, Springer.

Arzarello, F. (2008) 'The proof in the 20th Century', in P. Boero (ed.) *Theorems in Schools: from history, epistemology and cognition to classroom practices*, Rotterdam: Sense Publishers.

Arzarello, F., Olivero, F., Paola, D. and Robutti, O. (2008) 'The transition to formal proof in geometry', in P. Boero (ed.) *Theorems in Schools: from history, epistemology and cognition to classroom practices*, Rotterdam: Sense Publishers.

Baker, M. (2003) 'Computer-mediated interactions for the co-elaboration of scientific notions', in: J. Andriessen, M. Baker and D. Suthers (eds) *Arguing to Learn: confronting cognitions in computer supported collaborative learning environments*, Dordrecht, The Netherlands: Kluwer.

Balacheff, N. (1988) *Une etude des processus de preuve en mathématique chez des élèves de Collège*, Thèse d'Etat, Université Joseph Fourier, Grenoble.

Balacheff, N. (1991) 'The benefits and limits of social interaction: the case of mathematical proof', in A. Bishop, S. Mellin-Olson and J. van Doormolen (eds) *Mathematics Knowledge: its growth through teaching*, Boston: Kluwer.

Balacheff, N. (1999) 'Is argumentation an obstacle? Invitation to debate', in *International Newsletter on the Teaching and Learning of Mathematical Proof*, Grenoble: IMAG.

Boero, P. (2008) 'Theorems in school: an introduction', in P. Boero (ed.) *Theorems in Schools: from history, epistemology and cognition to classroom practices*, Rotterdam: Sense Publishers.

Boero, P., Garuti, R. and Mariotti, M. A. (1996) 'Some dynamic mental process underlying producing and proving conjectures', in L. Puig and A. Gutierrez (eds) *Proceedings of the 20th PME Conference*, Vol. 2:121–8, Valencia, Spain.

Chazan, E. (1993) 'High school geometry students' justification for their views of empirical evidence and mathematical proof', *Educational Studies in Mathematics*, 24:359–87.

Chi, M. T. H., Bassok, M., Lewis, M. W., Reimann, P. and Glaser, R. (1989) 'Self-explanations: how students study and use examples in learning to solve problems', *Cognitive Science*, 13:145–82.

Cobb, P. and Bauersfeld, H. (eds) (1995) *The Emergence of Mathematical Meaning: interaction in classroom cultures*, Hillsdale, NJ: Lawrence Erlbaum.

Cobb, P., Yackel. E., and Wood, T. (1989) 'Young children's emotional acts while doing mathematical problem solving', in D. B. McLeod and V. M. Adams (eds) *Affect and Mathematical Problem Solving: a new perspective*, New York: Springer.

de Villiers, M. (1998) 'An alternative approach to proof in dynamic geometry', in R. Lehrer and D. Chazan (eds) *Designing Learning Environments for Developing Understanding of Geometry and Space*, Hillsdale, NJ: Lawrence Erlbaum.

Douek, N. (2008) 'Some remarks about argumentation and proof', in P. Boero (ed.), *Theorems in Schools: from history, epistemology and cognition to classroom practices*, Rotterdam: Sense Publishers.

Driver, R., Newton, P. and Osborne, J. (2000) 'Establishing the norms of scientific argumentation in classrooms', *Science Education*, 84:287–312.

Duval, R. (1991) 'Structure du raisonnement déductif et apprentissage de la démonstration', *Educational Studies in Mathematics*, 22:233–61.

Ernest, P. (1994) 'The dialogical nature of mathematics', in P. Ernest (ed.) *Mathematics, Education and Philosophy*, London: Falmer Press.

Fischbein, E. and Kedem, I. (1982) 'Proof and certitude in the development of mathematical thinking', in A. Vermandel (ed.) *Proceedings of the Sixth PME Conference*, Antwerpen: Universitaire Instelling.

Goldberg, T., Schwarz, B. B. and Porat, D. (2008) 'Living and dormant collective memories as contexts of history learning', *Learning and Instruction*, 18:223–37.

Hadas, N., Hershkowitz, R. and Schwarz, B. B. (2002) 'Between task design and students' explanations in geometrical activities', *Canadian Journal of Research in Mathematics Education*, 2:529–52.

Hanna, G. (1990) 'Some pedagogical aspects of proof', *Interchange*, 21(1):6–13.

Hanna, G. (1995) 'Challenges to the importance of proof', *For the Learning of Mathematics*, 15:42–50.

Hanna, G. (1996) 'The ongoing value of proof', in L. Puig and A. Gutierrez (eds) *Proceedings of the 20th PME Conference*, Vol. 1:21–34, Valencia, Spain.

Hanna, G. (2008) 'The ongoing value of proof', in P. Boero (ed.), *Theorems in Schools: from history, epistemology and cognition to classroom practices*, Rotterdam: Sense Publishers.

Hershkowitz, R. and Schwarz, B. B. (1999) 'Reflective processes in a technology-based mathematics classroom', *Cognition and Instruction*, 17:66–91.

Hershkowitz, R., Hadas, N., Dreyfus, T. and Schwarz, B. B. (2007) 'Processes of abstraction from the diversity of individuals' constructing of knowledge to a group's 'shared knowledge'', *Mathematics Education Research Journal*, 19:41–68.

Inglis, M., Mejia-Ramos J. P. and Simpson, A. (2007) 'Modeling mathematical argumentation: the importance of qualification', *Educational Studies in Mathematics*, 66(1): 3–21.

Krummheuer, G. (1995) 'The ethnography of argumentation', in P. Cobb and H. Bauersfeld (eds) *The Emergence of Mathematical Meaning: interaction in classroom cultures*, Hillsdale, NJ: Lawrence Erlbaum.

Krummheuer, G. and Yackel, E. (1990) 'The emergence of mathematical argumentation in the small group interaction of second grades', in G. Booker, P. Cobb and T. N. de Mendicuti (eds), *Proceedings of the 14th PME Conference*, Vol. 3:113–20, Oaxtepec, Mexico.

Lakatos, I. (1976) *Proofs and Refutations*, Cambridge: Cambridge University Press.

Lemke, J. L. (2002) 'Mathematics in the middle: measure, picture, gesture, sign, and word', in M. Andersen, A. Saenz-Ludlow, S. Zellweger and V. Cifarelli (eds) *Educational Perspectives on Mathematics as Semiosis: from thinking to interpreting to knowing*, Ottawa: Legas Publishing.

Means, M. L. and Voss, J. F. (1996) 'Who reasons well? Two studies of informal reasoning among children of different grade, ability, and knowledge levels', *Cognition and Instruction*, 14:139–79.

Nemirovsky, R. (2003) 'Three conjectures concerning the relationship between body activity and understanding mathematics', in N. A. Pateman, B. J. Dougherty and J. T. Zilliox (eds) *Proceedings of the 27th PME Conference*, Vol. 1:103–35, Honolulu, Hawaii.

Pedemonte, B. (2007) 'How can the relationship between argumentation and proof be analyzed?', *Educational Studies in Mathematics*, 66:23–41.

Pólya, G. (1948) *How to Solve It: a new aspect of mathematical method*, New York: Doubleday.

Pólya, G. (1954) *Mathematics and Plausible Reasoning* (vol. I, Induction and Analogy in Mathematics, and vol. II, Patterns of Plausible Inference), Princeton, NJ: Princeton University Press.

Prusak, N. (2007) *The Analysis of Dialogues of Dyads of Pre-service Teachers Operating in an Activity Designed to Foster Argumentation: the case of dynamic geometry*, unpublished Masters thesis, The Hebrew University, Jerusalem.

Rav, Y. (1999) 'Why do we prove theorems?', *Philosophia Mathematica*, 7:5–41.

Sackur-Grivard, C. and Leonard, F. (1985) 'Intermediate cognitive organization in the process of learning a mathematical concept: the order of positive decimal numbers, *Cognition and Instruction*, 2:157–74.

Sarkar, S. (1996) *The Emergence of Logical Empiricism: from 1900 to the Vienna circle*, New York: Garland Publishing.

Schoenfeld, A. (1986) 'On having and using geometric knowledge', in J. Hiebert (ed.) *Conceptual and Procedural Knowledge: the case of mathematics*, Hillsdale, NJ: Lawrence Erlbaum.

Schwarz, B. B. (2009) 'Argumentation and learning', in A.-N. Perret-Clermont and N. Muller-Mirza (eds) *Argumentation and Education: theoretical foundations and practices*, New York: Springer Verlag.

Schwarz, B. B. and Asterhan, C. S. C. (in press) 'Argumentation and reasoning', to appear in K. Littleton, C. Wood, and J. Kleine Staarman (eds) *The Handbook of Education: the psychology of teaching and learning*, London: Emerald.

Schwarz, B. B. and Linchevski, L. (2007) 'The role of task design and of argumentation in cognitive development during peer interaction. The case of proportional reasoning', *Learning and Instruction*, 17, 310–31.

Schwarz, B. B., Newman, Y. and Biezuner, S. (2000) 'Two wrongs may make a right ... if they argue together!', *Cognition and Instruction*, 18:461–94.

Senk, S. L. (1985) 'How well do students write geometry proofs?', *Mathematics Teacher*, 78:448–56.

Thurston, W. P. (1994) 'On proof and progress in mathematics', *Bulletin of the American Mathematical Society*, 30:161–77.

Toulmin, S. (1958) *The Uses of Argument*, Cambridge: Cambridge University Press.

van Eemeren, F. H., Grootendorst, R., Henkenmans, F. S., Blair, J. A., Johnson, R. H, Krabb, E. C., Plantin, C., Walton, D. N., Willard, C. A., Woods, J. and Zarefsky, D. (1996) *Fundamentals of Argumentation Theory: a handbook of historical background and contemporary developments*, Hillsdale, NJ: Lawrence Erlbaum.

Yackel, E. (2002) 'What we can learn from analyzing the teacher's role in collective argumentation', *Journal of Mathematical Behavior*, 21:423–40.

Yackel, E. and Cobb, P. (1996) 'Sociomathematical norms, argumentation and autonomy in mathematics', *The Journal of Research in Mathematics Education*, 27:458–77.

Yackel, E. Rasmussen, C. and King, K. (2000) 'Social and sociomathematical norms in an advanced mathematics course', *Journal of Mathematical Behavior*, 19:275–87.

Yackel, E., Cobb, P., Wood, T., Wheatley, G. and Merkel, G. (1990) 'The importance of social interaction in children's construction of mathematical knowledge', in T. Cooney (ed.) *Teaching and Learning Mathematics in the 1990s (1990 Yearbook of the National Council of Teachers of Mathematics)*, Reston, VA: National Council of Teachers of Mathematics.

Zeilberger, D. (1993) 'Theorems for a price: tomorrow's semi-rigorous mathematical culture', *Notices of the American Mathematical Society*, 40:978–81.

Chapter 7

Dialogical interactions among peers in collaborative writing contexts

Sylvia Rojas-Drummond*, Karen Littleton**,
Flora Hernández* and Mariana Zúñiga*
*National Autonomous University of Mexico
and **University of Jyväskylä

Introduction

This chapter focuses on understanding the nature and quality of primary school children's talk while working on collaborative writing projects in the context of an innovative Mexican educational programme called *Learning Together*. With its roots in socio-cultural perspectives on learning and development, the programme has been designed specifically to foster the development of 'learning communities', within which participants co-construct knowledge and understanding, and promote social, cognitive, psycholinguistic and technological abilities in the children. The analytic work presented focuses on exploring the relations between the dialogical, collaborative writing processes of teams of fifth graders (10 to 11 years old) engaged in the production of two types of texts, namely emails and opinion articles. It is argued that divergent tasks, such as collaborative writing, require somewhat different dialogic styles of interaction than convergent tasks. The associated conceptual and educational implications are discussed in relation to understanding and enhancing oral and written communication in school settings.

Antecedents

Our work is underpinned by a commitment to a socio-cultural approach to conceptualizing and studying processes of development, teaching-and-learning and education and it contributes to recent developments in 'dialogic approaches' to learning and teaching in classroom settings (e.g. Alexander 2004; Lyle 2008; Skidmore 2006). Specifically, our interest is in understanding and promoting 'dialogic interactions' which, drawing on Alexander (2004), we define as interactions where pupils ask questions, explicate points of view and comment on ideas that emerge in lessons. They are supported in this by teachers who are sensitive to, and take account of, their ideas in developing the theme of the lesson, using talk to provide a cumulative, dynamic, contextual frame to ensure reciprocity and promote the students' continued involvement (Lyle 2008). Our primary interest is thus in the nature and significance of classroom talk. Though we recognize the importance in educational activity of, for example, the use of gesture and other non-verbal ways of interacting, our view is that the distinctive role of spoken language in learning and development justifies it being given particular consideration and attention.

Inherent in the socio-cultural approach is the notion that if we are to understand the nature of thinking, learning and development we need to take account of the fundamentally social and communicative nature of human life. Socio-cultural theory posits that intellectual development is achieved through dialogue and that education is enacted through the interactions between students and teachers, which both reflect and constitute the historical development, cultural values and social practices of the societies and communities in which educational institutions exist. Education and cognitive development are therefore seen as cultural processes, whereby knowledge and meanings are 'co-constructed' as joint interactional accomplishments. Knowledge is not only possessed individually but also shared among members of communities – with people constructing knowledge and understandings jointly, through their involvement in events and practices, which are shaped by cultural and historical factors. Within such cultural practices, language plays a key role as a mediator of activity, on both the social and psychological planes.

Vygotsky (1978) described language as both a cultural tool (for the construction and sharing of knowledge among members of a community or society on the social plane) and as a psychological tool (for structuring the processes and content of individual thought on the psychological plane). He proposed that there is an inextricable inter-relationship between these two kinds of use, which can be summarized in the claim that 'intermental' (social, interactional) activity forges 'intramental' (individual) cognitive functioning. The creation of meaning is thus both an inter-personal and intra-personal process, with ways of thinking being embedded in ways of using language (Wegerif and Mercer 1997). As Littleton and Mercer (this volume) note, the implication is that educational success, and failure, may be explained partly by the quality of educational dialogues rather than being just the result of 'the intrinsic capability of individual students, the didactic presentational skills of individual teachers, or the quality of the educational methods, materials and technologies that have been used' (p. 303) (Mercer 1995, 2000; Mercer and Littleton 2007; Rojas-Drummond 2000).

As well as being inspired by socio-cultural theory, our research has also been motivated by practical educational concerns and we have sought to explore two functional aspects of interaction in classrooms. The first is teachers' use of spoken interaction with children as a means for promoting guided participation and 'scaffolding' the development of their knowledge and understanding by providing the intellectual support of a relative 'expert' for the efforts of 'novices' in engaging with any learning task (Rogoff 1990, 2003). The second is the potential value of peer group interaction and dialogue as another means of promoting such development, but in this case by providing a more symmetrical environment for the co-construction of knowledge in which the inevitable power and status differentials between expert and novice are less likely to apply (Mercer 2000). It is this second facet of our work that is the focus of this chapter.

Researchers have differed in their assessments of the educational value of putting children into small groups to work and talk together. On the one hand, experimental and observational studies have demonstrated the distinctive value of collaborative talk in problem solving and learning, including curriculum related activities (Littleton and Häkkinen 1999; Littleton and Light 1999; Rojas-Drummond, Hernández, Vélez and Villagrán 1998; Teasley 1995). On the other hand, observers of collaborative activity in classrooms have reported that most of the talk observed was off-task, unco-operative and of little educational value (Alexander 2004; Bennett and Cass 1989; Galton, Simon and Croll 1980). But this is not quite the paradox that it seems. Closer consideration of relevant evidence suggests that some ways of talking in group activity are indeed of special educational value, but that such ways are relatively uncommon in classrooms. Our explanation for the relatively low educational value of much group talk in classroom contexts has been that children are neither commonly taught about, or explicitly inducted into, ways of talking effectively together, nor are they helped to develop specific dialogic strategies for thinking collectively (Mercer 1995; Mercer and Littleton 2007; Rojas-Drummond 2000; Rojas-Drummond and Mercer 2003; Wegerif, Rojas-Drummond and Mercer 1999). In contrast, the quality of children's discussion when engaged effectively in collaborative activities in the classroom can be captured in the notion of 'Exploratory Talk'. This is a way of using language for reasoning first identified by Douglas Barnes (e.g. Barnes and Todd 1995) which, although derived from the study of children's talk in groups without a teacher present, shares some of the characteristics of the type of teacher–student communication that Scott and colleagues (this volume) call 'dialogic-interactive'. According to Mercer:

> Exploratory Talk is that in which partners engage critically but constructively with each other's ideas. Relevant information is offered for joint consideration. Proposals may be challenged and counter-challenged, but if so reasons are given and alternatives are offered. Agreement is sought as a basis for joint progress. Knowledge is made publicly accountable and reasoning is visible in the talk.
>
> (Mercer 2000: 98)

Providing reasons, justifications, warrants and/or evidence to support one's opinions is part of argumentation, and is central to Exploratory Talk (Rojas-Drummond and Peon 2004). There are good reasons for wanting children to use this kind of talk in group activities, because it represents a distinctive social mode of thinking or 'interthinking' (Mercer 2000; Mercer and Littleton 2007). This constitutes a valuable kind of 'co-reasoning', with speakers following ground rules that help them share knowledge, evaluate evidence and consider options in a reasonable and equitable way.

In this respect, intervention work by Mercer and colleagues (e.g. Mercer and Littleton 2007; Mercer, Wegerif and Dawes 1999; Wegerif, Mercer and Dawes 1999) has enhanced the use of Exploratory Talk by British primary school children. Their results show that this enhancement had a positive effect on children's group and individual problem solving, as well as on performance in academic disciplines such as mathematics and social and natural sciences (see also Rojas-Drummond and Mercer 2003). Following these studies, research in Mexico by Rojas-Drummond and her colleagues (e.g. Rojas-Drummond, Gómez and Vélez 2008b; Rojas-Drummond and Peon 2004; Rojas-Drummond, Pérez, Vélez, Gómez and Mendoza 2003) has confirmed that Exploratory Talk is particularly effective in promoting group and individual reasoning, as well as argumentation abilities in primary school children.

Our most recent work, which we describe here, concerns the nature of children's collaborative writing processes. Writing is a socio-cultural process, with its learning taking place in specific cultural contexts and institutional settings. Learning to write involves becoming competent in the use of sophisticated communicative strategies – where the interaction between experts and novices is crucial. According to Flower and Hayes (1980), expert writers plan, compose and revise reflexively, while novice writers do so in a more rudimentary way. Similarly, Scardamalia and Bereiter (1986) claim that during writing, novices engage in writing but without much reflection, using mainly a linear 'knowledge telling' strategy. In contrast, expert writers move backwards and forwards continuously between a content and a rhetorical space using mainly a more sophisticated 'knowledge transforming' strategy. Sharples (1999) synthesized the previous models and proposed that writing is a process of 'creative design' where the writer chooses among many potential courses. During writing, planning, composing and revising take place in a cyclical and iterative fashion, and these processes in turn involve cycles of action and reflection.

It is important to stress that writing is not a solitary activity, even if it is undertaken by one person. The socio-cultural perspective emphasizes that writing is embedded in a complex social world, where already existent texts intermingle to create new ones, a process referred to as 'intertextuality' (Maybin 2003). If intertextuality is evident when the text is created by a lone writer, it is even more prominent when this writing is collaborative, since a new dimension is added: the referencing to each writer's discourse. Collaborative writing makes even more evident its dialogic and intertextual nature, because 'each utterance is part of a larger whole in which all possible meanings of a word interact, possibly conflict, and affect future meaning' (Dale 1994). Intertextuality is essential to collaborative writing given that participants are constantly blending their voices for a common purpose. At the same time, collaborative writing informs our understanding of intertextuality because it makes thinking about writing external and explicit.

More recently, conceptions of literacy have been greatly extended to incorporate the variety of uses of ICT that have permeated society as a whole and education in particular. In this context, authors now refer to the integration of the functional uses of this variety of psycholinguistic, technological and cultural artefacts as 'information literacy'; 'multiliteracies' or 'multimodal literacy' (e.g. Cassany 2003; Fairclough 2000; Jewitt 2005; Mercer, Fernández, Dawes, Wegerif and Sams 2003; Wegerif and Dawes 2004). Understanding the dialogical processes implicated in collaborative writing is the object of the present study. This research focus is particularly salient as collaborative writing is inherently dialogic (unlike, say, a concept in science) and thus the 'processes' and 'products' of such writing are interwoven and mutually constitutive. However, work such as this is also vital, given that functional and information illiteracy are very widespread among student populations, including in Mexico, as demonstrated by several international and national studies (e.g. Mazón, Rojas-Drummond and Vélez 2005; Organisation for Economic Cooperation and Development [OECD], 2001, 2004; Rojas-Drummond, Gómez, Márquez, Olmos, Peon and Vélez 1999). Thus, the programme to be described next was designed to contribute to understanding and tackling these problems for Mexican primary students.

The context of the study: the *Learning Together* educational programme

In the present study Mexican primary school children carried out various team projects involving dialogical interactions and collaborative writing. These projects were generated in the context of the implementation of an innovative educational programme called *Learning Together*. This has operated in a public primary school in Mexico City for over 8 years. The purpose of the programme is to establish 'learning communities' within primary schools, which foster the creation of close partnerships among children, teachers and university researchers. These communities encourage the active participation of all its members in meaningful activities involving the co-construction of knowledge. In addition, the programme seeks to promote social, cognitive, psycholinguistic, technological and academic abilities in primary students. Particular emphasis is placed on enhancing abilities and dialogic and literacy repertoires, which our research (among others) has demonstrated the children do not generally develop adequately as part of their regular school activities, but which are relevant for their competent participation in their communities of practice in and out of school. These include: collaboration, problem solving, as well as functional oral and written communication (see for example Mazón *et al.* 2005; Rojas-Drummond, Albarrán and Littleton 2008a; Rojas-Drummond *et al.* 2008b; Rojas-Drummond *et al.* 1998; Rojas-Drummond, Mazón, Fernández and Wegerif 2006; Rojas-Drummond *et al.* 2003).

The programme runs within school hours and the activities are carried out in parallel with those of regular school. However, the way the programme operates contrasts sharply with that of ordinary classrooms in most public primary schools in Mexico. The latter tend not to provide a rich social learning environment. Teaching in general tends to comply with traditional, recitational pedagogical methods that involve mainly directive and transmissional styles of interaction and 'monologic' talk (e.g. Mercado, Rojas-Drummond, Weber, Mercer and Huerta 1998; Paul 2005; Rojas-Drummond 2000). The State-provided textbooks are the main guide for a variety of routine exercises, and literacy practices tend to be void of meaning or function (Instituto Nacional para la Evaluación de la Educación [INEE] 2007). As Kaufman and Rodríguez comment, writing is performed 'for nothing and for nobody' (2001: 19).

In contrast with the school practices detailed above, our programme strives to create learning communities where all members participate actively in pursuing authentic and creative projects and solving a wide variety of engaging problems. Activities involve participants' immersion in diverse meaningful and functional oracy and literacy practices, including competent uses of cultural artefacts and technologies. These practices are relevant to children's active and autonomous participation in their communities inside as well as outside of the school context.

The programme *Learning Together* is implemented throughout the academic year with fourth-, fifth- and sixth-grade students (from 9 to 12 years old). Activities take place in a multipurpose room designed *ex professo* and equipped with modular furniture, a small library and computers connected to the Internet. The arrangement enables the teacher to orchestrate diverse whole-class and small group activities. Once a week, the respective students from each participating group come with their teacher to this setting for a 90-minute session. The sessions are co-ordinated by the teacher with the support of several university researchers. Before, during and after implementation of the programme, teachers and researchers work in close collaboration to design, carry out, review and refine all the activities, procedures and resources used in the sessions.

The programme comprises four modules designed to enhance diverse abilities in the students. In the first module, activities are intended to foster collaboration, effective ways of communication, including the use of Exploratory Talk, and problem solving strategies. Methods used include those developed by Mercer and colleagues in the UK for promoting Exploratory Talk (Dawes, Mercer and Wegerif 2000; Mercer 2000; Mercer and Littleton 2007). These have subsequently been adapted by Rojas-Drummond and colleagues for use with Mexican children (e.g. Rojas-Drummond *et al.* 2008a; Rojas-Drummond *et al.* 2003). Briefly, with adult guidance, children are encouraged to generate certain 'ground rules' or strategies for using Exploratory Talk. Then, throughout the programme, children apply and adapt these strategies to the solution of a wide variety of problems in different domains, with emphasis in the psycholinguistic domain.

In the remaining three modules, the focus is on the promotion of strategies for comprehending and producing texts of different genres, including literary, argumentative and informative texts. Emphasis is placed on the use of strategies for producing texts with local and global coherence, guided by the structure and rhetorical qualities of specific text genres (see van Dijk and Kintsch 1983). Methods followed include those developed by Rojas-Drummond and colleagues in previous studies related to literacy (e.g. Mazón *et al.* 2005; Rojas-Drummond *et al.* 2008a; Rojas-Drummond *et al.* 2008b; Rojas-Drummond *et al.* 1998; Rojas-Drummond *et al.* 2006). In particular, children carry out a variety of creative team projects, which require the dynamic use and integration of strategies for communicating through oral and written language effectively, using diverse technological tools. The projects involve: comprehension and production of literary texts in fourth grade; comprehension and production of communicative and argumentative texts in fifth grade, and comprehension and production of expository texts in sixth grade.

From these three grades, the projects generated particularly in fifth grade were selected for illustrative purposes and are the focus of the present study. As part of these projects children, organized in small teams, carry out email correspondence with Mexican-American 'pen-pals'. They also create periodistic texts for a school bulletin, including news reports, opinion articles, reviews and the like. This bulletin is published and disseminated, together with all the products of the projects carried out by the teams of each grade, at the end of the school year in a wide event called the 'cultural fair'. In it, children present to and discuss with the whole learning community, as well as a broader audience, the products of their projects. This event contributes to rendering the projects meaningful and functional, given their genuine communicative purposes and the interaction with real interlocutors.

Throughout the implementation of the *Learning Together* programme, researchers co-ordinate efforts with teachers in order to promote the use of diverse instructional and learning strategies, inspired in socio-cultural perspectives on learning and development. These include the following:

a   the creation of learning environments rich in social interactions where the diverse activities carried out are meaningful, purposeful and mediated by a variety of

cultural artefacts, including tools and sign systems (Cole 1996; Rogoff 2003);
b   guided participation between experts and novices where adults scaffold children's learning activities (Bruner 1978; Rogoff 1990);
c   collaborative learning where peers engage in diverse creative projects, joint problem solving and co-constructing knowledge (Brown, Palincsar and Ambruster 1984; Littleton, Miell and Faulkner 2004; Rojas-Drummond *et al.* 2008b; Rojas-Drummond *et al.* 1998); and
d   promotion of effective strategies for oral and written communication between children and adults, as well as among peers, including dialogic teaching and Exploratory Talk (Alexander 2004; Mercer 2000; Mercer and Littleton 2007).

Our team has conducted numerous quantitative and qualitative longitudinal, cross-sectional and micro-genetic research projects throughout the 8 years of the implementation of the programme. These have been framed by theoretical as well as practical concerns. The investigations have assessed, among other issues, the success of the programme in promoting the repertoires we seek to enhance. In general, our results have indicated that the programme has been highly effective in promoting social, cognitive, psycholinguistic and technological abilities in the children. In particular, children who participate in our programme, in comparison with peers matched on relevant characteristics, develop better collaboration and communication abilities, including the use of Exploratory Talk, argumentation, and other dialogical and co-constructive forms of interaction for solving a wide variety of problems (Rojas-Drummond *et al.* 2008a; Rojas-Drummond and Peon 2004; Rojas-Drummond *et al.* 2003; Wegerif, Pérez, Rojas-Drummond, Mercer and Vélez 2005). Similarly, the programme enhances literacy abilities in the students, including those dealing with the comprehension and production of literary, argumentative and expository texts (e.g. Guzmán and Ibarra 2003; Mazón *et al.* 2005; Peon 2004; Rojas-Drummond, Mazón, Gómez and Vélez forthcoming).

A parallel line of research has analysed the processes involved in children's appropriation of abilities related to collaboration, oral and written communication and problem solving (e.g. Fernández, Wegerif, Mercer and Rojas-Drummond 2001; Rojas-Drummond 2000; Rojas-Drummond *et al.* 2008b; Rojas-Drummond *et al.* 2006; Rojas-Drummond and Mercer 2003; Rojas-Drummond, Mercer and Dabrowski 2001).

One issue of particular concern in our research has been elucidating the collaborative contexts which promote the use of explicit reasoning in the form of argumentation that is characteristic of Exploratory Talk. In previous studies, Rojas-Drummond *et al.* (2006) found that children who participated in the *Learning Together* programme used argumentation extensively when solving a convergent task that demanded finding the correct answer to logical-mathematical problems. In contrast, argumentation was less frequently used for solving divergent tasks such as summarizing several related texts. (This latter task is divergent in the sense that it is more open and there is not one single correct answer for solving this task, as is the case for convergent tasks). Similarly, argumentation was not frequently used in other divergent tasks such as the creative collaborative writing of multimedia stories (Rojas-Drummond *et al.* 2008b). For divergent tasks, our studies have found that children use most commonly a type of talk we call 'co-constructive'. This seems to follow most of the basic ground rules of Exploratory

Talk, except that children do not necessarily make their reasoning visible in the form of explicit arguments. In co-constructive talk, children typically chain, integrate, elaborate and/or reformulate each other's contributions to negotiate meanings and jointly construct solutions to problems, including differences of perspectives.

Based on these recent studies, we argue that the nature of the task in terms of convergence versus divergence is one relevant factor for explaining the degree to which children make their reasoning explicit in the form of arguments, with convergent tasks particularly affording this use. In fact, most of the studies that have demonstrated the extensive use of Exploratory Talk by children, when this is explicitly promoted, have used convergent tasks such as those involved in solving logical, mathematical and science problems (for a review see Mercer and Littleton 2007; Rojas-Drummond *et al.* 2008a; Rojas-Drummond and Mercer 2003). However, divergent tasks such as collaborative writing have been much less studied in these contexts. Thus, analysing the dialogic styles children use when writing collaboratively is the object of the present study. Considering the scarce evidence so far, we hypothesize that divergent tasks like collaborative writing require somewhat different dialogic styles of interaction than convergent tasks. Furthermore, besides the nature of the task, the type of text children produce might be another contributing factor for explaining the degree to which they use argumentation. Therefore, in the next section we offer evidence of dialogical interactions of fifth-grade children producing collaboratively two contrasting types of texts, namely epistolary and argumentative. We would predict that the latter can create particularly favourable contexts where children can make their reasoning visible in their talk in the form of explicit arguments.

Dialogical interactions in two writing contexts

The data to be analysed here were drawn from a wider study of 48 fifth-grade children (10 to 11 years old) within a state primary school in Mexico City that takes part in the *Learning Together* programme. The data were collected in the context of the implementation of the module designed to promote comprehension and production of communicative and argumentative texts, which lasted 12 sessions. During this module children, organized in triads, carried out two main team projects: email correspondence with Mexican-American 'pen-pals', and the creation of a school bulletin, which contained a diversity of periodistic texts, including opinion articles, news reports, book and film reviews and letters of complaint. The projects reflected the work of the team and represented an ideal opportunity for enhancing oracy, literacy and functional uses of technology in an integrated and meaningful fashion.

For data collection, four focal triads were randomly selected and their collaborative work was videoed to enable a micro-genetic analysis of their interaction and discourse while they wrote the emails and periodistic texts. Five sessions were video recorded for each triad. Videos were transcribed verbatim together with a description of the context, following procedures developed by Edwards and Mercer (1987). Videos and transcripts were consecutively analysed qualitatively on the basis of the content, structure and communicative function of the dialogical interactions, as well as the micro and macro contexts surrounding these exchanges. At the same time, our analyses were guided by previous relevant work, including our own (e.g. Mercer 2000; Mercer and Littleton

2007; Rojas-Drummond 2000; Rojas-Drummond et al. 2008a; Rojas-Drummond et al. 2008b; Rojas-Drummond et al. 2006; Rojas-Drummond and Mercer 2003). In addition, the texts produced by the four focal triads were collected and analysed qualitatively and quantitatively using rubrics designed for the purpose.

To exemplify our approach to the in-depth micro-analyses of dialogues and texts mentioned above, we focus on representative examples of the dialogical and text production processes displayed by triad 1 while creating an email to their 'pen-pal', and triad 2 while producing an opinion article. Both triads comprised two girls and one boy (all the dialogues and texts provided were produced in Spanish by the children; the texts presented here are English translations of these original texts).

These two contexts were compared to establish the generalities and specificities in the dialogical and literacy processes involved in the production of two contrasting types of texts. On the one hand, emails represent informal texts with an expressive function where the focus is engaging in interpersonal exchanges, and the interlocutor(s) are well defined. On the other hand, opinion articles correspond to more formal texts with an appellative function where the focus is presenting a problem and defending a position; also, the interlocutor(s) are more loosely defined.

Participating in email correspondence

General context

Marisol, Dalia and Felipe are sitting together at a computer writing an email to Patricia, a Mexican-American 13-year-old girl living in California. In a previous email, Patricia had sent them her photo and told them about herself. The children are now responding to that mail. In Excerpt 1 they are discussing several questions they want to ask to Patricia. (After Excerpt 1, we present the email they sent to Patricia later in the same session.)

Excerpt 1: Asking about boyfriend

MARISOL: *(Starts writing on the computer using a word processor)* 'We're going to ask you some questions: Do you have a boyfriend?' ... Another could be 'At what age do you think you'll get married?'

FELIPE: *(Reading)* 'At what age?' Yeah.

MARISOL: Another question about boyfriends and getting married and all of that?

FELIPE: 'How many kids do you want?'

MARISOL: Yes

DALIA: But those are personal questions ...

MARISOL: It doesn't matter *(starts writing down the idea)*. 'How many kids do you want?'

DALIA: What? No! Don't write that question because ...

FELIPE: Yeah!

MARISOL: *(In agreement with Felipe)* It's to get to know how she is, depending on how many kids she wants is how she is ... *(she writes down the information)* 'Where do you want to go for your honeymoon?' *(While Marisol types, Dalia and Felipe chat)*

DALIA: To New York.

FELIPE: No.

DALIA: To Hollywood.

FELIPE: Or to Dallas.

MARISOL: (*Writes while reading aloud*) 'Honeymoon'.

FELIPE: Honeymoon? Why do people say 'going to honeymoon'?

DALIA: Mmmhh ... Oh, I know! Because it is very romantic and all that stuff.

FELIPE: Oh, you're right ...

DALIA: (*Reading*) 'How many kids do you want?' Let's say that ... But what if she is infertile?

MARISOL: Infertile? What do you mean?

DALIA: (*Speaking quietly*). That she can't have children. We shouldn't ask things like that.

MARISOL: But she can't know that.

DALIA: Why don't we ask her ... mmmhh ... 'Which pet do you want to have?'

FELIPE: ... 'Do you have a pet?' or 'Which pet would you like?' Yes.

DALIA: ... 'Which animal ...'

MARISOL: Why don't we ask only about boyfriends and getting married and all of that (*She reads all the questions written so far while Dalia and Felipe listen*). Another question could be 'When you turn fifteen years old, what will your dress look like?'

FELIPE: How about 'Which color will it be?'

MARISOL: Yes. 'Which color will your dress be?'

DALIA: Fifteen-year-old dress?

MARISOL: Yes, because the wedding dress must be white (*she writes the idea down*).

DALIA: (*She writes on the computer*) 'We send you lots of kisses ...' 'Sincerely, Marisol, Dalia and Felipe'.

FELIPE: Well, let's see. 'Hi Patty!' (*He reads aloud the entire letter while the girls read on the screen*)

Comments

The preceding dialogue shows the collaborative work of the children during the writing of an email to their 'pen-pal' Patricia. In turn 1 Marisol proposes that they ask Patricia personal questions. This initiative gives rise to an engaging discussion where Felipe and Marisol favour continuing to ask Patricia more personal questions (turns 2–5, 7, 9, 10 and 26), whereas Dalia expresses her objection and concern, arguing that these questions are too personal (turns 6, 8, 21 and 23). In turn 10 Marisol offers a counter-argument for maintaining the personal tone. These differences of opinion continue to underlie the triad's interaction throughout, surfacing intermittently. These exchanges indicate that the children have differing perspectives about the degree of privacy/intimacy that is socially acceptable in their correspondence with their 'pen-pal'. However, their dialogue also reflects a high level of intersubjectivity, as well as a commitment to negotiate their perspectives and move forward in writing their text (e.g. turns 1–10 and 19–33). In this sense, their talk is not disputational (as it is not characterized by conflict and individualized decision-making, see Littleton and Mercer this volume)

Hi Patty!

We just read your message, we enjoy writing among each
other but we don´t know what else we can tell you.
Ah! We have another thing to ask you: tell us exactly
what you think about this email exchange that teachers
have organized for us?

We'll ask you other questions...
Do you have a boyfriend?
At what age do you think you'll get married?
How many kids do you want?
Where do you want to go for your honeymoon?
Which color will your 15 year-old dress be?

We send you lots of kisses

Sincerely,
Dalia, Felipe and Marisol
The League of Justice

Figure 7.1 Text of Dalia, Felipe and Marisol's email to their 'pen-pal'.

but highly exploratory in orientation; that is, the different positions are not imposed
but offered as proposals for joint negotiation, and in some instances accompanied by
arguments and counter-arguments.

Besides this collaborative orientation, throughout the triad's discussion we can also
observe the expression of affection, as well as the externalization of personal, social
and cultural views (see turns 10–14, 16–18, 20–2, 26–30). These arose from the children's high level of involvement in the activity. For example, in turns 16–18 Felipe
and Dalia discuss the metaphoric use of the term 'honeymoon' to convey a sense of
romance. Also, in turns 20–2 Dalia and Marisol speculate on the personal concerns of
their interlocutor. The children also show sensitivity to Patricia's cultural context in
turns 10–14 and 26–30. Thus, the high level of intersubjectivity displayed by the triad
in their discussions is extended to their interlocutor: throughout the segment, Patricia
seems to be another participant, a fourth 'voice' present in a more extended dialogue
(Wertsch 1991). (Note also how the children continually use the second person – you
– when deciding what to ask Patricia; e.g. turns 1, 4,10, 23, 26 and 28).

At the end of the segment (turns 31 and 32), the children close down the email
with an affectionate good-bye and revise the text by reading it out loud. These actions
provide evidence of the triad's knowledge about the importance of revising a text that
will be read by others. The final version of the written text conforms to the typical
structure of an informal or personal letter and reflects the expressive function of the
epistolary genre. These aspects were reinforced by the inclusion of a pertinent image,
which worked as a semiotic device to highlight, in a condensed and attractive fashion,
some central meanings of their message (romance, marriage, etc.).

Further analyses of the relations between the children's dialogues, written text and image revealed complex and dynamic intertextual and intercontextual links (Maybin 2003). These include: 1) juxtapositions across different segments of the dialogue (e.g. see relations between turns 4 and 19); 2) various references to their interlocutor; 3) allusions to world knowledge (e.g. social and cultural conventions); 4) non-linear relations between the contents of the oral and written texts; and 5) overlapping references to certain central meanings in the dialogue, written text and image (e.g. romance, marriage, social celebrations and conventions, etc).

It is interesting to note that the children's rich peripheral (yet pertinent) discussions on a variety of topics occurred in parallel with making central decisions about what to say to their 'pen-pal' and how to say it, as well as typing the email in the computer. These parallel processes and activities, or 'parallel conversations', exemplify children's use of sophisticated writing strategies with engagement in cycles of action and reflection (Sharples 1999), moving backwards and forwards between a content and a rhetorical space (Scardamalia and Bereiter 1996).

Writing an opinion article for the school bulletin

General context

Estefanny, Leticia and Mauricio are sitting together at a computer writing an opinion article about the mistreatment of animals. In Excerpt 2 the children are discussing and writing about different situations in which animals are mistreated, as well as their stance on this problem. (After Excerpt 2, we present the opinion article they produced later in the same session.)

Excerpt 2: Discussing animal mistreatment

1. ESTEFANNY: There are animals (*starts writing*) 'that are …'
2. LETICIA: (*Reading*) that are (*adding*) 'mistreated in the streets by the …'
3. ESTEFANNY: By their owners.
4. MAURICIO: I don't hit my dog, only when he ate a marble.
5. ESTEFANNY: It would also be to abandon them in the street.
6. MAURICIO: They kill them, they use them …
7. ESTEFANNY: 'They use them for fights …'
8. MAURICIO: 'They make them fight.'
9. LETICIA: Also dogs without training, those dogs bite people.
10. ESTEFANNY: They leave them in the streets.
11. LETICIA: Yeah, one day I had a dog named (*inaudible*) and one day … and this dog bite my sister here (*points at her arm*).
12. ESTEFANNY: We write a colon, right? Colon and then we write: 'First, because they use them …'
13. LETICIA: For fighting, to leave them abandoned.
14. MAURICIO: They use them to leave them abandoned? (*questioning Leticia's phrase*).
15. ESTEFANNY: Mmmhhh … (*she corrects as she writes*) 'because they abandon them.'

16. LETICIA: Mmmhhh … 'It is unjust!'
17. MAURICIO: Ah, why, why?
18. LETICIA: Well, because animals should stay alive and be cared for by the … by their owners.
19. MAURICIO: Because they should not be used to …
20. ESTEFANNY: To fight and all those kind of things, etcetera.
21. LETICIA: In order to live and stay alive.
22. ESTEFANNY: Well, to live and to be cared for, protected, loved
23. MAURICIO: Yeah, not to be hit … so the … that their owners should protect them.
24. ESTEFANNY: Because animals should have freedom, right? Some of them should have their own space. They should …
25. LETICIA: Have their, their, how do you call it? … 'their adequate place.'
26. ESTEFANNY: (*Reads part of the text and then adds*) 'to receive love and protection, right?'
27. LETICIA: 'And protection by their owners.'
28. ESTEFANNY: 'And the necessary care?'
29. LETICIA: From their owners.
30. ESTEFANNY: On the part of their …
31. LETICIA: 'On the part of their owners.'
… (*Children take up previous topic about fights, and start talking about bull fights*) …
32. ESTEFANNY: Bull fights are unjust.
33. MAURICIO: No, 'cause sometimes bulls kill.
34. ESTEFANNY: Yeah, but because they tease them.

Comments

In Excerpt 2 children discuss, organize information and jointly construct the main body of their opinion article. The first part of their conversation (turns 1–15) relates specifically to generating, in a process of 'brainstorming', five central ideas as supporting evidence for the claim that animals are mistreated (i.e., they kill them, they use them for fighting, they abandon them, etc.). The second part (turns 16–31) deals with taking a personal (collective) position on the issue – namely that animal mistreatment is unjust – and jointly constructing a central argument supported by eight related justifications to back off their position (i.e. that animals should be cared for, protected, loved, etc.).

Throughout the dialogue we see evidence of a high degree of engagement with the activity by the three children, as well as the proposal of a wide range of contributions from their world knowledge to advance their written composition. The main thesis and supporting evidence, as well as the position, global argument and accompanying justifications, were jointly generated by displaying a wide variety of communicative acts indicative of a collaborative orientation (Hymes 1972). Among these were: proposing ideas, questioning, negotiating alternative perspectives, arguing and counter-arguing as well as chaining, elaborating, integrating and reformulating information. These observations provide evidence of a collaborative and co-constructive orientation to the task, as well as a high level of intersubjectivity among the participants. (For example, in turns 1–3, 6–8, 19–20 and 26–31 children chained their ideas by completing or

Animal mistreatment

There are animals that are mistreated by their owners: first because they use them for fighting and because they abandon them. Another way to mistreat them is to hunt them and to make some events where animals must fight such as the bull fights, rooster fights and dog fights. In some zoos the managers sometimes hit them and leave them without food.

It's unjust because animals should have an appropriate place, receive love, protection and the necessary care by their owners. We suggest that people who have animals as pets should give them all they need and if they are to abandon them it is better to give them away or sell them.

Authors:
MAURICIO ESCUTIA,
ESTEFANNY ORDUÑA
AND LETICIA GRISEL

Figure 7.2 Text of Estefanny, Leticia and Mauricio's opinion article.

reformulating each others' phrases, as if anticipating what the previous speaker was going to say and finishing the phrase for him/her). Similar communicative acts were also identified in the four focal triads for the whole corpus of data of the present study. Other communicative acts present in the whole corpus were: asking for and providing opinions, clarifications and/or explanations; joint elaboration of ideas; asking for agreement; agreeing with others; disagreeing with others; and evaluating information. All these communicative acts reflect a co-constructive style of dialogical interaction, similar to the style described in previous related studies (e.g. Rojas-Drummond *et al.* 2008b; Rojas-Drummond *et al.* 2006).

Alongside this collaborative orientation, children made extensive use of Exploratory Talk (see turns 5–15, 17–31, and 32–4). For example, in turns 5–15 the three children jointly propose supporting evidence for the claim that animals are mistreated. In addition, in turn 17 Mauricio asks for reasons for Leticia's position and in turn 18 Leticia provides an argument; this is followed by a series of additional justifications jointly constructed in turns 18–31. Furthermore, in turns 32–4 Estefanny and Mauricio express different perspectives on the subject of bull-fighting by making a claim as well as arguing and counter-arguing. These exchanges make evident children's disposition and openness to confront their ideas and solve conflicts in a critical but constructive fashion.

In parallel with deciding jointly what to say, children also negotiated how to write and engaged in writing their text. For example, in turn 12 Estefanny suggests organizing their contributions by writing a 'colon' followed by the connector 'first'. Then in turn 13 Leticia offers a phrase that is not very coherent; this is questioned by Mauricio in turn 14 and corrected by Estefanny in turn 15, who writes in turn a more coherent phrase.

All these examples evidence the children's knowledge about linguistic conventions, as well as engaging in planning, supervision and correction processes. This evidence in turn suggests that triad 2, as was the case of triad 1, used sophisticated writing strategies.

Also in parallel with the processes described above, children evoked previous related personal experiences, as well as externalized reflections about their own and others' behaviours, emotions, moral values and social and cultural practices (see turns 4, 11, 16 and 32–4). For example, in turn 4 Mauricio reflects on his own behaviour towards his dog, and in turn 11 Leticia recounts a related personal experience. Also, in turn 16 Leticia claims that animal mistreatment is unjust. In addition, in turns 32–4 Mauricio and Estefanny discuss bull-fighting, and argue about the animal's versus human responsibility for bulls' aggressive behaviour. These concomitant actions and reflections are reminiscent of the sophisticated 'parallel conversations' exhibited by triad 1.

In relation to the written text, an analysis of its content, structure and function revealed the use of a formal language characteristic of this modality (including the third person and impersonal phrases). Also, the text conforms to the typical structure of this genre: it includes a title; it starts with a problem/thesis, followed by an exposition of details of the problem/thesis; it further expresses a personal position supported by valid arguments, and closes with suggestions for how to solve the problem. Similarly, the text has local and global coherence, including the use of linguistic markers (e.g. first, another way, because, if, etc.) (van Dijk and Kintsch 1983). In addition, the text complies with the appellative function of this genre by using adequate rhetoric devices to convince a possible audience, including several back-ups to the main thesis in the form of supporting evidence and a well developed argument with several supporting justifications (see Halliday 1985). As was the case for the email, some central meanings of the text, in this case related to animal mistreatment, were underscored by the inclusion of a pertinent image in which some dogs are tightly enclosed in a cage[1]. In general, the text is very adequate and sophisticated when compared to those produced by children of similar age and socio-economic level (see Peon 2004).

As was the case for the emails, analyses of the relations between the children's dialogues, text and image for the opinion article revealed complex and dynamic intertextual and intercontextual links. These include: 1) juxtapositions across different segments of the dialogue (e.g. see the relations between Mauricio and Estefanny's discussion in turns 6–8 about animal fighting, and in turns 32–4 about bull-fighting); 2) implicit references to possible readers (e.g. suggestions to people with pets at the end of the written text); 3) allusions to world knowledge in personal, moral, social and cultural planes (e.g. animal rights and human values – justice, freedom, responsibility, etc.) 4) non-linear relations between the oral and written texts (e.g. contrast discussion of bull-fights in turns 32–4 with lines 2–4 of the text about bull, rooster and dog fights as examples of animal mistreatment); and 5) overlapping references to certain central meanings in the dialogue, written text and image (e.g. animal mistreatment, abandonment, lack of freedom, etc.).

Discussion

The dialogues analysed for triads 1 and 2, as well as most of those of the four focal triads studied, exhibited in general a collaborative orientation when writing texts of different genres, including emails and opinion articles. When differences of opinion or perspective arose, the triads tended to try to overcome these differences through negotiations using mainly co-constructive talk (although their attempts to solve the differences were not always successful).

Sometimes the confrontation of perspectives was accompanied by explicit arguments, in which case the conflict was addressed using mainly Exploratory Talk. When considering the whole corpus of data for the present study, we found that Exploratory Talk was salient when children wrote argumentative texts (including opinion articles and letters of complaint). Exploratory Talk was also used, although in a lesser degree, for writing other non-argumentative texts such as emails and news reports (for a complete report of the data, see Zúñiga 2007 and Hernández 2008). In the latter cases co-constructive talk was particularly evident, as was the case for the data reported in Rojas-Drummond *et al.* (2006) and Rojas-Drummond *et al.* (2008).

In summary, the results of all these studies in combination suggest that, children who have participated in programmes that explicitly induce the use of Exploratory Talk, (such as *Learning Together*), tend to confront convergent tasks by using Exploratory Talk extensively. On the other hand, with divergent tasks such as those involved in collaborative writing of texts of different genres (including summaries, stories, emails and opinion articles), their use of Exploratory Talk is more sporadic. This is because, unlike convergent tasks, in divergent ones, there is not one correct solution, nor are there definitive 'truths' involved in solving them. As Sharples (1999) argues, writing as creative design is open-ended since the writer can choose among many courses. Thus, in these divergent contexts children may or may not express differences of perspectives, and when these arise they may or may not address them through the use of explicit arguments, depending on different factors. One of these seems to be the type of text children write: argumentative texts seem to provide particularly fertile contexts for the use of Exploratory Talk (as was shown for the opinion article). Another factor might be the degree to which children adopt perspectives involving differences in personal values (as was the case in the example in Excerpt 1 where there was a clash of these different perspectives). An additional factor that has been identified in related studies is the writing phase children are engaged in: phases involving creative 'brainstorming' might not be suitable for making reasoning explicit, whereas more reflective phases where children review their texts might be more conducive (see Vass 2004 and Vass, Littleton, Miell and Jones 2008). As can be seen, elucidating the contexts that promote the use of explicit reasoning is an open and exciting field, which needs much more empirical underpinning than that which exists at present. However, taking the evidence so far in combination, it is reasonable to argue that divergent tasks like writing require somewhat different dialogic styles of interaction than convergent tasks.

Exploratory Talk was explicitly fostered as part of the *Learning Together* programme and was exhibited by the four triads under study. As discussed in the Antecedents section above, research in the area shows that, when not promoted directly, Exploratory Talk is very infrequently used by children in the school context. Given its clear educational benefits, there is a pressing need to enhance children's collaborative, co-constructive and exploratory orientation to solving jointly a wide variety of problems, as highlighted by the studies reviewed in this chapter.

The analytic work presented evidenced the complex 'parallel conversations' identified during the triads' dialogical interactions. Both triads engaged in iterative cycles of talking and writing, and in discussions about what to say and how to write it, in parallel with expressions of emotions, as well as a wide variety of personal, moral, social and cultural values, beliefs and knowledge. These complex processes in turn are indicative of the use of sophisticated writing strategies. These include 'knowledge transformation' strategies, that is, moving backwards and forwards between a content and a rhetorical space. In addition, they engaged in iterative cycles of action and reflection, as well as of planning, writing and correcting (Scardamalia and Bereiter 1996; Sharples 1999). These authors claim that such strategies are typically used by expert writers. Children also exhibited in their written texts subtle knowledge about the structure and function of different text genres, and showed sensitivity to the differences between emails and opinion articles in terms of these features, as well as the type of language to be used and the way to address their interlocutors. Previous data suggest that the use of these advanced oracy and literacy strategies is enhanced by the children's participation in the *Learning Together* programme, and is not typical of children of equivalent age and socio-economic level. In addition, the programme seems to foster argumentation and critical thinking in the children (e.g. Guzmán and Ibarra 2003; Mazón *et al.* 2005; Peon 2004; Rojas-Drummond *et al.* 2008a; Rojas-Drummond *et al.* 2008b; Rojas-Drummond *et al.* 2006; Rojas-Drummond and Peon 2004). In these studies we have found evidence that the benefits in oracy and literacy that children gain as a result of participating in the programme are generalized to new tasks and settings, different to those used as part of the programme. In addition, gains are starting to reflect in standard national student evaluations such as an achievement test called ENLACE.

Further evidence of the advanced oracy and literacy abilities of the children participating in the study stems from the analyses of the complex and dynamic intertextual and intercontextual relations holding between the children's dialogues, written texts and images (Maybin 2003). These included links within the dialogues, within the written texts, as well as among the dialogues, the written texts, the images and their knowledge of the world.

All the evidence reviewed in the present chapter supports the claim that authentic communicative activities such as those promoted in the *Learning Together* programme, including email correspondence and writing editorial articles to be published, create motivating and functional situations that enhance active participation, engagement, as well as the development of oracy and literacy (including reading and writing texts of different genres and for different communicative purposes). These types of practices are rare in more traditional classroom environments (INEE 2006; Rojas-Drummond 2000). Furthermore, data illustrate how these authentic activities also encourage children's engagement in rich and meaningful discussions and reflections. This engagement in turn illustrates how collaborative writing provides ideal settings for encouraging the use of language as a 'social mode of thinking' (Mercer 2000). In this context children can externalize their various perspectives, beliefs and thoughts spontaneously (i.e. without the need for induction by an adult or an experimenter). It is highly likely that these thoughts would not have been made explicit if the children had written the text individually. Thus, collaborative writing opens a window for analysing not only children's dialogues and texts, but also their thinking.

Lastly, results highlight the importance of considering the dynamic interrelations between the micro and the macro levels of analyses for a comprehensive understanding of the phenomena under investigation. In the case of the present study, these relations include links between the particular activities of the children during the dialogical inter-actions and writing processes at the micro-analytical level, on the one hand, and their wider world knowledge about personal, social and cultural practices and conventions at the macro-analytical level, on the other. They also include the relations between these collaborative activities and the wider context in which they were fostered, which corresponds to the *Learning Together* programme. Analyses of these inter-relations are essential in order to provide a fuller account of the processes by which children learn to write collaboratively by using diverse cultural artefacts including oracy, literacy and technologies, given that these processes are framed by the wider social and cultural settings in which these literacy practices are embedded.

Note

1 The original image accompanying the text had two dogs enclosed in a cage. However, this was taken by the children from the internet and therefore was not included in this published version, due to problems with copyright. Instead, the original image was substituted with the present one, which reflects some central ideas of the second part of the text, related to the need for animals to receive love from their owners.

References

Alexander, R. (2004) *Dialogic Teaching* (1st edn), Leeds: Dialogos.

Barnes, D. and Todd, F. (1995) *Communication and Learning Revisited: making meaning through talk*, Portsmouth, NH: Boynton/Cook Publishers.

Bennett, N. and Cass, A. (1989) 'The effects of group composition on group interactive processes and pupil understanding', *British Educational Research Journal*, 1:19–32.

Brown, A., Palincsar, A. S. and Ambruster, B. (1984) 'Inducing comprehension-fostering activities in interactive learning situations', in H. Mandl, N. Steinand and T. Trabasso (eds) *Learning and Comprehension of Texts*, Hillsdale, NJ: Lawrence Erlbaum.

Bruner, J. (1978) 'The role of dialogue in language acquisition', in A. Sinclair, R. Jarvella and W. J. M. Levelt (eds) *The Child's Conception of Language*, Berlin: Springer.

Cassany, D. (2003) 'La lectura electrónica', *Cultura y Educación*, 15:239–51.

Cole, M. (1996) *Cultural Psychology: a once and future discipline*, Cambridge, MA: Harvard University Press.

Dale, H. (1994) 'Collaborative writing interactions in one ninth-grade classroom', *Journal of Educational Research*, 87:334–44.

Dawes, L., Mercer, N. and Wegerif, R. (2000) *Thinking Together. A Programme of Activities for Developing Thinking Skills at KS2*, Birmingham: Questions Publishing Co.

Edwards, D. and Mercer, N. (1987) *Common Knowledge: the development of understanding in the classroom*, London: Methuen.

Fairclough, N. (2000) 'Multiliteracies and language: orders of discourse and intertextual-ity', in B. Hope and M. Kalantzis (eds) *Multiliteracies: literacy learning and the design of social futures*, Melbourne, Australia: Macmillan.

Fernández, M., Wegerif, R., Mercer, N. and Rojas-Drummond, S. M. (2001) 'Reconceptualizing "scaffolding" and the zone proximal development in the context of symmetrical collaborative learning', *Journal of Classroom Interaction*, 36:40–54.

Flower, L. and Hayes, J. (1980) 'Identifying the organization of writing processes', in L. Gregg and E. Teinberg (eds) *Cognitive Processes in Writing*, Hillsdale, NJ: Lawrence Erlbaum.

Galton, M., Simon, B. and Croll, P. (1980) *Inside the Primary Classroom (The ORACLE Report)*, London: Routledge and Kegan Paul.

Guzmán, C. K. and Ibarra, I. (2003) *Desarrollo de estrategias de colaboración y comprensión de cuentos dentro de una innovación educativa*, unpublished bachelor's thesis, National Autonomous University of Mexico.

Halliday, M. A. K. (1985) *An Introduction to Functional Grammar*, London: Arnold.

Hernández, F. (2008) *El proceso discursivo en la composición de textos argumentativos en alumnos de 5o año de primaria: una perspectiva teórica de Bajtín y Vigotsky*, unpublished bachelor's thesis, National Autonomous University of Mexico.

Hymes, D. (1972) 'Models of interaction in language and social life', in J. J. Gumperz and D. Hymes (eds) *Directions in Sociolinguistics: the ethnography of communication*, London: Basil Blackwell.

Instituto Nacional para la Evaluación de la Educación (INEE) (2006) *El aprendizaje de la expresión escrita en la educación básica en México*, Mexico: INEE. Available online at: http://www.inee.edu.mx/ (accessed 20 September 2007).

INEE (2007) *El aprendizaje en tercero de primaria en México*, Mexico: INEE. Available online at: http://www.inee.edu.mx/ (accessed 27 September 2007).

Jewitt, C. (2005) 'Multimodality, "reading" and "writing" for the twenty-first century', *Discourse: Studies in the Cultural Politics of Education*, 26:315–31.

Kaufman, A. M. and Rodríguez, M. A. (2001) *La escuela y los textos*, Buenos Aires: Santillana Aula XXI.

Littleton, K. and Häkkinen, P. (1999) 'Learning together: understanding the processes of computer-based collaborative learning', in P. Dillenbourg (ed.) *Collaborative Learning: cognitive and computational approaches*, Pergamon: Oxford.

Littleton, K. and Light, P. (eds) (1999) *Learning with Computers: analysis productive inter-action*, London: Routledge.

Littleton, K., Miell, D. and Faulkner, D. (eds) (2004) *Learning to Collaborate, Collaborating to Learn*, New York: Nova Press.

Lyle, S. (2008) 'Dialogic teaching: discussing theoretical contexts and reviewing evidence from classroom practice', *Language and Education*, 22:222–40.

Maybin, J. (2003) 'Voices, intertextuality and induction into schooling', in S. Goodman, S. Lillis, J. Maybin and N. Mercer (eds) *Language, Literacy and Education: a reader*, Staffordshire, UK: Trentham Books.

Mazón, N., Rojas-Drummond, S. M. and Vélez, M. (2005) 'Efectos de un programa de fortalecimiento de habilidades de comprensión de textos en educandos de primaria', *Revista Mexicana de Psicología*, 22:91–102.

Mercado, R., Rojas-Drummond, S. M., Weber, E., Mercer, N. and Huerta, A. (1998) 'La interacción maestro-alumno como vehículo del proceso de enseñanza-aprendizaje en la escuela primaria', *Morphé*, 8:15–16.

Mercer, N. (1995) *The Guided Construction of Knowledge: talk amongst teachers and learn-ers*, Philadelphia: Multilingual Matters.

Mercer, N. (2000) *Words and Minds: how we use language to think together*, London: Routledge.

Mercer, N. and Littleton, K. (2007) *Dialogue and the Development of Children's Thinking: a socio-cultural approach*, London: Routledge.

Mercer, N., Fernández, M., Dawes, L., Wegerif, R. and Sams, C. (2003) 'Talk about texts; using ICT to develop children's oral and literate abilities', *Reading, Literacy and Language*, 37:81–9.

Mercer, N., Wegerif, R. and Dawes, L. (1999) 'Children's talk and the development of reasoning in the classroom', *British Educational Research Journal*, 25:95–111.

Organisation for Economic Cooperation and Development (OECD) (2001) *Knowledge and Skills for Life: first results from PISA 2000*, Paris: OECD. Available online at: http://www.caliban.sourceoecd.org (accessed 27 January 2007).

OECD (2004) *Learning for Tomorrow's World: first results from PISA 2003*, Paris: OECD. Available online at: http://www.pisa.oecd.org/document/55/0,2340 (accessed 27 January 2007).

Paul, W. J. E. (2005) *Beliefs and practices of high school biology teachers: a case study of communities of practice*, unpublished doctoral thesis, Mexico: DIE-CINVESTAV-IPN.

Peon, M. (2004) *Habilidades argumentativas en alumnos de primaria y su fortalecimiento*, unpublished doctoral thesis, National Autonomous University of Mexico.

Rogoff, B. (1990) *Apprenticeship in Thinking: cognitive development in social context*, New York: Oxford University Press.

Rogoff, B. (2003) *The Cultural Nature of Human Development*, London: Oxford University Press.

Rojas-Drummond, S. M. (2000) 'Guided participation, discourse and the construction of knowledge in Mexican classrooms', in H. Cowie and D. van der Aalsvoort (eds) *Social Interaction in Learning and Instruction: the meaning of discourse for the construction of knowledge*, Exeter: Pergamon Press.

Rojas-Drummond, S. M. and Mercer, N. (2003) 'Scaffolding the development of effective collaboration and learning', *International Journal of Educational Research*, 39:99–111.

Rojas-Drummond, S. M. and Peon, M. (2004) 'Exploratory talk, argumentation and reasoning in Mexican primary school children', *Language and Education*, 18:539–57.

Rojas-Drummond, S. M., Albarrán, D. and Littleton, K. (2008a) 'Collaboration, creativity and the co-construction of oral and written texts', *Thinking Skills and Creativity*, 3:177 –91.

Rojas-Drummond, S. M., Gómez, L.M., Márquez, A. M., Olmos, A., Peon, M. and Vélez, M. (1999) 'Desarrollo de macroestructuras en niños de primaria', *Estudios de Lingüística Aplicada*, 17:13–32.

Rojas-Drummond, S. M., Gómez, L. and Vélez, M. (2008b) 'Dialogue for reasoning: promoting exploratory talk and problem solving in the primary classroom', in B. van Oers, W. Wardekker, E. Elbers and R. van der Veer (eds) *The Transformation of Learning. Advances in Cultural-Historical Activity Theory*, Cambridge, MA: Cambridge University Press.

Rojas-Drummond, S. M., Hernández, G., Vélez, M. and Villagrán, G. (1998) 'Cooperative learning and the acquisition of procedural knowledge by primary school children', *Learning and Instruction*, 3:37–61.

Rojas-Drummond, S. M., Mazón, N., Fernández, M. and Wegerif, R. (2006) 'Explicit reasoning, creativity and co-construction in primary school children's collaborative activities', *Thinking Skills and Creativity*, 1:84–94.

Rojas-Drummond, S. M., Mazón, N., Gómez, L. and Vélez, M. (forthcoming) 'Oracy and literacy in the making: the collaborative creation of macrostructures by primary school children', to be submitted to *Reading Research Quarterly*.

Rojas-Drummond, S. M., Mercer, N. and Dabrowski, E. (2001) 'Teaching-learning strategies and the development of problem solving in Mexican classrooms', *European Journal of Psychology and Education*, 16:179–96.

Rojas-Drummond, S. M., Pérez, V., Vélez, M., Gómez, L. and Mendoza, A. (2003) 'Talking for reasoning among Mexican primary school children', *Learning and Instruction*, 13:653–70.

Scardamalia, M. and Bereiter, C. (1986) 'Research on written composition', in M. Wittrock (ed.) *Handbook of Research on Teaching*, MacMillan: London.

Sharples, M. (1999) *How We Write: writing as creative design*, London: Routledge.

Skidmore, D. (2006) 'Pedagogy and dialogue', *Cambridge Journal of Education*, 36:503–14.

Teasley, S. (1995) 'The role of talk in children's peer collaboration', *Developmental Psychology*, 3:207–20.

van Dijk, T. A. and Kintsch, W. (1983) *Strategies of Discourse Comprehension*, New York: Academic Press.

Vass, E. (2004) 'Understanding collaborative creativity: young children's classroom-based shared creative writing', in D. Miell and K. Littleton (eds) *Collaborative Creativity*, London: Free Association Books.

Vass, E., Littleton, K., Miell, D. and Jones, A. (2008) 'The discourse of collaborative creative writing: peer collaboration as a context for mutual inspiration', *Thinking Skills and Creativity*, 3:192–202.

Vygotsky, L. S. (1978) *Mind in Society*, Cambridge, MA: Harvard University Press.

Wegerif, R. and Dawes, L. (2004) *Thinking and Learning with ICT: raising achievement in primary classrooms*, London: Routledge.

Wegerif, R. and Mercer, N. (1997) 'A dialogical framework for researching peer talk', in R. Wegerif and P. Scrimshaw (eds) *Computers and Talk in the Primary Classroom*, Clevedon: Multilingual Matters.

Wegerif, R., Mercer, N. and Dawes, L. (1999) 'From social interaction to individual reasoning: an empirical investigation of a possible socio-cultural model of cognitive development', *Learning and Instruction*, 9:493–516.

Wegerif, R., Pérez, J., Rojas-Drummond, S., Mercer, N. and Vélez, M. (2005) 'Thinking together in México and the U.K.: a comparative study', *Journal of Classroom Interaction*, 40:40–8.

Wegerif, R., Rojas-Drummond, S. and Mercer, N. (1999) 'Language for the social construction of knowledge: comparing classroom talk in Mexican pre-schools', *Language and Education*, 13:133–51.

Wertsch, J. V. (1991) *Voices of the Mind: a sociocultural approach to mediated action*, Cambridge, MA: Harvard University Press.

Zúñiga, M. (2007) *La escritura colaborativa de cartas en alumnos de 5º de primaria: un estudio de su correspondencia electrónica con alumnos méxico-americanos*, unpublished bachelor's thesis, National Autonomous University of Mexico.

Chapter 8

Philosophy for Children as dialogic teaching

Margaret Hardman and Barbara Delafield
Leeds Metropolitan University

Introduction

The wide variety of educational programmes promoting the development of children's critical thinking reflects concern about the changing nature of the skills needed in contemporary society (Trickey and Topping 2004). These programmes can be differentiated in various ways, including the extent to which they are incorporated into the existing curriculum, and their specific characteristics in terms of the tasks and methodology adopted to develop children's thinking. The *Philosophy for Children* programme (Lipman and Sharp 1978; Lipman, Sharp and Oscanyon 1980; Lipman 1981, 2003) is one of a group of multi-method educational programmes employed to develop critical thinking as either additional to the set curriculum, or more widely across the curriculum as an aspect of teaching subject specialisms such as English language and literature, personal or social education, maths, science and history. The programme is designed to develop critical, creative and caring thinking through a dialogical process whereby children are engaged in discussion and debate in a 'community of enquiry'. This differs from programmes employed separately from the rest of the curriculum, as in the case of the *Instrumental Enrichment* programme (Feuerstein, Rand, Hoffman and Miller 1980) using context-free pencil-and-paper exercises to develop children's critical thinking. It can also be differentiated from subject-based educational programmes, such as the *Cognitive Acceleration through Science Education* (CASE) programme (Adey and Shayer 1994), developing critical thinking skills through special lessons taught by science teachers.

In this chapter we first describe the distinctive and highly specified characteristics of the *Philosophy for Children* programme (Lipman and Sharp 1978; Lipman *et al.* 1980; Lipman 1981, 2003) before reviewing research concerned with evaluating and assessing the outcomes claimed to be achieved. In the latter, and more substantial, part of this chapter we then explore in more detail the process of dialogic teaching involved, its impact on dialogue and implications for practice.

Characteristics of the Philosophy for Children programme

Matthew Lipman devised the *Philosophy for Children* programme (Lipman and Sharp 1978; Lipman *et al.* 1980; Lipman 1981, 2003) with the aim of improving the reasoning skills, critical and creative thinking of children from primary school onwards. The programme has at its core the development of a 'community of philosophical enquiry' in which thinking is stimulated by means of philosophical questions and dialogue, with children critically discussing and debating concepts and ideas in which they have a personal interest.

Lipman's *Philosophy for Children* programme is underpinned by the adoption of what he terms the 'reflective paradigm of critical practice', whereby education is seen as the outcome of participation in a teacher-guided community of enquiry, among whose goals are the achievement of understanding and good judgment. In this supportive context children are prompted to think about the world when their knowledge is revealed to them to be ambiguous, equivocal, and otherwise open to question. The focus of the educational process is on the grasp of relationships within, and among, the subject matters under investigation rather than on the acquisition of information (Lipman 2003: 18). In a classroom community of enquiry 'students listen to one another with respect, build on one another's ideas, challenge one another to provide reasons for otherwise unsupported opinions, assist each other in drawing inferences from what has been said, and seek to identify one another's assumptions' (Lipman 2003: 18). The classroom discourse in this community of enquiry is allowed to transcend discipline boundaries but is structured along logical lines, and this process is then internalized to structure thinking.

In addition to proposing a new approach to education, Lipman draws on the discourse of 'philosophy as a disposition' (or lived philosophy) to propose that *Philosophy for Children* is a radical departure from traditional academic philosophy. The programme is designed to develop a 'philosophical disposition' through a process whereby children are engaged in discussion and debate about concepts they care about and are prepared to follow the reasoning wherever it may lead in a supportive, rather than competitive, environment where each child's views are sought and equally valued. 'Philosophy as a disposition', therefore, emphasizes how discussion and debate of differing ideas should be seen as essential in developing children's abilities to critically examine and share their own understanding and opinions of others, rather than as an end in itself with the outcome as 'winning' such a debate. Differences of opinion openly expressed in this co-operative, collaborative environment are seen as developmental opportunities, and the skills of reasoning learned through such social interaction turned inward for the benefit of further private reflection. The process engendered by this reflective paradigm of critical practice is described as dialogical in that it has a structure as a form of inquiry that is largely logical and is followed to wherever it leads. Lipman describes dialogue as being midway on the continuum between conversation and rhetoric in that it is not wholly free from purpose and may well involve arguments whose purpose is to persuade. Communities of enquiry are described as being characterized by dialogue that is disciplined by logic (Lipman 2003: 92).

The *Philosophy for Children* programme is now used worldwide, with the original material comprising philosophical novels, teacher guides and suggestions for further exercises translated into at least 20 different languages. The original programme employed a series of seven specially written novels relating to different age groups from 6–16 years. These novels and much of the subsequent material developed for use with the programme are described as 'philosophical' in the way in which they question 'open' concepts for which there are no single correct answers, such as fairness and justice, freedom and good/bad rules governing behaviour, friendship, and judgments on moral issues more generally. The novels are designed to prompt questions requiring children to draw on their own ideas to suggest possible solutions as the basis for philosophical discussion. A wide variety of children's texts, including traditional fairy tales and fables, together with new specially designed texts, are frequently now used as alternatives to the original seven novels. If it is not explicitly philosophical, the material used must be centred on a dilemma, containing ambiguities or paradoxes to encourage children to question and create a cognitive conflict in their minds to generate a process of enquiry.

While the texts for discussion and place in the curriculum may now be more varied, what is common to all *Philosophy for Children* programmes is the distinctive structure of the sessions involving 1) reading, 2) collecting questions, and 3) philosophical dialogue within a community of enquiry. Each session begins with the children sharing a reading from the novel, which can be read by the teacher or the children taking turns while the rest follow the text. The teacher then asks what interested or puzzled them, and what questions they would like to explore from the passage. These questions are collected and written up on the board, with the name of the child alongside the suggested question. When all the children have been encouraged to think of a question, the teacher asks the group to decide on the topic and question they would like to explore as a group. One of the basic tenets of the programme is the fallibility of the teacher and the discussion of questions that are problematic to both the teacher and the pupils. The teacher therefore encourages good philosophical questions described as 'questions likely to kindle the pupil's scepticism, doubt and questioning of beliefs, opinions and prejudices' (Daniel 2007: 146). In the ensuing discussion, the children's views hold as much weight as those of the teacher, and the teacher's ideas and interpretations of the points under discussion may be challenged.

In creating a 'community of enquiry', the teacher will encourage the children themselves to develop the ground rules for the sessions, typically writing these up as a reference point for consideration and revision where necessary as the sessions develop. Their role is crucial in facilitating and managing the process of the session to ensure that the discussion keeps running smoothly, that everyone has a chance to be heard, children learn to listen to each other and are sympathetic as well as critical listeners, where all members in the group are equal and each child's contribution is valued. Teachers are trained to encourage children to build on one another's ideas, to see the implications of what they say, make them aware of their own assumptions and find reasons to justify their beliefs.

The underlying principles of the *Philosophy for Children* programme pre-date and have much in common with the recently developed *Thinking Together* programme (Dawes, Mercer and Wegerif 2000; Mercer and Littleton 2007) described in this volume. Both programmes are multi-method educational programmes employed to develop critical thinking as either additional to the set curriculum, or more widely across the curriculum. Lipman's description of the philosophical dialogue promoted as children discuss and debate differing ideas and values is similar to that of 'Exploratory Talk' encouraged in the *Thinking Together* programme. Mercer and Littleton (2007) describe Exploratory Talk as representing 'a joint, coordinated form of co-reasoning in language, with speakers sharing knowledge, challenging ideas, evaluating evidence and considering options in a reasoned and equitable way' (Mercer and Littleton 2007:

62). In both programmes the educational value of this type of talk is emphasized as the dialogue is internalized. In *Philosophy for Children* this philosophical dialogue is seen as crucial to the development and structuring of critical, caring and creative thinking. Similarly, in the *Thinking Together* programme Exploratory Talk is described as a distinctive social mode of thinking – a way of using language that is both the embodiment of critical thinking and essential for successfully participating in 'educated' communities of discourse (Mercer and Littleton 2007: 66). Fundamental to both programmes is the development of a 'community of enquiry' with the ground rules developed by the children to provide a safe, co-operative, and collaborative context whereby differences of opinion openly expressed are seen as developmental opportunities. The teacher's role, in all sessions in *Philosophy for Children* and in the teacher-guided introductory and plenary sessions in the *Thinking Together* programme, is similarly to model the type of talk and questions for collaborative discussion and debate, and to facilitate this community of enquiry to ensure that the discussion runs smoothly with each child's views sought and equally valued.

Critical, creative and caring thinking as measurable outcomes

Lipman (2003) proposes that *Philosophy for Children* facilitates the development of three types or modes of thinking – critical, creative and caring thinking – as a trinity of criteria for so-called multidimensional thinking to be encouraged at all levels of education. Rather than providing a definition encapsulating this multidimensional thinking, he outlines the various aspects of thinking involved in each of the three modes of thinking together with five specified thinking skills and dispositions. *Critical thinking* involves being sensitive to the context, thinking that is dependent on specified criteria and self-correction. *Creative thinking* involves imaginative, holistic, inventive and generative thinking. *Caring thinking* has various forms linking emotions to thinking including appreciative, active, normative and empathic thinking. In addition, the programme is proposed to develop five specified thinking skills and dispositions. These latter include: *inquiry skills*, such as observation, description, narration skills; *reasoning skills* such as inductive, deductive, analogical reasoning skills; *concept formation skills* such as those involved in definition, classification; *translation skills* involving comprehension, listening, writing skills; and *critical dispositions* including 'wondering', asking for reasons, judging with criteria, and questioning.

One approach to evaluating the success of the programme has been to undertake experimental research, with pre/post-test designs, using established tests of cognitive thinking skills as outcome measures by which to assess its impact. Trickey and Topping's (2004) systematic review of research adopting this approach suggests that much of the experimental research undertaken lacks methodological rigour, with very few studies including control groups and pre/post-test measures. They identified ten evaluative studies with controlled experimental designs indicating a range of positive measurable outcomes. These included advances in logical reasoning, reading comprehension, mathematics skills, self-esteem, listening skills and expressive language, creative thinking, cognitive ability and emotional intelligence (Lipman and Bierman 1970; Haas 1976; Education Testing Service 1978; Williams 1993; Dyfed County Council 1994;

Sasseville 1994; Fields 1995).

Topping and Trickey (2007) report their own more recent research where they found that the use of the *Thinking through Philosophy* programme (based on Lipman's *Philosophy for Children* programme but using more contemporary practical programme materials) led to advances in measured verbal ability and generalized to gains in non-verbal and quantitative reasoning ability. They followed two cohorts of 10-year-old children in four different schools and found that 12 months after participating in the programme the intervention group continued to produce higher scores in reasoning tests compared with control group children. This enhanced reasoning transferred across domains of intelligence and was largely irrespective of pupil, school and class, pre-intervention ability and gender (Topping and Trickey 2007: 283).

Controlled outcome studies provide a range of evidence suggesting children from different cultural backgrounds and of different ages can gain significantly in measurable terms both academically and socially. However, there has been criticism that there are inherent problems in this type of research including the need to ensure appropriate control groups, short- or long-term follow up and choice of reliable and valid measurement instruments. This latter problem has been a particular concern because of the programme's wide-ranging goals without any obvious evaluative instruments, supporting claims that it is not only unrealistic but, more controversially, inappropriate to employ this type of evaluative research (Fisher 1999; Burden and Nichols 2000; Topping and Trickey 2004).

Thinking with and through dialogue

An alternative to employing controlled outcome studies is to examine the process of teaching and the dialogue involved in the sessions. A number of researchers, including Lipman himself, have employed an analysis of the discourse in the sessions in addition to controlled outcome measures, and there is an increasing number of studies using this approach as the only, and most appropriate, form of research evaluating the programme. The importance of taking this approach is reflected in the manner in which Lipman draws on the work of both Vygotsky (1962, 1978) and more particularly Bakhtin (1981, 1986), to describe the characteristics of the dialogic process of the interaction. Lipman thus describes how in 'solidifying' the community through dialogical enquiry, articulating disagreements and the quest for understanding and joining together in co-operative reasoning, the overt cognitive behaviours of the community are internalized, quoting Vygotsky's (1962, 1978) proposal of the 'intrapsychical reproduction of the interpsychical' (Lipman 2003: 102). Bakhtin's (1981, 1986) proposals are similarly drawn on and they provide a more critical perspective on the fundamental role of dialogue in understanding meaning and the creation of meaning.

According to Bakhtin, the essential characteristic of dialogue is in the social interchange of ideas that prompt further questions as 'if an answer does not give rise to a new question from itself, it falls out of the dialogue' (Bakhtin 1986: 168). Bakhtin emphasized the dialogic nature of our thinking and way of knowing (epistemology), suggesting that individuals' beliefs and understanding are developed through the identification and internalization of the different 'voices' of others in the dialogue. As we identify and reflect on these voices as different positions in the dialogue, we modify these words and ideas in our own discourse or voice. By selectively assimilating the words of others in our utterances, we change and retell them as our own words. He proposes that there are a number of ways in which utterances can be positioned on a dialogic to monologic continuum, and can vary according to the extent to which they are multi-voiced and 'open to the other' to be taken up in this manner. Not all voices are, therefore, open to interpretation. Bakhtin proposes the 'authoritative voice' (or 'official monoligsm') remains outside the individual and is not changed or challenged, but transmitted in its original form. In contrast, however, the 'internally persuasive' voice is 'affirmed through assimilation and tightly woven with one's own word' (Bakhtin 1981: 344–5) and enters inside the individual to organize and prompt new questions, new meanings and understanding. Dialogic thinking is seen as an enriching experience in the manner in which each voice in the dialogue speaks in anticipation of the answering, and different, voice of the other, and does not depend on accepting the other's position or in reaching consensus.

Bakhtin's (1981, 1986) proposals on the dialogic nature of our thinking and way of knowing provide a powerful endorsement for the need to teach students how to engage in dialogues through which knowledge is continually being constructed, deconstructed and re-constructed by all participants. One of the implications of drawing on the theoretical stance of both Bakhtin and Vygotsky to develop the *Philosophy for Children* programme is that it emphasizes the importance of evaluating the success of the programme as a form of dialogic teaching through a much closer analysis of the nature of the exchanges of views that take place in the sessions, and the construction of knowledge that occurs. Before exploring some of the research that has taken this approach, however, it is relevant here to briefly examine Alexander's (2008) proposals on the characteristics of dialogic teaching.

Dialogic teaching

Dialogic teaching has been described in many different ways in this volume and in recent literature more generally. Alexander (2008: 28) proposes that dialogic teaching involves the following five principles:

- *Collective*: teachers and children address learning tasks together, whether as a group or as a class, rather than in isolation.
- *Reciprocal*: teachers and children listen to each other, share ideas and consider alternative viewpoints.
- *Supportive*: children articulate their ideas freely, without fear of embarrassment over 'wrong' answers; they help each other to reach common understandings.
- *Cumulative*: teachers and children build on their own and each other's ideas and chain them into coherent lines of thinking and enquiry.
- *Purposeful*: teachers plan and facilitate dialogic teaching with particular goals in view.

As Alexander (2008) indicates, there are many forms of dialogical teaching that encapsulate these characteristics, and he quotes examples such as Bruner's (1996) 'mutualist and dialectical pedagogy' and Lindfors (1999) 'dialogue of enquiry'.

Research undertaken on the practice of *Philosophy for Children* suggests the programme has similar characteristics in the development of a 'community of enquiry' concerned with the conduct and ethos of classroom talk (collective, reciprocal and supportive) with teachers' aims (purposeful) to encourage children to build on their own and each other's ideas and chain them into coherent lines of thinking and enquiry (cumulative). Alexander (2008) has suggested that the principles of dialogic teaching concerned with the conduct and ethos of classroom talk are relatively easy to achieve in setting out the ground rules for speaking and listening, while those principles concerned with the content and meaning of talk as opposed to its dynamics are more challenging. The principle of cumulation is identified as being the most difficult to achieve, drawing on a teacher's professional skill, subject knowledge and understanding of the capacities of each pupil to further develop their learning. In order to explore these problems in more detail, and to provide some assessment of *Philosophy for Children* as a dialogic teaching programme, the following review of research undertaken by Daniel and her colleagues (Daniel 2007, 2008; Daniel, Lafortune, Pallascio, Splitter, Slade and de la Garza 2005) and our own research (Delafield 1999, 2003; Delafield and Hardman 2004) focuses on a more detailed analysis of the content of children's learning and types of exchanges through which this is manifested, and the teacher's role in the dialogic process.

Philosophy for Children and the development of dialogical critical thinking

The recent series of studies undertaken by Daniel and her colleagues (Daniel 2007, 2008; Daniel *et al.* 2005) examined how Lipman's proposals for so-called multidimensional critical, creative and caring thinking are reflected in the dialogue, and suggest that the development of this type of thinking requires regular sessions over some considerable time. As part of this research, they explored the discourse over a school year as groups of 10–12-year-old children engaged in *Philosophy for Children Mathematics* (P4CM) sessions in Australia, Mexico and Quebec. Grounded Theory (Glaser and Strauss 1967) was employed to analyse the transcripts of the verbal exchanges among the pupils at the beginning, middle and end of the school year. This involved four stages of coding and analysis of the children's critical thinking as manifested in the discourse, rather than on more traditional definitions of the concepts involved.

The first stage of their analysis involved coding and defining the inherent cognitive skills displayed (logical, creative, responsible, and metacognitive). The second stage involved coding and defining the manner in which the four identified modes of thinking increased in complexity as the exchanges progressed, moving from anecdotal or monological toward critical dialogical (epistemological perspectives named as egocentricity, relativism and intersubjectivity). The third stage involved cross-tabulating the cognitive modes (logical, creative, responsible and metacognitive) and epistemological perspectives (egocentricity, relativism and intersubjectivity) to distinguish between content and form. Finally, the four cognitive modes and three epistemological perspectives were then incorporated into a matrix as an instrument for analysing each group's transcripts to enable a fuller understanding of the development of critical thinking processes.

Five types of exchanges emerged from the analysis (Daniel *et al.* 2005: 338–41):

1   *Anecdotal* – where pupils were unconcerned by peer points of view.
2   *Monological* – where discussion focused on the question selected, with brief answers addressed to the teacher and difficulties in justifying viewpoints.
3   *Non-critical dialogical* – a dialogical exchange in which children listened to each other and integrated differing views to enrich their understanding, but without any evaluation of viewpoints.
4   *Semi-critical dialogical* – a dialogical exchange that was almost, but not fully, critical where children formulated criticisms, which were more or less well justified but which were unsuccessful in terms of influencing the outcome at the end of the exchange.
5   *Critical dialogical* – a dialogical exchange characterized as a negotiation of viewpoints, a transaction among pupils, an open process in which the conclusions, when they are spoken, are open and temporary, serving as a hypothesis for future reflection.

From their analysis of the different types of exchanges, modes of thinking and epistemological perspectives, Daniel *et al.* (2005) developed a model of the learning process of dialogical critical thinking with two fundamental criteria, described as multimodality of thought and epistemological complexity. Multimodality of thought referred to the four thinking modes (logical, creative, responsible and metacognitive) and the way in which they appeared to be inherently linked. Thus, metacognitive thinking was only observed when pupil exchanges were dialogical, and dialogical exchanges became critical only when the participants adjusted or modified their viewpoints as they became aware of the distinctions between the different perspectives. Creative thinking appeared to be instrumental in prompting a transition from monological to dialogical exchange, and the more the dialogue reflected the criteria for critical status, the more creative thinking became. Similarly responsible thinking was only present in the most critical exchanges, reflecting a concern for the development of moral rules. Epistemological complexity, as the second fundamental criteria of dialogical critical thinking, was reflected in the way this thinking only occurred when the four thinking modes were observed with the capabilities associated with intersubjectivity (conceptualization, transformation, categorization and correction).

Daniel and her colleagues (Daniel *et al.* 2005) report a similar pattern to the development of pupils' ability to conduct the different types of exchanges over the school year, regardless of pupils' language and culture. At the beginning of the year, the predominant form of exchange was monological, with mainly concrete logical thinking and an egocentric epistemology. At mid-year, exchanges were dialogical but non-critical, with mainly relativism characteristics in the accumulation of many different points of view. At the end of the school year semi-critical dialogical exchanges were much in evidence in the four different thinking modes. Children demonstrated both acceptance and evaluation of differing points of view, with an epistemology described as 'wavering' between relativism and intersubjectivity.

The results of this study suggest that dialogical critical thinking only gradually develops over regular weekly *Philosophy for Children* sessions, ideally spread over two consecutive years. The transition from simple thinking to dialogical critical thinking, as well as the intersubjectivity within which this type of thinking is based, has to be learnt and practised over a considerable period of time. Daniel and her colleagues (Daniel *et al.* 2005) suggest their findings have implications for practice in terms of teachers' effectiveness in stimulating and modelling appropriate questions, being aware of the type of exchanges taking place and of the intended goal of developing dialogical critical thinking.

Magistral, Socratic and Menippean dialogue

The complex nature of *Philosophy for Children* has also been explored in our own research (Delafield 1999, 2003; Delafield and Hardman 2004) that examined ways in which the socio-cultural context is played out in its practice and its impact on dialogue. The research project followed four groups of children, aged 7–9 years, from two different inner-city primary schools in Northern England. One group of children had been participating in *Philosophy for Children* for two years, while the other group had been participating for one year. A total of eight *Philosophy for Children* sessions were observed and recorded over a 12-month period. Detailed analysis was undertaken of transcripts from these sessions, interviews with two of the teachers and a small group of children from one of the schools, together with programme and educational policy documents.

The research used Critical Discourse Analysis (Chouliaraki and Fairclough 1999) to explore how the socio-cultural context impacts on, and is reflected in, the classroom dialogue in the sessions. Critical Discourse Analysis involves the identification of different 'elements' in the socio-cultural context that are brought together as 'moments'. Harvey (1996) proposed that in any social process there are six 'elements', including: discourse/language; power; social relations; material practices; institutions/rituals; and beliefs/values/desires. Critical Discourse Analysis enables exploration of how the different elements of the social practice come together to make particular discourses visible. It is this visibility of the discourse that is considered a 'moment' of that discourse, which is made explicit in the analysis.

The reason for adopting Critical Discourse Analysis was that this approach allowed us to fully explore the complex, interrelated, multifaceted nature of the socio-cultural context of *Philosophy for Children* through analysis of the discourses relevant to each element of its practice. This recognition of the socio-cultural context was an important issue in the development of the model of classroom practice (the Di-Med model, Delafield 2003). In this model, each of these six elements are likened to the facets of a precious stone. Just as different facets of the stone combine to produce the finished jewel, the different elements involved in the production of a classroom session depict the practice as it is carried out in the classroom.

Critical Discourse Analysis was, therefore, employed to explore each of the six elements or 'facets' of the practice of *Philosophy for Children* sessions in terms of: the ground rules used and developed in the session (social relations); the aims of the programme (discourse/language); the pedagogic discourse (power); the institutional discourse (institutions/rituals); the views of the participants (beliefs/values/desires); and the materials used (material practices). For the purpose of this research a 'moment' was defined as a section of dialogue in which various elements of social practice came together, thus creating a synergy that led to a force coming into play that had the effect of shaping the social activity being investigated.

In this summary of the research findings, we first illustrate how the socio-cultural context played out in the practice of *Philosophy for Children* impacted on dialogue when we explored the pedagogic discourse as the facet (or element). For this analysis, we drew on Bakhtin's (1981, 1986) theoretical stance on dialogue as a community of different and often conflicting voices that is motivated, and is productive, to the extent to which such differences are identified and discussed rather than being resolved. In order to explore the power relationships within the pedagogic discourse, and more specifically the incorporation of the 'third voice' of authority, we employed Cheyne and Tarulli's (1999) identification and definitions of three dialogical positions or types of dialogue, referred to as Magistral, Socratic and Menippean.

Magistral dialogue is authoritative dialogue, referred to by Bakhtin (1981: 344–5) as the 'authoritative voice' or 'official monoligms' that is always asymmetrical in terms of power as the superior voice exercises control over the other inferior or novice second voice. Bakhtin refers to the way in which this asymmetry is created by the authoritative voice drawing on a third 'voice' in its reference to representations of 'truth' and claims to universal truth, factual truth, or institutional truth, such as a set of rules, sacred text, the school curriculum.

Socratic dialogue is typified by the symmetry of power between the participants in the dialogue. It is a questioning dialogue in which all participants are able to take part as equal partners. Socratic dialogue is suspicious of consensus and allows a questioning of authoritative representations of 'truth'. Socratic dialogue is defined as a questioning dialogue in which there is no guarantee of resolution or consensus, truths are provisional and always open to further questions. Socratic questioning is integral to this type of dialogue and provides the means to progressively engage higher levels of literal, critical, creative and conceptual thinking (Fisher 2007). Good Socratic questioning therefore engages these types of thinking, with literal (or factual) questions asking for information (e.g. 'What is this about?'), analytic questions calling for critical thinking (e.g. 'What reasons can you give?'), divergent questions calling for creative thinking (e.g. 'What other viewpoints could there be?') and conceptual questions calling for abstract thinking (e.g. 'What criteria are we using to judge this (or test if it is true)?') (Fisher 2007: 153).

Menippean dialogue is characterized as the dialogue of carnival and creativity, where things may not be as they seem, which questions and allows the possibility of rejecting all potential authorities. As such, it has a creative quality as a vehicle for the spontaneous play and experimentation of ideas, but it also has the possibility of representing complete relativism, where nothing is accepted as truth, and can lead to disorder and anarchy.

Cheyne and Tarulli (1999) propose each of these dialogical positions can be shown to demonstrate different power relationships within the learning process, referring to the way in which these dialogical positions have potential to typify different phases or transformations of the Zone of Proximal Development (ZPD) as the voices, particularly the second voice, are transformed. Their account reflects Bakhtin's (1981, 1986) view of dialogue and culture as being a set of guidelines ever open to re-interpretation and under re-negotiation. As such they offer a more critical stance on the generally somewhat 'cosy' view of adults supporting role in the ZPD, recognizing that all three genres can be both productive but also have the capacity to dominate, discourage and oppress. Their proposals prompt a more critical appraisal of how each may be effective in supporting children's learning, and their definition of Socratic dialogue allows for the possibility of adults engaging in this type of dialogue. Cheyne and Tarulli (1999) note that their definition of Socratic dialogue differs from many accounts of 'Socratic method' in that the 'other' in this type of dialogue is not conceived exclusively as an expert or more competent other. Dialogue is said to become Socratic to the extent that the child's voice asserts itself in unpredicted and challenging ways and the opportunity arises for the role of the tutor to be modified, requiring an openness not only to the child but also to otherwise previously unquestioned prejudices guiding Magistral dialogue.

The use of Cheyne and Tarulli's (1999) three dialogical positions in our analysis of the classroom talk suggests there is a complex interplay of all three forms of Magistral, Socratic and Menippean dialogue in *Philosophy for Children* sessions, which support the aims of the programme and indicate some of the problems that teachers have in its practice.

We found that teachers drew on the Magistral voice of authority to provide a stable framework from which to promote Socratic dialogue until the participants were able to follow its inherent principles without guidance. The teacher's use of Magistral dialogue was found to be most evident at the beginning of the sessions when they established their authority over how the session was to proceed and at the end when, in summing up, they were the authority on the quality of the ideas and questions tackled in the session. Magistral dialogue was also evident at other points in the sessions, when, for example, the teacher needed to gain control of the group, either in matters of behaviour or by being the authority on the relevance of a contribution, or when she stepped in to assert her authority to prompt a change of dialogue as, for example, in allowing and encouraging the use of Menippean dialogue as an aid to creativity. Similar results were found by Fisher (2007), who employed the same three types of dialogue to explore the characteristics of *Philosophy for Children* sessions.

Although this is not fully explored in this chapter, we found good examples of Menippean dialogue in the sessions encouraging creativity and experimentation in the interplay of ideas and questions. Used in this way, the dialogue enabled the children to explore new ideas in a non-threatening way, thus supporting Lipman's proposals on the importance of encouraging creative thinking as part of the trinity of criteria for multidimensional thinking. We also found less positive examples of where Menippean dialogue, with its association with a breakdown in authority, resulted in the children refusing to abide by the ground rules they had developed, leading to disruption of the session.

The following excerpts illustrate the use of Socratic dialogue in the sessions and also illustrate 'moments' within *Philosophy for Children* sessions where the teachers' aims of promoting Socratic dialogue are in one case successful, and in the other unsuccessful. The first is taken from a session with a class of 7–8-year-olds, led by the school's head teacher. The children were discussing how people sometimes answered without really listening to what was said. Jane had proposed that she had never not listened to what she was told, and both the teacher and Mary challenged this.

Excerpt 1: the importance of listening

JANE: cos erm sometimes like people like they don't listen and then they er come back with something that their mum didn't ask them to get

TEACHER: So do you think it's important to listen?

JANE: Yea

TEACHER: Mary

MARY: Well in one way it is important but would you lis, like, for example would you listen if someone were repeating things again and again and again?

TEACHER: Are you asking me or Jane?

MARY: Well Jane

JANE: Well if they was really [deriding] I'd run up the stairs and slam the door

(LAUGHTER)

JANE: What I would do, what I would do right, I would, I would, I would just make as much noise as I can to not hear them, like playing my playing my computer or something

TEACHER: Do you not think that's the same, it, is that not ignoring them?

MARY: Well you said you would never ignore them, didn't you?

JANE: Yea but I can still hear them cos I've tried it and I can still hear them

In this excerpt, Jane is seen to draw on her own experiences and views to give reasons for, clarify and justify her responses. The teacher and Mary both use Socratic dialogue to question and challenge Jane's proposals. Mary's questions appear to be a more direct challenge to Jane than the teacher's, perhaps, gentler response. It does appear as if they are all at this moment equal partners in the dialogue, with no one contribution having more weight than any other.

It was less usual to see the teachers offer their own ideas and reasons for them, though there were times when this did occur, as illustrated in the second excerpt below. This was in session with another group of 7–8-year-olds, led by their class teacher. They were discussing the story of a little girl called Augusta who did not like her name and preferred to be called Gus. The discussion had become focused on whether or not Gus was actually a different name from Augusta.

Excerpt 2: Augusta is a girl's name

MARY: Er no because er Augusta is like a girl's name. The picture you have in your mind is, if you just heard Gus, is a bit like a boy's name

TEACHER: So it sounds a little bit like a boy's name then, Gus, so the way she's the way she's changed her name, she's changed it from, I would say if I was asked to imagine what Augusta would look like, I'd be thinking of a little girl with pigtails and freckles with cute little frocks on but if I was asked what a little girl called Gus looked like I might be thinking of dungarees and climbing trees. Do you think names are important? I'm sorry Jenny I've just gone straight across you. Go on

JENNY: I can picture Gus, er just a normal girl like, er us

TEACHER: Like you or me?

JENNY: Like er a scruffy girl on a bike and Augusta is, I can imagine a girl, like posh in what she's wearing

In this excerpt, we see the teacher taking up Mary's point and expanding it. The indication that this is a moment of Socratic rather than Magistral dialogue comes from the remark 'I would say if I was asked to imagine', indicating that this is the teacher's own view, and also by the way she finishes her turn by inviting other comments ('I'm sorry Jenny I've just gone straight across you. Go on'). Jenny's response may point to one of the reasons that teachers do not use the reason-giving strategy as often as a challenging one. Jenny appears to accept the teacher's interpretation by suggesting that different pictures are conjured up by the names ('Like er a scruffy girl on a bike') and Augusta ('a girl like posh in what she's wearing'). However, the extent to which this is prompted by her acceptance that the teacher's expressed view is the 'right' interpretation (and, therefore, an instance of Magistral dialogue) is difficult to determine in this example. The teachers interviewed reported that this is a difficulty they have in the running of the sessions as their traditional role as the source of information in the classroom makes it difficult to make suggestions without stifling the flow of the children's ideas.

Our analysis illustrated how the institutional view of what it means to be a teacher or a pupil can act as the authoritative 'third voice' in Magistral dialogue and can make it difficult for a teacher to participate in Socratic dialogue. Our results suggest this is a difficulty inherent in the practice of *Philosophy for Children*, which needs to be acknowledged and addressed. The excerpt above indicates that the teacher can overcome this and successfully engage in Socratic dialogue, but that it can be difficult to interpret the reasons why children accept their suggestions.

The institutional roles of teacher and pupil clearly impacted on the dialogue, as we have indicated above, but our analysis was also revealing in the manner in which the school curriculum affected the sessions, as teachers attempted to encourage dialogue that could fulfil the aims of both the *Philosophy for Children* programme and the National Curriculum. Similarly the materials used to generate discussion were also shown to have an effect on the interaction. The lack of closure in the Lipman novels encouraged the children to develop and question their own ideas. However, in the sessions where the teacher employed other video and storybook material the emphasis tended to be more on reaching the right answer in terms of their comprehension of the story, rather than a creative activity involving philosophical questioning to enable children to progressively engage in higher levels of thinking.

In conclusion, our analysis of the pedagogic discourse clearly demonstrated that all three forms – Magistral, Socratic and Menippean dialogue – supported the educational experience and aims of *Philosophy for Children*, but also highlighted some of the problems teachers experience. More generally, the methodological approach adopted highlighted the importance of taking into account the socio-cultural context and range of factors, such as institutional practice, the curriculum and materials used, which clearly impact on the process of the sessions and reveal some of the inherent problems in developing this programme and other forms of dialogic teaching intervention.

Concluding comments

In this chapter, we have attempted to demonstrate how *Philosophy for Children* can be described as a dialogic teaching programme with highly specified theoretical underpinnings that define its structure and practice. The research reviewed provides evidence in support of Lipman's claims that children's participation in the programme encourages the development of critical, creative and caring thinking. Of more significance in relation to current debates discussed by contributors to this volume, we suggest that the highly specified characteristics of the *Philosophy for Children* programme should be seen as an exemplar of dialogic teaching (as defined and described by Alexander 2008) with wider implications for practice. Thus, Daniel and her colleagues (Daniel *et al.* 2005) demonstrate how the programme develops modes of thinking and epistemological perspectives through the different types of dialogical exchanges. The features characteristic of critical dialogical exchanges are similar to the form of dialogue described as 'Exploratory Talk' in research on children's collaborative learning (Mercer 1995; Mercer and Littleton 2007). Such Exploratory Talk 'typifies language that embodies certain principles, notably those of accountability, of clarity, of constructive criticism and receptiveness to well-argued proposals' (Mercer and Littleton 2007: 66) and is seen as a 'distinctive social mode of thinking' that is essential for successful participation in educated communities of discourse.

The proposed model of the learning process of dialogical critical thinking (Daniel *et al.* 2005) is helpful in more clearly encapsulating and defining the so-called trinity of criteria for multidimensional thinking in terms of critical, creative and caring thinking promoted by the *Philosophy for Children* programme. There are clear links here to recent proposals on teaching dialogical reasoning and the speaking and listening skills children need in order to learn from each other in the *Thinking Together* approach (Dawes *et al.* 2000) and in the *Talk for Learning* programme (Alexander 2008).

Our own research reported here takes up the points and implications for practice in its exploration of the dialogic nature of the *Philosophy for Children* sessions, the power relationships played out in the sessions and manner in which the various facets of the socio-cultural context of its practice impact on dialogue (Delafield 1999, 2003; Delafield and Hardman 2004). Our findings indicate that all three forms – Magistral, Socratic and Menippean dialogue – can be played out in the sessions. We found that Magistral dialogue can be used in a supportive manner to scaffold the interaction. There were good examples of stimulating Socratic and Mennipean dialogue, as well as examples of less engaging, unproductive dialogue in the sessions, confirming previous research on the effectiveness as well as the variability of practice. Our analysis also has implications for practice in revealing some of the ways in which the dialogue is affected by various features, or facets, inherent in the socio-cultural context. Thus, the institutional role of the teacher, the school curriculum, and materials used can be drawn on as the authoritative 'third voice' in the dialogue, and need to be considered in any evaluation of its use and success as a dialogic teaching programme.

References

Adey, P. and Shayer, M. (1994) *Really Raising Standards: cognitive intervention and academic achievement*, London: Routledge.

Alexander, R. (2008) *Towards Dialogic Teaching: rethinking classroom talk* (4th edn), Cambridge: Dialogos.

Bakhtin, M. M. (1981) *The Dialogic Imagination*, Austin: University of Texas Press.

Bakhtin, M. M. (1986) *Speech Genres and Other Late Essays*, Austin, TX: University of Texas Press.

Bruner, J. (1996) *The Culture of Education*, Cambridge, MA: Harvard University Press.

Burden, R. and Nichols, L. (2000) 'Evaluating the process of introducing a thinking skills programme into the secondary school curriculum', *Research Papers in Education*, 15:293–306.

Cheyne, J. A. and Tarulli, D. (1999) 'Dialogue, difference, and the 'third voice' in the zone of proximal development', *Theory and Psychology*, 9:5–28.

Chouliaraki, L. and Fairclough, N. (1999) *Discourses in Late Modernity: rethinking critical discourse analysis*, Edinburgh: Edinburgh University Press.

Daniel, M. F. (2007) 'Epistemological and educational presuppositions of P4C: from critical dialogue to dialogical critical thinking', *Gifted Education International*, 22:135–47.

Daniel, M. F. (2008) 'Learning to philosophize: positive impacts and conditions for implementation', *Thinking*, 18(4): 36–48.

Daniel, M. F., Lafortune, L., Pallascio, R., Splitter, L., Slade, C. and de la Garza, T. (2005) 'Modeling the development process of dialogical critical thinking in pupils aged 10–12 years', *Communication Education*, 54:334–54.

Dawes, L., Mercer, N. and Wegerif, R. (2000) *Thinking Together: a programme of activities for developing speaking, listening and thinking skills for children aged 8–11*, Birmingham: Imaginative Minds.

Delafield, B. (1999) 'Lessons: philosophy for children' in I. Parker and the Bolton Discourse Network (eds) *Critical Textwork: an introduction to varieties of discourse and analysis*, Buckingham: Open University Press.

Delafield, B. (2003) *An exploration of the socio-cultural aspects involved in the introduction of classroom innovation*, unpublished doctoral thesis, Bolton Institute of Higher Education.

Delafield, B. and Hardman, M. (2004) 'Philosophy for children: collaboration and discussion in the classroom', paper presented at the BPS Developmental Psychology Conference, Leeds, September.

Dyfed County Council (1994) *Improving Reading Standards in Primary Schools Project*, Wales: Dyfed County Council.

Education Testing Service (New Jersey) (1978): Pomtom Lakes and Newark 1976–78, cited in 'Appendix B', M. Lipman, A. M. Sharp and F. Oscanyon (1980) (eds) *Philosophy in the Classroom*, Philadelphia, PA: Temple University Press.

Feuerstein, R., Rand, Y., Hoffman, M. and Miller, M. (1980) *Instrumental Enrichment: an intervention programme for cognitive modifiability*, Baltimore, MD: University Park Press.

Fields, J. (1995) 'Empirical data research into the claims for using philosophy techniques with young children', *Early Child Development and Care*, 107:115–28.

Fisher, R. (1999) *Teaching Thinking: philosophical enquiry in the classroom*, London: Cassell.

Fisher, R. (2007) 'Dancing minds: the use of Socratic and Menippean dialogue in philosophical enquiry', *Gifted Education International*, 22:148–59.

Glaser, B. and Strauss, A. L. (1967) 'The discovery of grounded theory: strategies for qualitative research', *Thinking*, 7(4): 13–15.

Haas, H. (1976) *Philosophical Thinking in the Elementary Schools: an evaluation of the education program 'Philosophy for Children'*: unpublished mimeo., Institute of Cognitive Studies, cited in 'Appendix B: experimental research in philosophy for children', in M. Lipman, A. M. Sharp and F. Oscanyon (1980) (eds) *Philosophy in the Classroom*, Philadelphia, PA: Temple University Press.

Harvey, D. (1996) *Justice, Nature and the Geography of Difference*, Massachusetts: Blackwell.

Lindfors, J. W. (1999) *Children's Inquiry: using language to make sense of the world*, New York: Teachers College Press.

Lipman M. (1981) 'Philosophy for children', in A. L. Costa (ed.) *Developing Minds: programs for teaching thinking*, Alexandria, VA: Association for Supervision and Curriculum Development.

Lipman M. (2003) *Thinking in Education* (2nd edn), Cambridge and New York: Cambridge University Press.

Lipman, M. and Bierman, J. (1970), a research study cited in 'Appendix B', in M. Lipman, A. M. Sharp and F. Oscanyon (1980) (eds) *Philosophy in the Classroom*, Philadelphia, PA: Temple University Press.

Lipman, M. and Sharp, A. M. (1978) *Growing up with Philosophy*, Philadelphia, PA: Temple University Press.

Lipman, M., Sharp, A. M. and Oscanyon, F. (eds) (1980) *Philosophy in the Classroom*, Philadelphia, PA: Temple University Press.

Mercer, N. (1995) *The Guided Construction of Knowledge: talk among teachers and learners*, Clevedon: Multilingual Matters.

Mercer, N. and Littleton, K. (2007) *Dialogue and the Development of Children's Thinking: a sociocultural approach*, Abingdon: Routledge.

Sasseville, M. (1994) 'Self-esteem, logical skills and philosophy for children', *Thinking*, 11(2):30–7.

Topping, K. J. and Trickey S. (2007) 'Collaborative philosophical enquiry for school children: cognitive effects at 10–12 years', *British Journal of Educational Psychology*, 77:271–88.

Trickey, S. and Topping, K. J. (2004) 'Philosophy for children: a systematic review', *Research Papers in Education*, 19(3): 363–78.

Vygotsky, L. S. (1962) *Thought and Language*, Cambridge, MA: Harvard University Press.

Vygotsky, L. S. (1978) *Mind in Society*, Cambridge, MA: Harvard University Press.

Williams, S. (1993) *Evaluating the Effects of Philosophical Enquiry in a Secondary School*, Derbyshire: Derbyshire County Council.

Part III

Social context

Introduction

The preceding chapters have clarified the forms of dialogue that support classroom learning. Information has been provided about the features that characterize those forms, and about the processes through which benefits are obtained. However, any teacher who has tried to promote the forms during routine classroom activities will be aware of variation between pupils in how they react. Take for instance so-called 'dialogic teaching' within whole-class contexts espoused by many of the contributors to this volume. Substantial variation occurs over which pupils are willing to stand out from their peers and make contributions to whole-class discussions (and which prefer to remain silent in the 'audience'), and over whether contributors are prepared to limit their input to the 'pupil response' slot (as opposed to joining with the teacher in initiating and providing feedback). Take also exchange of views during collaborative exercises among small groups of pupils, a dialogic form that has already emerged as potentially helpful. Many teachers will recall observing instances where all group members expressed their opinions, listened respectfully while each pupil contributed in turn, and ensured that disagreements were dealt with constructively. On the other hand, many teachers will also be familiar with instances where a subset of group members dominated the interaction, concerned primarily that their own opinions prevail, and ignoring or belittling the 'opposition' when challenges occur.

Recognizing such variation, there has been a great deal of research, stretching back at least 40 years, into the factors that predict it. The research is rich and multifaceted, and any attempt at synthesis is fraught with hazards. Nevertheless, in our view, much of the work can be regarded as following either or both of two broad approaches. The first approach emphasizes the *social goals* that pupils pursue during classroom interaction. Terminology varies from study to study, but two goals emerge repeatedly: goals relating to the achievement of power and goals relating to the achievement of solidarity (see Brown and Levinson [1978] for an ambitious attempt to develop this approach, albeit not concerned with classrooms). Following the first approach, pupils who push their views upon others during collaborative group work would most likely be interpreted as valuing power above solidarity. Pupils who facilitate balanced turn-taking might be regarded as emphasizing solidarity. The second approach to variation in participation patterns highlights *social identity*, i.e. the social groups that pupils see themselves as belonging to within the classroom context, and/or that others assign them to. From the multiplicity of possible identities (ethnicity, social class, scholastic ability, etc.), the one that has attracted the lion's share of research is gender.

Social goals and social identity are inter-related. For instance, there is considerable evidence that boys are more likely than girls to pursue a power agenda, while girls are more likely than boys to value solidarity (see Howe 1997). Nevertheless, the two constructs are not interchangeable. Conventionally, the pursuit of power in males is interpreted rather differently from the pursuit of power in females, even when the dialogic forms are equivalent. The same applies to the pursuit of solidarity. Thus, there is an important job to be done in working out how goals and identity interact to shape pupil dialogue, from the perspective both of anticipating how pupils will vary in their response to new initiatives and, where appropriate, of adopting strategies that allow such variation to be pre-empted. This is one of many areas where the four chapters that comprise the present section make a contribution, for collectively they can be regarded as addressing goals, identity and the association between these. This is not to say that the chapters only address these issues. As will become clear, they are all much richer than this. Equally, it is not to claim that the chapters highlight goals and identity explicitly. As noted already, there are countless perspectives upon the social context of dialogue, and the chapters vary in how closely they approximate the specific perspective we have adopted. Nevertheless, in our opinion, it is appropriate to employ the goal versus identity distinction to introduce the material that follows.

As well as contrasting over their adherence to the goal versus identity dichotomy, the chapters also differ over their analytic frameworks. They are variously anthropological, linguistic, philosophical, psychological, and sociological, and they vary greatly over the emphasis that they place upon interpretative analysis as opposed to teaching intervention, theoretical constructs as opposed to empirical data, and (when empirical) qualitative as opposed to quantitative assessment. Implicitly (and occasionally, explicitly), the chapters support the complementary functions of qualitative and quantitative analysis. Given their diversity, it would be a mistake to suggest that the chapters provide a unified message. Nevertheless, whatever their differences, there can be no doubt that collectively they contribute to our understanding of educational dialogue at the theoretical, empirical, practical and methodological levels, while simultaneously highlighting a social dimension that needs be considered when promoting productive forms. Insofar as the chapters' emphasis is practical, they also offer words of warning: addressing the social dimension takes time, with both teachers and pupils needing to adjust. Yet no matter what the timescale, the message is upbeat: adjustment is achievable, and evidence is already available to indicate what it should involve.

Chapter 9 from Adam Lefstein begins the section and provides a bridge between the two preceding sections and the chapters to follow. This is because Lefstein's chapter starts by discussing the emphasis on questioning, answering and the exchange of views that epitomizes the models discussed so far. It might not be distorting Leftsein's views too greatly to suggest that he regards these models as 'idealizing the ideational'. In any event, Lefstein shows how such idealization can be located within an intellectual tradition that is traceable to Socrates, and he accepts that the tradition is robust and compelling. Nevertheless, one of his key points is that because the tradition downplays the social dimension, it does not merely overlook a significant factor, it also ignores a potential source of conflict and tension. This is because questioning, answering and exchanging presuppose plurality, equality, and openness, when the social goals that pupils pursue in classrooms can include dominance and self-promotion. Lefstein does not refer to the contrast between 'power' and 'solidarity' but his argument is tantamount to suggesting that the ideational tradition presupposes solidarity, when in reality the emphasis in classrooms is as much upon power. Indeed, the two dimensions are inextricably linked and are implicitly or explicitly negotiated in all communicative encounters. Turning to pedagogical implications, Lefstein criticizes teaching interventions (some discussed in the section that follows this one) that revolve around conversational ground rules, for these interventions can sometimes be accused of paying too much attention to the ideational component, or more accurately taking a metacommunicative perspective upon this component. Nevertheless, social goals could, in principle, be addressed within a ground-rules approach, through requiring pupils to develop and implement rules that acknowledge the social dimension.

Although there is no mention of ground rules nor of power and solidarity in Chapter 10 from Peter Kutnick and Jennifer Colwell, this chapter can be interpreted as an attempt to foster social climates that are conducive to questioning, answering and exchanging. Kutnick and Colwell start by reviewing research relating to four influential theoretical perspectives, which has led them to emphasize positive social relations as a prerequisite for productive educational dialogue. Kutnick and Colwell include trust, mutuality, connectedness, and openness within their conception of positive relations, constructs that seem to indicate high solidarity and low power differentiation when interpreted within the framework that we are adopting, i.e. the relational approach seems linkable with the social goals dimension of the two that we have highlighted. Having justified a relational approach with reference to the literature, Kutnick and Colwell outline three studies that exemplify its application in genuine educational contexts. The first study is a large-scale intervention in English primary schools, where children who experienced relational training made significant gains not just in social behaviour but also in mathematics and reading. The second study was conducted in secondary schools located on two Caribbean islands. Once more, the relational approach was associated with gains in pupil attainment, and this time the research also included measures of teacher attitude, which over time became increasingly supportive of communication skills and group work. The final study focused on English pre-school children, looking specifically at the effects of a relationally oriented intervention upon joint activity and patterns of communication. Again, results proved positive. As Kutnick and Colwell acknowledge, it would be premature to make strong claims about causation from their current results: their relational approach addresses many aspects of the educational context in addition to social relations. Nevertheless, the research described in Kutnick and Colwell's chapter provides a pioneering example of the approach that might be taken if pupil social goals are to be taken seriously in teaching practice.

With Patrick Leman's chapter (Chapter 11), the section shifts from being purely concerned with goals to also addressing social identity, specifically gender identity. Key issues are how gender identity influences the dynamics of pupils' interactions when working collaboratively with other pupils, and whether this influence extends to the learning and development that results from these interactions. Adopting a theoretical perspective that is largely social psychological, Leman amasses a broad range of evidence for gender effects upon communicative behaviour. This evidence includes Leman's own research, where pairs of children were recorded while they engaged in problem solving. Three styles of interaction were identified, with the styles proving to be aligned with gender composition. There was also an unmistakable hint of contrasting social goals. In particular, girl-girl pairs were relatively likely to adopt a collaborative style. Interaction within boy-boy pairs was typified by dominance and conflict, while within mixed pairs one child (often the boy) dominated the other child (often the girl), who was passively compliant. The implication is that boys typically attempt to dominate regardless of their conversational partner, but their attempts are more likely to prevail when the partner is female. On the other hand, girls' behaviour changes qualitatively as a function of their partner's gender, indicating that identity is interacting with goals in some fairly conscious process of adjustment. As regards the influence of such differences upon learning and development, Leman is suitably circumspect. Most research has been limited to describing gender differences in dialogue rather than charting their consequences. The few studies to have grappled with the issue often take a short-term perspective, and even then typically find limited evidence for an impact on outcome. On the other hand, to the extent that the learning process involves dialogue and patterns of dialogue differ, even equivalent outcomes are educationally significant, for they signify a need for sensitivity to a plurality of routes. The need for such sensitivity was of course a key theme across the chapters that comprised this book's first and second sections.

The focus of Kutnick and Colwell's and Leman's chapters is upon dialogue during collaborative work within small groups of pupils. With Chapter 12, contributed by Ben Rampton and Roxy Harris, the emphasis shifts to whole-class, teacher-led interaction, and inevitably to the IRF format. Using dialogues recorded in London secondary schools, Rampton and Harris argue that, although it remains possible to detect the format during classroom interaction, roles within the format have become more loosely defined in recent years. Nowadays, it is not uncommon for pupils to 'assist' with initiation, e.g. by anticipating and completing what their teacher was going to say, and such pupils are also far from reticent in providing evaluative feedback. Rampton and Harris suggest that relations between pupils and teachers have become increasingly informal, and it is this informality that underpins the patterns of dialogue. At the same time, the authors move beyond the exclusively interpersonal level, and argue that informality in classrooms is part and parcel of broader cultural changes. On the other hand, they do not suggest that cultural changes have resulted in all pupils engaging vociferously in initiation, response and evaluation. On the contrary, engagement is typically restricted to some boys. Other boys keep relatively quiet, and some girls are transparently disaffected. Moreover, gender differences in 'rules of engagement' are shown to be part of one teacher's explicit frame of reference: this teacher deliberately (and unsuccessfully) calls on the girls *as girls* to make contributions. Rampton and Harris's ethnographic approach is very different from the social psychological perspective that Leman adopts in his chapter. Nevertheless, in highlighting this teacher's behaviour, Rampton and Harris seem to be confirming the interplay between identity and goals for girls in particular, which as noted above, Leman also reports.

References

Brown, P. and Levinson, S. (1978) 'Universals in language use: politeness phenomena', in E. N. Goody (ed.) *Questions and Politeness*, Cambridge: Cambridge University Press.
Howe, C. J. (1997) *Gender and Classroom Interaction: a research review*, Edinburgh: Scottish Council for Research in Education.

Chapter 9

More helpful as problem than solution

Some implications of situating dialogue in classrooms

Adam Lefstein
Institute of Education, University of London

This volume is part of a broad convergence of interest in and enthusiasm for dialogue from across a variety of disciplinary and practical domains. The dialogic ideal is proposed as remedy for irrationality, false consciousness, multicultural strife, misunderstanding, civil society, and post-modern ethics. In education, dialogue is promoted as a means of improving teaching and learning (e.g. Alexander 2005; Nystrand, Gamoran, Kachur and Prendergast 1997), advancing democratic values and pupil voice (e.g. Fielding 2004, 2007), facilitating intercultural understanding (e.g. Delpit 1988), empowering the disenfranchised (e.g. Freire 1986), and cultivating thinking and argumentation (e.g. Fisher 2007; Osborne, Erduran and Simon 2004). Recent English policy endorses teaching through dialogue (e.g. DfES 2004; QCA 2005). In short, dialogue has come into fashion. Having crossed every other threshold, one is tempted to conclude, its entrance into our classrooms is merely a matter of time.

Yet, studies repeatedly find that the overwhelming majority of classroom interactions adhere to the infamous Initiation-Response-Evaluation (IRE) framework (Cazden 2001).[1] In this deeply ingrained pattern, teachers *initiate* discourse by lecturing or asking predominately predictable, closed questions, usually designed to test pupils' recall of previously transmitted knowledge and/or to discipline inattention. Pupils *respond* with one- or two-word answers. Teachers *evaluate* student responses, praising correct answers ('well done!') and censuring error ('you haven't been paying attention!'). Teachers dominate talk by controlling the topic and allocation of turns, by speaking more often than pupils and for longer periods of time and, indirectly, by privileging pupil contributions that are essentially a re-voicing of previous teacher utterances.

The persistence of non-dialogic teaching in the face of so much enthusiasm should give us pause: Why hasn't dialogue become a common form of classroom discourse? True believers round up the usual suspects: 'inept' teachers, an over-crowded curriculum, managerialism, the audit society, 'youth today'. While each of these explanations may account for part of the failure to make schools more dialogic, I am troubled by this general line of reasoning, in which theories of dialogue themselves remain largely unquestioned. In this chapter, I seek to shift the focus: rather than positing a dialogic ideal and decrying schools for not living up to that standard, I question prevailing common sense about educational dialogue against the background of current structures and cultures of schooling.[2] I argue that *idealistic* models of dialogue are ultimately inimical to formal educational practice, and outline the issues confronting a *situated* model of dialogue, sensitive to the tensions inherent in dialogic interaction and appropriate to contemporary school contexts.

This chapter is organized in two sections: the first is a critical review of the dialogic ideal, including connotations, constitutive image, core dimensions and inherent tensions. In particular, I highlight three central concerns in discussions of dialogue – metacommunicative, ideational and interpersonal – and explore the ways in which tensions between them are negotiated. In the second section I discuss the implications of situating dialogue in schools, especially in whole-class settings, which among other issues introduces into the discussion a fourth, aesthetic concern: how participation in dialogue often also involves performance for an audience.

The chapter's primary object is to explore thinking about educational dialogue and productive interaction in schools: what it should include and how it should be conducted. My argument can be summarized in the following three claims:

1   Both dialogue and teaching, as communicative activities, involve multiple dimensions, including the ideational, interpersonal, metacommunicative and aesthetic. Thinking about educational dialogue or productive interaction is incomplete without taking all four communicative dimensions into account.
2   Communication, including dialogue, involves tensions: between participants, between ideas, and between the concerns raised by each dimension. These tensions are inherent to dialogue, and therefore thinking about productive dialogue needs to accept and work with the tensions rather than ignoring them or wishing them away.
3   The institution of schooling constrains the ways in which dialogue can be conducted within its domain. Thinking about productive dialogue needs to accept and work with these constraints rather than ignoring them or wishing them away.

In terms of disciplinary perspectives, I focus primarily on philosophical approaches to dialogue, especially drawing on Burbules (1990, 1993, 2000) and Gadamer (1998); in the latter part of the chapter I also build on insights from the ethnography of communication. One aim of this eclectic review is to bring these philosophical and linguistic anthropological perspectives into contemporary discussions about educational dialogue, which are principally informed by socio-cultural psychology (especially Vygotsky), Bakhtin and comparative educational research (Alexander 2000).

The dialogic ideal

A plurality of theories of dialogue reflects the lengthy genealogy of the concept and the plurality of issues and contexts to which it has been and is applied (Burbules and Bruce 2001). Nevertheless, most theories share some core qualities and address similar concerns. In the following discussion I explicate those commonalities, and highlight the tensions between and within central approaches.

On the occasion of invoking 'dialogue'

Before discussing the content of the concept 'dialogue', it is useful to look at the contexts and manners in which it is commonly employed. I follow Bauman (2001: 1), who notes that 'words have meanings: some words, however, also have a "feel".' Like 'community', which is the focus of Bauman's study, 'dialogue' feels good. Even prior to agreeing about what it means – or perhaps *because* agreement has not yet been attempted – there is general consensus that 'dialogue' is beneficial, an ideal worth striving toward, and that it doesn't happen as often as it ought.

What goods are implied by 'dialogue'? What are the 'bads' that occasion its invocation? 'Dialogue' suggests plurality and equality in opposition to authoritarian voices that try to dominate all others; it suggests openness and thoughtfulness as antidotes for the combativeness and dogmatism that commonly characterize argument and debate; and it offers a path toward understanding in instances in which interlocutors have become deaf to one another's concerns.

These oppositions construct an *idealized* dialogue, which excludes the aforementioned 'bads' by ascribing them to 'monologism'. Gurevitch (2000: 246) criticizes this approach, which he finds prevalent in Bakhtinian theory:

> By insisting on dialogue as a remedy, it tends to oversimplify the instability and threat inherent in dialogue ... Even in the more competent, good willing and compatible encounter, the 'other side of dialogue' does not disappear. Illuminating only the blessed plurality and semioticity, [dialogue] leaves out of the picture of sociality the Other side, that of strain, tension and silence.

Having been purified of threats and tensions, idealized dialogue appears as a solution, equal to problems posed by any and all contexts. As such, it can serve as a powerful image with which to critique current practice. It is less useful, I argue below, as a guide for how to conduct that practice.

The Socratic legacy

The roots of the dialogic ideal can be traced back to the image of Socrates. Although there is little consensus about his method (and whether 'method' is an apt characterization), Socrates stands out as the archetypical dialogic instigator, participant and guide (see Burbules 1990; Haroutinian-Gordon 1989; Reich 1998; and Sichel 1998 for interpretations of the Socratic legacy). And what does Socrates do? He seeks out conversational partners and inquires into their ideas. He questions them at length, subjecting their ideas and commonly held doctrines to intense critical scrutiny. He is driven to dialogue by passion for knowledge coupled with awareness of his own ignorance. He does not always infect his interlocutors with that passion, but he invariably provokes thinking.

In the following passage, from Plato's *Gorgias,* Socrates reflects on 'the sort of person' he is, and on the sort of discussion he prefers to engage in. Prior to this passage Socrates has been questioning Gorgias about the nature of rhetoric, and takes a break in his examination in order to check with Gorgias whether to continue the conversation:

You, Gorgias, like me, have much experience in arguments, and have undoubtedly noticed that they don't always end well. Disagreements arise, each accuses the other of misrepresentations, passions erupt, they begin to quarrel.

Both sides think that the other is guided by personal animosity rather than interest in the actual question in dispute. And sometimes they abuse one another such that everyone present regrets having been privy to the discussion.

Why do I mention this? Because I cannot help feeling that what you just said is inconsistent with your initial statements about rhetoric. But I'm afraid to point this out, lest you think that I harbour ill will toward you, and that I am motivated by jealousy rather than pursuit of truth.

Now, if you are the sort of person I am, I would like to cross-examine you. But if not I prefer to let the matter rest. And what sort of person am I? I am ready to be refuted if I say something untrue, and ready to refute anyone else who speaks wrongly. But I prefer to be refuted than to refute, for I believe that the former poses the greater benefit, since it is better to be cured of an evil than to cure another. And I imagine that there is no greater evil than to be mistaken in the matters about which we speak.

So if you claim to be like me, let us continue the discussion. But if you would rather be done, no matter – let's stop here.

(Plato 1924: §457–8)[3]

In this passage Socrates addresses the three concerns central to the various treatments of dialogue I discuss below. First, the immediate, explicit topic of Socrates' intervention is *metacommunicative*: he directs attention to the nature of the conversation itself, questioning whether – and, implicitly, how – the discussion should continue. Second, he highlights the *interpersonal* dimension, recalling some of the ways in which interpersonal animosity can obstruct or derail dialogue's progress.[4] Third, the impetus for his intervention is *ideational*: he wishes to examine further what he perceives to be a contradiction in Gorgias' ideas. In what follows I review the different ways theories of dialogue attend to these three dimensions – the metacommunicative, interpersonal and ideational – and the relationships between them.

The metacommunicative dimension: dialogue as interactional structure

At first glance the question of whether an activity should be considered 'dialogue' appears to be a question of discourse patterns and associated norms. In this 'formal' or 'structural' orientation, a few people discussing an idea through questions, answers and the exchange of ideas would appear to be dialogue, while two people shouting insults at one another, or a teacher lecturing a group of docile pupils, or a candidate in a job interview being grilled by a panel, or a group of people meditating in silence would likely not count as dialogue.

I implicitly invoked such a formal approach in the beginning of this chapter when I claimed that current classroom discourse tends to be non-dialogic because it is structured according to the Initiation-Response-Evaluation (IRE) pattern. IRE contradicts some key expectations for dialogue: for example, that discursive rights and responsibilities be equitably distributed, or that questions lead to genuine inquiry into the topic at hand (rather than examination of pupil knowledge and attention). Many dialogic models specifically use the presence or absence of these and related features as a way of gauging relative dialogicality. For example, Nystrand and colleagues (1997) measured discourse data in terms of questions' sources (teacher or student), authenticity, response and cognitive demand, and the extent to which teachers engaged in 'uptake' and evaluation of student responses. Similarly, Alexander's (2003: 37) indicators of 'dialogic teaching' include numerous structural features (alongside other dimensions), for example:

- questions are structured so as to provoke thoughtful answers, and – no less important –
- answers provoke further questions and are seen as the building blocks of dialogue rather than its terminal point;
- individual teacher-pupil and pupil-pupil exchanges are chained into coherent lines of enquiry rather than left stranded and disconnected.

Dialogic measures and indicators can be readily converted into communicative procedures or rules to guide participants in the normative conduct of dialogue. For example, Mercer and colleagues have demonstrated the efficacy of creating metacommunicative ground rules, and their explicit modelling and instruction by teachers, for promoting 'Exploratory Talk' among pupils (e.g. Mercer and Littleton 2007). While these ground rules are developed collaboratively with pupils, others employ a more top-down approach. So, for example, a recent DfES (2003: 22) *Handbook* directs teachers' behaviour by a list of *Dos* (e.g. 'expect children to speak for all to hear' and 'vary your responses to what children say … in order to extend the dialogue') and *Don'ts* ('routinely repeat or reformulate what children have said' and 'just ask questions').

In a more philosophical treatment of dialogic norms, Burbules (1993: 80–2) posits three rules: participation ('engagement … must be voluntary and open to active involvement by any of its participants'), commitment ('engagement … must allow the flow of conversation to be persistent and extensive across a range of shared concerns …') and reciprocity ('engagement … must be undertaken in a spirit of mutual respect and concern … what we expect of others we must expect of ourselves').

Focusing on external forms, procedures or rules may be problematic inasmuch as it overlooks those elements of the dialogic *spirit* that discourse patterns are assumed to reflect: the substance of the talk, the conversational context, and, perhaps most importantly, participants' motivations and dispositions. Thus, in a review of theory and research on teaching as dialogue Burbules and Bruce (2001: 1110) call for going

> beyond the idea that dialogue can be simply characterized as a particular pattern of question and answer among two or more people. Many instances of pedagogical communicative relations that might have this external form are not dialogical in spirit or involvement, while interactions that may not have this particular form can be.

Burbules and Bruce's emphasis on dialogue's internal spirit is consistent with their categorization of dialogue as primarily a *relation* (see also Burbules 1993). While I agree that the tendency to reduce dialogue to patterns or procedures is too simplistic, it is problematic to view discourse patterns only as an external manifestation of relations. Indeed, there is an implicit tension in interaction between an emphasis on structures and rules on the one hand, and attention to relationships on the other. This tension becomes apparent, for example, when one tries to invoke a rule in an intimate relation, or to develop a friendship in a highly bureaucratic environment. A corollary: the more fragile the relationships between partners in dialogue, the more important rules and procedures become.

The ideational dimension: dialogue as cognitive activity

Educationalists have been attracted to dialogue as a means of improving cognition, developing understanding and learning (e.g. Hicks 1996; Mercer 2000; Nystrand *et al.* 1997; Wells 1999). There are many ways to interpret this process. In the *Theaetetus* Plato uses the metaphor of midwifery: Socrates recognizes when his interlocutor is pregnant with thought; instigates, intensifies and allays the pains of labour; and thereby delivers ideas. The 'highest point of [Socrates'] art is the power to prove by every test whether the offspring of a young man's thought is a false phantom, or instinct with life and truth' (Plato 1957). In this final sense, dialogue is a method for testing hypotheses – a thinking laboratory for conjectures and refutations.

The significance of dialogue as a means of learning lies not only in the quality of its offspring, but also in the very participation in the process. If, as Vygotsky (1978) claims, 'all the higher [cognitive] functions originate as actual relations between human individuals', then participation in high quality interpersonal dialogue is expected to lead to the development of high quality cognitive abilities. Higher order, critical thinking is internalized dialogue.[5]

In this socio-cultural psychological approach, as I have (simplistically) outlined it, dialogue is valued primarily for its potential role in the development of cognitive abilities and acquisition of conceptual tools (reflecting Vygotsky's psychological interest). But there is another way in which dialogue underlies learning: not only appropriation of the tools of thought, but also formation of the product, knowledge. Inasmuch as understanding happens – including self-understanding – it occurs in a process of dialogue with Others (including texts). Gadamer (1998) employs the metaphor of *fusion of horizons* to illuminate this process. According to Gadamer, each interlocutor brings to dialogue their own unique perspective, or *horizon* of assumptions, prejudices, expectations and ideas. Participants can only 'see' what is on their horizon – i.e. participants' prejudices limit their thinking and understanding. But the horizon is also enabling; without it, thinking and understanding would be impossible. Another person's unique horizon has the potential to reflect back to me my own prejudices, and thereby to help me become more conscious of the boundedness of my own understanding.

Dialogue entails a back-and-forth movement, between my own and the Other's horizons. I am distanced in dialogue from my own prejudices, suspending them in order to engage with the Other. But if prejudices remain forever suspended, then one might be described as 'politely listening', but not truly *engaged*. Engagement implies returning to my prejudices, using the Other's perspective as leverage for self-understanding and, ultimately, revision of my own horizon. Thus, dialogue necessitates maintaining the tension between two forms of openness, to the Other and to oneself. This tension can be characterized as a tension between speaking (or, asserting one's own horizon) and listening (suspending one's own prejudice in order to be addressed by the Other's horizon).

At the end of a key paragraph describing the fusion of horizons, Gadamer emphasizes that horizons only '*supposedly* [exist] *by themselves*' (1998: 306, emphasis in original). In a sense, they are actually tips of a collective iceberg called tradition. Because our horizons have been nurtured by a shared culture, each meeting with the Other might be better described as a 'deepening' (in the sense of getting to the roots of tradition or base of the iceberg) than as a 'broadening'. Either way, what's important for my purpose is to note that dialogic activity also by definition implies understanding of and participation in cultural tradition.

Viewed in this way, dialogue is not about method or form of interaction, but is most fundamentally an epistemological position. Freire repeatedly emphasizes this theme in clarifications of his pedagogy (e.g. Freire and Macedo 1995; Shor and Freire 1987). According to Freire, dialogue is not a better technique for the effective transmission of positive knowledge determined prior to and outside of the learning encounter; rather, knowledge – at least knowledge of society, culture and self – is itself formed in the dialogic process.

Being conscious of and accepting this epistemology leads to *humility* – recognizing one's own ignorance, the inherent limitations of one's own knowledge – and *openness* to the Other. Consider two extremes, both of which reflect an essential closedness of mind: 1) I assume that relative to me the Other is an all-knowing authority on the matter under consideration, and do not speak, only listen; and 2) I assume a position of authority, believing that relative to me the Other is utterly ignorant, and only speak, do not listen. Dialogic openness happens between these two extremes: I assume that both my partner's and my own horizons are necessary for greater understanding. (Complete understanding is impossible, so openness always seeks more partners and more varieties of difference.)

The epistemological stance underlying dialogue guides participants' general orientation toward the content of the conversation – a subversive, questioning orientation. Indeed, perhaps one of the reasons the IRE cycle is so repugnant to educational sensibilities is that teachers' initiations – although often linguistically adhering to the form of questions – are antithetical to questioning as a cognitive activity. A genuine question is one that *problematizes*, i.e. that transforms commonly accepted facts or answers into problems to be explored, thereby opening knowledge up to thinking. Since 'the significance of questioning consists in revealing the questionability of what is questioned' (Gadamer 1998: 363), an emphatic yet controversial statement or subversive narrative can have a more powerful questioning effect than a series of predictable utterances capped with question marks (see also Dillon 1988).

Interlocutors oriented toward the questionability of the subject matter tend to gravitate toward controversy and difference, to problematize seemingly straightforward topics and to be sceptically disposed toward their own and others' ideas. Their nemesis is unthinking conformity to the majority opinion.

> Plato shows in an unforgettable way where the difficulty lies in knowing what one
> does not know. It is the power of opinion against which it is so hard to obtain an

admission of ignorance. *It is opinion that suppresses questions.* Opinion has a curious tendency to propagate itself. It would always like to be the general opinion, just as the word that the Greeks have for opinion, doxa, also means the decision made by the majority in the council assembly.

(Gadamer 1998: 366, emphasis added)

This critical, subversive attitude to dominant ideologies, which contributed to Socrates' demise in Athens, accounts for part of the appeal of dialogue to Freire and fellow critical pedagogues.

Questioning is being open, not only to the possibility that my own or the general opinions are wrong, but also to the possibility that they may be right. For this reason, Gadamer calls questioning an 'art of strengthening' (1998: 367). There is a basic tension inherent in this orientation, between sceptical questioning that strives to refute an idea, and supportive questioning that strives to understand and strengthen an idea, or to use Ricoeur's (1970) terms, between a hermeneutics of faith and a hermeneutics of suspicion. A related tension is between convergent and divergent forces in dialogue: on the one hand, dialogue is forever aimed at creating agreement between interlocutors; on the other hand its continuation is dependent on the persistence of difference.

In concluding this discussion of the ideational dimension, I should briefly draw attention to differences between the largely Gadamerian approach outlined above and many currently influential models of dialogue (e.g. Alexander 2005; Mercer 2000; Wells 1999). In these latter models, the dominant image of pedagogic interaction is one of co-operative inquiry, in which participants build on one another's ideas in a generally harmonious process of constructing shared knowledge and understanding. While such processes clearly have a place in educational dialogue, the preceding discussion highlights the potential benefits of dialogue that starts from difference and proceeds through critical argument to competing understandings and further inquiry.[6]

So, for example, in Alexander's (2005) model dialogic content is defined as *purposeful*, i.e. guided by educational goals, and *cumulative* in the sense that participants respond to and build upon one another's ideas. In light of the above discussion of dialogue as fusion of horizons, epistemological stance and questionability, two further criteria might be added:

- *critical*: participants identify and investigate open questions and points of contention within the group; and
- *meaningful*: participants relate the topic of discussion to their own horizons of meaning, and bring those horizons to bear upon one another (and the curricular content) in developing new understandings.

The interpersonal dimension: dialogue as relation

My discussion until this point has tended to treat dialogue as a meeting of *minds*, without body, emotion or extra-intellectual interests. But ignoring these non-cognitive aspects of human interaction leads to an incomplete and even distorted view of dialogue. Burbules points out that the 'cognitive interest is not all that attracts us to the dialogical encounter, or keeps us in it when it becomes difficult or contentious'. This is one of the reasons that, for Burbules, dialogue is chiefly a relation, which thrives on emotions such as 'concern, trust, respect, appreciation, affection, and hope – [which] are crucial to the bond that sustains a dialogical relation over time' (Burbules 1993: 41). These emotions are of course closely related to the cognitive openness described above: one is more inclined to respect and appreciate someone from whom one learns and with whom one engages in productive dialogue.

The importance of emotional relations in dialogue lies in the latter's unpleasant or dangerous 'other side' noted by Gurevitch (2000). Openness to the other implies a threat to one's own identity. Our ideas are invested with emotional energies: extending the midwife metaphor, we become attached to the ideas we have conceived as parents love their children. Few are as Socrates and happy to have them refuted. Most, contrary to the view espoused by Socrates above, prefer winning to losing an argument. Partly for this reason, discourse is rarely the co-operative, orderly and attentive affair commonly evoked by the word 'dialogue'. Indeed, attention to emotional and relational factors is important specifically because dialogue is also implicated with competition, argument, struggle to be heard, persuasion, 'ego' and – like other social arenas – power relations.

The concern with power relations is central to criticisms of dialogue. Habermas, for instance, criticizes Gadamer's hermeneutic model of understanding as lacking the vantage point from which one can come to terms with power and ideology, which systematically distort communication. He quotes Wellmer (1971) in this regard: 'The Enlightenment knew what a philosophical hermeneutic forgets – that the "dialogue" which we, according to Gadamer, "are," is also a context of domination and as such precisely no dialogue …' (Habermas 1990: 266).

Paradoxically, a similar concern motivates Freire's use of dialogue. He decries so-called 'revolutionaries' who would use 'banking methods of domination (propaganda, slogans – deposits) in the name of liberation' (1986: 66). For Freire the only way to truly enable the oppressed to liberate themselves from domination is to engage with them in dialogue. Because dialogue is fundamentally respectful of the Other's humanity – including experience, intellect and freedom – it is potentially empowering.

However, critical pedagogy's recourse to dialogue can also be experienced as repressive. 'Why doesn't this feel empowering?' asks Ellsworth (1989) in the title of an essay that draws attention to the way in which the call to dialogue is also an exercise of power, with its accompanying assumptions and expectations regarding teacher authority, communication norms, legitimate forms of participation, and privileged differences and identities. Discussion of uneven power relations leads to fundamental questions about the very possibility of dialogue at this particular historical moment.

At one point Ellsworth suggests that 'the only acceptable motivation for following Others into their worlds is friendship' (Ellsworth 1989: 317, in reference to Lugones and Spelman 1983). This principle coincides with Noddings' (1994) concerns in advancing what she calls 'ordinary conversation' as an important yet neglected form of educational discourse:

> Perhaps most significantly of all, in ordinary conversation, we are aware that our partners in conversation are more important than the topic. Participants are not trying to win a debate; they are not in a contest with an opponent. They are

conversing because they like each other and want to be together. The moment is precious in itself.

(Noddings 1994: 115)

This tension, between care for the participants and concern for the topic, is especially acute in situations in which consensus seems beyond reach. At some point in such conversations, if participants are committed to one another in a dialogic relation, they 'almost say to each other: "Let us change the topic. We all know what we all know. We have our disagreements, but let us have a small talk as a token of our mutual understanding beyond the subjects that divide us"' (Sidorkin 1999: 76). The tension between care for participants and topic is paralleled by a tension between gravity and levity in conversational tone. Sidorkin, drawing on Bakhtin, juxtaposes the light and 'nurturing atmosphere of a carnival, where all things seem to be possible and all becomes laughable' to the gravity, discipline and high stakes of formal discussion or debate (cf. Wegerif 2005, on 'playful talk').

However, there is no escaping the issue of power: while carnival levity may alleviate the oppressiveness of argumentative, truth-seeking discourse for some, it can become repressive for others. Similarly, regarding conversational partners as more important than the topic is problematic in cases in which care for the other obliges us to disagree (for example, when we believe that their position will harm them), or when the topic is inextricable from interlocutors' identities (for example, in a discussion of 'Britishness' among a culturally diverse group). Indeed, Callan (1995) argues that dialogue about issues of serious moral consequences necessarily involves such complications, since our moral commitments are constitutive of our selves and at the heart of our care for others.

The back-and-forth movement of this discussion, between the various approaches to power in dialogue, suggests its conclusion: power relations are implicated in all human intercourse, and attempts to dismiss them from dialogue serve some interests while harming others, and are therefore ultimately self-defeating. Burbules and Bruce (2001:1117) therefore include reflexivity as an integral part of their definition of dialogue:

> the element of reflexivity puts within the concept of dialogue the possibility of renegotiating, as part of an ongoing dialogical engagement, questions of inclusiveness, linguistic difference, bias, domination, and so forth. None of this guarantees the success of such attempts to identify, critique, and renegotiate those limits; but one need not necessarily step outside of the dialogical relation in order to challenge them.

Reflexivity, or dialogue about dialogue, returns us of course to the metacommunicative dimension.

Dialogic tensions

Throughout the preceding discussion I highlighted principal points of contention between different approaches to dialogue, and argued that these differences reflect fundamental tensions inherent in any robust conception of dialogue for education. Some of these tensions are basic to human sociality – e.g. between self and other, between speaking and listening – while others are more specific to epistemology – e.g. hermeneutics of faith versus suspicion. Metacommunicative and interpersonal concerns are in tension (i.e. rules versus relationships), as are interpersonal and ideational concerns (i.e. care for participants versus pursuit of truth, levity versus gravity).

How should participants in dialogue navigate these tensions? How should those who would design, facilitate or direct dialogue (e.g. as teaching activity) address the tensions?

Most current interest in educational dialogue is focused on the ideational dimension, i.e. on dialogue's potential utility to improve learning and cognition. But, unfortunately, as Socrates pointed out to Gorgias, interpersonal issues often interfere with the free exchange of ideas, and passions can cloud thinking. So, a common strategy among dialogue advocates is to design metacommunicative rules that neutralize or at least minimize interpersonal conflict, thereby keeping the passions in check.

In assessing such a strategy – and in theorizing the relationships between metacommunicative, interpersonal and ideational concerns – Scollon's (1998) research on the structuring of (business telephone) conversations may be helpful. Scollon (1998: 19, 78) argues that conversational participants are guided by the following 'maxims of stance':

1 Attend to the definition of the situation (including the channel).
2 When the channel is established, attend to the relationships and identities.
3 When identities are established, attend to topics.

These maxims construct a hierarchy of concerns in dialogue, according to which the ideational can be successfully addressed only after participants attend to metacommunicative and interpersonal issues. If Scollon is correct, then assisting participants, for example, to develop ground rules makes sense as a way of clearing out a space to attend to relationships and topics. However, such a move still poses problems. First, metacommunicative rules do not resolve or make less relevant interpersonal issues, rather they structure the field in which participants negotiate these issues and provide participants with resources for use in ongoing interpersonal struggles (cf. Swann 2007). Moreover, the distribution of these resources may be unequal, as ground rules legitimate some pupils' communicative repertoires and styles while sanctioning (and thereby alienating) others (cf. Lambirth 2006).[7] Second, while analytically it may be possible to separate interpersonal and ideational concerns, for participants these issues are almost always interwoven; interlocutors communicate their feelings, negotiate their social positions, exercise and resist power, define the communicative situation and entertain themselves and others at the same time that they contribute ideas to the academic discussion (cf. Wortham 2006). Finally, even if it were possible to wish away participants' interpersonal concerns, it would not necessarily be for the better: dialogue's social dimension may at times interfere with the exchange of ideas, but it is also very often that which drives participants' engagement.

Acknowledging that dialogic tensions cannot be resolved marks a significant shift away from idealistic thinking about dialogue. Rather than viewing dialogue as an ideal that we should aim to achieve – as a pre-determined solution – I argue that dialogue should be viewed as a problem – riddled with tensions – with which we are constantly confronted. Navigating these tensions is usually not a matter of choosing between dialogue or monologue, but between competing dialogic concerns. Moreover, while a (dialogic) move may encourage, empower and foster growth for some participants, it may also silence and alienate others. Educators and researchers need to be cognizant of and sensitive to such tradeoffs: as Alexander (2004: 25) argues, problems encountered in teaching dialogue should be thought of as 'dilemmas, not deficits'.

Situating dialogue in classrooms

At the beginning of this chapter I noted that classroom discourse is dominated by the non-dialogic IRE pattern, and questioned why the many attempts to 'dialogicize' pedagogy have been so inconsequential in practice. Burbules (1993) concludes his penetrating *Dialogue in Teaching: theory and practice* with consideration of this question. After touching on problematic aspects of communication in the larger society, Burbules focuses attention on 'the antidialogical school', including structural conditions that make 'dialogue on any general scale ... simply impracticable' (Burbules 1993: 161–2). Among the impediments he lists are pressures to cover curriculum, time constraints, standardized testing, over-crowded classrooms, the valuation of control and discipline, and teacher authority and privileges. Burbules concludes,

> Indeed, it appears that if we were designing institutions from scratch with a primary goal of *guaranteeing* that there would be few incentives to pursue dialogue and even fewer opportunities to do so, we could not do much better than the typical public school.
>
> (Burbules 1993: 162, emphasis in original)

While I do not want to ignore those problematic aspects of school structure that could and should be changed (and not only because they inhibit dialogue), the net effect of this way of thinking could be termed the *anti-school theory of dialogue*. Instead of adapting their ideas to existing structures of schooling, idealists theorize about dialogue in such a way that its application in school becomes an impossibility, something to dream about doing after the abolition of schooling as we know it. Not only is such an idealistic approach to school dialogue unhelpful, Ehlich (1985: 408) notes that it may be damaging to teachers 'who perceive their own *institution-adequate* actions as subjective *failures*' (emphasis in original).

In contrast, I propose to 'pedagogize' dialogue, that is, to work toward developing models of dialogue that are appropriate to contemporary school contexts. Such work needs to be carried out with teachers and pupils in classrooms and, indeed, many of the chapters in this book reflect such efforts. Julia Snell and I have recently begun collaborating with teachers in one London primary school in an attempt to work through some of the issues discussed here and the challenges of changing classroom interaction more generally.[8] It is beyond the scope of this chapter (and the current stage of our work) to present an elaborated situated model for classroom dialogue. Instead, I briefly discuss here some of the problems that such models need to address. Schools differ, of course, and while I expect that my comments here will pertain to most formal educational settings, I should note that as I write I have in mind the sites of my recent and current research: Key Stage 2 Literacy lessons in southern English primary schools.

What are the implications of situating dialogue in classrooms? In what follows I explore three issues: class size, curricular content and institutional roles. Each of these issues further complicates the multidimensional conceptualization of dialogue that I developed in the preceding section. The discussion of teacher role serves to pull the entire chapter together, as competing dialogic concerns are translated into competing functions the teacher is called upon to perform.

Implications of large class size: dialogue and audience

An obvious difference between idealistic accounts of dialogue and actual classroom encounters is that the former are much less populated than the latter. This disparity is especially striking in scholarly articles that report on 'classroom' dialogues between the teacher and two or three participants or in instructional demonstration videos. Where are the other 30+ pupils? What's happening out of frame? Granted, it is possible to organize classroom situations in which pupils converse in pairs or small groups; and, indeed, these situations do afford dialogic possibilities and should be exploited. However, current UK policy emphasizes 'whole class interactive teaching', which poses a greater challenge to dialogue, and elements that are central to it are also relevant (though less obviously so) in smaller group conditions.

What are the ramifications of the whole-class situation, with 30–40 'participants', for engagement in dialogue? First, not everyone can contribute actively and meaning-fully to a particular discussion. Thus, it is reasonable to expect that only a portion of a large group will be intensely involved as speakers at any one time, while the majority participate as audience. Contrary to the common expectation that teachers involve as many pupils as possible in every discussion, it may make more sense to focus dialogue on three or four pupils – provided, of course, that the same three or four pupils do not dominate every discussion.

Second, this division of participants into interlocutors and audience entails a rethink-ing of the communicative situation, including the introduction of a fourth, aesthetic dimension alongside the metacommunicative, interpersonal and ideational dimen-sions discussed above. The terms 'participants' and 'interlocutors', which I have been using up until now, are insufficient to capture the complexity of a classroom of pupils with different levels of involvement and diverse interests. Speakers do not direct their utterances only toward their direct addressees' interests and horizons, they also must take account of an audience of side-participants, targets, eavesdroppers and bystanders (Goffman 1981). When thinking about dialogue in the classroom, we must replace the image of two or three conversants, leaning toward one another in intimate conversa-tion, with that of a performance:

> Performance in its artful sense may be seen as a specially marked way of speaking, one that sets up or represents a special interpretive frame within which the act of speaking is to be understood. In this sense of performance, the act of speaking is put on display, objectified, lifted out to a degree from its contextual surroundings, and

opened up to scrutiny by an audience. Performance makes one communicatively accountable; it assigns to an audience the responsibility of evaluating the relative skill and effectiveness of the performer's accomplishment.

(Bauman and Sherzer 1989: xix)[9]

For a performance to succeed, it must not only be satisfying and edifying for the directly involved conversants, it also needs to be aesthetically pleasing and/or intellectually meaningful for the audience.

For pupils to successfully participate in performances on the classroom stage, they must vie for the floor, be attentive to their various audiences and direct their speech in such a way that it will be appropriate for all concerned. Moves that work well in an intimate, relatively audience-free situation become problematic in a performance dialogue – for example, posing a question can lead to losing the floor.[10]

This performance view complicates the idea of dialogue as a fusion of horizons. Not only does it raise the question of whose horizons are involved, it also draws attention to the fact that dialogues occur in rhetorical situations, in which interlocutors adapt their speech to their audience(s). Thus, the distinction between speaking and listening is made more complex – as I speak I also listen, in order to represent my own horizon in a way which will be comprehensible and/or palatable to my direct and indirect interlocutors.

Finally, the large number of participants arguably necessitates that someone – typically, the teacher – act as moderator or facilitator of the discussion. This task entails responsibility not only for allocation of the floor, but also for the discussion's aesthetic qualities, i.e. for ensuring that pupils' performances sustain their classmates' attention and interest (more on this in discussion of teacher's role below).

Implications of the curriculum: dialogue and official knowledge

Dialogue in school is driven and bounded by pre-determined curricular content and objectives, which at least in the current English context are typically cast as a set of answers to be grasped or skills to be mastered. As such, they appear inimical to dialogue, which thrives on epistemological openness and uncertainty. Moreover, by demarcating the topics of conversation, and directing them toward clear objectives, the curriculum further constrains the breadth of discussion and participants' freedom to draw in other concerns (cf. Burbules' commitment rule). Thus, it is tempting to see dialogue as primarily appropriate for discussions of current events or Personal, Social and Health Education (PSHE). Such an approach, however, relegates dialogue to the margins of the school day. The challenge is how to reframe the core curricular subjects in such a way that they are amenable to and stimulating of dialogue.

Building on Gadamer's conceptualization of dialogue (discussed in the section on the ideational dimension above), I find it helpful to think about curriculum as conversation (cf. Applebee 1986) or, more precisely as two interweaving conversations. First, the curriculum can be viewed as the site of an ongoing conversation of each generation with its cultural tradition. What appear as answers today first entered this conversation as questions, and vice-versa: current conventional thinking may one day be the subject of heated disagreements. Pupils can be invited to engage in this curricular conversation as active participants: taking sides, contributing new perspectives, and raising questions about issues that appear to have been settled. Of course, pupils' attention is not only focused on this conversation: pupils also participate in ongoing (extra-curricular) conversations with their friends, family, and classmates about a wide range of everyday concerns and issues, including what they saw on television last night, who is friends with whom, and what they want to be when they grow up. The curriculum can enter this 'classroom conversation' as another set of voices, as another perspective on the issues occupying pupils' lives.

How can teachers (and curriculum designers, textbook authors and the like) both engage pupils in the curriculum as conversation and bring the curriculum into ongoing classroom conversations? Here I briefly touch upon three processes: opening up the curriculum, weaving curricular and everyday knowledge, and enabling pupil voices.

Conversations end when all the questions have been answered. Framing the curriculum as an ongoing conversation involves opening it up to active engagement by identifying and drawing attention to what is questionable – to areas of mystery, uncertainty and controversy. For example, I recently collaborated with a group of teachers in planning a unit on E. B. White's *Charlotte's Web* for Year 5 (10-year-olds). One of the teachers brought to the meeting a series of comprehension questions, conveniently divided by chapter, which she had downloaded from a popular teacher resource website.[11] Most of these questions seem to have been designed to examine pupils' literal understanding of the text, or to direct pupils to arrive at a predictable interpretation. For example, the questions for Chapter 3, 'Escape', include 'Why is the barn described using smells?' and 'How does Wilbur like his new home?' With an eye toward opening this chapter to productive discussion, the teachers posed the questions, 'Where do you think Wilbur would be happier: penned up in the barn or able to roam free in the woods? Where would you be happier?' The question is potentially open inasmuch as the text is ambivalent with regard to this issue; an issue that, indeed, touches upon basic human dilemmas regarding our desire for and yet fear of freedom (cf. Fromm 1942).

The question is *potentially* open, since openness is a function of the teachers' epistemological stance – they perceived that there is no one correct answer – but also of the actual situation in which it is encountered by a certain group of pupils in a particular context. To what extent do they hold different and conflicting positions on this question? Mapping pupil positions allows the teacher to tweak or refocus the question such that it highlights the key points of contention in the group, or to introduce the content in such a way that its questionability is revealed or recreated.

A second way of engaging pupils in the curriculum as conversation is to 'weave' curricular and everyday knowledge. Weaving is a term used by Dennis Kwek and colleagues to describe the phenomenon – unfortunately rare in their sample of lessons in Singapore – of teachers and pupils using everyday experiences, concepts and discourse to make sense of and build academic knowledge (Luke, Kwek and Cazden 2006). So, for example, a teacher in our research used an episode from a popular television programme to explain the notion of a cliffhanger, and a pupil told a story about her own family in order to make sense of a story about two sisters. Similarly, in the questions about Chapter 3 of *Charlotte's Web*, the teachers did not only pose a question about Wilbur, but also asked pupils to apply the same sort of question to their own situation, in essence weaving their reading of the text with their own experiences. In the Gadamerian terms introduced here, such weaving is a potentially productive way of bringing pupil and curricular horizons into dialogue with one another.

A third means of enhancing pupils' engagement in the curricular conversation is to give pupils' voices a privileged position. For example, rather than focusing on pupil writing as an opportunity to demonstrate relative success or failure in achieving assessment criteria, pupil-produced texts can be subjected to the sort of critical inquiry that is normally reserved for canonical texts. In such a way pupils are positioned as active contributors of knowledge, their voices are given a hearing alongside those of the official curriculum.

Implications of institutional roles: the teacher and dialogue

The institution of schooling shapes the identities and roles participants can legitimately inhabit in it. Inherent in these roles are imbalances in the distribution of resources for the exercise of power: teachers are mandated to limit pupils' movement and speech, assign pupils tasks and determine the quality of pupils' activity (thereby classifying the pupil as 'successful' or 'failing'). Teachers are also vested with epistemic authority – the teacher's curricular knowledge has been officially authorized; school is ostensibly designed to cure pupils of their ignorance. In this setting, complete reciprocity, in which 'what we expect of others we must expect of ourselves', is an impossibility, and epistemological openness is threatened.

One idealistic approach to this power imbalance is to attempt to dissolve or transcend the traditional teacher role, e.g. by assuming the role of facilitator. While I agree with Burbules and Bruce (2001: 1111) that 'the roles of teacher and student … must be viewed as historical artifacts, discursively constructed and institutionalized, not as inherent concepts that define the educational endeavour', the roles are still very real and durable. Even though they do not define all educational endeavours, pupil and teacher roles are inherent to schooling as a compulsory institution, in which the former's attendance is coerced, and the latter are bound by legal and contractual obligations.

So, instead of trying to eliminate the teacher, the question is how to negotiate the various role demands of teaching through dialogue. Consider, for example, the following roles, roughly divided according to the four dimensions discussed in this paper:

Metacommunicative
1   Establishing and maintaining communicative norms – for example through the negotiation of ground rules, through modelling, and through enforcement of rules that have been established.
2   Encouraging and facilitating reflexivity – for example by inviting criticism of and participation in direction of the dialogue.

Ideational
3   Opening the curriculum – for example by exhibiting an open epistemological stance, revealing questionability, directing the conversation to points of contention, and weaving academic and everyday domains.
4   Maintaining conversational cohesion – for example by relating pupils' contributions

to one another, drawing together and summarizing conversational threads, and making explicit the logic of the developing argument(s).

5   Calling into question prevailing orthodoxies – for example, by probing and challenging pupils' ideas, by making space for or even strengthening minority positions, and by introducing ideas that subvert conventional classroom thinking.

Interpersonal

6   Building classroom community – for example by attending to relationships, modelling caring behaviours, and facilitating the productive management of conflict.

7   Encouraging broad participation – for example, by ensuring fairness in access to the floor, by protecting (socially and/or academically) 'weak' pupils, and by organizing tasks and structuring discussions in such a way that maximizes the chances that pupils will have something significant to say.

Aesthetic

8   Setting the stage for engaging discussion – both in terms of the way the topics of discussion are laid out, and also vis-à-vis the organization of physical and social spaces.

9   'Orchestrating' pupil participation – for example, by coaching pupils' rhetoric, attending to 'audience' needs, and injecting humour and drama into the proceedings.

Note that some of these functions contradict one another, as dialogic tensions are manifested in teacher role conflicts. For example, opening up curricular content and maintaining conversational coherence may involve denying pupils the floor. Similarly, protecting pupils' social needs may involve not probing their thinking (in public). Affording 'wait time' for pupils to think and prepare ideas can detract from the conversational flow and coherence. As noted in the discussion of dialogic tensions above, there is arguably a hierarchy of priorities, according to which metacommunicative and interpersonal concerns take precedence over ideational issues, so consequently emphases on different teacher functions may change as the classroom community evolves.

Conclusion

I opened this chapter by observing that 'dialogue' has come into fashion in educational circles and beyond. What will be the fate of the widespread expectation that teaching and learning in classrooms become more dialogic? The answer to this question depends at least in part on what we mean by 'dialogue' and how we approach its importation into classrooms. In this chapter I have argued that idealistic thinking about dialogue in schools is counter-productive, and instead have promoted a situated approach to dialogue, sensitive to the tensions inherent in dialogic interaction and firmly grounded in the realities of contemporary school contexts.

I have reviewed a number of influential ways of thinking about dialogue, exploring the multiple concerns they address – the ideational, interpersonal, metacommunicative and aesthetic – and arguing that thinking about educational dialogue or productive interaction is incomplete without taking all four of these dimensions into account. I have highlighted the numerous tensions inherent to dialogue, and argued that thinking about productive dialogue needs to accept and work with these tensions rather than ignoring them or wishing them away. Finally, I have examined central features of the school setting – in particular, class size, the curriculum and institutional roles – and have drawn attention to the implications and challenges they pose for dialogue. The chapter has not offered solutions to the problems raised by situating dialogue in schools, but I hope it will contribute to thinking about dialogue and productive interaction by clarifying the range of problems to be confronted, and the various issues to be considered in coming to terms with them.

Coda: revisiting idealistic dialogue

In this chapter, I have critiqued idealistic approaches to dialogue, arguing that they are inadequate – even counter-productive – as guides to practice in schools. The argument has proceeded on the assumption that the dialogic ideal is appropriate for most contexts, and thus only its applicability to school has been questioned. However, consideration of dialogue in school raises questions about the adequacy of idealistic theories for other contexts also. Issues highlighted by the classroom context – institutional roles and audience – may have farther-reaching implications.

By way of illustration, I return to the scene from the *Gorgias* quoted at the beginning of the chapter. Socrates tells Gorgias that he has detected some inconsistencies in the latter's exposition, and wants to make sure that Gorgias, like Socrates himself, is committed to the truth instead of to winning the argument. Gorgias replies, 'Personally, Socrates, I would claim to be just the sort of person you have indicated, but perhaps we ought to consider the rest of the company … it may be that we are keeping some of them when they have other things to do.' Gorgias' comments remind the reader what Socrates pretends to ignore: a crowd is present, and they have assembled in order to hear Gorgias, the visiting teacher, speak. Gorgias appeals to the audience to give him an excuse for breaking off the dialogue without losing face.

This effort backfires, however, and we are informed by Chaerephon that the audience has signalled with applause that they would like the dialogue to continue. Callicles also voices his delight. Socrates agrees to continue, but again questions Gorgias' willingness. Gorgias responds:

> It would be a disgrace for me not to be willing, Socrates, after my spontaneous offer to reply to any question. So, if our friends approve, go on with the conversation and ask me anything you like.
>
> (Plato 1924: §458)

Socrates has set a trap for Gorgias, compelling co-operation and raising the stakes before delivering his knockout blow. After Socrates' trap, Gorgias' refusal to continue would be publicly humiliating. Moreover, consideration of Socrates' and Gorgias' institutional roles serves to complete the picture. Both Socrates and Gorgias are teachers who purport to contribute to their students' betterment. The contents of their teachings, however, are diametrically opposed. Gorgias is from out of town, and has succeeded in attracting a big crowd. Given the context, Socrates' questions seem geared more toward winning over the crowd than ascertaining the truth of the matter.[12]

Read the scene from Gorgias' perspective: he came to town to teach rhetoric. He was challenged to a verbal duel by Socrates, a disgruntled local teacher-competitor. Rather than exchanging speeches, Gorgias' area of expertise, Socrates changes the rules of engagement to those of Dialogue. Being unaccustomed to this interactional genre, Gorgias is literally dumbstruck by it.

Acknowledgements

An earlier version of these ideas appears in Lefstein (2006). I am grateful to Robin Alexander, Richard Andrews, Valerie Coultas, Sharon Gilad, Christine Howe, Karen Littleton, Yael Ofarim, Ben Rampton, David Reedy, Julia Snell and participants at the Philosophy of Education Society of Great Britain Annual Conference (2004) and Institute of Education Philosophy of Education seminar (2008) for helpful comments on previous drafts.

Notes

1 Recent UK studies of primary school discourse include: Burns and Myhill (2004); Galton, Hargreaves, Comber, Wall and Pell (1999) and Smith, Hardman, Wall and Mroz (2004). But see Rampton (2006), and Rampton and Harris's chapter in this volume for evidence that in London secondary schools this communicative regime is shifting.

2 To clarify: I am not suggesting that problems with our models of dialogue are the only or even the primary factor in the failure to make schools more dialogic. Elsewhere I examine other, more significant factors, highlighting in particular reasons for the inherent durability of classroom interactional genres (Lefstein 2008).

3 In the interests of brevity, clarity and accessibility, I have liberally edited Jowett's translation of the dialogue.

4 And, I should add, by putting his philosophical ideas into the mouths of dramatis personae, Plato constantly reminds the reader of the ways in which the conceptual is bound up with the social.

5 Hicks (1996: 106–7, citing also Wertsch and Stone 1985) argues that this common interpretation does not reflect the central place of learner agency in Vygotsky's theory. In her interpretation, the child does not passively internalize cultural tools, but also actively transforms them. In this sense, Vygotsky's approach to the individual's encounter with her or his society and culture is closer to Gadamer's.

6 Cf. Burbules (1993) on four types of dialogue: conversation (inclusive-divergent), inquiry (inclusive-convergent), debate (critical-divergent) and instruction (critical-convergent).

7 See also Mercer and Littleton's (2007) response to this criticism (pp. 108–11).

8 The ESRC-funded 'Towards Dialogue: A Linguistic Ethnographic Study of Classroom Interaction and Change' project (RES-061-25-0363).

9 Bauman and Sherzer (1989: xix) clarify that performance is a relative category: 'To the extent that the skill and effectiveness of expression may become the focus of attention in any act of communication, the potential for performance is always present'. See Rampton (2006) for an application of these ideas to analysis of classroom interaction.

10 Perelman (1982) sees the difference in audience size as constitutive of the difference between dialogue and (monological) speech-making: 'the Socratic technique of question and answer will appear ... as suited to argumentation before one person or a small number of people, while long speeches are necessarily given before large audiences.' Further, he argues that ultimately both are rhetorical forms, aimed at persuasion. He

continues: 'But, it is not necessary to transform into a difference of nature a difference of argumentative technique imposed, essentially, by circumstances, and which concerns only the adherence, more or less assured an explicit, to the arguments developed' (Perelman 1982: 16).

11 The website is http://www.primaryresources.co.uk. The teachers used the characteristics of a 'fertile question' (Harpaz and Lefstein 2000) as a planning tool.

12 Comparison of the *Gorgias* and the *Phaedrus* can be instructive here. Socrates' style is more 'philosophical' – in the sense of self-critical and reflective – in the latter, i.e. in the intimacy of a one-on-one conversation beyond the city walls (and thus outside of the public eye). Moreover, away from the crowd Socrates' attitude toward rhetoric is much more conciliatory. See Kennedy (1980) for a comparison of the two dialogues.

References

Alexander, R. J. (2000) *Culture and Pedagogy: international comparisons in primary education*, Oxford: Blackwell Publishers.

Alexander, R. J. (2003) *Talk for Learning: the first year*, North Yorkshire County Council.

Alexander, R. J. (2004) *Talk for Learning: the second year*, North Yorkshire County Council.

Alexander, R. J. (2005) *Towards Dialogic Teaching: rethinking classroom talk* (2nd edn), Cambridge: Dialogos.

Applebee, A. N. (1996) *Curriculum as Conversation: transforming traditions of teaching and learning*, Chicago: University of Chicago Press.

Bauman, R. and Sherzer, J. (1989) *Explorations in the Ethnography of Speaking* (2nd edn), Cambridge: Cambridge University Press.

Bauman, Z. (2001) *Community: seeking safety in an insecure world*, Cambridge: Polity Press.

Burbules, N. C. (1990) 'Varieties of educational dialogue', *Philosophy of Education*, 1990:120–31.

Burbules, N. C. (1993) *Dialogue in Teaching: theory and practice*, New York: Teachers College Press.

Burbules, N. C. (2000) 'The limits of dialogue as a critical pedagogy', in P. P. Trifonas (ed.), *Revolutionary Pedagogies: cultural politics, instituting education, and the discourse of theory*, New York: Routledge.

Burbules, N. C. and Bruce, B. C. (2001) 'Theory and research on teaching as dialogue', in V. Richardson and American Educational Research Association (eds), *Handbook of Research on Teaching* (4th edn), Vol. 4, Washington, DC: American Educational Research Association, pp. 1102–21.

Burns, C. and Myhill, D. (2004) 'Interactive or inactive? A consideration of the nature of interaction in whole class teaching', *Cambridge Journal of Education*, 34:35–50.

Callan, E. (1995) 'Virtue, dialogue, and the common school', *American Journal of Education*, 104:1–33.

Cazden, C. B. (2001) *Classroom Discourse: the language of teaching and learning*, (2nd edn), Portsmouth, NH: Heinemann.

Delpit, L. D. (1988) 'The silenced dialogue – power and pedagogy in educating other people's children', *Harvard Educational Review*, 58:280–98.

DfES (Great Britain Department for Education and Skills) (2003) *Speaking, Listening, Learning: working with children in Key Stages 1 and 2: handbook*, London: DfES.

Dillon, J. T. (1988) *Questioning and Teaching: a manual of practice*, New York: Teachers College Press.

Ehlich, K. (1985) 'School discourse as dialogue?', in M. Dascal and H. Cuyckens (eds), *Dialogue: an interdisciplinary approach*, Amsterdam: Benjamins.

Ellsworth, E. (1989) 'Why doesn't this feel empowering – working through the repressive myths of critical pedagogy', *Harvard Educational Review*, 59:297–324.

Fielding, M. (2004) 'Transformative approaches to student voice: theoretical underpinnings, recalcitrant realities', *British Educational Research Journal*, 30:295–311.

Fielding, M. (2007) 'Beyond 'voice': new roles, relations, and contexts in researching with young people', *Discourse: Studies in the Cultural Politics of Education*, 28:301–10.

Fisher, R. (2007) 'Dialogic teaching: developing thinking and metacognition through philosophical discussion', *Early Child Development and Care*, 177:615–31.

Freire, P. (1986) *Pedagogy of the Oppressed*, New York: Continuum.

Freire, P. and Macedo, D. P. (1995) 'A dialogue – culture, language, and race', *Harvard Educational Review*, 65:377–402.

Fromm, E. (1942) *The Fear of Freedom*, London: Kegan Paul & Co.

Gadamer, H. G. (1998) *Truth and Method* (trans. J. Weinsheimer and D. G. Marshall, 2nd edn), New York: Continuum.

Galton, M. J., Hargreaves, L., Comber, C., Wall, D. and Pell, A. (1999) *Inside the Primary Classroom: 20 years on*, London: Routledge.

Goffman, E. (1981) *Forms of Talk*, Oxford: Blackwell.

Gurevitch, Z. (2000) 'Plurality in dialogue: a comment on Bakhtin', *Sociology*, 34:243–63.

Habermas, J. (1990) 'The hermeneutic claim to universality', in G. L. Ormiston and A. D. Schrift (eds) *The Hermeneutic Tradition: from Ast to Ricoeur*, Albany, NY: State University of New York Press.

Haroutunian-Gordon, S. (1989) 'Socrates as teacher', in P. W. Jackson and S. Haroutunian-Gordon (eds) *From Socrates to Software: the teacher as text and the text as teacher*, Chicago, IL: NSSE.

Harpaz, Y. and Lefstein, A. (2000) 'Communities of thinking', *Educational Leadership*, 58:54–7.

Hicks, D. (1996) *Discourse, Learning and Schooling*, Cambridge: Cambridge University Press.

Kennedy, G. A. (1980) *Classical Rhetoric and its Christian and Secular Tradition from Ancient to Modern Times*, Chapel Hill: University of North Carolina Press.

Lambirth, A. (2006) 'Challenging the laws of talk: ground rules, social reproduction and the curriculum', *The Curriculum Journal*, 17:59–71.

Lefstein, A. (2006) 'Dialogue in schools – toward a pragmatic approach', *Working Papers in Urban Language and Literacies*. Available online at: http://www.kcl.ac.uk/content/1/c6/01/42/29/paper33.pdf (accessed 27 July 2009).

Lefstein, A. (2008) 'Changing classroom practice through the English National Literacy Strategy: a micro-interactional perspective', *American Educational Research Journal*, 45:701–37.

Lugones, M. C. and Spelman, E. V. (1983) 'Have we got a theory for you! Feminist theory, cultural imperialism and the demand for 'the woman's voice'', *Women's Studies International Forum*, 6:573–81.

Luke, A., Kwek, D. and Cazden, C. (2006) 'Weaving in classroom discourse', paper presented at the American Educational Research Association 2006 Annual Meeting, San Francisco, CA.

Mercer, N. (2000) *Words and Minds: how we use language to think together*, London: Routledge.

Mercer, N. and Littleton, K. (2007) *Dialogue and the Development of Children's Thinking: a sociocultural approach*, London: Routledge.

Noddings, N. (1994) 'Conversation as moral education', *Journal of Moral Education*, 23:107–18.

Nystrand, M., Gamoran, A., Kachur, R. and Prendergast, C. (1997) *Opening Dialogue: understanding the dynamics of language and learning in the English classroom*, New York: Teachers College Press.

Osborne, J., Erduran, S. and Simon, S. (2004) 'Enhancing the quality of argumentation in school science', *Journal of Research in Science Teaching*, 41:994–1020.

Perelman, C. (1982) *The Realm of Rhetoric*, Notre Dame, Indiana: University of Notre Dame Press.

Plato (1924) *The Dialogues of Plato* (trans. B. Jowett, 3rd edn). London: Oxford University Press. First published 1871.

Plato and Cornford, F. M. (1957) *Plato's Theory of Knowledge: The Theaetetus and the Sophist of Plato*, New York: Liberal Arts Press.

Qualifications and Curriculum Authority (QCA) (2005) Opening up talk [DVD], London: QCA.

Rampton, B. (2006) *Language in Late Modernity: interaction in an urban school*, Cambridge: Cambridge University Press.

Reich, R. (1998) 'Confusion about the Socratic method: Socratic paradoxes and contemporary invocations of Socrates', *Philosophy of Education*, 1998: 68–78. Available online at: http://www.ed.uiuc.edu/EPS/PES-Yearbook/1998/reich.html (accessed 12 March 2009).

Ricoeur, P. (1970) *Freud and Philosophy: an essay on interpretation*, New Haven: Yale University Press.

Scollon, R. (1998) *Mediated Discourse as Social Interaction: a study of news discourse*, London: Longman.

Shor, I. and Freire, P. (1987) *A Pedagogy for Liberation: dialogues on transforming education*, South Hadley, MA: Bergin & Garvey Publishers.

Sichel, B. A. (1998) Your Socrates, my Socrates, everyone has a Socrates, *Philosophy of Education*, 1998: 79–81.Available online at: http://www.ed.uiuc.edu/EPS/PES-Yearbook/1998/sichel.html (accessed 12 March 2009).

Sidorkin, A. M. (1999) *Beyond Discourse: education, the self, and dialogue*, Albany, NY: State University of New York Press.

Smith, F., Hardman, F., Wall, K. and Mroz, M. (2004) 'Interactive whole class teaching in the National Literacy and Numeracy Strategies', *British Educational Research Journal*, 30:395–411.

Swann, J. (2007) 'Designing 'educationally effective' discussion', *Language and Education*, 21:342–59.

Vygotsky, L. S. (1978) *Mind in Society: the development of higher psychological processes*, Cambridge: Harvard University Press.

Wegerif, R. (2005) 'Reason and creativity in classroom dialogues', *Language and Education*, 19:223–38.

Wellmer, A. (1971) *Critical Theory of Society*, New York: Herder and Herder.

Wells, C. G. (1999) *Dialogic Inquiry: towards a sociocultural practice and theory of education*, Cambridge: Cambridge University Press.

Wertsch, J. V. and Stone, A. (1985) 'The concept of internalization in Vygotsky's account of the genesis of higher mental functions', in J. V. Wertsch and Center for Psychosocial Studies (eds), *Culture, Communication, and Cognition: Vygotskian perspectives*, Cambridge: Cambridge University Press.

Wortham, S. E. F. (2006) *Learning Identity: the joint, local emergence of social identification and academic learning*, New York: Cambridge University Press.

Chapter 10

Dialogue enhancement in classrooms

Towards a relational approach for group working

Peter Kutnick, King's College London
and Jennifer Colwell, University of Brighton

Theories that posit a relationship between dialogue and understanding are predominantly psychological, but are associated with diverse perspectives. Minimally, four types of theory comment on this relationship: socio-cognitive, socio-cultural, social psychological and developmental/relational. These theories provide pertinent insights as to why dialogue may be related to understanding *and* why this relationship is rarely found in classrooms. Using studies conducted by the authors, this chapter will show that theory, combined with an awareness of classroom realities, can increase children's within-class dialogue – impacting upon children's understanding/attainment, participation and social inclusion.

Theories underlying dialogue in classrooms: socio-cognitive, socio-cultural and social psychological

Socio-cognitive and socio-cultural theories focus on the role of talk among children (and teachers) and its association with enhanced cognitive development. In the main, these theories are updates and applications inspired by Piaget (1971) and Vygotsky (1978). Studies by Piaget (1928, 1932) and neo-Piagetians (for example, Doise and Mugny 1984; Howe and Tolmie 2003; Light and Littleton 1994; Perret-Clermont 1980) focus on mutual peer interaction during problem-solving tasks. As such, they are distinct from 'instructional' interpretations of Vygotskian socio-cultural theory, which often focus on the relationship between an expert (knower) and novice (an individual within the 'zone of proximal development' [Luria 1976]).

Drawing upon the potential mismatch between knowledge-based perspectives of individuals during joint problem-solving tasks, socio-cognitive theory declares that socio-cognitive conflict (the acknowledgement of differences between one another's perspectives) leads to higher order understanding. Damon and Phelps (1989) note that as long as the partners are not influenced by an inequality in power, the overcoming of differences in perspectives is likely to lead to more complex understanding than either of the partners was able to contribute originally. They further explain that complex understanding is gained through terms such as 'mutuality' and 'connectedness' where (peer-based) social interaction ensures that both partners are equally participative and they maintain a relational obligation to work together.

Classroom-based studies have shown that cognitive development (often associated with understanding within a curriculum area) can be enhanced when activities are undertaken in pairs or small groups and children are able to work independently from their teacher (Cohen, Lotan and Leechor 1989; Kutnick and Thomas 1990) towards a problem resolution that can be empirically tested (Howe and Tolmie 2003). These studies show the need to move beyond a simple interpretation of Piaget's theory as an ordering of progressively more complex cognitive stages (Davis 1991). The studies acknowledge, often tacitly, that particular social conditions must exist wherein socio-cognitive conflict (and the joint resolution of problems) is likely to be encouraged (Doise 1990; Light and Littleton 1994; Perret-Clermont 1980). From this theoretical approach, cognitive problem solving requires the ability to share perspectives in the joint/social resolution of new and challenging problems. Expecting that children can resolve a problem collaboratively without considering social conditions ignores research on social comparison within cognitive development. Monteil (1992), as well as Salonen, Vauras and Efklides (2005), acknowledge that the nature of children's social pairings (or relationships used to promote cognition) will be affected by the children's emotional and social responses to working with one another. In particular, Salonen *et al.* (2005; similar to Cazden, Cox, Dickinson, Steinberg and Stone 1979) identify that cognitive tasks undertaken within small groups of children can only be successful if group members are able to mutually co-regulate their cognitive *and* relational interactions – the absence of one will limit the effectiveness of the other. Similarly, if the relationships between children can be structured to allow successful cognitive interaction (Webb and Farivar 1994), then children from very different backgrounds who are asked to work together can also produce socially inclusive as well as successful cognitive results (Cohen 1994; Perret-Clermont 1980).

The occurrence of cognitive and relational interaction between children is associated with mutual (symmetrical) relationships (described predominantly by Piaget 1932) and asymmetrical (expert/novice) relationships (described predominantly by Vygotsky 1978). Children's ability to draw upon symmetrical and asymmetrical relationships is: 1) strongly correlated to the type of problem presented (Kutnick 1994); 2) reminiscent of evolutionary relationships (Hinde 1997); and 3) the basis for a 'social' pedagogy discussed later in this chapter. Typically, within socio-cognitive theory, open-ended problems are more likely to be resolved in symmetrical, mutual interaction while close-ended/instructional problems are more likely to be resolved in the asymmetrical interaction between a knower and a learner. Both of these problem resolution approaches rely on the importance of talk between individuals in some form of 'dialogue-based' relationship. Talk is generally considered as evidence of active construction and co-construction of cognitive knowledge (see Donaldson 1978; Littleton and Mercer this volume).

One should not assume that talk is the natural result of bringing together a number of children or seating them near one another (characterized in classrooms). In socio-cognitive and socio-cultural theories, talk (Mercer 2000; Webb 1989) must encourage children's communication beyond simple description, confirmation or disagreement; moving towards 'elaborations' that add new cognitive perspectives and clarify existing information. Elaborated talk does not simply occur when children (or others) are asked to undertake a task together. Classroom studies have found most peer-based talk to be of low cognitive value (for example, Webb 1989; Wegerif, Mercer and Dawes 1999). Studies that recognize the importance of elaborated talk (Mercer and Littleton 2007; Gillies 2008) also recommend that children should be instructed and supported in the use of their elaboration. Only rarely, though, do these theories acknowledge the importance of the quality of the relationship between interactors (as previously identified by Salonen *et al.* 2005). The relationship between cognitive partners may facilitate or discourage interaction (Light and Littleton 1994); a key issue identified in descriptions of pupil groups in classrooms (Galton 1990). In basic terms, if individuals do not have a positive, supportive social relationship during their communication then they are unlikely to engage in the elaborated discussion required for cognitive development. This relational qualification opens questions as to whether relationships that support high-level cognitive talk are a prerequisite for cognitive advancement, whether children can be trained for relational skills/support or whether supportive relationships are simply an outcome of joint cognitive tasks (Azmitia and Montgomery 1993; Jarvelä, Lehtinen and Salonen 2000; Kreijens and Kirschner 2005).

While working from a different theoretical basis, the social psychology that underlies co-operative learning (Johnson and Johnson 2003a; Slavin 1995) also acknowledges a relational basis in enhancing classroom learning (and, presumably, cognitive growth). Initial insight into the relational basis is derived from contact theory (Allport 1954) and interpersonal aspects of motivation (Deutsch 1949). Associating relationship and learning is not straightforward, though, as it is unclear whether a positive relationship is a prerequisite for co-operation or the outcome of a successful interaction (Slavin 1990). Contact theory appears to identify relationships as a prerequisite, using terms such as positive 'social interdependence' (noting that each individual's goals are affected by the actions of others that surround the individual; Johnson and Johnson 2003b). On the other hand, Slavin (1995) recognizes that interpersonal relationships (such as liking of group members) can be enhanced as a result of co-operative tasks, but only when tasks are successfully completed. In noting the importance of this relational outcome, Slavin recommends that co-operating groups be structured to represent a 'heterogeneous' cross-section of all individuals in the classroom; thus facilitating social inclusion in a manner similar to Cohen (1994). The social psychology associated with co-operative learning also acknowledges (from Bossert, Barnett and Filby 1985) that the learning tasks drawn upon must be of sufficient (cognitive) challenge to encourage engagement without under- or over-estimating the ability of group members. Thus, co-operative learning studies emphasize (like Salonen *et al.* 2005) that cognitive task success is based upon cognitive and relational interactions. These studies, though, are not clear in identifying whether relational interaction is a prerequisite or result of the co-operative experience.

Relational approaches

Relational theory combines aspects of socio-cognitive and social psychological theory. Relational theory assumes the importance of positive relationships in the facilitation of social interaction for productive dialogue and cognitive development, and explores how relationships can be promoted and where positive relationships should be integrated in the promotion of dialogue. A background to relational approaches acknowledges the importance of interpersonal sensitivity and emotional development for wellbeing and learning in classrooms (Hall 1994). Kutnick and Manson (1998) consider that a relational approach should be based on social and cognitive developmental (psychological) principles. Social and cognitive development can be described as a sequence of stages found in children's relationships with adults and peers. The stages emerge in the social contexts within which children interact. Co-construction of relationships between the child with peers or adults is fundamental. Small-scale experimental studies show that the development of these relationships may be 'scaffolded' in classroom and other environments (Hall 1994; Kutnick and Brees 1982; Thacker, Stoate and Feest 1992), acknowledging that positive and supportive relationships are a prerequisite for the development of cognitive and social understanding.

Development of relationships is described in a stage-like sequence resulting from a child's quality interactions with specific individuals. An initial attachment-like stage (similar to that described by Ainsworth, Bell and Stayton 1974; Stayton, Hogan and Ainsworth 1971) establishes a mutual bond of trust, dependency and security, which provides a basis for joint communication, interdependence and further ability to solve relational and other problems (Damon 1977; Selman 1980; Youniss 1992). The attachment-like stage is followed by stages of interpersonal dependency, cognitive characterization of rules for dependence and interdependence, reflective understanding of contexts and qualities of relationships and autonomous relational understanding (Kutnick and Manson 1998; from Selman 1980 and Sullivan 1953). Traditionally, relational development descriptions have focused on the close child-adult relationship (attachment) and have been described as a necessary condition for effective learning (Barrett and Trevitt 1991) and development of relationships with others. Relational development rarely considers early relations between child and peers (especially within Western cultures) except in specific regard to friendship (Kessen 1991; Youniss 1978). Nevertheless, some studies indicate that early, close relationships can be developed among very young children (Howes 1983; Vandell and Mueller 1980) when children are provided quality exposure to peers. This peer-oriented dependency/close friendship has been characterized as developing trust, sensitivity and reciprocal communication at its base (Hartup 1978; Maxwell 1990; Youniss 1980), although it is rarely found among children.

We propose that the potential for relational development can be facilitated among children and peers if stages of trust/dependence, communication/responsiveness and joint relational problem solving are scaffolded into their activity (particularly classroom activity). If children are given the opportunity to develop close peer relationships, then cognitive and social benefits should accrue, similar to those benefits found in close child-adult relationships. While young (Western) children may only have limited opportunities to develop relational activities with peers at home, the onset of schooling allows this opportunity to extend and 'scaffold' quality peer relations (Kutnick, Blatchford and Baines 2002; Kutnick, Ota and Berdondini 2008).

Pupil groupings and the promotion of dialogue in classrooms

It would be naive to assume that elaborated dialogue will be a natural part of children's interaction within the classroom. A child's ability to engage in dialogue (and related small group work) may be limited by previous interaction experiences of working with others, liking of/support for others in dialogue, ability to engage with the teacher, and general 'cultural' support for dialogue in the classroom (Cowie and Ruddock 1988; Galton 1990; Galton, Hargreaves, Comber, Wall and Pell 1999; Webb and Mastergeorge 2003). Studies that focus on the frequency and use of naturally occurring pupil groupings in classrooms consistently identify that these groupings do not feature as contexts for collaboration or cognitive development. Galton, Simon and Croll (1980) and Galton *et al.* (1999) note that while pupils are often seated in small groups, they are rarely assigned co-operative or collaborative tasks where dialogue is encouraged. Many of the learning tasks that are assigned to pupil groups have low levels of cognitive challenge (Bennett 1994; Bossert *et al.* 1985). And, studies concerning cognitive challenge in 'classroom talk' (Fuchs, Fuchs, Hamlett, Phillips, Karns and Dutka 1997; Mercer 2000; Webb and Mastergeorge 2003) rarely find examples of the high levels of cognitive-based communication (i.e. exploratory and elaborated talk) necessary for promoting cognitive understanding. Naturalistic 'mapping' of classroom groups and activity also indicates that size and composition of pupil groupings (social pedagogy) are unlikely to facilitate dialogue or communication, and that teachers lack the knowledge and skills to promote and support dialogue in class (Kutnick *et al.* 2002).

Applications of relational approaches in the classroom

Consideration of classrooms as a social pedagogic context draws together theories previously described and their application within classrooms – noting that the teaching/learning (pedagogic) relationship is undertaken within a social context that may promote or inhibit dialogue and communication. A review of naturalistic studies of classrooms (Baines, Blatchford and Kutnick 2008) shows little evidence of elaborated talk (often associated with effective group work); and this analysis contrasts with the potential for cognitive enhancing dialogue that may be engendered via relationally based group work. Yet, classroom dialogue and communication studies rarely consider or seek to develop children's relational skills (involving communication and interpersonal support) as fundamental to the promotion of communication and support for dialogue in children's learning and development. Only limited training or support for the development of close relationships and group work among children is found in classrooms (in primary schools, Kutnick *et al.* 2002; secondary schools, Kutnick, Blatchford and Baines 2005; or pre-schools, Kutnick, Colwell and Canavan 2006).

In response to the limited number of studies concerning the role of relationships and dialogue, a number of social pedagogic research projects have been developed recently. Particular relational approaches reported here were co-developed with teachers (based upon relational approaches described above) and implemented in their classrooms. These studies explored, in particular, whether a relational approach would 1) enhance dialogue and communication skills among young children; 2) positively affect teacher perceptions and pupil participation; 3) improve achievement; and 4) effect inclusion as a whole-class phenomenon. Three studies are described below and the impact of the approach on classroom dialogue considered. While each of these studies identifies the successful implementation of a relational approach, it should be noted that the approaches were integrated with the more general implementation of group work in classrooms. Within current analyses it is not possible to disaggregate the success of the relational approach from the group work context, and discussion at the end of the chapter indentifies this issue for further consideration.

Study 1: Establishing a relational approach and its effect on dialogue and communication with young children in primary school classrooms

This study was undertaken as part of a large, funded project (known as 'SPRinG' – Social Pedagogic Research into Groupwork; see Blatchford, Galton, Kutnick and Baines 2005) and focused on children aged 5 to 7 years (school-based Years 1 and 2; see Kutnick *et al.* 2008). In a quasi-experimental design, teachers co-developed and implemented a sequence of relational activities to improve the effectiveness of group working and communication among pupils over a full school year. Control class teachers were given an equivalent amount of time/support to develop and implement their own approaches to classroom learning (some involving group work). The relational activities that were introduced to the experimental classes drew upon a developmental sequence that began with an emphasis on trust and support (described more fully by Pfeiffer and Jones 1983), including activities such as blindfold walks and mirroring. The sequence continued with communication skills (described by Leech and Wooster 1986), including activities such as partnered discussions of favourite actions and leading to partnered socio-emotional consideration of 'what makes me happy, sad, etc.'. The third component of the sequence involved joint problem solving (Thacker *et al.* 1992), including activities such as joint drawings, co-operative shapes and letters, etc. As children became more competent in these relational activities, their teachers were able to adapt the activities to support work across the curriculum. It should be noted that the relational activities were not designed to coincide with any specific curriculum area in schools although particular communication/dialogue skills and curricular/ cognitive understanding were assessed as described below.

In total, 980 children (from 17 experimental and 21 control classes) were assessed and compared for attainment (reading and mathematics) and communication actions at the beginning and end of a school year. Analysis, using multi-level modelling, found that children in the experimental classes showed significantly greater improvement in their mathematics and reading scores over the year than children in control classes. Improvement was evident at all levels of attainment in experimental classes within Years 1 and 2 with regard to reading. With regard to mathematics, only pupils in Year 2 showed statistically significant improvement (see Table 10.1; supplemented by means and standard deviations in Table 10.2).

Acknowledging the significant cognitive/achievement improvement in the experimental classes as a backdrop, we focus on children's dialogue and communication effects. While there were few differences between experimental and control classes at the start of the year, classroom observations showed that experimental children had increased opportunities to participate in group work over the year (control classes increased their group work between autumn and spring, but this did not continue to increase in the summer term). Children in experimental classes displayed higher levels of within-group involvement and lower levels of dependence on the teacher than children

Table 10.1 Multi-level analysis of reading and mathematics attainment scores: significant main effect variables and interactions associated with reading/literacy and mathematics scores over the school year with coefficients and levels of probability (Study 1)

Subject	Explanatory Variable	Group/Term	Coefficient (SE)	P-value
Reading/Literacy	Reading/Literacy	Linear Term	0.76 (0.06)	<.001
	Group	Control	0.0	
		Experimental	0.23 (0.10)	<.02
Mathematics	Mathematics	Linear	0.81 (0.06)	<.001
	Year 1	Control	0.0	
		Experimental	0.0 (0.13)	NS
	Year 2	Control	0.0	
		Experimental	0.71 (0.13)	<.001

Source: Kutnick *et al.* (2008).

in control classes. And, where it could be recorded, communication between pupils in the experimental classes was significantly more likely to take place at an elaborated/high level than pupils in control classes (see Kutnick *et al.* 2008 for fuller explanation).

To assess particular developments in dialogue and communication, we asked all children in the experimental and control classes to draw concept maps of current curriculum topics while working as a pair during the spring term and again in the summer term. Concept maps were selected to provide a focus for paired discussion based on a (teacher-defined) curriculum relevant topic. Concept maps allow 'the nature of children's understanding and development' to be identified (Pearson and Somekh 2003), especially children's 'negotiation of meaning' (Anderson-Inman and Ditson 1999). Asking children to plan and write joint concept maps allows the recording of dialogue as well as assessment of complexity of concepts used in the maps (Jonassen, Carr and Yuch 1998) and the basis to compare these assessments over time. Children were randomly allocated their partners by their teachers.

Given the complexity of recording the concept map writing process and associated dialogue, only one pair of randomly selected children could be recorded per class. The same pair of children was recorded in the spring and summer terms. Analysis drew upon Fogel's (1993) categories of mother-infant dialogue, these being adapted to analyse child-peer conversations. The categories defined 'frames' (contexts) and 'qualities' of communicative interaction. The main frame was 'On-task – Off-task'. Communicative interaction categories included: 'Co-regulation' (each member of the dyad actively participates through verbal and non-verbal actions, and this may be undertaken through symmetrical or asymmetrical interactions); 'Unilateral regulation' (one member dominates the activity, usually ignoring the other member of the dyad); whether one member of the dyad 'Disrupted' their joint work; and whether partners were 'Disengaged' (dyad members do not share any aspect of the activity, each member has a different focus).

Table 10.2 Mean of start (pre-test) and end-of-year (post-test) results by year in school and subject for SPRinG and Control (standard deviations in brackets) (Study 1)

Year Group		Subject Reading Pre-test	Post-test	Mathematics Pre-test	Post-test
Year 1					
	SPRinG	43.49	23.99	22.59	12.26*
		(36.43)	(14.40)	(9.62)	(5.73)
		N = 170	N = 147	N = 170	N = 147
	Control	45.80	22.81	21.92	12.15*
		(33.42)	(13.52)	(8.54)	(5.42)
		N = 214	N = 162	N = 214	N = 165
Year 2					
	SPRinG	21.24	55.18**	9.14	23.21
		(13.43)	(29.45)	(6.37)	(8.17)
		N = 218	N = 152	N = 218	N = 175
	Control	23.29	51.02	12.93	22.38
		(11.97)	(27.18)	(5.51)	(7.49)
		N = 243	N = 194	N = 243	N = 199

Source: Kutnick *et al.* (2008).

Notes:
* Year 1 mathematics post-test was scored on a different scale from the pre-test, hence the lower average scores for SPRinG and Control classes.
** One SPRinG class was withdrawn from this analysis. The teacher allowed data to be collected, but did not participate in the training programme or introduce group work methods in her class.

Coding of videotapes was based on the total time to complete the concept map, recorded in seconds. From this total time, two proportions were calculated: 1) Framing: on- and off-task accounted for 100 per cent of total time; and 2) Communicative interaction: co-regulation, unilateral, and disengagement accounted for 100 per cent of total time. Using percentages of time allowed for standardization between classes. The percentages were assessed for distribution (normalcy and homogeneity), allowing parametric analyses to be undertaken. In total, 23 pairs of pupils were represented in the spring/summer analyses (11 experimental and 12 control pairs; although 38 pairs were recorded in the spring, a number of the pairs could not be included in the analyses because children selected for observation were not present on the day of the summer recording). As (spring term) pairs were randomly selected for inclusion, the reduction in number of pairs (in the summer term) should not have affected analyses/results. Average Cronbach's alpha for the coding of the proportions of communicative interaction was 0.74 (ranging from 0.83 to 0.79 among the separate qualities of communicative interaction). Table 10.3 shows changes over the two school terms. Pupils from the experimental classes increased their proportion of 'On-task' activities while pupils from the control classes decreased. Pupils from the experimental classes also displayed significantly higher proportions of 'Co-regulation' in both spring and summer terms than pupils from the control classes.

Table 10.3 Comparison of experimental and control classes by category in spring and summer terms; means of percentages presented (standard deviations in brackets) (Study 1)

		Category On-task	Co-regulation	Unilateral	Disengaged
Spring term					
	Experimental	82.35	60.57	11.73	24.88
		(12.29)	(24.78)	(6.25)	(23.22)
		N = 11	N = 11	N = 11	N = 11
	Control	84.41	40.52	8.35	50.83
		(8.62)	(18.31)	(7.28)	(18.46)
		N = 12	N = 12	N = 12	N = 12
	F	1, 22 =	1, 22 =	1, 22 =	1, 22 =
		0.22	4.93	1.42	8.88
		NS	p<.04	NS	p<.007
Summer term					
	Experimental	90.49	65.73	7.92	19.78
		(6.57)	(27.89)	(8.88)	(16.50)
		N = 11	N = 11	N = 11	N = 11
	Control	80.19	36.72	10.24	52.88
		(14.24)	(21.12)	(9.94)	(20.43)
		N = 12	N = 12	N = 12	N = 12
	F	1, 22 =	1, 22 =	1, 22 =	1, 22 =
		4.81	8.00	0.34	18.05
		p<.04	p<.01	NS	p<.0001

Source: Kutnick et al. (2008).

There were no significant differences with regard to 'Unilateral' between experimental and control pairs in either term, although pupils from the experimental classes decreased their proportion while pupils from the control classes increased this over time. Pupils from the experimental classes showed significantly lower 'Disengagement' than pupils from the control classes in each of the spring and summer terms. Furthermore, over the two terms, experimental pupils lowered 'Disengagement' while pupils from the control classes increased. In an analysis of covariance (with spring term scores as covariates of summer term scores) pupils from the experimental classes spent a higher proportion of time 'On-task' [F(1, 19) = 5.51, p<.03, d (Cohen's d) = .85], and interacted with higher proportions of 'Co-regulation' [F(1, 19) = 3.70, p<.05, d = .67] than pupils from the control classes. In a recent re-analysis of statistics in Table 10.3 (Kutnick and Berdondini 2009) 'Co-regulation' was broken down into its symmetrical and asymmetrical components. For the experimental children, virtually all of their co-regulated increase between spring and summer terms was explained by symmetrical co-regulation, while asymmetrical co-regulation remained constant; suggesting that it is the symmetric mutual/connectedness (Damon and Phelps 1989) that is most likely to support the dialogue associated with improved classroom achievement.

Study 1 findings show that, over time, the pupils from the experimental classes became more task-focused, engaged and aware of their partners in communication than the pupils from the control classes. The findings indicate that, while everyday classroom processes are likely to allow children to engage in dialogue and communication, focusing on the development of a relational approach among pupils allowed 1) development of a higher proportion of co-regulated communication (communication in which partners actively focus their dialogue on one another in a mutually supportive manner); 2) greater 'on-task' focus; and 3) association of these skills with higher levels of academic/cognitive development within a school year. It should be understood that this relational development is unlikely to take place in the short term and it is difficult to disaggregate the particular effects of the relational approach from the general context of increased levels of group work in the experimental classes. It is also noteworthy that this study was undertaken with children aged 5 and 6 years, an age range often associated with egocentrism in understanding and speech (Battisch and Watson 2003; Davis 1991; Littleton, Mercer, Dawes, Wegerif, Rowe and Sam 2005).

Study 2: A relational approach in secondary school classrooms; promoting participation, attainment and teachers' perceptions in the Caribbean

The islands of Trinidad and Barbados were the site of this action research study. These islands were selected because of their concern for pupil underachievement in secondary schools (Kutnick, Layne and Jules 1997; Layne and Kutnick 2001); wherein traditional, teacher-dominant pedagogic methods characterize classroom activity. Concern has been expressed about the lack of participation (especially communicative interaction) and low attainment in classrooms. Into these traditional classrooms a social pedagogic method based on a relational approach for group working among pupils was introduced. The study aimed to assess whether improved dialogue and communication was a result of relational activities and greater opportunities for group working, and whether relational activities would affect participation within classrooms as well as the attitudes and understanding of teachers. Twelve in-service social studies teachers participated in this study. Teachers held positions across the achievement range of secondary schools in Trinidad and Barbados. Teachers co-adapted and applied the relational approach for group work (described previously) for their classrooms and were provided with supportive visits by a research officer between December and July of a school year. Data were collected from nearly 300 pupils in December and July in social studies classes among 2nd Formers (children aged 13–14 years).

The study allowed teachers to introduce and record aspects of the relational approach in their classrooms during spring and summer terms of a school year. As with any action research study (in education), classroom-based initiatives only assessed change over time with regard to the teachers' 12 classrooms; quasi-experimental/control group comparisons were not possible in this research method. Measures of pupil attainment and teacher attitudes to pupils in the classroom were collected at the start of the spring and end of summer terms (see Layne, Kutnick, Jules and Layne 2008 for fuller explanation). The measures included 1) pupil attainment scores assigned by individual teachers that were standardized on the basis of end-of-term examinations (December and July); and 2) a teacher questionnaire concerning classroom behaviours regarding each child in class (December and July). The questionnaire included nine items (general knowledge, reactions when confronted with a problem in class, mode of speaking to the teacher, amount of attention paid in class, ability to work in a group, classroom autonomy, reliance on the teacher, popularity with peers and bossiness with peers) set out as semantic differentials. The questionnaires had been developed and validated in the Caribbean (Kutnick 1992). Supplemental information was gained from post-study interviews with teachers and pupils.

Results from Study 2 initially consider the development of subject attainment (in this case, social studies) within classrooms between December and July. Standardized attainment (z) scores allowed pupils to be divided into one of four attainment quartiles for each class. Drawing upon these quartiles, Table 10.4 displays means and standard deviations for December and July examinations as well as identifying the amount of change in attainment that characterized pupils in each quartile after undertaking the relational programme for group work within their social studies classes.

As expected, Table 10.4 shows that the 'top' quartile in December had the highest mean [$F(3, 288) = 100.65$, $p<.0001$; eta = .51] when compared to the means of other quartiles. This distribution of means also characterized the quartiles in July [$F(3, 259) = 20.89$, $p<.001$; although the effect size was substantially reduced, eta = .20]. Comparing results for the two attainment dates shows that all quartiles gained in attainment, but pupils in the 'lowest' quartile made the most significant gains between December and July; the difference in these 'change' scores was significant [$F(3, 259) = 14.54$, $p<.001$; eta = .15], with Scheffé *post hoc* analyses showing that pupils in the (initial) lowest quartile improved significantly more than top-performing pupils.

The teacher questionnaire showed that pupils in the highest (December) attainment quartile also scored highest for most of the nine items. Questionnaire items were factor analysed and two factors were found to have sufficiently high reliability in the separate December and July administrations (Table 10.5). In December, Factor 1 positively associated 'General Knowledge' of pupils with their ability to 'Pay Attention' in class

Table 10.4 Means of 'raw' within-class attainment scores, divided by December quartiles of attainment, for December and July assessments, and change of score between December and July (standard deviations in brackets) (Study 2)

| | Attainment scores | | |
	December	July	Change
December Quartile			
Lowest	37.32	53.02	14.56
	(13.92)	(18.81)	(15.10)
	N = 74	N = 61	N = 61
Low-mid	49.97	62.38	11.80
	(13.53)	(16.48)	(11.72)
	N = 76	N = 69	N = 69
High-mid	60.06	69.07	8.32
	(10.83)	(13.66)	(10.61)
	N = 65	N = 56	N = 56
Highest	71.70	73.22	1.55
	(11.80)	(12.52)	(11.03)
	N = 77	N = 73	N = 73

Source: Layne *et al.* (2008).

and to 'Work in a Group'. Factor 2 negatively associated pupils 'Dependent on the Teacher', with those who did not get on well with peers ('Bossy') and having poor 'General Knowledge'. Factor 1 was strongly associated with standardized performance scores from the December examination ($r = .75$, p<.001), with the high-attaining pupils scoring most highly on this factor. The Factor 2 association with attainment was less strong ($r = .14$, p<.05). In the July factor analysis, Factor 1 was negatively loaded and associated poor 'General Knowledge' with poor 'Concentration' and poor 'Pay Attention' in class. Factor 2 was positive and associated good 'General Knowledge' with the ability to 'Work in a Group' and 'Popularity with Peers'. By the end of the school year, teachers now associated knowledge with a positive use of social and communication skills (good peer relations and ability to work with/in a classroom group). In December, poor social skills ('Bossy' with peers) had been associated with poor 'General Knowledge'. In July, poor 'General Knowledge' was now associated with poor levels of 'Pay Attention' and 'Concentration'. Each of the July factors was significantly associated with school achievement (Factor 1, $r = .58$, p<.001, and Factor 2, $r = .85$, p<.0001). One particular change with regard to the individual items on the

Table 10.5 Reliable factors identified in Education Questionnaire, December and July (Study 2)

	Factor	Eigen Value	Variance	Cronbach's alpha	Characteristics
December					
	1	4.58	41.62%	0.89	General knowledge Pay attention Demands of group work
	2	1.29	11.72%	0.68	Dependence of teacher (-) Bossy with peers (-) General knowledge (-)
July					
	1	3.46	31.43%	0.86	General knowledge (-) Pay attention (-) Concentration (-)
	2	2.61	23.73%	0.76	General knowledge Demands of group work Popular with peers

Source: Layne *et al.* (2008).

questionnaire showed a decrease in 'Dependence on Teacher' by children in the lowest quartile [$F(3, 259) = 5.42$, $p<.001$].

Over the two terms of Study 2, the 12 teachers became more aware of the importance of communication and interpersonal skills – and these skills were seen to allow higher levels of participation and attainment for all pupils in their classes. When they reflected on the changes in their classes over the two terms, the teachers did not identify (in particular) the enhanced relational skills used by the pupils. Rather, they focused on how relational development was associated with general knowledge, the ability to get along with peers and dialogue/communication skills. Teachers were particularly impressed with the improvement in attainment of their pupils, with one stating: 'Overall results for terms 2 and 3 showed a steady improvement in 90 per cent of pupils, with the remaining 10 per cent exhibiting negligible declines.' Teachers also noted that the increased level of communication and participation in their classrooms was associated with less absenteeism and withdrawal from classroom discussion. The relational approach for group work was seen to encourage a network of social support processes that built trust and cooperation among pupils:

Group [relational] work helped to create new alliances both academic and social. It gave the pupils the opportunity to put forward and discuss their opinions and learn from each other. It enabled them to be self-reliant, thus depending less on the teacher. Ultimately it has contributed to an improved academic performance as they relinquish some of their inhibitions, like shyness, and become more asser-tive. Pupils who did not get a chance to speak in a whole-class situation became more vocal in a small group setting.

Similarly, another teacher stated:

> More student-to-student interaction took place. In class discussions, more students responded to their classmates. A few of the more reserved students began to partici-pate in class discussion, volunteer answers and ask questions. High ability students showed independence [from the teacher] ... they also demonstrated patience with group members of low ability. Students began taking more responsibility for their own learning and for their classmates' learning.

The relational approach for group work allowed a more inclusive classroom atmosphere wherein a range of high- and low-ability children were seen to engage in dialogue with peers and teachers. While increased levels of participation and communication were observed by teachers across all classrooms, there was also a strong association with improved (cognitive) attainment – especially among the (initially) lowest-attaining pupils. Teachers' understanding of the relationship between participation and under-standing was also found among the pupils. One boy, initially identified as low-attaining stated benefits of the approach: 'You will get more information when you are in a group instead of by yourself.' Another boy commented on his increased liking for schooling: 'Because I learn to communicate with other people, and also to develop work. I also learn to have courage and strength I learn to work better. I also build self-esteem.'

Study 3: Developing a relational approach to peer-based, pre-school experience: establishing the bases for dialogue and inclusion during 'learning' time

This study focuses on pre-school children, especially their interaction and communication with others during (classroom) time devoted to cognitive/learning activities. There has been comparatively little research undertaken concerning dialogue and communication with this age group and, as one may expect, the results presented are indicative rather than representative of development in pre-school. Again, this was an action research study with no control classes. The study was undertaken in 16 nursery and reception classrooms of children aged 4 to 5 years in England over a school year. It assessed communicative and interactional effects associated with the implementation of an age-appropriate relational approach to group work (similar to the two previous studies reported). The study was also based on the need to establish the range and type of social pedagogic contexts in which young children engaged when undertaking cognitive/learning tasks, and served as a complement to 'playground-based' research that focused on children of a similar age in the United States (Buysse, Goldman and Skinner 2003; Kontos and Herzog-Wilcox 1997). Playground research showed a strong tendency towards social exclusion in children's play behaviours and groupings and raises questions regarding the role of social inclusion within dialogue and communication. In addition, the play and exclusion literature also notes that relationships that develop among young children are dominated by gendered, ability and ethnicity-based friendships of similarity, and these relationships may inhibit dialogue and communication (associated with cognitive development) among some children (Kutnick and Kington 2005).

The main research measure employed in this study was the 'classroom map'; a phenomenographic tool designed by Kutnick and Blatchford (Kutnick *et al.* 2002). Classroom mapping is based on a physical plan of a classroom that is drawn at the beginning of a school day. At a pre-selected time (during cognitive/learning activities) the researcher records the physical place of all children and adults in the room on the map, and then circles are placed around all groupings of peers and children with adults. Each grouping is then assessed for group size and composition, activity being undertaken and communicative interaction. Communicative interaction was categorized by type of interpersonal activity (from Parten and Newhall 1943) and included 'Joint' (mutual between partners in any grouping); 'Parallel' (simultaneous actions among partners but no evidence of working together); and 'Solitary' (no attempt to interact, even when in the presence of a partner). Each of these communicative interactions types also noted whether reciprocal verbal communication between group members took place or not. Two data collection points were used in the study: 1) a 'mapping' phase at the beginning of the school year; and 2) a final 'mapping' at the end of the school year. Between the autumn and summer mappings, the relational approach (described previously) for group work was co-adapted with teachers and implemented. Teachers were supported in their implementation of the relational approach by termly meetings and half-termly visits by a research officer.

A minimum of four mappings was completed per classroom in each of the autumn and summer terms. Mappings within each data collection point showed a high degree of consistency (see Kutnick *et al.* 2006 for further explanation). Autumn term mapping clearly identified that children engaged in two separate social pedagogic worlds during cognitive/learning (within classroom) time; the worlds were related to teachers and peers respectively. Within their teacher-groups, children undertook learning activities in groups of six to eight children. Child-groups were composed of two to three children. The larger teacher-groups were likely to represent a cross-section of the class, including boys and girls, friends and non-friends and various ages[1] of children. Interaction and communication categories showed that a majority of interpersonal activity between teacher and child was characterized by 'Reciprocal Communication' (for example, an initiated question or statement and a relevant reply). This accounted for nearly 75 per cent of interactions within these groupings. Communication types included 'Joint' (37 per cent of the observations made); 'Parallel' (52 per cent); and 'Solitary' (15 per cent not interacting with anyone). Child-groups tended to be exclusively composed of children that were same sex, friends and of a single age. There was little or no adult presence in child-groups. 'Reciprocal Communication' was lower than teacher-groups, approximately 57 per cent of the observations. There was a high proportion of 'Solitary' activity observed (31 per cent of observations). Other communication types included 'Joint' (36 per cent); and 'Parallel' (34 per cent). Thus, in these classrooms, most exposure to high levels of communicative activity (associated with cognitive development) took place within teacher-groups, and the potential for child-groups to achieve communication-based cognitive development was limited.

Table 10.6 displays changes in types of communicative activity between autumn and summer terms for child- and teacher-groups. Table 10.7 collapses the types of interpersonal activity (in Table 10.6) to show whether these activities took place with or without reciprocal communication. Within the autumn term, Table 10.6 displays a relatively high rate of 'Solitary' activity (approximately 33 per cent) and Table 10.7 shows relatively low rates of 'Reciprocal Communication' (60 per cent). Table 10.6 highlights that there was a significant change in the nature of communication (combined) between autumn and summer terms [χ^2 (5, N = 817) = 31.14, p<.001]. 'Joint' activity with reciprocal communication increased most dramatically, from 30.2 per cent in the autumn to 41.8 per cent. All forms of interpersonal activity without reciprocal communication decreased. Differences between activity with and without reciprocal communication over the year changed significantly (Table 10.7) with communication within interpersonal activity increasing significantly [χ^2 (1, N = 817) = 17.41, p<.001].

Within teacher-group activities (Table 10.6) 'Solitary' and 'Parallel' interpersonal activity with reciprocal communication decreased from autumn to summer, while 'Joint' with reciprocal communication increased. In child-group activities there was a decrease in all interpersonal activity categories without reciprocal communication and increases in the two categories 'Parallel' with reciprocal communication and 'Joint' with reciprocal communication. 'Solitary' activity decreased generally over the year. While the changes in teacher-groups did not achieve statistical significance, changes in the child-groups were significant [χ^2 (5, N = 637) = 23.26, p<.001]. These changes in interpersonal communication for child-groups were further associated with greater social inclusion: an analysis of interaction within their social relationships revealed that the category 'Joint' with reciprocal communication increased for 'friends' (51.6 per cent to 81.5 per cent), 'not-friends' (28.6 per cent to 46.7 per cent) and 'mixed friends/ not friends' (38.2 per cent to 53.6 per cent).

Comparative changes in the children's and teachers' classroom actions over the year showed a decrease in average size of teacher-groups (from 9.3 to 5.9) and an increase in child-groups (from 2.2 to 2.4). While composition remained similar in teacher-groups, the slight increase in child-groups indicated a move towards greater inclusion (these larger groups were more likely to be composed of mixed-age, mixed-sex and combined friend and non-friends).

In addition, teachers involved in the project perceived a number of changes in their practice, classroom behaviour and children's relationships over the year. Several teachers anecdotally noted that the 'improvement' in children's interpersonal relationships made their work (as teachers) easier, as there were fewer incidents of exclusion that concerned children and greater amounts of joint activity/engagement on tasks: 'It has helped to bring together a class with very wide ranging difficulties and skills from learning difficulties to exceptional intelligence.' And: 'my children are happy to socialize, play and work together – inclusive of gender, race and learning difficulties.' Many teachers also changed their approach in grouping children, overcoming the ideas that it is best to group by friendship: '[We are] more aware of how we pair children – previously we would pair friends without thinking about it.' They also developed strategies to avoid the risk of new groupings where things may 'go wrong'. They felt more confident in

Table 10.6 Nature of interpersonal activity within child- and teacher-groups across autumn and summer terms (% in brackets) (Study 3)

Activity	Child-groups Autumn	Summer	Teacher-groups Autumn	Summer	Combined Autumn	Summer
Solitary with communication	28 (8.1)	16 (5.5)	6 (8.1)	6 (5.7)	34 (8.1)	22 (5.5)
Solitary without communication	94 (27.2)	66 (22.7)	11 (14.9)	15 (14.2)	105 (25.0)	81 (20.4)
Parallel with communication	69 (19.9)	81 (27.8)	21 (28.4)	23 (21.7)	90 (21.4)	104 (26.2)
Parallel without communication	43 (12.4)	18 (6.2)	7 (9.5)	4 (3.8)	50 (11.9)	22 (5.5)
Joint with communication	99 (28.6)	108 (37.1)	28 (37.8)	58 (54.7)	127 (30.2)	166 (41.8)
Joint without communication	13 (3.8)	2 (0.7)	1 (1.4)	0 (0.0)	14 (3.3)	2 (0.5)
Total	346 (100)	291 (100)	74 (100)	106 (100)	106 (100)	397 (100)

Source: Kutnick, Colwell & Canavan, 2006.

Table 10.7 Communication within interpersonal activity across both school terms (% in brackets) (Study 3)

Activity	Terms Autumn	Summer	Total
Activity with communication	251 (59.8)	292 (73.6)	543 (66.5)
Activity without communication	169 (40.2)	105 (26.4)	274 (33.5)
Total	420 (100)	397 (100)	817 (100)

Source: Kutnick, Colwell & Canavan, 2006.

'standing back' to allow children to express their views and solve problems among themselves: 'I now encourage children to find solutions rather than me resolving them.' By the end of the year, teachers described their children as demonstrating: increased questioning and joint problem-solving; increased collaboration and negotiation within relational activities; increased confidence and self-esteem; an ability to resolve their own disputes; a widening of friendships; and support for each other in terms of learning and feelings. Teachers particularly noted increases in children's self-esteem: 'those with low self-esteem have found a place where they feel comfortable.' And: 'the children's confidence has continued to grow and I believe they have become more caring about each other – asking question about how others are feeling.'

Findings from this pre-school study indicate that implementation of a relational approach in classrooms was associated with lower levels of solitary activity and increased reciprocal communication skills among peers and with teachers. In addition, teachers' reflections identified that children overcame early interpersonal problems, were able to (socially) include a wider range of peers within their interactions and be more sensitive to the needs and feelings of peers. While there is no direct correspondence between these communicative/interpersonal developments and cognitive development, the study identifies that the communicative conditions wherein cognitive-based dialogues were enhanced with regard to teachers and especially among peers. Further, readers may be circumspect as to whether these findings may be attributed to the implementation of a relational approach over a school year as opposed to normal development of pre-school children. A fuller exposition of this study (Kutnick *et al.* 2006) compared autumn and summer term maps in this implementation year with maps of the same teachers (but different children) made in the previous summer term. Correlation analyses found that the communication and types of activities engaged in the (previous) summer to be of greater similarity to the (mapped) autumn term as opposed to the summer term of the relational implementation year.

Conclusion

The three studies described are based on the premise that classroom dialogue is fundamental for cognitive/learning development. The studies stress that dialogue needs to be understood within the social pedagogic context of the classrooms (and the groupings that children find themselves in during 'learning' activity time) and challenge the assumption that working in groups without relational preparation is likely to promote 'dialogue'. The studies note that the potential for high (elaborated) levels of dialogue requires participation by children and relational support to overcome threats to participation, status differences and stereotypical (often friendship-based) preferences. To overcome problems associated with low levels of cognitive communication and types of interaction that characterize many current classrooms, the studies drew upon aspects of social and developmental psychologies to develop a relational theory and co-construct a sequence of relational activities. The application of the sequences of relational activities in classrooms was associated with increased cognitive/attainment, participation and interpersonal communication. Underlying these studies, a range of issues have been identified that may further establish the role/use of relational approaches within classrooms.

The issues that arise include development of relational theory and practice. Theoretically, we questioned whether relationships are a prerequisite, a process or a product of the interaction that enhances the quality of dialogue. We began with the premise that positive relationships do not simply arise from children's friendships and other social experience, and posed that some relational training may be required to produce high levels of dialogue. With regard to the social pedagogic context within which dialogue takes place, we are concerned about the types of peers (and others) with whom the child interacts. Finally, we suggest that the teacher should have a role in development and support of relational development (for dialogue) of their children.

Relational approach. Each of the studies began with the assumption that children's dialogue would benefit from development of relational approaches within classrooms. We have, until now, avoided questioning whether positive relationships need to be pre-established or are developed as an outcome of dialogue and other relational activities. Our stance on this issue is 'a bit of both'. We recognize that inclusion of relational approaches in classrooms provides a process similar to the cognitive/interpersonal co-regulation advocated by Cazden *et al.* (1979) and Salonen *et al.* (2005). Beyond this, Study 1 showed that early relational training accounted for some early differences in the amount and type of dialogue engaged in between experimental and control classes. By the spring term communication analysis, enhanced reciprocal dialogue among the experimental children appeared to be the basis for further development of 'co-regulated' dialogue through the summer term. Simply stating that a training programme (Jarvelä *et al.* 2000) is necessary does not identify why the relational approach was effective. We see that the early (in a school year) establishment of positive relationships between classroom peers thus becomes a basis for greater amounts of high-level cognitive interaction among children (seen in Studies 1 and 2) during the school year – allowing a 'spiral' of interactions that facilitate further dialogue and cognitive understanding. Having supportive relationships becomes a substantive basis to expand the use of high levels of dialogue among children. The spiral acknowledges a dynamic between prerequisite relational skills coupled with supportive practice within the classroom. It is of further interest that the type of reciprocal dialogue most associated with enhanced cognitive/attainment was symmetrical (or similarly referred to as mutual or connected from Damon and Phelps 1989; and identified in Studies 1 and 2) as opposed to instructionally based asymmetrical or unilateral.

Social pedagogic context. Similar to calls for 'heterogeneous' grouping by Slavin (1995) and Cohen (1994) (to overcome status, gender, friendship preferences among children), the relational approach was designed to allow children experience of working with peers beyond their preferred partners. A fundamental aspect of the social pedagogic context in classrooms is the composition and support of pupil groupings. While it may be assumed that working with a teacher is inherently a socially inclusive activity (especially in Study 3), much of children's cognitive/learning time is spent away from the teacher and in group situations that may support social exclusion or threaten children's ability to work with one another (Galton *et al.* 1999; Kutnick *et al.* 2005). If high levels of dialogue (associated with elaborated talk) are to be promoted and sustained in classrooms, this dialogue must be undertaken with a range of other children in a non-threatening manner. Study 2 provided evidence that even (initially) low-attaining children can benefit from improved dialogue (leading to increases in their attainment) via working supportively with others and their teachers need to realize that this dialogue is not just arbitrary 'talk' but talk that is associated with knowledge and the ability to share ideas with others. Study 3 also showed that relational support encouraged more joint interaction with communication in child-groups, a corresponding decrease of solitary activity and greater levels of social inclusion within these groupings.

Role of the teacher. Within the three studies, it is important to give further consideration to the teachers who co-constructed, implemented and supported relational activities in their classrooms. Teachers are responsible for the physical setting of their classrooms, provide opportunities for children to engage in relational activities, model and support these activities, and reflect on these activities with their children. In Study 2, changes in teacher attitudes towards relational activities coincided with greater levels of participation and dialogue among their pupils. Similar results (not described here) were also found in Studies 1 and 3 – where higher levels of teacher implementation of relational activities were associated with increased dialogue, communication, participation and attainment. Involvement of teachers in the implementation and support of relational approaches shows that a positive theory still demands positive practices in classrooms and over a lengthy period of implementation – from initial relational activities to continuing support and modelling in class.

Note

1   When 'age' is referred to in these analyses, only children in mixed-age nursery classes were included. The full sample also included children in reception classes, these classes were excluded from 'age' analyses because they were composed of a single age group.

References

Ainsworth, M., Bell, S. and Stayton, D. (1974) 'Infant-mother attachment and social development: "socialisation" as a product of reciprocal responsiveness to signals', in M. Richards and P. Light (eds) *Integration of a Child into a Social World*, Cambridge: Cambridge University Press.

Allport, G. (1954) *The Nature of Prejudice*, Cambridge, MA: Addison Welsley.

Anderson-Inman, L. and Ditson, L. (1999) Computer-based concept mapping; a tool for negotiating meaning, *Learning and Leading with Technology*, 26:7–13.

Azmitia, M. and Montgomery, R. (1993) 'Friendship, trans-active dialogues, and the development of scientific reasoning', *Social Development*, 2:202–21.

Baines, E., Blatchford, P. and Kutnick, P. (2008) 'Pupil grouping for learning: developing a social pedagogy of the classroom', in R. Gillies, A. Ashman and J. Terwel (eds) *The Teacher's Role in Implementing Co-operative Learning in Classrooms*, New York, NY: Springer.

Barrett, M and Trevitt, J. (1991) *Attachment Behaviour and the School Child*, London: Routledge.

Battistich, V. and Watson, M. (2003) 'Fostering social development in pre-school and early elementary grades through co-operative classroom activities', in R. M. Gillies and A. F. Ashman (eds), *Co-operative Learning: the social outcomes of learning in groups*, London: RoutledgeFalmer.

Bennett, N. (1994) 'Co-operative learning', in P. Kutnick and C. Rogers (eds) *Groups in Schools*, London: Cassell.

Blatchford, P., Galton, M., Kutnick, P. and Baines, E. (2005) *Improving the Effectiveness of Pupil Groups in Classrooms*. End of award report to the Economic and Social Research Council. Available online at: http://www.spring-project.org.uk/spring-Publications. htm (accessed 11 September 2006).

Bossert, S., Barnett, B. and Filby, N. (1985) 'Grouping and instructional organisation', in P. Peterson, L. Wilkinson and M. Hallinan (eds), *The Social Context of Instruction*, Orlando, FL: Academic Press.

Buysse, V., Goldman, B. D. and Skinner, M. L. (2003) 'Friendship formation in inclusive early education classrooms: what is the teacher's role?', *Early Childhood Research Quarterly*, 18:485–501.

Cazden, C. B., Cox, M., Dickinson, D., Steinberg, Z. and Stone, C. (1979) 'You all gonna hafta listen: peer teaching in a primary classroom', in W. A. Collins (ed.), *Children's Language and Communication: the Minnesota Symposia on Child Psychology*, 12, Hillsdale, NJ: Lawrence Erlbaum.

Cohen, E. (1994) 'Restructuring the classroom: conditions for productive small groups', *Review of Educational Research*, 64:1–35.

Cohen, E., Lotan, R. and Leechor, C. (1989) 'Can classrooms learn?', *Sociology of Education*, 62:75–94.

Cowie, H. and Rudduck, J. (1988) *Cooperative Group Work: an overview*, London: BP Education Service.

Damon, W. (1977) *The Social World of the Child*, San Fransisco, CA: Jossey Bass.

Damon, W. and Phelps, E. (1989) 'Critical distinctions among three approaches to peer education', *International Journal of Educational Research*, 58:9–19.

Davis, A. (1991) 'Piaget, teachers and education: into the 1990s', in P. Light, S. Sheldon and M. Woodhead (eds), *Learning to Think*, London: Routledge.

Deutsch, M. (1949) 'A theory of cooperation and competition', *Human Relations*, 2:129–52.

Doise, W. (1990) 'The development of individual competences through social interaction', in H. Foot, M. Morgan and R. Shute (eds) *Children Helping Children*, Chichester: Wiley.

Doise, W. and Mugny, G. (1984) *The Social Development of the Intellect*, Oxford: Pergamon Press.

Donaldson, M. (1978) *Children's Minds*, London: Fontana.

Fogel, A. (1993) *Developing through Relationships: origins of communication, self and culture*, London: Harvester-Wheatsheaf.

Fuchs, L., Fuchs, D., Hamlett, C., Phillips, C., Karns, K. and Dutka, S. (1997) 'Enhancing students' helping behaviour during peer mediated instruction with conceptual mathematical explanations', *The Elementary School Journal*, 97:223–49.

Galton, M. (1990) 'Grouping and groupwork', in C. Rogers and P. Kutnick (eds), *The Social Psychology of the Primary School*, London: Routledge.

Galton, M., Hargreaves, L., Comber, C., Wall, D. and Pell, A. (1999) *Inside the Primary Classroom: 20 years on*, London: Routledge.

Galton, M., Simon, B. and Croll, P. (1980) *Inside the Primary Classroom*, London: Routledge and Kegan Paul.

Gillies, R. (2008) 'Teachers' and students' verbal behaviours during cooperative learning', in R. Gillies, A. Ashman and J. Terwel (eds) *The Teacher's Role in Implementing Cooperative Learning in the Classroom*, New York, NY: Springer.

Hall, E. (1994) 'The social relational approach', in P. Kutnick and C. Rogers (eds) *Groups in Schools*, London: Cassell.

Hartup, W. (1978) 'Children and their friends', in H. McGurk (ed.) *Issues in Childhood Social Development*, London: Methuen.

Hinde, R. (1997) *Relationships: a dialectical perspective*, Hove: Psychology Press.

Howes, C. (1983) 'Patterns of friendship', *Child Development*, 53:217.

Howe, C. and Tolmie, A. (2003) 'Group work in primary school science: discussion, consensus and guidance from experts', *International Journal of Educational Research*, 39:51–72.

Jarvelä, S., Lehtinen, E. and Salonen, P. (2000) 'Socio-emotional orientation as a mediating variable in the teaching-learning interaction: implications for instructional design', *Scandinavian Journal of Educational Research*, 44:293–306.

Johnson, D. W. and Johnson, F. (2003a) *Joining Together: group theory and research*, Boston, MA: Allyn and Bacon.

Johnson, D. W. and Johnson, R. T. (2003b) 'Student motivation in co-operative groups: social interdependence theory', in R. M. Gillies and A. F. Ashman (eds) *Co-operative Learning: the social outcomes of learning in groups*, London: Routledge Falmer.

Jonasson, D. H., Carr, C. and Yuch, H.-P. (1998) Concept-mapping as cognitive learning and assessment tools, *Journal of Interactive Learning Research*, 8:289–308.

Kessen, W. (1991) 'The American child and other cultural inventions', in M. Woodhead, P. Light and R. Carr (eds) *Growing up in a Changing Society*, London: Routledge/OU.

Kontos, S. and Wilcox-Herzog, A. (1997) 'Influences on children's competences in early childhood classrooms', *Early Childhood Research Quarterly*, 12:247–62.

Kreijns, K. and Kirschner, P. A. (2005) 'Sociable CSCL and CSCoP environments: warming-up cold CSCL and CSCoP environments', paper presented at the European Association for Research on Learning and Instruction 11th Biennial Conference, Nicosia, Cyprus.

Kutnick, P. (1992) *Preschool Attendance and Primary School Performance in Trinidad, MPC*, St. Augustine, Trinidad: University of the West Indies.

Kutnick, P. (1994) 'Use and effectiveness of groups in classrooms: towards a pedagogy', in P. Kutnick and C. Rogers (eds) *Groups in Schools*, London: Cassell.

Kutnick, P. and Berdondini, L. (2009) 'Can the enhancement of group working in classrooms provide a basis for effective communication in support of school-based cognitive achievement in classrooms of young learners?', *Cambridge Journal of Education*, 39:71–94.

Kutnick, P. and Brees, P. (1982) 'The development of cooperation: explorations in cognitive and moral competence and social authority', *British Journal of Educational Psychology*, 52:361–5.

Kutnick, P. and Kington, A. (2005) 'Children's friendships and learning in school; cognitive enhancement through social interaction?', *British Journal of Educational Psychology*, 75:521–38.

Kutnick, P. and Manson, I. (1998) 'Social life in the classroom: towards a relational concept of social skills for use in the classroom', in A. Campbell and S. Muncer (eds), *The Social Child*, Hove, East Sussex: Psychology Press.

Kutnick, P. and Thomas, M. (1990) 'Dyadic pairings for the enhancement of cognitive development in the school curriculum; some preliminary results on science tasks', *British Educational Research Journal*, 16:399–406.

Kutnick, P., Blatchford, P. and Baines, E. (2002) 'Pupil groupings in primary school classrooms: sites for learning and social pedagogy?', *British Educational Research Journal*, 28:189–208.

Kutnick, P., Blatchford, P. and Baines, E. (2005) 'Grouping of pupils in secondary school classrooms: possible links between pedagogy and learning', *Social Psychology of Education*, 8:349–74.

Kutnick, P., Colwell, J. and Canavan, J. (2006) *Developing a Relational Approach to Peer-based, Pre-school Experience: establishing bases for inclusion and educational achievement*, final report for the Esme Fairbairn Foundation.

Kutnick, P., Layne, A. and Jules, V. (1997) *Gender and School Achievement in the Caribbean*, Department for International Development, Education Paper No. 21.

Kutnick, P., Ota, C. and Berdondini, L. (2008) 'Improving the effects of group working in classrooms with young school-aged children: facilitating attainment, interaction and classroom activity', *Learning and Instruction*, 18:83–95.

Layne, A. and Kutnick, P. (2001) 'Secondary school stratification, gender and other determinants of academic achievement in Barbados: a longitudinal study', *Journal of Education and Development in the Caribbean*, 5:81–101.

Layne, A., Kutnick, P., Jules, V. and Layne, C. (2008) 'Academic achievement, participation and groupwork skills in secondary school classrooms in the Caribbean', *International Journal of Educational Development*, 28:176–94.

Leech, N. A. and Wooster, A. (1986) *Personal and Social Skills: a practical approach for the classroom*, Exeter: Religious and Moral Education Press.

Light, P. and Littleton, K. (1994) 'Cognitive approaches to groupwork', in P. Kutnick and C. Rogers (eds), *Groups in Schools*, London: Cassell.

Littleton, K., Mercer, N., Dawes, L., Wegerif, R., Rowe, D. and Sam, C. (2005) 'Thinking together at Key Stage 1', *Early Years: An International Journal of Research and Development*, 25:165–80.

Luria, A. R. (1976) *Cognitive Development: its cultural and social foundations*, Cambridge, MA: Harvard University Press.

Maxwell, W. (1990) 'The nature of friendship in the primary school', in C. Rogers and P. Kutnick (eds) *The Social Psychology of the Primary School*, London: Routledge.

Mercer, N. (2000) *Words and Minds*, London: Routledge.

Mercer, N. and Littleton, K. (2007) *Dialogue and Development in Children's Thinking: a sociocultural approach*, London: Routledge.

Monteil, J.-M. (1992) 'Towards a social psychology of cognitive functioning', in M. von Granach, W. Doise and G. Mugny (eds), *Social Representation and the Social Bases of Knowledge*, Berne: Hubert.

Parten, M. B. and Newhall, S. M. (1943) 'Social behaviour of preschool children', in R. G. Barker, J. S. Kounin and H. F. Wright (eds) *Child Behaviour and Development*, New York, NY: McGraw-Hill.

Pearson, M. and Somekh, B. (2003) 'Concept mapping as a research tool; a study of primary children's representation of information and communication technologies', *Education and Information Technologies*, 8:5–22.

Perret-Clermont, A.-N. (1980) *Social Interaction and Cognitive Development in Children*, London: Academic Press.

Pfeiffer, J. W. and Jones, J. E. (1983) *Handbook of Structured Exercises for Human Relations Training*, La Jolla, CA.: University Associates.

Piaget, J. (1928) *Language and Thought of the Child*, London: Routledge and Kegan Paul.

Piaget, J. (1932) *The Moral Development of the Child*, London: Routledge and Kegan Paul.

Piaget, J. (1971) *The Science of Education and Psychology of the Child*, London: Longman.

Salonen, P., Vauras, M. and Efklides, A. (2005) 'Social interaction: what can it tell us about metacognition and coregulation in learning?', *European Psychologist*, 10:199–208.

Selman, R. (1980) *The Growth of Interpersonal Understanding*, New York, NY: Academic Press.

Slavin, R. (1990) *Co-operative Learning: theory, research and practice*, Englewood Cliffs, NJ: Prentice Hall.

Slavin, R. (1995) *Cooperative Learning* (2nd edn), Boston, MA: Allyn and Bacon.

Stayton, D., Hogan, R. and Ainsworth, M. S. (1971) 'Infant obedience and maternal behaviour: the origins of socialization reconsidered', *Child Development*, 42:1057–69.

Sullivan, H. S. (1953) *The Interpersonal Theory of Psychiatry*, New York: Norton.

Thacker, J., Stoate, P. and Feest, G. (1992) *Using Group Work in the Primary Classroom*, Exeter: Southgate Publishers Ltd.

Vandell, D. L. and Mueller, E. C. (1980) 'Peer play and friendship during the first two years', in H. C. Foot, A. J. Chapman and J. R. Smith (eds) *Friendship and Social Relations in Children*, Chichester: John Wiley.

Vygotsky, L. (1978) *Mind and Society: the development of higher mental processes*, Cambridge, MA: Harvard University Press.

Webb, N. (1989) 'Peer interaction and learning in small groups', *International Journal of Educational Research*, 13:21–39.

Webb, N. M. and Farivar, S. (1994) 'Promoting helping behaviour in cooperative small groups in middle school mathematics', *American Educational Research Journal*, 31:369–95.

Webb, N. M. and Mastergeorge, A. (2003) 'Promoting effective helping behaviour in peer-directed groups', *International Journal of Educational Research*, 39:73–97.

Wegerif, R., Mercer, N. and Dawes, L. (1999) 'From social interaction to individual reasoning: an empirical investigation of a possible socio-cultural model and cognitive development', *Learning and Instruction*, 9:493–516.

Youniss, J. (1978) 'The nature of social development: a conceptual discussion of cognition', in H. McGurk (ed.) *Issues in Childhood Social Development*, London: Methuen.

Youniss, J. (1980) *Parents and Peers in Social Development*, Chicago, IL: University of Chicago Press.

Youniss, J. (1992) 'Parent and peer relations in the emergence of cultural competence', in H. McGurk (ed.) *Childhood Social Development: contemporary perspectives*, Hove, East Sussex: Lawrence Erlbaum.

Chapter 11

Gender, collaboration and children's learning

Patrick J. Leman
Royal Holloway, University of London

Gender and the social context of peer collaboration

Beliefs about gender differences in intelligence, education or cognitive ability permeate society. Such beliefs also appear in academic discourses. For instance, Baron-Cohen (2004) has recently argued that the different cognitive styles of men and women (systemizing and empathizing, respectively) suit them to different domains of academic study and career. Whether we agree with such arguments or not, it is difficult to imagine that these and other commonly held perceptions of the genders do not tie in to processes of communication and collaboration in some way or other. This 'tie-in' might operate in two directions: for instance, differing expectations and stereotypes of gender may affect how children communicate and collaborate with one another. But gender differences in communication may also create or reinforce these expectations and stereotypes (Maccoby 1988, 1998). Of course, the two possibilities are not mutually exclusive, and it is often assumed that there is an intimate inter-relationship between gendered patterns of communication and gender attitudes and stereotypes (Leaper and Ayres 2007). Given this close relationship it should not be surprising that gender differences in classroom communication have been presented as strong candidates for explaining variations in educational outcomes.

The core focus of the present chapter is on how gender influences the dynamics of children's conversations and collaborations, and whether this influence extends to the outcomes of collaboration – learning and development. The chapter begins with an examination of possible sources of gender differentiation in communication and learning; first by describing how gendered messages that teachers send to children may affect learning, then by exploring how parents, peers, and children's own gender knowledge can influence communication in terms of learning and education. Having reviewed the broader context in which gender knowledge and communication is embedded, the focus moves to children's own peer relations and how gender frames the dynamics of children's conversations. The section concludes with a review of theoretical accounts of the relation between gender and conversation.

The chapter then turns to examine the relation between gender and peer collaboration, beginning with an examination of how different approaches to collaborative learning may (or may not) incorporate a role for gender. Next, the focus turns to details of specific research (Leman, Ahmed and Ozarow 2005) and details ways in which the social dynamics of interaction differ. Three different types of collaborative engagement are proposed: *collaborative*, *dominance-conflict*, and *dominant-compliant* interaction. These styles link with gender and the gender relations that arise between children engaged in conversation. Lastly, we consider how gender can operate as a source of constraint or grounds for resistance in interaction.

The final section explores how gender may inform understanding of collaboration and of interventions to promote effective classroom interaction. First, the question of how far gender affects the outcomes of collaboration in single- and mixed-sex interactions is addressed. Then the focus moves to how other aspects of identity – notably ethnicity and friendship – can combine with gender to affect collaboration and learning. Lastly, directions for future research are proposed.

Gendered education, gendered communication

Gender differences in communication may send boys and girls, and men and women, subtle (or sometimes not so subtle) messages about what is expected of them in an educational context. This is, albeit expressed with greater sophistication than is possible here, the core claim of socially contextualized accounts of gender differences in education (e.g. Walkerdine 1998), which see the roots of gender differences in achievement as social (societal or cultural) rather than biological. For these accounts, communication is *the* vehicle through which children can become empowered or disempowered (enfranchised or disenfranchised) within educational contexts. Communication is key because it is through classroom interactions that teachers communicate how academic domains or discourses are gendered: so a teacher may have differing expectations for boys and girls that she conveys to the child, and the child internalizes, with subsequent educational consequences.

Socially contextualized or social constructionist accounts are compelling because they offer researchers a means of linking broader social structures, norms and stereotypes with the micro-genetic process through which knowledge is communicated and constructed in the classroom. However, a sense that social and cultural norms of interaction are transmitted from adults to children is implicit in many social constructionist approaches. Consequently, these accounts may leave little room for children to understand or construct an understanding of their own and others' gender (Lloyd and Duveen 1992) or of the nuances of gender relations. Moreover, a primary focus on the content of these messages (e.g. 'Maths is not for girls') neglects to consider how children may find opportunities to overturn or contradict these adult expectations in their own interactions with their peers. Of course, that is not to say that children may not frequently reproduce gender stereotypes in their conversations, arguments and collaborations with peers. But peer interaction offers an opportunity to test out ideas in a forum that is independent of adult supervision, where outcomes can be demonstrably independent of prior expectations (e.g. counter-intuitive findings in a science task) and where, away from adults' watchful gaze, children can appreciate for themselves that the messages they receive regarding gender roles and expectations do not always reflect a complex reality.

Like social constructionist approaches, accounts of development and learning from a socio-cultural perspective place the notion of identity at the centre of their theory. For instance, Lave and Wenger's (1991) account of situated learning emphasizes the importance of meaning-making and learning as reflexive processes. These processes necessarily take place within social interaction. Again, communication and interaction are at the heart of such accounts. However, it is identity as a learner (or participant) that is central to these approaches (Wenger 1998), rather than identity as a boy or as a girl. Of course, discourses of gender are one important factor in determining how far one participates and is a member of a learning community, and notions of gender are transmitted from one generation of learners to the next (Kotthoff and Baron 2001). Yet few empirical studies in this tradition seek to link the specifics of interaction and collaboration to gender and to learning outcomes. Thus an important and outstanding issue concerns understanding the specifics and dynamics of children's interactions; it is in such interactions that the seeds for learning may be sown and begin to germinate, and it is within these interactions that educators can intervene to stimulate more effective collaboration and learning.

Gender is an important influence on conversation and interaction dynamics as well as educational processes and outcomes. In many respects, this influence should not be surprising since gender is a ubiquitous and binary social category (Lloyd and Duveen 1992) that often operates as a means of organizing classroom life; for instance, in many schools boys and girls will wear different clothes, or have coat pegs or seats arranged in some way dependent on gender. Moreover, gender differentiation may arise from within children's peer relationships themselves through gender cleavage in children's friendship preference that is evident from pre-school onwards (see Maccoby 1998). However, perhaps as a consequence of this ubiquity and importance as a social category, gender may not always function psychologically in the same way as other social 'variables' (Deaux 1984; Maccoby 1988). Individuals often have a subtle and complex understanding of gender and gender roles, which may mean rules and laws that might be applied to simple intergroup phenomena do not so readily apply to gender.

The research literature points to a need to recognize the ways in which gender is embedded in numerous aspects of children's everyday lives and interactions. Consequently there is a corresponding need to understand children's collaboration as involving a complex web of different processes, including how children make sense of their own and others' gender, their cognitive capabilities, and a variety of further sources of influence including the media, parents, and peers.

Parents, peers and gender socialization

Of all the sources of gender differentiation to which children are exposed, the earliest and most impactful are probably their parents. Empirical studies provide compelling evidence that parents frequently differentiate between boys and girls in the beliefs they have about their abilities and the language they use to teach them. So, for instance, parents often have differing beliefs about their sons' and daughters' aptitude for science subjects, and as a consequence may use more conceptually complex language when explaining scientific concepts to a son compared with a daughter (Crowley, Callanan, Tenenbaum and Allen 2001; Tenenbaum and Leaper 2003). In other domains (e.g. more feminine-typed areas such as languages) parent-child communication patterns may be affected in other ways. In the domain of mathematics achievement at least, it appears that mothers' beliefs correspond more closely than fathers' to their children's estimations of their own ability (Frome and Eccles 1998). Differences in parents' expectations of the achievement of boys and girls also increase with age, which is consistent with the prediction from the *gender intensification hypothesis* (e.g. Crouter, Manke and McHale 1995) that proposes that in adolescence pressures to adhere to traditional gender roles increase – both from a child's peer group and possibly also from parents.

The context of parental beliefs about children's aptitudes and abilities is important because it may provide grounding for children's beliefs about themselves and interactions at school. Moreover, if there are differences at home in how parents communicate with sons and daughters, children may either reproduce these in interactions with peers or expect such differentiation to be a feature of academic discussions. Thus these variations in parents' language use are doubtless crucial for understanding how gender and other aspects of identity may influence educational outcomes.

Once at school, teachers may also interact in different ways with boys and girls. In a meta-analytic review, Kelly (1988) found that teachers tended to pay slightly more attention to boys on a host of measures of classroom interaction (including total time, responding to questions) even though girls tended to volunteer (put their hands up) more often. However, the most marked gender differences were related to evaluations of behaviour: boys were criticized almost twice as frequently as the girls. Kelly's findings, although rather dated, resonate with the more general observation that, in the early years at least, girls tend to benefit from paying more attention and complying more with teachers' demands and classroom rules (Serbin, Zelkowitz, Doyle and Wheaton 1990). Even when training draws attention to the need to be sensitive to gender issues in the classroom, teachers may not be immune to demonstrating the same gender differences in expectations and communication that have been observed in parent-child interaction (Jones, Evans, Byrd and Campbell 2000).

Adult-child interactions doubtless provide an important source of gender information for young children, and serve as a backdrop to many aspects of peer interactions. However, as we have seen, there are good reasons for viewing adult-child and peer interaction as qualitatively different. These differences have important implications in terms of how collaboration between children may lead to benefits in terms of learning and development. In a study of children's moral reasoning, Kruger (1992) observed that children were less vocal participants and showed fewer benefits on post-test when they interacted with an adult compared with a peer. Authority and asymmetry in expertise and status characterize much adult-child interaction, whereas in peer interaction children may feel freer to ask questions, explore, and construct an understanding of phenomena for themselves. In this respect, the alternative dynamics of adult-child and peer interaction would appear to relate to rather different learning opportunities.

Peer collaboration thus offers children a different sort of opportunity for learning compared with adult-child interaction. In peer collaboration children may have more opportunity to explore or use apparatus, be more willing to ask questions or to articulate their own (incomplete) understanding, be more critical of another's ideas and generally engage in more child-friendly (child-relevant) language and discourse. In terms of gender, children's peer collaboration may involve the reproduction of gender differences that they observe in adult-adult interaction. They may also be influenced by gendering in how adults communicate with children. Collaboration is also affected by children's own gender schema and emerging gender knowledge. However, the relative freedom of peer collaboration may mean that gender affects interaction in distinctive ways that could present particular challenges or opportunities for collaborative learning in the classroom. Thus, before turning to consider the impact of gender on the learning outcomes of collaboration, it is important to explore how far gender affects the dynamics of peer collaboration specifically and interaction more generally.

Gender and the context of children's conversations

A great deal of research has charted consistent gender differences in adults' talk (e.g. Carli 1989; Leaper and Ayres 2007). Recently, there has been a research focus on the origins and developmental pathways that are associated with these differences. Leaper and Smith (2004) conducted a meta-analytic review of gender variations in children's language use. Their analysis confirmed that children, like adults, exhibit gender differences in conversational style. Girls use more affiliative speech, whereas boys use more assertive speech. The strongest effect sizes were associated with gender differences in the use of affiliative speech. Moreover, there was some evidence that differences were symptomatic of underlying changes in gender-related cognition and identity formation, with gender differences in affiliative speech diminishing during middle childhood, but re-emerging in adolescence.

Gender differences in some aspects of language use appear early on in life. From 12 months, for instance, there is some evidence that girls are more talkative than boys (DeLoache and DeMendoza 1987), although it remains uncertain whether these gender effects reflect differences in innate language abilities or are the consequence of different socialization experiences. By around 5 years there are only minimal gender differences in talkativeness. Whatever the initial causes, it is unarguable that by school-age children have an emerging knowledge of gender and gender relations (Martin, Ruble and Szkrybalo 2002) that can influence their attitudes, behaviour and reasoning both explicitly and implicitly (Davis, Leman and Barrett 2007). Throughout childhood, male and female conversational styles may become entrenched as boys and girls tend to play with children of the same gender, and engage more often in own gender-typed activities. Thus gendered communication styles are reinforced.

It is certainly the case that, by early childhood, children reproduce gendered conversational styles in their interactions with others. Their gender knowledge and experiences also guide their behaviour and conversations with their peers. By pre-school, children may react to the gender of a conversation partner and modify their conversations accordingly (Killen and Naigles 1995). Thus gender impacts on conversation dynamics.

Leman *et al.* (2005) explored the relation between gender and children's conversational styles in the context of a classroom-based problem-solving task. Children were given different shaped counters (circle, triangle, square) and then were individually told that each type of counter was associated with a different value (i.e. 10, 20 and 50). They were then asked to add counters together to make 100 in a pair with another child. However, unknown to both children, each child in a pair had been told conflicting information about the values associated with different counters. When asked to add the counters together, the differences in values created a conflict between children's perspectives, which led to discussion as children sought to agree a mutually acceptable solution. In the discussion, as expected, children used gendered styles of communication; specifically, 8-year-old girls' conversations were more marked by affiliative talk and less interruption than 8-year-old boys' conversations. Importantly, however, the children reacted to the gender of a conversation partner. Specifically, children subtly adapted their conversational styles between same-sex and mixed-sex (cross-sex) conversations: the most notable difference was that boys tended to interrupt a girl far more often than they interrupted another boy.

A further important consideration is in the influence of context on conversation dynamics. Leaper and Smith (2004) argued that activity context accounted for many gender differences in conversations between children. For instance, on feminine-typed games (e.g. playing 'home' or 'Mums and Dads') girls often assume a lead compared with the boys who were participating, whereas for masculine-typed games (e.g. 'superheroes') boys are more frequently dominant. Children, even from a young age, appear sensitive to the context of interaction and respond if that context is gendered in some way.

Variations in the effects of gender in different contexts are profoundly relevant in an educational context. For instance, in a classroom task where boys are perceived (or perceive themselves) to be more able or motivated, boys might dominate apparatus and interaction in collaborative engagements in mixed-sex classrooms. In a task where girls are viewed as more able, girls might control key aspects of a task. Even in same-sex collaborations we may expect that children could be inhibited in expressing ideas at risk of appearing to act in counter-stereotypical ways (perhaps as a consequence of *stereotype threat*, e.g. Steele 1997). Context differences suggest that it would be simplistic to view male and female interactional styles as inevitable and universal, or that one gender will inevitably prevail over the other.

There are other ways in which gender influences on children's interaction might be affected by context. In early work on the *contact hypothesis*, Allport (1954) suggested that contact between individuals from different racial groups was more effective in reducing prejudice if interaction (contact) focused on a shared or superordinate goal rather than participants merely engaging in free talk. Connected with this, the *contextual interactive model* (Deaux and Major 1983) has proposed that gender differences in adult communication will be greatest when there is no shared goal or conversation focus. If the contextual interactive model translates to children's interaction we might expect that collaborative problem solving, and classroom tasks with a clearer and more defined focus, might result in fewer differences in communication between boys and girls. Conversely, more open-ended tasks, or ones that do not demand or attract children's attention, may result in greater gender differentiation.

Theoretical approaches to gender and interaction

Research into conversational dynamics has examined a range of divergent aspects of conversation across a variety of contexts including everyday disagreements (Carli 1989), children's moral discussions (Leman and Duveen 1999), and play (Leaper, Tenenbaum and Shaffer 1999). The measures employed are every bit as varied as the contexts studied: they include turn-taking (Sacks, Schegloff and Jefferson 1974), the use of interruption (Zimmerman and West 1975), talkativeness and 'air time' (Mehl, Vazire, Ramirez-Esparza, Slatcher and Pennebaker 2007), topic change and transition (Maynard 1980), and conversation initiation (Psaltis and Duveen 2007), as well as more global measures of assertiveness and affiliation (Leaper 1991).

Studies suggest that different elements of conversation correspond to (or reveal) different aspects of dynamics in conversation. These aspects may be automatic and not controlled or strategically deployed in conversation by those interacting. For instance, more conversational 'air time' (i.e. spending more time talking or occupying more turns in a conversation than a partner) is often taken as an indicator of social dominance. Interruptions can also mark dominance but appear to operate in rather complicated ways and often researchers distinguish different forms of simultaneous speech such as positive and negative interruption and overlapping speech (see again Leman *et al.* 2005).

From a methodological perspective, there are several alternative means of establishing conversation dynamics. In the quantitative tradition conversational elements are, almost invariably, coded syntactically (West and Zimmerman 1983). That is, elements of discourse are identified and coded outside of the semantic context in which they occur. However, Murray (1985) has argued that syntactic coding fails to capture the meanings that conversation participants make of interruptions. In other words, by excluding or ignoring the content of talk, researchers miss the ways in which individuals may tolerate or view the seriousness of different interruptions. Murray's point extends beyond work on interruption to the more general quantitative (turn-taking) model of conversation analysis.

The charge that disregarding the role of content when considering the use of different aspects of speech is a potentially serious one, because it suggests that it may be difficult to generalize quantitative findings to a range of conversations of a particular type. And, of course, it is clear that no two conversations will share identical dynamics because individuals are complex and this complexity will inevitably transfer to affect interpersonal communication. However, the suggestion that the complexity of interaction makes it impossible to study behavioural laws that chart those dynamics (e.g. Dillenbourgh, Baker, Blaye and O'Malley 1996) does not seem warranted. From an empirical perspective at least it may be possible to separate out dynamics from content in conversations. Okamoto, Rashotte and Smith-Lovin (2002) found little difference between syntactic and content-linked approaches to coding in terms of their effectiveness in capturing the dynamics of interaction. Thus the content of a conversation may lead to variations in the use of different aspects of conversation, but these variations appear to stem from changes in underlying dynamics rather than changes in the function of the elements of conversation themselves.

Many researchers have taken these aspects of conversations, and the differences in social dynamics that they correspond to, as the product of underlying social status differences. This approach is common to a series of studies concerning what has been labelled *expectation states theory* (e.g. Berger, Conner and Fisek 1974). Expectation states theory grew out of classic small group research (e.g. Bales 1951), and proposes that if a group expects one of its members to be more competent, the group will allow that individual to participate more and afford that member greater influence than others.

An important adjunct to expectation states theory is *status characteristics theory* (Berger, Hamit, Norman and Zelditch 1977; Berger, Rosenholtz and Zelditch 1980). Status characteristics theory proposes that if social categories (such as race or gender) are deemed relevant to task expertise in interaction, these characteristics will affect conversation dynamics. So in mixed-gender interaction, if conversation participants assume that gender is a relevant consideration in terms of expertise, conversation dynamics will alter accordingly to reflect this assumption.

Of course, it is not merely gender that can act as a source of status in interaction. The conversational consequences of status characteristics have been observed in a variety of settings for both 'natural' and 'artificial' categories of social life. For instance, alongside classic studies of gender as a status characteristic in conversation (e.g. Smith-Lovin and Brody 1989), status characteristics have been studied in doctor-patient consultations (Ohtaki, Ohtaki and Fetters 2007), juror and courtroom deliberation (Scherer 1979), and naturally occurring managerial discussions in the workplace (Gibson 1988, cited in Okamoto and Smith-Lovin 2001).

While status characteristics theory anticipates that categories of social life such as gender and race might influence dynamics in conversation, subsequent researchers also recognized that these categories may not always be salient or activated in interaction. Thus, Skvoretz and Farraro (1996) proposed that differences in the status of conversation participants can arise endogenously, even in initially status-equal groups. Moreover, if a high-status individual fails to make an expected contribution, the status dynamics can change. These processes are referred to as endogenous group dynamics (see again Okamoto and Smith-Lovin 2001). Thus, more recent incarnations of expectation states theory and status characteristics theories acknowledge that the dynamics in interaction can evolve in response to behaviour of group members.

The social roots of peer collaboration

Theoretical work into the influence of gender on conversation dynamics demonstrates a need to take social processes seriously when seeking to understand what goes on within collaboration. Alongside this work on dynamics sits theoretical and empirical work into collaboration processes. Although both areas have led to a considerable amount of research, the two research literatures rarely intersect. Yet a full consideration of this intersection is important if we are to understand fully what makes for effective, peer collaboration.

In a review, Slavin (1996) suggested four broad categories of explanation for the benefits of collaborative interaction. First, collaborating in a group increases *motivation* because participants recognize that a group can achieve more than an individual. A second, related explanation is that collaboration works because individuals are motivated not by achievement, but by a desire for *social cohesion*. Thus more altruistic and social concerns drive involvement in an activity and a positive outcome of this is better achievement.

On the face of things, the motivation and social cohesion accounts might suggest only minimal influence of gender and other social factors on conversation outcomes, given that success or social cohesion are of such fundamental importance. Moreover, there is no really clear evidence from adult studies on whether gender and aspects of social identity affect levels of motivation and the desire for social cohesion in interaction (Shaw and Barrett-Power 1998). Although the motivation and social cohesion accounts speak to social psychological work on decision-making, they are not well suited to explain processes of learning. In the classroom, more often than not, success is defined not only in terms of being able to reach a decision, but reaching the right decision and acquiring knowledge or developing understanding in some way. Thus motivation and social cohesion accounts may do a good job of explaining why children enjoy interacting in groups and learning together, but they do not articulate a clear account of why collaboration is associated with learning – longer-term, enduring changes in cognition and understanding of the reasons for the right answer – rather than decision-making.

Slavin (1996) also identified cognitive developmental perspectives as a further explanation for the benefits of collaboration. These included, for instance, Doise and Mugny's (1984) account of development through socio-cognitive conflict where the acquisition of knowledge is driven by intersubjectivity and the integration of divergent perspectives. Alongside Doise and Mugny's neo-Piagetian approach, neo-Vygotskian approaches (e.g. Wertsch 1991) would also fall under Slavin's banner of *cognitive developmental* theories. Finally, related to the cognitive developmental accounts, there are *cognitive elaboration* perspectives (King 1988) where any developmental work done by the child is undertaken on an individual level. In this case, the benefits of interaction arise from elaborating or articulating one's own position (or a set of arguments) to others in an interactive setting (Verba 1998).

Cognitive developmental and elaboration accounts are more clearly focused on learning outcomes and are certainly better suited to explaining how collaboration leads to learning than social cohesion and motivational accounts. The key question, then, for those interested in how gender relates to collaboration, is how its influence on the dynamics of interaction may filter in to influence cognitive processes. In this respect, the relationship between conflictual dynamics and collaboration is a particularly notable one. Given that research has revealed consistent conversational effects of gender, and given that gender is a source of intergroup (gender group) differentiation, one might anticipate that gender could be a source of conflict in interaction. This conflict could, in turn, jeopardize the chances of successful collaboration (Damon and Killen 1982). Of course, not everyone sees disadvantages to conflict in interaction. For instance, the idea of socio-cognitive conflict was at the heart of Doise and Mugny's (1984) account of learning through interaction, wherein socially marked conflict between alternative perspectives motivates developmental change. It is at least possible that conflict might be beneficial in collaboration or that it may lead to positive learning outcomes.

The significance of social dynamics in collaborative learning

There is a wealth of research charting communication and learning within an educational perspective (see for instance Doise and Mugny 1984; Mercer 2000). This work has unpicked how argumentation and communication can improve understanding, reasoning and thinking skills, but has not focused on how the dynamics of interaction and aspects of social identities might affect processes of persuasion, communication, and learning. From an educational perspective, the focus has tended to be on argument content rather than conversation dynamics.

The focus on conceptual content in communication is clearly important, but it is not the whole picture. For a long time social psychologists have demonstrated that processes of communication, influence, and persuasion are intimately tied to the social dynamics of interaction (Carli, LaFleur and Loeber 1995) or the behavioural style of those interacting (Moscovici, Mucchi-Faina and Maas 2004; Mugny and Papastamou 1982).

Moreover, there are grounds for believing that a simple distinction between argument content and argument dynamics cannot easily be sustained in the cut-and-thrust of conflictual interaction. Social dynamics therefore have a potential influence on collaboration; maybe by inhibiting discussion, or by bringing about an unproductive type of discussion. And any account of learning through discussion and collaboration needs to include a role for such dynamics.

Research on small groups, together with studies exploring expectation states and status characteristics theories, underscores the importance of considering the social dynamics of collaborative encounters. As we have seen, gender can be an effective ingredient in influencing those dynamics. For instance, boys' interaction may be characterized by dominance and girls' by affiliation, whereas boy-girl interaction can be characterized by asymmetry that stems from the contrasting expectations and styles of boys and girls (see again, Leman *et al.* 2005). Of course, it is important to remember that while certain styles may typify male and female interaction, boys can engage in productive affiliation and girls can be dominating in conversations too.

Social dynamics are important because they can affect whether and how arguments are adopted and discussed during peer collaboration. For instance, the opportunity to bring a fresh or divergent perspective may be suppressed if one child feels dominated by another, or conversation may not reach beyond the point of social conflict if both children dominate or seek to dominate interaction. Two children may also merely fail to communicate at all.

In order to illustrate the extent of potential differences in conversation and collaboration, three conversation examples from the study discussed earlier are presented below (Leman *et al.* 2005). The intention is not to present these as exclusive exemplars of male, female, or mixed-gender conversation types, although there appears to be a preponderance of certain types in the different types of interaction. Rather, the intention is to illustrate different conversation dynamics and how these give discussions a distinctive character.

The first excerpt features a conversation between Jamie (boy) and Sarah (girl). Again, both 8-year-old children were discussing how to use different value counters to add to 100. However, unknown to each of them, Jamie and Sarah had been told to associate different values to the triangle and square (either 20/50 or 50/20).

Excerpt 1

JAMIE All right, so, that's 50 [square] and if that was 50 [square] … makes 100.
SARAH No …
JAMIE So …
SARAH No. Well, I … Well … No … I think … I think triangle's 50. 'Cos first … I think … first I thought a square was 50, and now I think a triangle's 50. 'Cos I remember … I think … But now I think a triangle is best. Two triangles.
JAMIE It's not.
SARAH Yes.
JAMIE I think it's these two … But, what one do you think it is?
SARAH I think it's the triangles.
JAMIE All right then … so what are these?

SARAH You mean, you mean what cost?
JAMIE Yeah.
SARAH These ... these ... circles cost 10.
JAMIE 1, 2, 3, 4, 5, 6, 7, 8, 9, 10. [counts out counters]
SARAH Yeah.
JAMIE You agree with me?
SARAH Yeah.

Jamie and Sarah's conversation has many features of successful and 'typical' collaboration. Although both children are initially surprised by their differing expectations about the values of the counters, Sarah (line 4) challenges Jamie's assertion with a fuller explanation. Although Jamie initially rejects Sarah's assertion, in line 7 he acknowledges there is a difference of opinion. Then, in lines 9–11, Jamie outlines the route to a compromise deal where the pair choose ten circles (both children were told that circles were worth 10) to make 100. This style of conversation could be described as *collaborative* because both children, after initial disagreement, engage freely in a conversation strategy that is aimed at solving the task effectively. In terms of dynamics, the impression is of a balanced interaction where both children are focused on getting the answer right.

In contrast, the all-boy interaction between Sean and Mikey (below) is characterized by *dominance-conflict* in communication and argument.

Excerpt 2

SEAN Made one
MIKEY What, No! that's 50 ...
SEAN 50, 50 ...
MIKEY No!
SEAN 20, 10 ...
MIKEY Oh yeah
SEAN See I told yah
MIKEY Is that 50? I thought that was ...
SEAN (laughs) No, that's ...
MIKEY No, that's 50!
SEAN This is 50 ...
MIKEY That's 50!
SEAN That's 20!
MIKEY This is 50!
SEAN And that's 10!
MIKEY That's 50!
SEAN No, that's 50.
MIKEY That's 50!
SEAN 50, 20 ...
MIKEY No
SEAN And that's 10
MIKEY That's 50

SEAN No it ain't
MIKEY Is
SEAN Ain't
MIKEY Is, it is 50!
SEAN It ain't!
MIKEY Well, do your own way of making it then
SEAN All right then
MIKEY I made one. 10, 20, 30, 40, 50, 60, 70, 80, 90, 100
SEAN ... 60, 70, 80, 90, 100

It is difficult for the conversation to move forward from the initial recognition of disagreement (lines 1–2), and even when this disagreement is acknowledged (lines 8–9) the boys find it hard to address this difference but merely restate their own perspectives (lines 10–11). Only after repeatedly restating their own positions do the pair seek a compromise solution (lines 28–9), eventually agreeing on the same 10 × 10 counters solution that the first pair agreed on. Thus the pair overcomes their conflict but both boys seek to dominate and the interaction as a whole is marked by this disagreement.

A final pairing, Ashok (boy) and Jenny (girl), have a type of interaction that could be characterized as *dominant-compliant*.

Excerpt 3

ASHOK 50 and a 20, now we have to make 100, yeah, Jenny?
JENNY Yeah.
ASHOK We start from 50.
JENNY 50.
ASHOK 50 and 20.
JENNY Makes 70.
ASHOK 50, 20, 30, so we need a 10.
JENNY 100.

Although Jenny had been told that the counters were different values, she never raises an objection to Ashok's initial remarks (line 1). Ashok's dominance of the conversation is achieved by compliance on Jenny's part. There is little discussion of different perspectives before the solution is reached (line 8).

In this study, all-boy conversation tended to be characterized by the dominance-conflict type of interaction; in fact, of the 20 all-boy pairs in the study, 11 conversations could be classified as being the dominance-conflict type. All-girl interaction tended to be more akin to classic ideas of collaboration; 14 of the 20 all-girl pairs fell into this category. (But note that our example of collaborative interaction, above, was in fact between a boy and a girl. So it is important to stress, once again, that while we may see trends for certain types of interaction that follow gendered lines, the dynamics of interaction may depend on a complex interplay of different factors including expertise, social status, and ethnicity.) The final conversation between Ashok and Jenny represents an asymmetry in interaction that might be associated with dominant-compliant conversation types, and 11 of the 20 boy-girl pairs showed this interaction type. However, perhaps counter to intuitions, in six of those pairs it was the girl who dominated, whereas the boy was dominant in only five pairs. It is also worthwhile noting that there may be different forms of dominant-compliant conversations when the boy or the girl dominates. For instance, Leman and Duveen (1999) suggested that when girls dominate in mixed-gender interaction they may invoke circumspect forms of persuasion where aspects of conversation dynamics are more subtly, but just as forcefully, controlled.

Conversation dynamics, on the face of things at least, appear to correspond to markedly different learning experiences. However, it is worth noting that in these three examples (and across pair types in the study) there were no differences in terms of whether children in different gender configurations could solve the task. Thus the short-term outcomes of the task were unaffected by conversation dynamics.

Gender, collaboration and resistance

It is maybe easy to imagine why the collaborative type of conversation – giving and asking for reasons, questioning and seeking agreement – might be an effective opportunity for learning. It is also possible to consider how dominant-compliant type conversations might lead to effective learning in a more formal, instructional sense if one child gives information to his or her (less able) conversation partner. However, it is difficult to view the dominance-conflict type of conversation as offering a productive means of engagement. Yet, as we have seen, several theorists have viewed conflict as a potentially useful ingredient for learning through peer interaction. Conflict might not be considered the most obvious candidate for promoting effective collaboration or learning. On the one hand conflict can obstruct communication and it would seem, on the face of things at least, that this could act as a barrier to learning. On the other hand, however, if learning is about coming to new understandings and overturning misconceptions and misunderstandings, a degree of conflict may be necessary to shake out old ideas or routines or to motivate engagement in a topic. As we have seen, different forms of communication (collaborative, dominance-conflict and dominant-compliant) may all involve a sense in which conflict is both social and cognitive. So perhaps only when social conflicts are overcome can children learn effectively from interaction (see Ames and Murray 1982). It is interesting to consider how children can overcome social conflict that can obstruct successful collaboration in order to identify forms of conflict that may play a positive role in learning and development.

From a related perspective, since collaboration is not always productive, learning about what happens when conflict inhibits learning can inform our understanding of what it *is* that makes collaboration productive. Several studies have tried to establish the extent to which resistance in interaction can obstruct collaboration. For instance, Leman (2002) found that when 9-year-old children discussed a moral problem together, most children's reasoning advanced. However, in cases where children's reasoning did not advance, conversations were distinguished by a particular dynamic; specifically, in these conversations, less advanced children argued for their position far more fervently, and rebutted their partner's arguments far more frequently, than in other discussions. By adopting a particular behavioural style – by offering sustained resistance – some less advanced children were able to convince their conversation partners to agree to adopt a less advanced position.

In a similar vein, Duveen and Psaltis (2008) and Psaltis and Duveen (2006) found gender effects in terms of conversation dynamics on conversation tasks involving an expert converser and non-expert (non-converser) aged 6–7 years. They argued that resistance to arguments was important in terms of development, i.e. those children who questioned and challenged the statements and arguments of their conversation partners tended to improve conversation skills compared with those who merely complied. However, development was greatest where there was an explicit recognition, in a conversation, of the reasons why the conversing solution was more appropriate. This explicit recognition occurred mostly in conversations involving female conversers (experts). A lack of resistance was most notable in interaction involving male conversers (experts).

Psaltis and Duveen (2006) link gender to resistance and conversation dynamics, and in turn to developmental changes in conversation ability. But it seems that this link diminishes with age. Leman and Duveen (1996) asked children to discuss whether lines in a visual illusion were the same or different lengths. Older children (11 years) had collaborative conversations, where children were interested in establishing the right or correct answer in its own right. They asked their partners more questions and volunteered explanations to support their own judgments. Younger children had more conflictual conversations. For younger children the conversation appeared to be more about 'winning' (akin to the dominance-conflict type of conversation) and less to do with establishing facts of the matter. Although gender was not a consideration in the study's design, it was noticeable that this conflict in the younger pairs tended to be drawn along gender lines. Subsequent studies (e.g. Leman and Duveen 1999) suggested that this may have been a result of younger children's specific difficulties in recognizing female expertise.

There seems to be an important age-related shift away from overt conflict in conversation and collaboration (progressively onwards from around 7–8 years, see Leman and Oldham 2005). That is not to say that interactions between older children are always less conflictual. Rather, older children seem more able to recognize that conflict need not always result in negative social outcomes and that people can disagree on a task in the process of solving a problem, or merely because they hold contrasting positions, without damaging their relationship in the longer term (Howe and McWilliam 2006). Thus it remains an open question, even if gender acts as a source of conflict in interaction, whether gender inevitably feeds through either to help or hinder learning at all ages. Consequently, some researchers have suggested that a key developmental task for children involved in interaction may be differentiating the influence of social dynamics of interaction from epistemic aspects of a problem or task (Leman and Duveen 1996, 1999).

Whether it is the co-construction of understanding (e.g. Doise and Mugny 1984) or the internalization of knowledge (Tudge 1992), an emphasis on developmental outcomes as a measure of success in interaction tends to ignore that in interaction children are negotiating (or grappling with) both a conceptual and a social process (Duveen 1997). However, comparatively few accounts have sought to explore the inter-relations between social and cognitive factors in any great depth, and theoretical accounts of how any inter-relations may operate are under-developed.

Gender and collaboration in the classroom

Although there is a dearth of research elaborating the mechanics of the link between cognitive and social processes in conversation, a good deal of work has explored the relative benefits of collaboration in same- and mixed-sex groups. This research has charted the different ways in which gender influences the dynamics of interaction in classroom collaboration. The focus of this research is on immediate outcomes of interaction (problem solving or participation) and a systematic empirical investigation of learning outcomes over time is often not pursued as a research goal.

Several studies in the area have explored how gender dynamics vary between children when they use computers together. For instance, Keogh, Barnes, Joiner and Littleton (2000) compared gender differences in behaviour on similar tasks in paper form and on the computer. Gender differences emerged only on the computer task where boys dominated interactions and use of key resources (i.e. the computer mouse) in mixed-sex pairs. Underwood, Underwood and Wood (2000) found similar gender dynamics in another computer-based task where there was less collaboration and sharing of resources in mixed-sex interaction compared with same-sex interaction, but few performance effects (aside from a general finding that those who engaged in collaborative interaction outperformed those who did not).

Results from Keogh *et al.*'s (2000) and Underwood *et al.*'s (2000) studies highlight a concern that one gender (i.e. boys) dominates both the dynamics of interaction and the learning resources. Of course, this domination may arise from the gender-marking of a particular type of task (use of computers) and predate any specific episode of interaction. In fact, gender differences in computer-based learning have been seen to be highly context sensitive (Littleton, Light, Joiner, Messer and Barnes 1998). Similarly, gender differences in use of equipment in science teaching may relate to differences in classroom dynamics and orientations to learning but not necessarily to learning outcomes in the longer term (Jones, Brader-Araje, Wilson-Carboni, Carter, Rua, Banilower and Hatch 2000).

Gender differences in the use of resources in mixed-sex pairs is a clear and concrete way in which gender dynamics visibly relate to interaction in the classroom. However, gender may also affect the extent to which children can ask questions of others, or may inhibit children from asking questions, articulating opinions or proposing explanations. Both Lockhead and Harris (1984) and Webb (1991) report studies where girls received fewer explanations or answers to questions from boys in collaborative tasks. Hakkarainen and Palonen (2003) observed a difference in contributions to a computer database among 11- to 12-year-old children. In one class, where girls outnumbered boys by a ratio of more than two to one, discussions focused on explanatory issues. However, in a comparison classroom where there were twice as many boys as girls, discussions focused on factual information. Moreover, although the boys in the majority-female class had some difficulty contributing to group discussion, in computer-supported collaborations the boys dominated interactions.

Studies illustrating gender differences in classroom interactions and collaborative learning are often taken as evidence for inequality in learning, and are cited as sources of possible gender differences in achievement. However, surprisingly few studies have considered how differences between mixed- and same-sex collaboration might feed into longer-term development and learning. The evidence from the few studies that there are indicates that gender differences in interaction do not readily translate into gender differences in learning. For instance, Barbieri and Light (1992) examined how children in mixed- and same-sex pairs solved a computer task together, and tested performance one week later. Although gender effects were observed in interaction, and boys appeared to outperform girls in the post-test, there were no links between gender dynamics or the gender-mix of pairs in interaction and outcome measures.

Alongside the paucity of hard research evidence for any longer-term, enduring relation between gender and learning outcomes, there is a further problem with extending research on gender dynamics in the classroom to account for longer-term changes in learning. Specifically, studies have had little success in establishing a link between learning outcomes and features of conversation such as contribution, argumentation, and argument quality when examining changes in understanding in the longer term.

Although some researchers have found evidence of links between learning and behavioural or conversation style (e.g. Psaltis and Duveen 2007), the failure to demonstrate a consistent connection between aspects of conversation and learning presents a real problem for those who emphasize that gender acts as a status dynamic in conversation which, in turn, has educational implications. (In truth, it presents a problem beyond questions of the role of social identities and conversation dynamics in collaborative learning.) Yet while there has been difficulty establishing with consistency which features of conversation or collaboration connect with learning, few studies find no benefits of collaboration over and above benefits of individual learning. It may be that merely engaging in peer collaboration (even unsuccessful collaboration) is sufficient to stimulate individual reflection and learning in the longer term (see Howe, McWilliam and Cross 2005).

The dynamics of interaction are doubtless different in same- and mixed-sex conversations. However, at present the question of how far mixed- and single-sex collaboration affects longer-term outcomes remains unanswered. There may be important methodological differences between studies that can account for some of the apparent contradictions in findings. For instance, many studies of mixed- versus single-sex collaboration explore only short-term gains or focus on dynamics of interaction and infer learning outcomes. It may also be the case that the widely observed gender differences in interaction do not have any lasting effect on learning outcomes.

Social identities and collaboration in educational contexts

In terms of the influence of social identity and peer learning, by far the greatest research focus has been on the role of gender on collaboration. However, status characteristics approaches would anticipate that any aspect of identity that can generate an asymmetry in status has the potential to affect conversation dynamics. For instance, Howe and McWilliam (2001) found that socio-economic status and gender affected children's use of arguments in different educational settings.

Race or ethnicity has also been found to affect children's conversation dynamics in marked ways. The relation between ethnicity and conversation, like gender, operates both in terms of baseline differences in conversation style and in terms of reactions to a conversation partner's ethnicity. The link between ethnicity and conversation is important in terms of collaborative learning because, again like gender, ethnicity has been implicated as a source of variation in educational achievement. Leman and Lam (2008) explored 7-year-old children's discussions about choosing a possible friend. There were subtle, yet consistent variations in the use of language and the dynamics of interaction between boys and girls from European (white), African-Caribbean (black) and South Asian (predominantly, Bangladeshi and Pakistani) ethnic groups. Generally, European boys tended to be most assertive, and South Asian girls least assertive. Yet gender was also an effective ingredient in interaction and moderated the effects of ethnicity. European girls were more affiliating (closer to the gendered norm for interaction) and European boys were more assertive (again, closer to the gender norm).

It is interesting and important to note that at this age ethnicity can affect conversation dynamics, because if we see this translating to collaborative interaction we may see, again, different learning opportunities for boys and girls from different ethnic groups. The finding also hints at the sophistication in young children's abilities to react to aspects of their own and others' social identity in conversation. A further finding from that study also gives a clue as to how aspects of identity may come to influence conversations; although children could choose potential friends from a series of photographs, same-ethnic pairs almost always chose a playmate from the ingroup. However, these children almost never voiced ethnicity as a consideration in their choice. Rather, the decision appeared to be made on the basis of implicit understanding or attitudes. Thus implicit processes may guide interaction (see Dovidio, Kawakami and Gaertner 2002 for similar work with adult intergroup prejudice). It may therefore be difficult to remove entirely social influences on interaction. Similarly, it is important to remember that collaborative encounters at school are still social encounters between children that will also entail social consequences in terms of peer group relationships and status. Indeed, children may focus on (and learn more from) these social outcomes than on the learning that may arise from collaboration.

Another social factor that may have a bearing on collaborative processes is friendship. Friends are more likely to volunteer to sit with one another during classroom activities and are also more familiar with one another, which may diminish or accentuate status differences in interaction and collaboration. Kutnick and Kington (2005) observed social dynamics in boys' and girls' same-sex pairs solving a science task together. Girls paired with a female friend performed best, followed by boys in acquaintance pairs and then girls in acquaintance pairs. Boys paired with a male friend performed worst of all. The authors argued that greater affiliation, collaboration and disclosure between female friends contributed towards the success of female friendship pairs on the task. In contrast, boys' friendship is characterized by a general action orientation that militated against successful collaboration. However, research on friendship among slightly older children (e.g. Azmitia and Montgomery 1993; Miell and MacDonald 2000) finds no gender differences in this context. Kutnick and Kington's results could reflect slightly slower maturation on the part of the boys.

An association between levels of friendship and gender in terms of the effectiveness of collaboration is an intuitively appealing one, and makes an important contribution to our understanding of dynamics in real-life classroom settings where issues such as friendship often dominate children's choices about potential collaborators. In such settings social problems may arise in collaborations, over time, which affect the effectiveness of working together (Strough, Berg and Meegan 2001). Moreover, while friendships have many positive factors and appear to assist (girls at least) in collaborative problem-solving activities, there are often other factors such as gender, socio-economic status and race that are confounded with friendship choices, and this confound may blur our understanding of how far friendship rather than other social factors underlies processes of collaboration (Zajac and Hartup 1997).

A key element in understanding the role of social factors in peer learning is the context in which collaborative activity occurs. Even from pre-school (5 years) children alter the types of behaviour they display in terms of gender (Killen and Naigles 1995) and task (Holmes-Lonergan 2003). It may also be the case that children learn regardless of the disruptions to conversation dynamics and access to resources that have been observed in studies of gender differences. In this respect, some tasks may be gender-marked in ways that others are not and, consequently, some classroom tasks focus attention on a set of problems or questions that allow children to overcome (or work around) disruptions to conversation dynamics that are caused by gender.

This suggestion fits with the contextual interaction approach to gender effects in conversation, which argues that how gender operates in talk is determined largely by social and contextual factors (see again Leaper and Ayres 2007). However, it is important to remember that there may be other consequences of gender differences in interaction that educators need to consider. Even if most children are able to benefit from collaboration by learning to negotiate the disruptive effects of gender on conversation and associated inequities in access to resources, there may be consequences for ongoing social relationships and interactions in the classroom and beyond that are difficult to detect with any single research study (Howe 1997; Scanlon 2000).

Classroom perspectives and future directions

The research findings indicate that gender, as well as other aspects of social identity, can affect conversation dynamics and processes of collaboration. The extent of any gender influence varies by context including task, children's expectations, background, ability and social experiences as well as the developmental level of children involved in any collaboration. Moreover, it remains to be seen whether any disruption to the social dynamics of collaboration that is caused by gender has a lasting influence on learning in the longer term. Thus research in the area faces three major challenges.

The first challenge is to chart what features of the social or activity context are important in determining how far gender has an effect on collaboration, and why these features activate gender in children's conversations. For instance, the observation that computer-related tasks tended to favour male dominance during collaboration (Littleton *et al.* 1998) suggests that such contexts trigger gender as a status characteristic that either one or all participants in the collaboration accede to. Other contexts may be more female-marked, while others still may not be marked at all. Since both genders often coalesce to make gender an active ingredient in conversations, educators need to devise learning materials and manage interactions between children in ways that help children to overcome barriers to effective (or maybe, non-gendered) communication in gender-marked tasks. In this respect, thought and attention need to be given to considering how and when mixed- and single-sex groups and pairs can collaborate most effectively.

The second, major challenge is to gather robust and reliable evidence about whether gender influences on the dynamics of collaboration have any bearing on longer-term educational and developmental outcomes. This challenge (and the previous one) might be met, in due course, by meta-analyses of existing literature. However, given that existing findings suggest some uncertainty, it may only be possible to establish with confidence if there is a link between gender, collaboration and learning through experimental or quasi-experimental methods.

Such research is important: many studies have demonstrated how gender can disrupt collaborative interactions without exploring the important question of how far this impacts on learning. If there is no impact, it might be tempting to disregard gender in considerations of what makes for effective collaborative learning. Yet, as we have seen, to ignore gender altogether would be unwise because there may be other consequences of inequality in interaction that are more insidious. For instance, as Leman *et al.* (2005) suggest, children may 'work around' gender differences in interaction to solve a problem and achieve a short-term goal. But by reinforcing 'male' and 'female' conversational styles certain routes to interaction, argument, and conversational leadership may be closed off to one or both genders. Learning outcomes need to be broadly understood in future research in the area. In this respect, while children may, from a young age, reproduce and react to gender in conversation (e.g. Killen and Naigles 1995), they may also learn very quickly to compensate for this influence to ensure they gain some benefits from collaboration or to achieve desirable goals. A focus on learning outcomes should not exclude a consideration of outcomes in terms of children's social relationships.

The third and final challenge is to establish how far other aspects of identity influence collaboration dynamics and the outcomes of collaborations. It is important to explore whether different aspects of identity interact with one another, and with gender, to influence conversation dynamics and learning. Early research evidence suggests that even at 7 years children can react in complex ways to different aspects of identity, such as race, in conversation and decision-making (Leman and Lam 2008). In a modern, diverse classroom, children often need to negotiate a complex web of peers with a range of different social identities. Research is needed to establish whether the task of negotiating the effects of these identities in conversation affects processes of collaboration and learning at different ages. Findings here could help teachers to guide children's interactions in ways that ensure all participants have the same opportunities to receive the undoubted benefits of peer collaborative learning.

Gender and other aspects of a child's social identity have an influence on the content and dynamics of children's collaborative interactions in different contexts. However, the question of how far these influences feed in to affect longer-term educational outcomes remains open. And although it is necessary to develop tasks and strategies for managing effective peer collaboration, it is important to remember that what distinguishes peer interaction from adult-child interaction is that the former often offers opportunities for learning in a freer, less constrained environment. This environment not only offers a chance for children to learn but to learn how to collaborate successfully. In this respect peer interaction can also provide valuable opportunities for children to learn more about how gender affects their own and others' interaction, and to overcome any barriers to learning that this might present.

Acknowledgements

I am grateful to Gabrielle Ivinson and Bethan Skone for their advice and assistance.

References

Allport, G. W. (1954) *The Nature of Prejudice*, Cambridge, MA: Addison-Wesley.

Ames, G. J. and Murray, F. B. (1982) 'When two wrongs make a right: promoting cognitive change by social conflict', *Developmental Psychology*, 18:894–7.

Azmitia, M. and Montgomery, R. (1993) 'Friendship, transactive dialogues, and the development of scientific reasoning', *Social Development*, 2:202–21.

Bales, R. (1951) *Interaction Process Analysis: a method for the study of small groups*, Cambridge, MA: Addison-Wesley.

Barbieri, M. S. and Light, P. H. (1992) 'Interaction, gender, and performance on a computer-based problem solving task', *Learning and Instruction*, 2:199–213.

Baron-Cohen, S. (2004) *The Essential Difference: men, women and the extreme male brain*, London: Penguin.

Berger, J., Conner, T. L. and Fisek, H. (1974) *Expectation States Theory: a theoretical research programme*, Cambridge, MA: Winthrop.

Berger, J., Hamit, F., Norman, R. Z. and Zelditch, M. (1977) *Status Characteristics in Social Interaction: an expectation states approach*, New York: Elsevier.

Berger, J., Rosenholtz, S. J. and Zelditch, M. (1980) 'Status organizing processes', *Annual Review of Sociology*, 6:479–508.

Carli, L. L. (1989) 'Gender differences in interaction style and influence', *Journal of Personality and Social Psychology*, 56:565–76.

Carli, L. L., LaFleur, S. J. and Loeber, C. C. (1995) 'Nonverbal behavior, gender, and influence', *Journal of Personality and Social Psychology*, 68:1030–41.

Crouter, A. C., Manke, B. and McHale, S. M. (1995) 'The family context of gender intensification in early adolescence', *Child Development*, 66:317–29.

Crowley, K., Callanan, M. A., Tenenbaum, H. R. and Allen, E. (2001) 'Parents explain more often to boys than to girls during shared scientific thinking', *Psychological Science*, 12:258–61.

Damon, W. and Killen, M. (1982) 'Peer interaction and the process of change in children's moral reasoning', *Merrill-Palmer Quarterly*, 28:347–67.

Davis, S. C., Leman, P. J. and Barrett, M. (2007) 'Children's implicit and explicit ethnic group attitudes, ethnic group identification, and self esteem', *International Journal of Behavioral Development*, 31:514–25.

Deaux, K. (1984) 'From individual differences to social categories: analysis of a decade's research on gender', *American Psychologist*, 39:105–16.

Deaux, K. and Major, B. (1983) 'Putting gender into context: an interactive model of gender-related behavior', *Psychological Review*, 94:369–89.

DeLoche, A. S. and DeMendoza, O. A. P. (1987) 'Joint picturebook interactions of mothers and 1-year-old children', *British Journal of Developmental Psychology*, 5:111–23.

Dillenbourg, P., Baker, M., Blaye, A. and O'Malley, C. (1996) 'The evolution of research on collaborative learning', in E. Spada and P. Reiman (eds) *Learning in Humans and Machines: towards an interdisciplinary learning science*, Oxford: Elsevier.

Doise, W. and Mugny, G. (1984) *The Social Development of the Intellect*, Cambridge: Cambridge University Press.

Dovidio, J. F., Kawakami, K., and Gaertner, S. L. (2002) 'Implicit and explicit prejudice and interracial interaction', *Journal of Personality and Social Psychology*, 82:62–8.

Duveen, G. (1997) 'Psychological development as a social process', in L. Smith and J. P. Tomlinson (eds) *Piaget, Vygotsky and Beyond*, London: Routledge.

Duveen, G. and Psaltis, C. (2008) 'The constructive role of asymmetry in social interaction', in U. Müller, J. I. M. Carpendale, N. Budwig and B. Sokol (eds), *Social Life and Social Knowledge: towards a process account of development*, New York: Lawrence Erlbaum.

Frome, P. M. and Eccles, J. S. (1998) 'Parents' influence on children's achievement-related perceptions', *Journal of Personality and Social Psychology*, 74:435–52.

Hakkarainen, K. and Palonen, T. (2003) 'Patterns of female and male students' participation in peer interaction in computer-supported learning', *Computers and Education*, 40:327–42.

Holmes-Lonergan, H. A. (2003) 'Preschool children's collaborative problem-solving interactions: the role of gender, pair type, and task', *Sex Roles*, 48:505–17.

Howe, C. (1997) *Gender and Classroom Interaction: a research review*, Edinburgh: Scottish Council for Research in Education.

Howe, C. and McWilliam, D. (2001) 'Peer argument in educational settings', *Journal of Language and Social Psychology*, 20:61–80.

Howe, C. and McWilliam, D (2006) 'Opposition in social interaction between children: why intellectual benefits do not mean social costs', *Social Development*, 15:205–31.

Howe, C., McWilliam, D. and Cross, G. (2005) 'Chance favours only the prepared mind: incubation and the delayed effects of peer collaboration', *British Journal of Psychology*, 96:67–93.

Jones, K., Evans, C., Byrd, R. and Campbell, K. (2000) 'Gender equity training and teacher behavior', *Journal of Instructional Psychology*, 27:173–7.

Jones, M. G., Brader-Araje, L., Wilson-Carboni, L., Carter, G., Rua, M. J., Banilower, E. and Hatch, H. (2000) 'Tool time: gender and students' use of tools, control, and authority', *Journal of Research in Science Teaching*, 37:760–83.

Kelly, A. (1988) 'Gender differences in teacher-pupil interactions: a meta-analytic review', *Research in Education*, 39:1–23.

Keogh, T., Barnes, P., Joiner, R. and Littleton, K. (2000) 'Gender, pair composition and computer versus paper presentations of an English language task', *Educational Psychology*, 20: 33–43.

Killen, M. and Naigles, L. R. (1995) 'Preschool children pay attention to their addressees: effects of gender composition on peer disputes', *Discourse Processes*, 19:329–46.

King, A. (1998) 'Transactive peer tutoring: distributing cognition and metacognition', *Educational Psychology Review*, 10:57–74.

Kotthoff, H. and Barron, B. (2001) 'Preface', in B. Baron and H. Kotthoff (eds) *Gender in Interaction: perspectives on femininity and masculinity in ethnography and discourse*, Amsterdam: John Benjamins Publishing Company.

Kruger, A. C. (1992) 'The effect of peer and adult–child transactive discussions on moral reasoning', *Merrill-Palmer Quarterly*, 38:287–315.

Kutnick, P. and Kington, A. (2005) 'Children's friendships and learning in school: cognitive enhancement through social interaction?', *British Journal of Educational Psychology*, 75:521–38.

Lave, J. and Wenger, E. (1991) *Situated Learning: legitimate peripheral participation*, Cambridge: Cambridge University Press.

Leaper, C. (1991) 'Influence and involvement in children's discourse: age, gender, and partner effects', *Child Development*, 62:797–811.

Leaper, C. and Ayres, M. M. (2007) 'A meta-analytic review of gender variations in adults' language use: talkativeness, affiliative speech, and assertive speech', *Personality and Social Psychology Review*, 11:328–63.

Leaper, C., and Smith, T. A. (2004) 'A meta-analytic review of gender variations in children's talk: talkativeness, affiliative speech, and assertive speech', *Developmental Psychology*, 40:993–1027.

Leaper, C., Tenenbaum, H. R. and Shaffer, T. G. (1999) 'Communication patterns of African-American girls and boys from low-income, urban backgrounds', *Child Development*, 70:1489–503.

Leman, P. J. (2002) 'Argument structure, argument content and cognitive change in children's peer interaction', *Journal of Genetic Psychology*, 163:40–57.

Leman, P. J. and Duveen, G. (1996) 'Developmental differences in children's understanding of epistemic authority', *European Journal of Social Psychology*, 26:683–702.

Leman, P. J. and Duveen, G. (1999) 'Representations of authority and children's moral reasoning', *European Journal of Social Psychology*, 29:557–75.

Leman, P. J. and Lam, V. L. (2008) 'The influence of race and gender on children's conversations and playmate choices', *Child Development*, 79:1330–44.

Leman, P. J. and Oldham, Z. (2005) 'Do children need to learn to collaborate? The effects of age and age differences on children's collaborative recall', *Cognitive Development*, 20:33–48.

Leman, P. J., Ahmed, S. and Ozarow, L. (2005) 'Gender, gender relations, and the social dynamics of children's conversations', *Developmental Psychology*, 41:64–74.

Littleton, K., Light, P., Joiner, R., Messer, D. and Barnes, P. (1998) 'Gender, task scenarios and children's computer-based problem solving', *Educational Psychology*, 18:327–40.

Lloyd, B. and Duveen, G. (1992) *Gender Identities and Education: the impact of starting school*, Hemel Hempstead: Harvester Wheatsheaf.

Lockhead, A. E. and Harris, A. M. (1984) 'Cross-sex collaborative learning in elementary classrooms', *American Educational Research Journal*, 21:275–94.

Maccoby, E. E. (1988) 'Gender as a social category', *Developmental Psychology*, 24:755–65.

Maccoby, E. E. (1998). *The Two Sexes: growing up apart, coming together*, Cambridge, MA: Belknap Press.

Martin, C. L., Ruble, D. N. and Szkrybalo, J. (2002) 'Cognitive theories of early gender development', *Psychological Bulletin*, 128:903–33.

Maynard, D. (1980) 'Placement of topic changes in conversation', *Semiotica*, 30:263–90.

Mehl, R. M., Vazire, S., Ramírez-Esparza, N., Slatcher, R. B. and Pennebaker, J. W. (2007) 'Are women really more talkative than men?', *Science*, 317: 82.

Mercer, N. (2000). *Words and Minds: how we use language to think together*, London: Routledge.

Miell, D. and MacDonald, R. (2000) 'Children's creative collaborations: the importance of friendship when working together on a musical composition', *Social Development*, 9:348–69.

Moscovici, S., Mucchi-Faina, A. and Maas, A. (eds) (2004) *Minority Influence*, London: Nelson-Hall.

Mugny, G. and Papastamou, S. (1982) *The Power of Minorities*, Michigan: Academic Press.

Murray, S. O. (1985) 'Toward a model of members' methods for recognizing interruptions', *Language in Society*, 14:31–40.

Ohtaki, S., Ohtaki, T. and Fetters, M. D. (2007) 'Doctor–patient communication: a comparison of the USA and Japan', *Family Practice*, 20:276–82.

Okamoto, D. G. and Smith-Lovin, L. (2001) 'Changing the subject: gender-, status-, and the dynamics of topic change', *American Sociological Review*, 66:852–73.

Okamoto, D. G., Rashotte, L. S. and Smith-Lovin, L. (2002) 'Measuring interruption: syntactic and contextual methods of coding conversation', *Social Psychology Quarterly*, 65:38–55.

Psaltis, C. and Duveen, G. (2006) 'Social relations and cognitive development: the influence of conversation type and representations of gender', *European Journal of Social Psychology*, 36:407–30.

Psaltis, C. and Duveen, G. (2007) 'Conversation and conversation types: forms of recognition and cognitive development', *British Journal of Developmental Psychology*, 25:79–102.

Sacks, H., Schegloff, E. and Jefferson, G. (1974) 'A simple systematics for organization of turn-taking for conversation', *Language*, 50:696–735.

Scanlon, E. (2000) 'How gender influences learners working collaboratively with science simulations', *Learning and Instruction*, 10:463–81.

Scherer, K. R. (1979) 'Voice and speech correlates of perceived social influence in simulated juries', in H. Giles and R. St. Clair (eds) *Language and Social Psychology*, Oxford: Blackwell.

Serbin, L. A., Zelkowitz, P., Doyle, A.-B. and Wheaton, B. (1990) 'The socialization of sex-differentiated skills and academic performance: a meditational model', *Sex Roles*, 23:613–28.

Shaw, J. B. and Barrett-Power, E. (1998) 'The effects of diversity on small work-group processes and performance', *Human Relations*, 51:1307–25.

Skvoretz, J. V. and Farraro, T. J. (1996) 'Status and participation on task groups: a dynamics network model', *American Journal of Sociology*, 101:136–49.

Slavin, R. E. (1996) 'Research on cooperative learning and achievement: what we know, what we need to know', *Contemporary Educational Psychology*, 21:43–69.

Smith-Lovin, L. and Brody, C. (1989) 'Interruptions in group discussions: the effects of gender and group composition', *American Sociological Review*, 54:424–35.

Steele, C. (1997) 'A threat in the air: how stereotypes shape intellectual identity and performance', *American Psychologist*, 52:613–29.

Strough, J., Berg, C. A. and Meegan, S. P. (2001) 'Friendship and gender differences in task and social interpretations of peer collaborative problem solving', *Social Development*, 10:1–22.

Tenenbaum, H. R. and Leaper, C. (2003) 'Parent-child conversations about science: the socialization of gender inequities?', *Developmental Psychology*, 39:34–47.

Tudge, J. R. H. (1992) 'Processes and consequence of peer collaboration: a Vygotskian analysis', *Child Development*, 63:1364–79.

Underwood, J., Underwood, G. and Wood, D. (2000) 'When does gender matter? Interactions during computer-based problem solving', *Learning and Instruction*, 10:447–62.

Verba, M. (1998) 'Tutoring interactions between young children: how symmetry can modify asymmetrical interactions', *International Journal of Behavioral Development*, 22:195–216.

Walkerdine, V. (1998) *Counting Girls Out: girls and mathematics*, London: Falmer Press.

Webb, N. M. (1991) 'Task-related verbal interaction and mathematics learning in small groups', *Journal for Research in Mathematics Education*, 22:366–89.

Wenger, E. (1998) *Communities of Practice: learning, meaning, and identity*, New York: Cambridge University Press.

Wertsch, J. V. (1991) *Voices of the Mind: a sociocultural approach to mediated activity*, Cambridge, MA: Harvard University Press.

West, C. and Zimmerman, D. H. (1983) 'Small insults: a study of interruptions in cross-sex conversations between unacquainted persons', in B. Thorne, C. Kramarae and N. Henley (eds) *Language, Gender and Society*, Rowley, MA: Newbury House.

Zajac R. J. and Hartup, W. W. (1997) 'Friends as coworkers: research review and classroom implications', *The Elementary School Journal*, 98:3–13.

Zimmerman, D. H. and West, C. (1975) 'Sex roles, interruptions and silences in conversation', in B. Thorne and N. Henley (eds) *Language, Sex and Dominance*, Rowley, MA: Newbury House.

Chapter 12

Change in urban classroom culture and interaction

Ben Rampton and Roxy Harris
King's College London

In a recent QCA sponsored discussion of classroom discourse (QCA 2003), a leading researcher proposed that

> most classroom talk ... involves a centralized communication system. Teachers direct the talk by doing most of it themselves, combining lengthy exposition with many questions, allocating the right or obligation to answer those questions and evaluating the answers. The transmission of knowledge creates very unequal communication rights to those who know and those who do not. This is why the sequence of (teacher) initiation – (pupil) response – (teacher) evaluation has emerged from so many research studies as the 'essential teaching exchange'.
>
> (Edwards 2003: 38; see also Edwards and Westgate 1994: 40, 46; Mehan 1979; Cazden 1985)

But if public and political debates are any indication, teaching through the Initiation-Response-Evaluation discourse sequence – the 'IRE' – is rather less straightforward than this quotation suggests. In an account of the education policy of the British Conservative party from 1979–94, Lawton notes that

> ... by 1979 many [members of the Conservative Party] had gained the impression that schools were chaotic and teachers were lax, or – worse still – militant egalitarians who used the classroom for subversive political activities. The right wing feared that schooling had ceased to be a means for promoting order and obedience, and had taken on the role of encouraging the young to be critical of authority and disrespectful [...] [In general the Tories expressed] a wish to return to traditional curricula and teaching methods.
>
> (Lawton 1994: 47, 147)

The perception that schools were faltering in the delivery of traditional forms of instruction was echoed by the Labour Party in the run-up to the 1997 British general election, and indeed, when it came to power afterwards, it introduced a minute-by-minute programme for a 'Literacy Hour' in primary schools, prescribing whole-class teaching, with pupils' eyes and ears tuned to the teacher, as the main component (*c.* 40 minutes) (Rampton 2006:1).

So what is going on here? Is this a case of populist politicians stoking moral panic to their own advantage, or is educational research out of tune with a reality that politicians and public are rather more alert to? This chapter tries to provide a nuanced view. Yes, there undoubtedly are a substantial number of secondary schools where classroom discourse *does* correspond to the standard patterns described in research, but we also have strong evidence that there are quite a lot of others where it doesn't. But that evidence does not justify a 'classroom chaos' rhetoric, or warrant a top-down 'back-to-basics' policy, premised on the view that teachers in these classrooms are lax and/or incompetent. It is vital not to romanticize the kind of classrooms we shall discuss, but humans tend to produce some kind of order in their habitual activity together – even though it may be hard for outsiders to recognize – and in many urban classrooms, rather than chaos, it is more accurate to speak of a different way of operating, or a 'new settlement'. Similarly, efforts to change and improve learning conditions are much more likely to succeed if they are based on an understanding rather than on a denial of this environment.

In reaching this view, 'linguistic ethnography' is our main methodology. Linguistic ethnography uses linguistics and discourse analysis as sensitizing tools in the analysis of interaction and it combines this with the perspectives and field strategies of ethnography, which involve among other things, a commitment to understanding everyday practice in context, to identifying patterns and systems without losing sight of local particularities, and to extensive data-collection in environments uncontrolled by the researcher.[1]

Our mode of argumentation is also ethnographic, and moves from particular description to wider cultural claims (cf. Burawoy 1998; Erickson 1985). The account starts off with what Hymes calls a 'contrastive insight' (1996: 5), the apprehension of a disparity between a) claims about social life circulating in prevailing discourses and b) what one can actually see in social life as it really seems to happen. In our case, this was a gap between on the one hand, the views of classrooms in policy and research sketched above, and on the other, our own observation of 13–15-year-olds in two inner London comprehensive schools. To follow up on this initial insight, our account first dwells on a particular set of practices in the data from one of these two schools, 'Central High', and it describes the non-canonical initiations, responses and evaluations of a prominent group of boys in Class 9A (Section 1), their embellishment of the teacher's discourse (Section 2) and the subordinated non-participation of girls (Section 3). In the two sections after that, we attempt to bring these empirical observations together in a more general characterization of local institutional processes (Burawoy 1998: 14–15,17–19; Erickson 1985: 145–53). In Section 4, we propose a model of how these elements fitted together during teacher talk, and then in Section 5 we delineate this genre's specificity within classroom activity more generally, concluding with a characterization of teacher-centred discourse that is founded on the observation of pupil practices and that looks rather different from the one offered by Edwards and others (cf. Burawoy 1998: 5 on reformulating existing theory). In the section after this (Section 6), we try to situate our case-study findings in a larger landscape, using historical comparison with classroom ethnographies from the 1970s and 80s to identity those aspects of local practice that represent cultural change, and then, in Section 7, we use other studies and further research of our own to assess the wider contemporary relevance of our claims. Our conclusion returns to the starting point, drawing out the implications for educational research and policy (Section 8).

We will start with Class 9A at Central High, where in all, fieldwork lasted about 1 year, and data-collection involved: interviews; participant observation; *c.* 37 hours of radio-microphone recordings of the everyday interaction of four youngsters (2M, 2F) in a tutor group of about 30; and participant retrospection on extracts from the audio recordings.[2] After initial observation sitting in lessons for several weeks, we selected students who seemed to represent different groupings within the class, asking each of them in turn to wear a lapel radio-microphone for several days, starting at the beginning of school and often continuing in break and lunchtime periods as well as class-time. This resulted in between 8 and 16 hours of spontaneous speech data on each inform- ant, and it was supplemented with audio recordings made with an omni-directional microphone located in the equipment bag carried by Rampton, who also sat at the side or the back of the classroom.

1. Classroom authority and the IRE

On the whole at Central High, teachers seemed to find it rather hard operating the conventional IRE pattern of classroom discourse. Both in instructional and regulative/ disciplinary talk, authority seemed to have been pluralized, and there was one group of boys in particular who took a lot of interactional turns that traditionally belong to the teacher. They sometimes jumped in, for example, to complete their teacher's sentences, and they encouraged the teacher to carry on when he seemed to be flagging.

Excerpt 1

An English lesson. Mr Newton is about to tell the class about league tables compar- ing the performance of different schools (Radio-microphone (Rm): Simon. Blex 33; n19:210). (Transcription conventions can be found in the Appendix.)

MR N: if you look at the big newspapers today (1.0) You'll find that they've all got
       these erm
JOHN: **car crashes**
MR N: charts: (1.5) [they're called the league tables
ANONM: [**of schools**
MR N: about all the primary schools
JOHN: **of schools good and bad yeh**

Excerpt 2

Tutor period in the morning. There has been an incident in the school and Mr Alcott is talking about racism to the class, who are listening quite quietly. (Rm: Joanne. n42:209)

MR A: (1.5) I seem– I seem to be doing lots of talking ((*quietly:*)) I'm sorry
BOY: [**no you're not**

ANON: [(((*light laugh*))
SIMON: **no go on**
ANON M: **carry on**
ANON: ((*light laugh*))
SIMON: **it's very interesting**
BOY: ((*in a funny voice:*)) **go on** (   )
SIMON: ((*light laugh*))
MR A: okay but you're the ones who are experiencing: (.) this erm: (1.0) this
    situation

The students actively back-channelled and provided evaluative feedback, and they also
sometimes contradicted and criticized what their teacher was saying, contesting the
teacher's comments on their conduct, and complaining if he ignored them.

Excerpt 3

English lesson. Mr Newton is telling the class about underachievement at the school
(Rm: Simon. n19:210: BL2:141–2)

MR N: most of the students in this school (.) the biggest number of students got
    Level Four (.)
HANIF: ((*quite loud:*)) **eh?**
ANON: ((*quieter:*)) **huh?**
MRN: Level 4 in English is the most popular level too the– most common level that
    students got
HANIF?: >what about now?<

Excerpt 4

Tutor period at the start of the day. Mr Alcott is talking to the class about the exams
coming up. (The Rm is being worn by Joanne. n47:279; BL73:117)

MR A: HANG ON there are no: (.) language (.) SA[Ts
HANIF: [**there are**
SEVERAL: ((*chorally:*)) **there are**
ANON: (   )
ANNA: (it)
MR A: thank you (.) there are no: (.) language S:AT:s okay

Excerpt 5

English. Mr Newton is giving the class guidelines on their oral assessment tasks, and
he appears to single out John. (Rm: Hanif. n14:290ff; '15':1362)

MR N: the way you get a high score (.) is by actually encouraging others to speak
    and valuing their opinions (1.0) NOT (1.)

GIRL: ((*with exaggerated delivery:*))being ru:(de   )
GUY: ((*funny voice:*)) saying (they're)
MR N: running them down at all
BOY: yeh
MR N: so–
JOHN: **hey what did I do why are you pointing at me**
MR N: listen ((*sound of other pupils' voices is increasing*))
HANIF: [what?
MR N: [shshsh

And lastly, these boys often told other pupils to shut up or to do as they were told:

Excerpt 6

English lesson (Rm: Hanif. n14:290ff; '15':1330)

MR N: is (.) (say back) in 1590 (.)
ANONF: ooh ooh ((*giggles*))
MR N: just suppose (1.5) they [had such a thing as a coroner's inquest
BOY: [**(can't) you two shut up**
?: (ooo)
MR N: we gonna do it in groups (.)

The relationship between this activity and the IRE is summarized in Table 12.1.

It would be an exaggeration to say that traditional IRE relations had collapsed and that teachers and pupils now had an equal role determining the course of each lesson.[3] Even so, these deviations from the traditional structure were more than just temporary blips in instructional interaction – on the contrary, some of them helped to carry the lesson forward, and they usually went unreprimanded. Nor, indeed, were these boys particularly disruptive and alienated – on the contrary, they were generally very keen in class, and teachers rated Hanif as the star student. So can we just attribute all this to their communicative incompetence/inexperience, agreeing, for example, with Mr Poyser, their humanities teacher, who kept telling them that they needed to improve their 'listening skills'? Unlikely, and this becomes clear if we move past the IRE to a more student-centred analysis.

2. A contrapuntal aesthetic

In whole-class teaching, teachers are supposed to work with their students to try to build a cumulative public record of authoritative knowledge (Heap 1985), and although many stylistic, interpersonal and institutional dynamics are obviously always also in play when teachers teach the whole class, teachers normally attach special importance to the articulation of conceptually relevant, lexico-grammatical propositions. But this did not seem to be sufficient for some of the boys in Class 9A, and instead of simply taking classroom talk for what it contributed to the cumulative-construction-of-inter-subjective-mental-models-of-the-curriculum-topic, allowing it to transport them 'past

Table 12.1 The IRE, teachers and Hanif and co.

Type of act	The canonical incumbents	Non-canonical incumbents and acts at Central High
Initiation	Teacher	Students (boys) provide the teacher with (unsolicited) 'utterance completers' Students (boys) tell other students to keep quiet and do what they're told
Response	Student	
Feedback/ Evaluation	Teacher	Students (boys) evaluate the answers given by other students Students (boys) provide unsolicited feedback on what the teacher is telling them

the [classroom], the occasion, and the speaker into the subject matter upon which the [lesson] comments' (Goffman 1981: 166), these boys looked beyond just the content and attended very closely to the talk's formal, interactional and stylistic properties, emphasizing these as additional or alternative points of focus for the class.

So, for example, the boys often treated the utterance they had just heard as an opportunity for formal linguistic recoding, and they would then pick up pieces of relatively ordinary classroom talk and rework them into forms that were conspicuously different from the original and often incongruous in the immediate context. These repetitions added little to the development of the propositional argument, and instead, they drew out the poetic rather than the referential potential of the words that they responded to (Jakobson 1960). More specifically, ordinary utterances in instructional and regulative exchanges were transcoded into song, into German, into non-standard accents, into a different tempo, prosodic contour, word-stress, etc.:

Excerpt 7[4]

In an English lesson. Mr Newton, the English teacher, is calling the class to order.

```
8 MR N:  erm DONT WASTE – time everybody
9        js look this way (1.5)
10       thank you (.)
11       er we've      [finished- ((5.0 till turn 15))
12 HANIF((QUITE LOUD:)) [danke ((trans: thank you))
13 ANON: is that gum or () (.)
14 HANIF: gu[m
15 MR N:    [can I please have–
16 MR N: can I please have some complete attention everybody
17        cos I want to talk for about 5 or 10 minutes
```

Excerpt 8

Humanities lesson with Mr Alcott.

MR A: shsh, RAFIQ THAT WASN'T actually very <u>reli::vent</u>
SEVERAL BOYS IN CHORUS: it was (**i::relevant**)
MASUD?: yeah **IRRelevant**
HANIF: oo:::::h
MR A: right okay erm

The boys also often appreciatively recycled anomalous utterances – musical blurts, bits of German, incongruous back-channelling, obtuse comments – and in doing so, they iconically revivified a comic or dramatic moment, savouring some aspect of the very recent here-and-now, attending *precisely* to the 'felicities or infelicities of the presentation' that ought, according to Goffman, remain secondary in an academic setting.

Excerpt 9

The English lesson. (Rm: Hanif – '15' n14)

MR N: as I've said before I get a bit fed up with saying (.) shshsh
JOHN?: LOU[DER
MR N: [you're doing your SATs now
HANIF: VIEL LAUTER SPRECHEN VIEL LAUTER SPRECHEN ((*German:*
    '*speak much louder*'))
MRN?: [(((*emphatic:*)) sshh
JOHN: [(((*smile-voice:*)) **lauter spricken** (.) whatever that is

In both parallel and echoic utterances like these, the students were closely tracking the main discourse on the classroom floor. At the same time, both types of repetition impacted on the lesson's momentum. The boys lingered on utterances beyond the point of comprehension where words yielded their contribution to the development of a propositional argument, and in this way, they appeared to insist that it was not simply the rational and disciplinary requirements of the curriculum that propelled the unfolding of activity. Indeed, these utterances displayed an interest in artful 'performance' as an option within the official lesson.[5] In repetitions with contrast, students pushed themselves momentarily into the spotlight, bidding for acclaim for their quick wits, resourcefulness or droll humour, while in 'echoings' they acted as the responsive audience that performance plays to.

Overall, these practices can be characterized as a kind of contrapuntal aesthetic, pulling against the lesson's prioritization of semantic propositions, working tangentially to the normative drive for intellectual relevance to the curriculum topic. Rather than tuning out from the main proceedings in class, these boys appeared to intensify their enjoyment by embellishing the proceedings, seizing on a wide range of different aspects of the talk they were listening to. If we add to this the evidence of the previous section, where we saw them finishing sentences for their teachers and peers etc., then rather than seeing these boys as generally inattentive, or lacking adequate 'listening skills', it looks as though they were often actually *hyper-involved*, positively *over-exuberant* in their lesson participation.

Indeed, the performance of Hanif and his circle often provided a sharp contrast to others in the class. In Mr Alcott's words during one lesson:

> I'm sorry – look, these people are bursting with enthusiasm, right
> I'd like that to happen on this table too …
> ((*a little later:*))
> by the way,
> I – I've noticed that these four girls haven't answered
> ((*slowly, stressing each word:*))
> one single question all morning (.)
> ((*faster:*)) I noticed that
> you're very difficult to ignore in the centre

In fact, the combination of decentred authority and hyper-involvement was a significant factor in the exclusion of most of the girls from whole-class discussion.

3. The exclusion of girls

The English and humanities teachers at Central High worried quite a lot that the girls in 9A generally kept quiet in their lessons, and whenever there was a class discussion, the two girls that we recorded with radio-microphones spent most of their time talking quietly to each other about other issues. It was clear that they did not like speaking in front of the rest of the class, and there was ample evidence of boys putting pressure on them whenever they had to do so.[6]

Excerpt 10

In the corridors. (Rm: Ninnette. nr34:187)

NINNETTE: no we ain't got a test in Humanities today we got it tomorrow but we
    gotta read (1) today (2) we gotta report back to the studid idiotic class (.)
GIRL: (and people) are say(in') ((*half-laughing:*)) are you thick or something
NINNETTE: (yes)I know I know

Excerpt 11

English lesson on *Romeo and Juliet* with Mr Newton (Hanif wearing the Rm. Gex4:116; n14)

2 MR N: ((*light voice:*))first of all
3   can I have a couple of girls hands up (1.5)
5 JOHN: **the girls are (.) embarrassed**
6 MR N: [erm (.) let's try

7 ANONF: [(   )
8 MR N: (we)'ve had the feud already
9   Ninnette, you (   ) about these characters
10   Ninnette (.)
11 ANON: feudal system
12 GUY: [**Ninnette don't know**
13 MR N: [Ninnette (.)

In fact, the girls must have often felt that the boys and the teacher were acting in concert – the adult using his power to put them in the spotlight so the boys could prance around them (so to speak) – and certainly, rather than targeting Hanif and his crew, Ninnette and Joanne directed a lot of their discontent towards the teachers when they were being drawn into the main class business, or when they were interrupted in their independent conversations.

Excerpt 12

Humanities class. Mr Alcott is asking the class to name the four factors leading to the abolition of slavery. Ninnette, who is sitting next to Joanne (wearing the Rm) has evidently been making a (relatively rare) bid for his attention (n42:348).

1 NINNETTE: [becau:se
2 MR A: [Joanne's table
3 ((*to the rest of the class:*)) SHSH
4 NINNETTE: becau:se
5 MR A: can you give me another factor
6 NINNETTE: because the slaves rebelled
7 MR A: excellent
8 JOANNE: ((*in a whisper:*)) **Joanne's table!**
9 MR A: so action by the [slaves
10 JOANNE: [(((*whispering:*)) **fucking bastard** ((*light laugh*))

Mr Alcott described Joanne as quite alienated, and when Ninnette said Central High was 'a shitty school' on separate occasions during the recordings, Joanne certainly did not argue. Overall, the challenge to school authority presented by Joanne, Ninnette and some of the other girls seemed to carry rather different implications from Hanif and co.'s. The disagreements articulated by Hanif and his friends were part of a more general pattern of close attention to what the teacher was trying to do, and this sometimes turned into vocal support. So their challenges seemed to be framed within a wider acceptance of the importance of the matters on hand. In contrast, these girls' dissent was off-set by very few signs to reassure the teachers of any broader interest and commitment to the proceedings. Their challenges seemed more profound, questioning the relevance and legitimacy of the classroom enterprise as a whole.

At the same time, it is important not to oversimplify, providing nothing but a picture of over-keen boys and alienated girls. At this point, it is worth stepping back, first to suggest some links between the different elements described here, clarifying the part that gender played in all this, and second to emphasize the specificity of the genre we are addressing.

4. Power relations and the classroom settlement

There certainly was a *broad* contrast between boys talking and girls keeping silent, but the situation was actually more complex since:

a   there were a number of other boys who kept rather quiet in class discussion;
b   there were a lot of quiet girls who were far less disaffected than Ninnette and Joanne.

So the male-female split wasn't absolute, and as a matter of theoretical principle, it is important to consider how this relationship between gender and discourse might be shaped by the kinds of activity that they were all engaged in (Goodwin and Goodwin 1987: 241).

So far, three features have been identified in teacher-fronted, whole-class talk in Class 9A: decentred authority, over-exuberance, and refusal. These three characteristics could well have been mutually reinforcing, and the emergence of an at least partial classroom settlement might be modelled as follows:

1   For many reasons – including the school's commitment to mixed ability teaching – it was quite hard for everyone in the class to work together to meet the institutional demands. Some kids were keen and very clever; there was a substantial turnover of pupils (with new ones arriving at different times); some had only recently arrived in the country; a few were seriously disaffected; and all this was set against a background of the material disadvantage, which often intensifies conflict over educational power relations (Davies 2000: 3–22).

2   For one reason or another, the traditional IRE structure of classroom talk did not work very well at Central High. Maybe the teachers had tried it but found it unworkable with such a mixed group of students, or maybe it ran contrary to their professional philosophies – there is obviously a long tradition of educational thought that sees the IRE pattern as a constraint on authentic communication (e.g. Barnes, Britton and Rosen 1969; Edwards 2003), and freed up from the IRE, there certainly were some really scintillating intellectual debates in these classrooms.

3   But if you give students more space to express themselves, they often say things that either don't fit the official agenda, or fit it only tangentially. In Class 9A, there was a group of boys who attended very closely indeed to whole-class discussion, but rather than sticking strictly to thematic relevance and lexico-grammatical propositions, they milked the main line of talk for all its aesthetic potential, recoding the official discourse into melody, German, non-standard accents, etc. On top of that, these hyper-attentive youngsters also made noisy, disparaging comments about others in the class, some of whom did not want to participate at all.

4   Rather than putting a stop to this over-exuberance, the teachers seemed much more preoccupied by the conduct of the youngsters who were conspicuously

disengaged. Indeed, faced with their persistent refusal, it is easy to imagine the teachers becoming increasingly dependent on the hyper-involved ones for reassurance. More than that, in situations where interested students felt that the teacher was getting distracted, it is not hard to understand them lending a hand (in whatever way) to get the lesson back on track, exacerbating the alienation of the classroom's 'others'.

5   In sum, we can see the teacher and the keen students developing a strategic alliance that managed to hold the lessons more or less on course. Within the alliance, teachers were inclined to be tolerant of the excesses of apparently keen students, and this is likely to have intensified the exclusion of the disengaged, but as long as the alliance held up, at least some sense of progress and value could be derived from the lessons.

Certainly, *gender* was factored into this interactional 'system' in very significant ways. Culturally gendered dispositions may well have made it harder for the girls to participate; it was fairly obvious that quite a bit of the boys' attentiveness to the girls was animated by sexual interest; and participants sometimes invoked gender to try to make sense of what was going on. Even so, it seems unlikely that either sexism or gendered dispositions per se can explain the development of this classroom dynamic, and instead, the main source of this interactional polarization can be very plausibly located in the pressures, opportunities and constraints of the institutional activity in which they were all engaged.[7]

That is a hypothesis about how the elements of classroom discourse we have described hung together. It is now worth turning to the generic specificity of whole-class instruction fronted by the teacher.

5. The generic distinctiveness of whole-class teacher talk

Ninnette and Joanne generally chatted to each other during whole-class discussion, but when they had written tasks to do, they were a lot more attentive to curriculum business. In fact, this was quite general, and as their German teacher declared to the class as a whole:

> 'How come every time we do oral work, you get out of hand. The only time this class can actually be manageable is when we do writing.'

There was also a good deal of structured role-play at Central High, and when students watched their peers as an audience they were also much more attentive. So there are significant contrasts here: the class was either over-exuberant or obdurately disengaged when it came to whole-class discussion, but they were much more compliant with curriculum demands when it came to writing and role-plays.

In the first instance, this contrast helps once again to rule out certain explanations for the patterns of classroom discourse described earlier on: Joanne and Ninnette were not completely alienated, and under different conditions, they were perfectly capable of participating in activities that involved an element of semiotic narrowing, capable of following the logo-centric rationality of the curriculum, capable of focusing their minds on curriculum ideas and turning these into writing. Equally, any suggestion that there was an endemic inability to participate in orderly collective events can be discounted by referring to the evidence of role-play.

But maybe more important, it invites reflection on what features of writing and role-play are most likely to have influenced these differences in students' conduct, pointing to the properties in teacher talk that are likely to have made it particularly problematic (cf. Rampton 2006: Ch. 2.6).

Assessment is one factor. Whereas writing results in recorded assessments of individual performance that accumulate over time and are consequential for students' overall school careers (and beyond), the evaluative acts in a fast-flowing IRE are relatively fleeting and trivial, and comparatively inconsequential for the documentary profile of individuals.

The *demands of audienceship* are another factor. During whole-class teacher-talk, you may think that what has just been said is ridiculous, dull or stupid, but you are expected to subordinate your assessment to the evaluative criteria and curriculum knowledge possessed by the teacher. In role-play, you can attend to many different aspects of the performance and there is leeway to respond as you want to the proceedings. Rather than being disruptive, laughter, gasps and maybe even comments can enhance the general activity, and if you are asked for your views at the end, the aesthetic framing of the activity gives more scope for a take-it-or-leave-it response.

The *expectations of linguistic production* are a third factor. During teacher-talk, the IRE involves you in cycles of spotlighting, performance and evaluation that are both rapid and insistent, not just cramping you within evaluative criteria you do not control but also nagging you to participate. In contrast, in writing on the one hand, individuals are not generally made the single focus of attention for the whole class, and there is time to review, revise and indeed even enjoy one's own product prior to both its completion and its assessment by somebody else. And on the other, while role-plays are in progress, the boundary between performance and audience is fairly clear and you have a better sense of how long you can relax in an audience identity. Indeed, moving on from this itemization of teacher-talk's generic differences from writing and role-play, we can suggest that in its canonical, unadulterated form, teacher-led discussion involves a *jostling but expressively depleted style of communication that marginalizes students' own judgment but threatens to drag them onto the platform with curriculum-scripted performances, which in the end do not actually count for very much.*[8]

This description is obviously rather different from the characterization of whole class discussion provided by Sinclair and Coulthard (1975), Mehan (1979), Edwards and Westgate (1994) or Edwards (2003), but it builds on the evidence of how students actually did and did not participate in Class 9A, and it attempts to reflect *their* experience and perspective on this genre. Most obviously, it suggests that in its canonical form, whole-class teacher-fronted discussion was rather distasteful to the students, and this raises a larger question. Is there now a new kind of pedagogic settlement in contemporary urban classrooms, represented by the kinds of the communicative practice we saw in Class 9A? Or was what we have seen simply business-as-usual in working-class education in Britain?

6. Historical changes in the genre

In the 1970s and 80s, the British sociology of education produced a flurry of classroom ethnographies.[9] How far do their portraits of classroom life resemble the descriptions in this chapter? Has the discursive organization of classroom discourse in urban secondary schools stayed much the same over the last 30 years, or were there new ingredients in Class 9A that pointed to cultural change?

Although there are methodological issues complicating the comparison,[10] a number of similarities show that there were continuities between the classrooms described in the 1970s–80s and Class 9A in 1990s. So, for example, both in the 1970s and late 1990s, work and non-work activity were often closely intertwined in class, and a certain level of routine non-conformity was treated as acceptable – 'laughter, talking in class, running in school, jostling in line, fidgeting, staring out of windows, not listening to teacher, failure to hand in work, failure to "try your best" etc' (Pollard 1979: 83).[11] At the same time, two quite substantial differences stand out. In British classroom ethnographies of the 1970s and 1980s:

1   There was generally a basic contrast between, on the one hand, lessons as a place/ period for work, and on the other, the high priority that young people attached to enjoyment. In working-class areas, pupil peer groups were seen as normatively oriented to pleasure and amusement, to the extent that keen students felt pressure to conceal their commitment to schoolwork.
2   In addition, ethnographies in the 70s and 80s painted a picture in which academic work went hand-in-hand with orderly talk along the lines directed by the teacher. In general, when pupils prioritized their own concerns, moving outside the terms of reference/engagement offered by the teacher, this was open to interpretation as 'deviance'.

In contrast, at Central High in the late 1990s:

1   Instead of being defensive about an interest in the lesson, pupils were often quite aggressive in trying to keep the lesson on track, making space for curriculum work by challenging the unofficial activity of other pupils.
2   Rather than following a teacher-led IRE lockstep, students displayed their interest in academic work by taking over a lot of the speech turns that are traditionally reserved for their teachers

In the 1970s and 80s, British classroom ethnographies assumed or reported a set of normative oppositions and links, which can be loosely described as:

lessons + work versus peer group + fun

and

orderly talk ↔ deference to teachers ↔ respect for knowledge and learning

At Central High in the late 1990s, these patterns appeared to be less stable. Talk among peers could be aggressively *school*-oriented, while at the same time, there was often a noticeable *lack* of deference in the way pupils spoke to the teacher about session topics. Valued classroom knowledge was no longer inextricably tied to a procedural decorum managed by the teacher.[12]

So even though comparison with the 1970s and 1980s shows that classroom interaction in the late 1990s at Central High had not changed beyond all recognition, there seemed to be a noticeable difference in the interactional demeanour with which students approached the business of learning. How far, though, is it possible to generalize beyond this particular dataset?

7. How typical was Central High, and how significant is this non-deferential commitment to learning?

As well as studying inner-city Central High in the 1990s, we also investigated Westpark, a suburban school with a rather different demographic profile. At Central High, more than half of the students received free school meals, almost a third were registered as having special educational needs and, in 1999, when our informants eventually took their school-leaving exams at 16, less that 20 per cent got five or more 'GCSE' A*–C results. In contrast, at Westpark only about a quarter of students received free school meals, only 15 per cent were registered as having special educational needs, and 60 per cent of the cohort we investigated achieved five or more A*–C results at GCSE in their school-leaving exams in 1999. These demographic differences were matched by discursive differences in class. In contrast to the patterns described above, Westpark teachers could generally talk to the class for substantial periods relatively free from interruption or distraction by the pupils; there were few difficulties maintaining the conventional IRE pattern of classroom discourse; unauthorized talk between students was largely hidden from the teacher; and pupils generally maintained a public show of willingness to participate in class as directed. So does this mean that the claims and descriptions above are really only relevant to Central High, or at best, to a small group of the most disadvantaged schools?

Certainly, there could have been a range of local contingencies shaping the particular settlement identified in Class 9A (relationships, personalities, interactional histories, etc.) and it seems unlikely that decentred authority, over-exuberance and refusal would be found in every other class at Central High, or that they would coalesce in the same way. Nevertheless, there are very good grounds for saying that IRE problems, routine disengagement and non-deferential enthusiasm are *not* simply confined to only the most underachieving schools and that they extend quite far beyond.

During 2005 and 2006, we used the same methodology to study 13–15-year-olds at another secondary school, 'London Community School' (LCS), where GCSE results were twice as good as those at Central High.[13] Although we have not systematically analysed the teacher-centred classroom discourse in this location, observation over 2 years suggested that discourse practices broadly similar to Class 9A were very common. Indeed, much more relevant to the question of generalizability, we also used the radio-microphone recordings from LCS to elicit the perceptions of a wider group of urban school teachers.

Deliberately excluding more spectacular episodes (e.g. watching music videos during Art; looking at internet porn during IT), first we selected four relatively routine 2- to 4-minute excerpts that raised issues about the boundaries between teachers and students, and/or involved teachers trying to elicit class- and task-participation from pupils who did not offer immediate compliance.[14] Then we played these excerpts to 39 professionals with over 500 years of classroom experience in predominantly urban areas (mean: 13 years; median: 11 years), eliciting their reactions in seven groups. When they first heard the extracts, these teachers quite often criticized the staff involved for their classroom management shortcomings, but this soon gave way to more general reflections:

'[the relationship between] staff and students is so different than it was ten years ago. The difference is that you can't get in their faces. I remember when I started teaching … seventeen years ago and you got in [a] kid's face and that was accepted as the norm. You could not do that here and I'm so glad they would be – they'd be quite entitled to go and complain about you. You would lose respect, you would lose all – you know, that would spread and you would be seen as this person and would stand out amongst this school as this – as someone who tried to rule by fear and we cannot do that again.'

(Tom, 40–50. MFL (Asst. Head). 17 years' classroom experience)

'In my experience, any lesson in which the students come in and you start off saying "we are going to pick up from the last lesson" is bound to be unsuccessful in this school, in an environment where teachers are – have to be most of the time red-hot. You have to be – it is all a continual performance. My unsuccessful lessons this week ((*laughs*)) are ones where I am quite happy to say "right we'll continue from last lesson".'

(Gethin, 20–30. English. 3 years' classroom experience)

'I think it [the relationship between adults and children] has become far less formal, you know, the idea that you know, the adult is right and the students do what they are told has broken down in wide areas of society – certainly in my little bit.'

(Caroline, 40–50. EAL. 24 years' classroom experience)

Traditional order might still be found in some schools:

'I can remember teaching at grammar school – humanities, you know, you could have lively discussions but they'd be as strict as hell, and once the discussion's over you work in silence and nobody's gonna mess about, you know, nobody would be leaning over the radiator or anything like that.'

(Joe, 50–60. English. 31 years' classroom experience)

But this experience of an environment where there could be 'lively discussions … strict as hell' was very far from typical in the accounts provided by these teachers. Overall, they said, classroom relations had changed over time; communication with pupils relied on negotiation rather than authority; pupils knew their rights; lessons had to entertain; and digital culture presented a continual challenge. Indeed, when the teachers were asked to indicate whether they were familiar with episodes like the ones we played them, 86 per cent of their 149 responses indicated that they saw them as either 'fairly' or 'very' recognizable.

Turning to non-deferential enthusiasm for learning as a fairly new classroom phenomenon (Section 6 above), the last 10–15 years have produced a number of studies describing students whose curriculum interest combines with a lack of respectful obedience to their teachers – this is reported among 14–15-year-olds in Los Angeles (Gutiérrez, Rymes and Larson 1995), among 15–16-year-olds in Perth, Australia (Lee 1996), 10–11-year-olds in Mexico City (Candela 1999), and 9–10-year-olds in the US Mid-west (Kamberellis 2001). In fact, if we want to understand what keeps urban teachers going in the school environments where they find themselves, then this combination of an interest-in-learning with disregard for traditional classroom decorum may be particularly important. In environments where interest equates with obedience, it is likely to be rather hard reconciling the personal mission to educate with problems operating the IRE, holding the class's attention or establishing a working silence, but this certainly was not the situation at Central High, and even in the absence of canonical order during whole-class teacher talk, the hyper-exuberant kids showed that they were listening/engaged. Their involvement might not be disciplined in quite the ways that governments might dream of, but at least teachers were not talking in a vacuum. And although there was no question of their being wholly at ease in these conditions, there were signs that our 2006 teacher-informants were adjusting to this:

> 'Children are bright now. You know, we have got a whole different climate now. Children know what they are entitled to. Children will tell you "that was a crap lesson, it was boring, you read that story with no feeling". But they are right to do that if we are crap, you know, whereas I wouldn't have dreamed of saying anything. I would have sat and be bored.'
>
> (Deborah, 50–60. RE/humanities. 20 years' classroom experience)

> 'Some kids are responding to that [curriculum topic], even if not ((*laughs*)) very enthusiastically, and here yeah the teacher's a bit disappointed, but nobody gets sort of really upset about it, do you know what I ((*laughs*)) – you know, if … it's sort of like a social occasion in some ways.'
>
> (Maureen, 50–60. English and drama. 29 years' classroom experience)

So a comparatively unruly interest in the lesson topic is, it seems, at least one of the newer elements in contemporary classroom culture that was far from unique to Class 9A. What could account for its emergence?

Logically anyway, growing attention to students' non-deferential curriculum involvement could just reflect a shift in academic fashion, and there are parallels here to the move in the humanities and social sciences from 'structuralism' to 'post-structuralism', particularly with the latter's concern for the carnivalesque, the agency of subordinates, and the co-construction of social systems (cf. Rampton 2006: Ch. 1.2). But to attribute all this to academic fashion, we would first have to dismiss what Fairclough calls the 'conversationalisation of public discourse' (1995: 137–8), ignoring the growing separation of formality and seriousness in public culture generally, both in Britain and elsewhere. Second, to hold to a no-change, business-as-usual view of classroom discourse, we would have to assume that socio-linguists and language educationalists who have advocated the value of pupil talk and oracy – scholars such as Labov (1969), Trudgill (1975), Barnes, Britton and Rosen (1969) – have had absolutely no impact on schooling over the last 30 years. This is counter-intuitive, and certainly at Central High, it is objectively at odds with the history of local curriculum change. And third, we would have to ignore the influence of digital new media, which, in the words of one of our teacher-informants, generates

> 'the issue of us playing catch up with young people today, realizing that they inhabit a world in which we are always uh playing catch up with, you know, the mobile phones. Five-six years ago, it was clear cut – mobile phones were not allowed. But they are so ubiquitous that we have to give in, and we haven't accommodated them properly. So every now and then the school takes a hard line on it, and everybody's singing from the same hymn sheet – all members of staff – and they know that it's gonna to be okay for a while. Then, you know, priorities shift cos we've got other things to do, and then like Daryl's saying no [to handing over his mobile phone] to me a couple of weeks after, and I was instrumental in putting this policy forward. ((*laughing*)) So I feel a right idiot, uh to some degree we've just gotta learn how to accommodate it.'
> (Tom, 40–50. MFL (Asst. Head). 17 years' classroom experience)

According to Holmes and Russell, new media and the Internet are 'much more decen-tred, democratic and empowering than an adolescent's subjection to … institutional life via … classrooms' (1999: 71), and Sefton-Green suggests that 'young people who regularly "surf the Net" at their own pace may well find the regimented structure of a teacher-led curriculum tedious' (1998: 12). Since we have not specifically investigated the links between digital culture and interactional learning styles, we cannot engage empirically with proposals like these, but with Caroline Dover, we did conduct quantita-tive surveys of students' classroom media engagement practices in the radio-microphone datasets from 1997–8 and 2005 and 2006, and this provides clear evidence of the increasing classroom significance of interactive media technologies.[15]

In the 80 hours of recordings we surveyed from 1997–8, there were only 19 epi-sodes where students used or talked about digital media (PCs, pagers, mobiles, email, the Internet, electronic games) – 7 per cent of *c.* 275 popular and new media cultural engagements, averaging out at about once every 4 hours.[16] In contrast, in the 80 hours from 2005 and 2006, there were 138 references to digital media (mobiles, mp3s, PCs, the Internet, MSN, electronic games) – a quarter of all popular cultural engagements, on average about once every half-hour.[17] Indeed, when 2005 and 2006 are compared, there was also a noticeable shift in the classroom presence of portable digital hardware – in 2005, a mobile phone was audibly used just a couple of times in class for texting (by one informant), but in 2006, there were 22 instances of the non-coursework use of mobiles, PSPs, mp3 players in class (3 informants), an increase that can be at least partly linked to the availability and uptake of media products on the market.[18] The classrooms we examined in 2005 and 2006 did not appear to be 'swamped' by new digital hardware – at least, not audibly – but there was clear evidence of innovations in communications technology working their way into young people's classroom lives, validating the attention our teacher-informants gave to this.

Were lessons and learning being undermined? In the 80 hours of radio-microphone recordings from 2005 and 2006, there were only nine episodes where students themselves volunteered a link between the curriculum and popular and new media culture. But this lack of an active link does not mean that curriculum learning and popular digital culture are necessarily at odds, or that commitment to one entails rejection of the other. Of the five young people we tracked in our survey, Nadia talked about popular culture and used digital technologies far more than anyone else – on average, she audibly engaged with popular and new media culture about 15 times an hour. But she was seldom challenged or reprimanded by teachers, and she was also the highest achiever among our informants, included in the school's 'Gifted and Talented' programme.

Quite how and with what consequences teachers and students like Nadia negotiate the different demands and attractions of schooling and popular digital culture requires a good deal more analysis, not only judiciously looking for links between the details of interaction and the kinds of wider issue raised by our teacher-informants (including the discourse of consumer rights), but also attending, of course, both to youngsters who are relatively successful/engaged and to youngsters who aren't. But to conclude, two larger points stand out.

8. Conclusion

Our central argument is that in contemporary urban secondary classrooms, the patterns of discourse described as typical by education research and canonized in government policy are often highly problematic. Schools are hard to isolate from widespread cultural change, and we have adduced a range of additional sources of evidence to propose that the kinds of interaction seen at Central High were not unique. Nor are these patterns likely to be restricted to very low-achieving institutions – our teacher-informants had experience of working across a range of urban secondary schools – and although pupils at the school we studied in 2005–6 engaged with popular and new media culture with greater average frequency than the youngsters at Central High, their GCSE results were twice as good. This leads to two conclusions.

First – and more interrogatively, as this lies well beyond our own areas of expertise – it would seem to be something of a weakness, at least prima facie, if educational and psychological research committed to 'understanding and promoting productive interaction' screens out classroom dynamics like those we have described. Packer and Goicoechea maintain that 'mind is not from the outset a distinct ontological realm, but a cultural and historical product' (2000: 235), and they quote Lave (1988: 1) saying that cognition 'is a complex social phenomenon ... distributed – stretched over, not divided among – mind, body, activity and culturally organized settings' (2000: 229). Indeed, according to Packer and Goicoechea (2000: 238), Vygotsky himself referred to 'the atmosphere of tense social struggle' in classrooms, declaring that 'education and creativity are always tragic processes, inasmuch as they always arise out of "discontent", out of troubles, from discord'. If that is correct, then the kinds of cultural and interactional environment found in Class 9A are potentially rather significant for socio-cognitive studies of dialogue. Though their neglect may simplify the practice of research, it may also undermine the theory.

A second, much more emphatic set of implications relates to professional development and education policy more generally. We are certainly not suggesting that interactional dynamics like those in Class 9A generate ideal learning environments, and recommendations for practical action lie well beyond the scope of what we have investigated. Even so, a lot of easy explanations for the behaviour in this class fall by the wayside when we look at the proceedings more closely. 'Defective listening skills', 'gender and sexism', 'student alienation' and 'an inability to handle context-reduced' communication might all be invoked to account for what went on, but when we try to look at how things work in such environments, we can see that these explanations are either wrong or at best only partial. More obviously and most crucially: if you do not have a realistic account of the ways in which teachers and pupil actually manage to get by in their everyday lives, pedagogic interventions are bound to flounder. At present, public debate and official policy treat contemporary urban classrooms as nothing more than the chaotic outcome of incompetent pedagogy, or describe them with euphemisms like 'challenging', and there is no space for teachers to reflect on their work with anything other than feelings of failure and shame. Social science research can help to reset some of the terms of public debate by pointing to how things actually seem to operate. In the process, we can recognize the difficulties that students and teachers work under, give some credit to their hard-won achievements, and start to understand the adaptive utility of the strategies they develop in their interactions. Effective educational intervention depends, in short, on open and intelligent discussion tuned to the realities of the urban working environment, and in this chapter, we have tried to make a contribution towards this.

Notes

1   Linguistic ethnography draws on a number of traditions in applied and socio-linguistics: Ethnography of Communication, Interactional Sociolinguistics, New Literacy Studies, Conversation Analysis, Critical Discourse Analysis, Multimodal Semiotics. The UK Linguistic Ethnography Forum provides an arena for researchers pursuing this line of work (http://www.ling-ethnog.org.uk) and the 'Ethnography, Language & Communication' programme provides training for interested social scientists, funded under the ESRC Researcher Development Initiative (http://www.rdi-elc.org.uk). An account of linguistic ethnography's coherence, and of the ways in which some of the methods and perspectives in US linguistic anthropology have been adapted and changed in the process of appropriation in the UK, can be found in Rampton 2007 (see also Rampton 2006: Ch. 10)

2   The data come from a 28-month ESRC project entitled 'Multilingualism and Heteroglossia in and out of School' (R-000-23-6602; 1997–9).

3   It was the teachers who knew most about curriculum requirements, who had planned the lesson, who gave out marks, and who could quickly call on institutional punishments; students never spoke to the whole class for a protracted period on their own initiative, unlicensed by the teacher; and indeed in the excerpts above, even if the names had been

removed from the transcripts, it still wouldn't be very hard to identify who the teacher was.

4   Here and in a number of excerpts in this section, underlining points to the elements being transcoded while bold indicates the new form.

5   'Performance' in Richard Bauman's sense: 'Performance in its artful sense may be seen as a specially marked way of speaking, one that sets up or represents a special interpretive frame within which the act of speaking is to be understood. In this sense of perform-ance, the act of speaking is put on display, objectified, lifted out to a degree from its contextual surroundings, and opened up to scrutiny by an audience. Performance thus calls forth special attention to and heightened awareness of the act of speaking and gives licence to the audience to regard it and the performer with special intensity. Performance makes one communicatively accountable; it assigns to an audience the responsibility of evaluating the relative skill and effectiveness of the performer's accomplishment' (Bauman 1987: 8).

6   In Excerpt 11, for example, Mr Newton calls for girls to participate and nominates Ninnette. John flags up the girls' potential embarrassment (line 5), and then he and others 'embellish' Mr Newton's questions with disparaging comments on Ninnette's knowledge (line 12), proceeding from there to facetious remarks about dating, compet-ing for her speaking turn (see Rampton 2006: Ex. 2.21).

7   Indeed, if we refer to pressured situations rather than types of person to account for the kinds of classroom discourse we have seen, it is possible to conceive of *other* social category memberships becoming salient in these processes of micro-institutional polari-zation, and in fact, loosely comparable accounts where *ethnicity* gets foregrounded can be found in e.g. Foley (1990: Ch. 4) and in McDermott and Gospodinoff (1981).

8   Rampton (2006: Chs 2.6, 3.7 and 3.8) gives a much more extensive account of whole-class teacher-talk as a genre, drawing on linguistic anthropology (cf. Hanks 1987, Bauman 2001).

9   For example, Hammersley (1974, 1976), Furlong (1976, 1985), Pollard (1979, 1985), Turner (1983), Measor and Woods (1984), Hammersley and Woods (1984), Beynon (1985) and Woods (1990).

10   The studies being referred to generally relied heavily on field-note observations, and without radio-microphones, they were unable to gain the kind of intimate insight into classroom life we achieved at Central High (cf. Edwards and Westgate 1994: 44). Beyond that, there was very little systematic discourse analysis in these studies, since discourse analysis itself was only in a very rudimentary stage of development in the 1970s. Instead, they relied very heavily on what pupils said in interview, taking folk categories at face value and using them for the description and analysis of classroom practices.

11   Classroom discourse at Central High in the 1990s also resembled the patterns reported in the 1970s and 1980s to the extent that the latter showed:

  • how classes were often split between those who wanted to work and those who didn't;
  • how both the most deviant and the most conformist students varied in the extent to which they conformed or deviated, with lots of people in the middle;
  • how quite a lot of pupil acts looked both ways, satisfying the demands of both school and peer group – either doing the work without any show of enthusiasm, or putting on shows of enthusiasm that peers understood to be digressive, ironic and/or subversive;
  • how teachers drew the line differently, with different classes at different moments (deliberately ignoring a lot of the goings-on).

12   Ethnographers in the 1980s were certainly interested in the possibility of a respect for learning getting separated from deference to school as an institution, and Hammersley and Turner suggest, for example, that 'with recent changes in attitudes to children

and in the social organisation of the family, there may be a mismatch between the way pupils are treated in school and outside: outside, certainly among some strata, they are increasingly treated as "semi-adults"' (1984: 169). Even so, it is difficult to find anything similar to the combination of disorderly talk with intellectual engagement that emerged at Central High, though there is an early glimpse of the destabilization of these normative patterns in the accounts of black girls at school provided by Furlong (1976), Fuller (1984) and Mac An Ghaill (1988) (see Rampton 2006: 84–5 for elaboration).

13 'Urban Classroom Culture and Interaction' (ESRC, 2005–8, RES-148-25-0042).
14 The episodes included sequences like these:

Excerpt 13

Thursday morning, 10 minutes into Period 2 of a Year 10 GCSE maths class with Mr Graves. Otis is sitting in front of Jerome and Jermaine who have both recently purchased Sony PSP (Play Station Portable) consoles, and he wants them to tell him how to use Photoshop to import images.

5. MR G: ((*loudly, to the whole class:*)) Oh guys I wanna sign where you've got to
6.   today ((*some side comments from students*))
7. OTIS: ((*to Jermaine in a low voice*)): I wanna do Photoshop do some graffiti
8.   writing on my thing, innit (2) for my–
9. MR G: ((*moving closer to Otis and co*)): guys (.) [I've asked you (.)
10. JERMAINE ((*TO OTIS*)):   [if we can get in your website
11.   we can sort it out
12.MR G: three times now to get your coursework out
13.   if you don't you'll all be staying behind at break
14.   ok?
15. JEROME: Sir-[(   )
16. OTIS: [oh:: sh – don't tell me I lost my coursewo–

Excerpt 14

Wednesday morning, Period 3, in a Year 9 humanities lesson focusing on World War II. Mr Ross is a long-term supply teacher from Australia, standing in for Mrs Barrett. Basheera, Lola and Joel are friends (aged 13 and 14), and they are supposed to be working with Nita and Zane on rationing:

2. MR ROSS: alright Nita might do her, uh part of rationing (.) through a diary entry
3. GIRL: ((*giggles*))
4. MR ROSS: [ok
5. BASHEERA: [why do we have to do [that
6. MR ROSS: [shshsh
7. BASHEERA: (with) Ms Barrett, we had to do just like a normal essay why do you
8.   keep making it harder for us
9. MR ROSS: this is what every other–
10. JOEL: it's true
11. MR ROSS: this is what every other [class is doing
12. BOY: [where's Mrs Barrett man
13. ZANE: she got pregnant
14. BASHEERA: ((*laughs*))
15. MR ROSS: thank you
16. BASHEERA: ((*laughing*)) she had a baby

17. JOEL: (oh my days)

18. BASHEERA: the baby's a boy

19. GIRL: what's his [name

20. MR ROSS: [guys I wanna see some work actually done today

21. GIRL: (   )

22. MR ROSS: or you're not going to lunch

23. BASHEERA: it weighs a stone

24. LOLA: you want it finished?

15 For details, see Rampton, Harris and Dover (2002), Rampton (2006: Ch. 3) and Rampton, Harris, Georgakopoulou, Leung, Small and Dover (2008). The surveys sought to describe who engaged with what aspects of popular and new media culture, how, when, where at school, and against what background obstacles and opportunities. To achieve this, Dover listened to *c.* 80 hours of the radio-microphone recordings of nine informants from two schools in the 1997–8 dataset, and to *c.* 80 hours from the radio-microphone recordings of five informants in 2005 and then 2006. In both cases, she identified episodes in which the informants audibly used, referred to or performed music, TV, mobiles, mp3s, PSPs, PCs, the Internet, electronic games, magazines, or newspapers. In all, she identified *c.* 275 episodes in the 1997–8 recordings and 531 episodes in the datasets from 2005–6. An episode was defined as a sequence of talk introducing and often sustaining a popular or new media cultural theme, bounded by periods of talk and activity devoted to other matters, and as silent media engagements (e.g. reading text-messages) might well have been undetected in our radio-microphone recordings, actual engagements might well have been more numerous. The research was carried out over the course of two projects: 'Interaction, Media Culture and Adolescents at School' (Spencer Foundation, 2001–2) and 'Urban Classroom Culture and Interaction' (ESRC, 2005–8).

16 This was just before the massive uptake of mobile phones among young people. 'In October 1999, one in three young people aged 13–16 had their own mobile, up six-fold on the previous year' (Annual Childwise Monitor (*ChildWise Insights: Boys Kick the Reading Habit*)). Available online at: http://www.childwise.co.uk/reading/htm (accessed 9 May 2002).

17 In fact, this was mirrored by a decline in the proportional salience of TV in young people's talk. In 1997–8, about 25 per cent of the episodes orienting to popular and new media culture referred to TV (68 out of 275 episodes), whereas in 2005–6, this dropped to just 7 per cent (36 out of 531 episodes).

18 3G mobiles have been available in the UK market since 2004 but did not become very popular or affordable until 2006, after the first phase of our fieldwork. Similarly, PSPs became available in the UK at the end of 2005. In fact it was also during the second phase of fieldwork that social networking sites started to take off among young people in the UK. Hi5 (referenced by one student) launched in 2004, Bebo launched in 2005 and Facebook became available to everyone in 2006.

References

Barnes, D., Britton, J. and Rosen, H. (1969) *Language, the Learner and the School*, Harmondsworth: Penguin.

Bauman, R. (1987) 'The role of performance in the Ethnography of Speaking', *Working Papers and Proceedings of the Center for Psychosocial Studies 11*, Chicago: University of Chicago.

Bauman, R. (2001) 'Genre', in A. Duranti (ed.) *Key Terms in Language and Culture*, Oxford: Blackwell.

Beynon, J. (1985) *Initial Encounters in the Secondary School*, Lewes: Falmer Press.

Burawoy, M. (1998) 'The extended case method', *Sociological Theory*, 16:4–33.

Candela, A. (1999) 'Students' power in classroom discourse', *Linguistics and Education*, 10:139–63.

Cazden, C. (1985) 'Classroom discourse', in M. Wittrock (ed.) *Handbook of Research on Teaching* (3rd edn), London: Macmillan.

Davies, N. (2000) *The School Report: why Britain's schools are failing*, London: Vintage.

Edwards, A. and Westgate, D. (1994) *Investigating Classroom Talk* (2nd edn), Lewes: Falmer Press.

Edwards, T. (2003) 'Purposes and characteristics of whole-class dialogue', in Qualifications and Curriculum Authority (QCA) *New Perspectives on Spoken English in the Classroom*. Available online at: http://www.qca.org.uk/qca_5746.aspx (accessed 23 April, 2007).

Erickson, F. (1985) 'Qualitative methods in research on teaching', in M. Wittrock (ed.) *Handbook of Research on Teaching* (3rd edn), New York: Macmillan.

Fairclough, N. (1995) *Critical Discourse Analysis*, London: Longman.

Foley, D. (1990) *Learning Capitalist Culture*, Philadelphia: University of Pennsylvania Press.

Fuller, M. (1984) 'Black girls in a London comprehensive school', in M. Hammersley and P. Woods (eds) *Life in School: the sociology of pupil culture*, Milton Keynes: Open University Press.

Furlong, V. (1976) 'Interaction sets in the classroom: towards a study of pupil knowledge', in M. Hammersley and P. Woods (eds) *The Process of Schooling*, London: Routledge and Kegan Paul.

Furlong, V. (1985) *The Deviant Pupil*, Milton Keynes: Open University Press.

Goffman, E. (1981) *Forms of Talk*, Oxford: Blackwell.

Goodwin, C. and Goodwin, M. (1987) 'Children's arguing', in A. Grimshaw (ed.) *Conflict Talk*, Cambridge: Cambridge University Press.

Gutiérrez, K., Rymes, B. and Larson, J. (1995) 'Script, counterscript and underlife in the classroom', *Harvard Educational Review*, 65:445–71.

Hammersley, M. (1974) 'The organisation of pupil participation', *Sociological Review*, 22:355–68.

Hammersley, M. (1976) 'The mobilisation of pupil attention' in M. Hammersley and P. Woods (eds) *The Process of Schooling*, London: Routledge and Kegan Paul.

Hammersley, M. and Turner, G. (1984) 'Conformist pupils?' in M. Hammersley and P. Woods (eds) *Life in School: the sociology of pupil culture*, Milton Keynes: Open University Press.

Hammersley, M. and Woods, P. (eds) (1984) *Life in School*, Milton Keynes: Open University Press.

Hanks, W. (1987) 'Discourse genres as a theory of practice', *American Ethnologist*, 14:668–92.

Hannerz, U. (1987) 'The world in creolisation', *Africa*, 57:546–9.

Harris, R., Leung, C. and Rampton, B. (2001) 'Globalisation, diaspora and language education in England', in D. Block and D. Cameron (eds) *Globalisation and Language Teaching*, London: Routledge.

Heap, J. (1985) 'Discourse in the production of classroom knowledge: reading lessons', *Curriculum Inquiry*, 15:245–79.

Holmes, D. and Russell, G. (1999) 'Adolescent CIT use: paradigm shifts for educational and cultural practices?', *British Journal of the Sociology of Education*, 20:69–78.

Hymes, D. (1996) *Ethnography, Linguistics, Narrative Inequality*, London: Taylor & Francis.

Jakobson, R. (1960) 'Concluding statement: linguistics and poetics', in T. Sebeok (ed.) *Style in Language*, Cambridge, MA: MIT Press.

Kamberellis, G. (2001) 'Producing heteroglossic classroom (micro)cultures through hybrid discourse practice', *Linguistics and Education*, 12:85–125.

Labov, W. (1969) 'The logic of non-standard English', in J. Alatis (ed.) *Georgetown Monographs on Language and Linguistics* 22, Washington: Georgetown Press.

Lave, J. (1988) *Cognition in Practice: mind, mathematics and culture in everyday life*, Cambridge: Cambridge University Press.

Lawton, D. (1994) *The Tory Mind on Education 1979–94*, London: Falmer Press.

Lee, A. (1996) *Gender, Literacy, Curriculum*, London: Taylor & Francis.

Mac An Ghaill, M. (1988) *Young, Gifted and Black*, Milton Keynes: Open University Press.

McDermott, R. and K. Gospodinoff (1981) 'Social contexts for ethnic borders and school failure', in H. Trueba, G. Guthrie and G. Au (eds) *Culture and the Bilingual Classroom*, Rowley: Newbury House.

Maybin, J. (2006) *Children's Voices: talk, knowledge and identity*, Basingstoke: Palgrave.

Measor, L and Woods, P. (1984) *Changing Schools: pupil perspectives on transfer to a comprehensive*, Milton Keynes: Open University Press.

Mehan, H. (1979) *Learning Lessons*, Cambridge, MA: Harvard University Press.

Packer, M. and Goicoechea, J. (2000) 'Sociocultural and constructivist theories of learning: ontology, not just epistemology', *Educational Psychologist*, 35:227–41.

Pollard, A. (1979) 'Negotiating deviance and "getting done" in primary classrooms', in L. Barton and R. Meighan (eds) *Schools, Pupils and Deviance*, Driffield: Nafferton Books.

Pollard, A. (1985) *The Social World of the Primary School*, London: Holt, Rhinehard, Winston.

Qualifications and Curriculum Authority (QCA). *New Perspectives on Spoken English in the Curriculum*. Available online at: http://www.literacytrust.org.uk/research/oracy reviews.html (accessed 12 October, 2009).

Rampton, B. (2006) *Language in Late Modernity: interaction in an urban school*, Cambridge: Cambridge University Press.

Rampton, B. (2007) 'Neo-Hymesian linguistic ethnography in the UK', *Journal of Sociolinguistics*, 11:584–607.

Rampton, B., Harris, R. and Dover, C. (2002) 'Interaction, media culture and adolescents at school: end of project report', *Working Papers in Urban Language and Literacies* 20. Available online at: http://www.kcl.ac.uk/content/1/c6/01/42/29/paper20.pdf

Rampton, B., Harris, R., Georgakopoulou, A., Leung, C., Small, L. and Dover, C. (2008) 'Urban classroom culture and interaction: project report', *Working Papers in Urban Language and Literacies* 53. Available online at: http://www.kcl.ac.uk/content/1/c6/04/20/06/53.pdf

Sefton-Green, J. (1998) 'Introduction: being young in the digital age', in J. Sefton-Green (ed.) *Digital Diversions: youth culture in the age of multimedia*, London: University College London Press.

Sinclair, J. and Coulthard, M. (1975) *Towards an Analysis of Discourse*, Oxford: Oxford University Press.

Trudgill, P. (1975) *Accent, Dialect and the School*, London: Arnold.

Turner, G. (1983) *The Social World of the Comprehensive*, London: Croom Helm.

Varenne, H. and McDermott, R. (1998) *Successful Failure*, Colorado: Westview Press.

Woods, P. (1990) *The Happiest Days? How pupils cope with school*, London: Falmer Press.

Transcription conventions

(.)	pause of less than a second
(1.5)	approximate length of pause in seconds
[[	overlapping turns
CAPITALS	loud
>text<	more rapid speech
( )	speech inaudible
(text)	speech hard to discern, analyst's guess
((text:))	'stage directions'
bold	words and utterances of particular interest to the analysis
<u>text</u>	words and utterances subsequently repeated by someone else in an utterance (in **bold**) that is of particular analytic interest

Part IV

Promoting productive educational dialogues

Introduction

Throughout Parts 1 to 3 we have seen that underpinning many researchers' interest in exploring and conceptualizing educational dialogues is the idea that we need to understand how better to support teachers and learners' collective endeavours, such that we can promote effective opportunities for, and design strategies to support, productive interaction. This desire to create effective opportunities for dialogue in educational settings has brought about a significant shift in research. Increasingly, in addition to studying how certain forms or modes of interaction may promote learning, researchers are also asking how dialogue can be supported and resourced. They are also asking how efficacious forms of dialogue might be learned, in order to ensure that talk in educational settings becomes a valuable opportunity for learning. This concern to promote productive educational dialogues appears to reflect a belief that the quality of talk in educational contexts is profoundly important and yet its character and context need somehow to be transformed (Alexander 2005; see also Mercer and Hodgkinson 2008).

This imperative for transformation and change reflects, in part, a recognition that in schools, the normative environment for talk in most classrooms is incompatible with children's active and extended engagement in using language to construct knowledge and understanding (Mercer and Littleton 2007) and

> ... if we are not careful, classrooms may be places where teachers rather than children do most of the talking; where supposedly open questions are really closed; where instead of thinking through a problem children devote their energies to trying to spot the correct answer, where supposed equality of discussion is subverted by ... the 'unequal communicative rights' of a kind of talk which remains stubbornly unlike the kind of talk that takes place anywhere else. Clearly if classroom talk is to make a meaningful contribution to children's learning and understanding it must move beyond the acting out of such cognitively restricting rituals.
>
> (Alexander 2005: 10)

How then are we to move beyond the acting out of 'cognitively restricting rituals' such that the power of classroom talk is harnessed for learning and the joint construction of knowledge and understanding? Each of the four chapters in this section of the book report work designed, from a socio-cultural perspective, to address this thorny issue.

The authors are all grappling with the complex pedagogic challenges that arise when designing for dialogue and they explore: how children can be inducted into ways of talking and thinking together in small groups; the ways in which teachers can create 'space' for dialogue to support the development of students' disciplinary knowledge, and the significance of new technologies for resourcing and supporting fruitful educational dialogues. The contributors each acknowledge that what students learn from talk in classrooms (and other educational contexts) and how significant it is for their educational progress, depends crucially on the nature and quality of the dialogues in which they engage. There is certainly much more to discover about the ways in which language experience in educational contexts contributes to the development of learners' abilities to communicate, learn and reason. However, what is currently known provides a well-informed basis for the creation of more effective educational practice and there are already practical ways of making this happen – as testified by the chapters in this section.

The section opens with Chapter 13 by Karen Littleton and Neil Mercer, whose starting point is a concern with the nature and quality of children's small group work and the findings, from both 'classic' and contemporary classroom-based research, that point to the paradox of children being seen to work everywhere *in* groups, but rarely *as* groups – suggesting that much everyday classroom-based talk among children is of limited educational value. As discussed in the previous section (see Chapter 10), some studies have suggested that the quality of collaboration can be improved if attention is given to developing an atmosphere of trust and mutual respect. However, from Littleton and Mercer's perspective children have to do more than engage with each other in a positive and supportive way. They also should become able to use language to 'interthink', such that they can build constructively and critically on each others' ideas. As this does not happen 'naturally', through participation and immersion in ongoing classroom life, the argument is that children need to be explicitly inducted into ways of talking and working together – such that the 'ways with words' and 'ground rules' implicated in, educationally effective, Exploratory Talk become familiar and accessible to them. The chapter describes the principles underpinning the pedagogy and design of the *Thinking Together* classroom-based intervention programme, designed to induct children into effective ways of talking and working together. It also details the evaluation work, undertaken with children in the 8–11-year age range, which evidences the positive effects of the programme in respect of children's talk and their collective and individual performance on non-verbal reasoning tests.

While the positive findings arising from this intervention work are compelling, the idea that we should be encouraging children to take up a new set of norms (the 'ground rules') for their classroom discussions has attracted some critical commentary (see Chapter 9) and is proving to be controversial in some quarters. Lambirth (2006), for example, has argued that the 'ground rules' associated with Exploratory Talk have no intrinsic value as a basis for collaborative activity, they simply reflect the language habits of the more privileged, educated members of society. Having to make a shift from existing sets of ground rules (those that may operate in the child's out-of-school experience) to those related to Exploratory Talk will, he suggests, undermine the linguistic identities and communicative self-confidence of many children. While the 'subtraction' model of language learning (which proposes that adding any new language genre to a child's language repertoire must involve the deletion of some existing genre) that is implicit in this critique has no scientific foundation, it signals that for some educators there are strong ideological reasons why they would not advocate adopting a 'ground rules' approach to the promotion of productive educational dialogues.

Educational intervention work is just one response to the challenge of promoting productive educational dialogues. Phil Scott, Jaume Ametller, Eduardo Mortimer and Jonathan Emberton, who are committed to fostering dialogic teaching in science, suggest in Chapter 14 that there is much also that teachers can learn from careful consideration and engagement with examples of current good practice. Arguing that dialogic learning cannot be designed for *directly*, Scott and colleagues venture that it can be designed for *indirectly* by opening the kinds of 'dialogic spaces' that support it. So from Scott and colleagues' perspective, dialogic 'teaching routines', such as the one exemplified in their chapter, need to be opened up for appraisal by other practitioners and put to use by other teachers with their classes, with some foresight concerning what may occur. Of course the sharing of good practice is part and parcel of the professional teacher's work and figures prominently in ongoing professional development. Yet witnessing and engaging with examples of good practice does not mean that such practices can be easily appropriated by someone keen to develop their own professional practice. There are a multitude of challenges to be faced – not least those that are involved in getting to know the discipline-specific, intellectual terrain for a particular piece of teaching. Indeed, Scott and colleagues' analyses of dialogic teaching in science suggest that if a teacher is to be able to promote effective educational dialogues in their classroom, the endeavour needs to be underpinned by a secure understanding of the discipline area being taught and the obstacles to understanding that students face, along with knowledge of appropriate activities around which the dialogues might be staged.

A recurrent theme in the section concerns the potential of new technologies, notably computers, to resource and support productive educational dialogues. Since they were first introduced into classrooms, computers have been predominantly conceived of as a means for individual learners to access sources of information or to practise skills, rather than being seen as a tool for enabling them to work jointly and consider ideas with others. Computers have sometimes even been represented as offering learners routes to 'personalized learning', which could liberate them from the teacher-guided, collective endeavours of the conventional classroom (Papert 1980; Gee 2003, 2004). In contrast with this stance and rooted in the premise that 'thinking is always about dialogue across difference', with engagement in dialogue being an important 'end' of and in itself, Rupert Wegerif elaborates a dialogic framework for teaching thinking with technology.

Although one must be careful not to assume that technical interactivity automatically, and unproblematically, equates to pedagogic interactivity, in Chapter 15 Wegerif suggests that the affordance of *interactivity* enables the design of software that can simulate multiple perspectives and points of view – enabling learners to be inducted into the 'field of dialogue'. His characterization of the Internet as a cacophony of voices offering innumerable opportunities for dialogic engagement with multiple perspectives on topics suggests that if educators are to harness the potential of the Internet then a key pedagogic design challenge will concern the scaffolding of dialogic encounters between multiple 'voices'. In addition to inducting learners into dialogue, Wegerif argues that ICT can play a valuable role in both '*broadening or expanding dialogic space*' (which entails increasing the degree of difference between perspectives in a dialogue while maintaining the dialogic relationship) and '*deepening dialogic space*' (which involves increasing the degree of reflection on assumptions and grounds). Based on his construction of dialogue as the relationship between voices or perspectives, Wegerif also highlights the ways in which ICT affords opportunities for exploring the dialogue between meanings in different modes.

When considering the issue of how to foster productive educational dialogues in the context of group work, many researchers have emphasized the significance of task design (see Mercer and Littleton 2007). It is important that group tasks should be designed such that learners *need* to work together on them. Therefore tasks should not be too simple, for if each person can easily solve the problem or complete the task alone, then there is no imperative for joint working. Equally, if the task is too complex for the learners, then they will struggle to create understanding and meaning. A group task is one that requires resources no single individual possesses and is one in which students work interdependently and reciprocally – the exchange of ideas and information being vital to success. It is perhaps not surprising, then, that open-ended, challenging tasks tend to be more effective in facilitating productive interaction than more closed tasks focused on finding one right answer. A clear task structure and provision of feedback is also important and this might be one of the best ways in which computer technology can resource joint activity (Howe and Tolmie 1999). It is this concern with effective task design and the technological resourcing of joint activity and productive educational dialogues that sits at the heart of the final contribution by Keith Sawyer and Kenneth Goldman. These authors explore the role played by the mediating artefact of a computer application, the Java Programmer's Interactive Environment (JPie), in scaffolding educational dialogues between pairs of novice computer science university students. The work suggests that the provision of 'visual scaffolds', when they are specifically designed to promote dialogue about core concepts (rather than syntax), can resource exchanges of explanations and justifications that foster learning. Indeed there appears to be something very powerful about the visual nature of JPie, as it enables learners to externally represent conceptual understanding and communicate these understandings, even at a phase in their studies when they have not mastered the relatively advanced concepts, terminology and the ways of speaking associated with programming. Of course, it is not simply a case of 'getting the task right' – JPie is implicated in and integral to the broader endeavour of a 'concepts-first' curriculum. So while computer resources and applications can and do enter into, and distinctively shape and support educational dialogues, it is important to recognize the significance of the wider pedagogic framework within which particular collaborative computer activities are situated and framed.

References

Alexander, R. (2005) *Towards Dialogic Teaching: rethinking classroom talk*, Cambridge: Dialogos.

Gee, J. P. (2003) *What Video Games Have to Teach Us about Learning and Literacy*, London: Palgrave Macmillan.

Gee, J. P. (2004) *Situated Language and Learning: a critique of traditional schooling*, London: Routledge.

Howe, C. and Tolmie, A. (1999) 'Productive interaction in the context of computer supported collaborative learning in science', in K. Littleton and P. Light (eds) *Learning with Computers: analysing productive interaction*, London: Routledge.

Lambirth, A. (2006) 'Challenging the laws of talk: ground rules, social reproduction and the curriculum', *The Curriculum Journal*, 17:59–71.

Mercer, N. and Hodgkinson, S. (2008) *Exploring Talk in School*, London: Sage.

Mercer, N. and Littleton, K. (2007) *Dialogue and the Development of Children's Thinking: a sociocultural approach*, London: Routledge.

Papert, S. (1980) *Mindstorms: children, computers and powerful ideas*, New York: Basic Books.

Chapter 13

The significance of educational dialogues between primary school children

Karen Littleton, University of Jyväskylä and Neil Mercer, University of Cambridge

Introduction

Drawing on our own and others' research we suggest that that there is evidence to support the view that, with teachers' guidance, working and talking together can provide a powerful support for children's cognitive development and learning. However, the evidence also shows that much of the talk in collaborative activity in classrooms is unproductive – with children working everywhere *in* groups but rarely *as* groups, and with teachers often seemingly unaware of how to maximize the quality of children's collaborative work. Arguing that there is a need to explicitly induct children into ways of talking and working together, we highlight work from our ongoing programme of classroom-based research explicitly designed to enhance the quality of children's talk and joint activity. Most of our research has been with the primary (8–11 years) age group, and so we will draw on examples and evidence accordingly. We show how a well-designed programme of language-based classroom activities can make an important contribution to the development not only of children's language and communication skills, but also to their reasoning and learning.

Socio-cultural theory and the significance of interaction

Within educational research, a particular theoretical perspective has become influential over recent decades, from which education and cognitive development are seen as cultural processes. From this socio-cultural perspective, knowledge is not considered to be only possessed individually, but also created by and shared among members of communities and the ways in which knowledge is created are seen to be shaped by cultural and historical factors. This does not mean that socio-cultural researchers boldly assert that intellectual achievement is determined entirely by social experience rather than heredity; they recognize that innate factors play an important part in development, but share the view that we cannot understand the nature of thinking, learning and development without taking account of the intrinsically historical, social and communicative nature of human life.

Detailed explanations of the socio-cultural approach to education (which is also sometimes called 'cultural-historical') can be found in Wells and Claxton (2002) and Daniels (2001), but to summarize, from this perspective education is seen as a 'dialogic' process, with intellectual development being shaped to a significant extent through interaction. In educational settings it is not only the interactions between students and teachers that are regarded as being of significance and consequence, but also those among students. Such interactions inevitably reflect the historical development, cultural values and social practices of the societies and communities in which schools and other educational institutions exist, as well as the more local cultures and practices within particular schools and classrooms. An important implication of this perspective is that we are encouraged to look for the basis of educational success, and failure, in the nature and quality of the social and communicative processes of education rather than in the intrinsic capability of individual students, the didactic presentational skills of individual teachers, or the quality of the educational methods, materials and technologies that have been used.

From a socio-cultural perspective, language is one of the principal tools for constructing knowledge. Vygotsky (1962, 1978), whose work provided the foundations for socio-cultural theory, argued that the acquisition and use of language transformed children's thinking. He described language as both a cultural tool (for the development and sharing of knowledge among members of a community or society) and as a psychological tool (for structuring the processes and content of individual thought). He also proposed that there is a close relationship between these two kinds of use, which can be summed up in the claim that 'intermental' (social, interactional) activity forges some of the most important 'intramental' (individual, cognitive) capabilities, with children's involvement in joint activities generating new personal understandings and ways of thinking. From a socio-cultural perspective, then, language acquisition and use are seen as having a profound effect on the development of thinking (Mercer 2000, 2008; Wells 1999). This gives the study of talk in educational settings a special significance, and implies that its effective use in classrooms is important.

Although ideas have changed to some extent in recent years, pupil-pupil talk is still regarded with unease by many teachers (see for example, Fisher and Larkin 2008). As any teacher will confirm, one way that they feel their competence is judged by senior staff is: Can they keep their class quiet? Of course, the reasonable explanation for the traditional discouragement of pupil-pupil talk is that, as an incidental accompaniment to whole-class chalk-and-talk teaching, it is indeed disruptive and subversive. Even in less formal regimes, teachers have an understandable concern with limiting the amount of 'off-task' talk that goes on. Thus while working and learning with other people is quite common in everyday life outside school, educational practice has implicitly argued against it and collaborative activity among children has rarely been incorporated into the mainstream of classroom life. One of the motivations for our research has been to change this situation.

Learning as a collaborative enterprise

In everyday life, the terms 'collaboration' and 'co-operation' are often used in very loose and general ways to indicate that people are working together to get something done. In the research literature, however, there has been considerable debate about how to define terms such as collaboration and collaborative learning (for example, Dillenbourg 1999). Nevertheless, it is usually agreed that collaboration means something more than children working together in a tolerant and compatible manner. 'Collaborating' or being engaged in collaborative learning means that participants are engaged in a co-ordinated, continuing attempt to solve a problem or in some other way construct common knowledge. It involves a co-ordinated joint commitment to a shared goal, reciprocity, mutuality and the continual (re-)negotiation of meaning (as described by Barron 2000; Nystrand 1986). Participants in collaboration may experience what Ryder and Campell (1989) call 'groupsense' or a feeling of shared endeavour. Such co-ordinated activity depends upon the collaborators establishing and maintaining what Rogoff (1990) and Wertsch (1991) have termed *intersubjectivity*. It will necessarily involve them maintaining a shared conception of the task or problem. Partners will not only be interacting, as they might in co-operative activity, but also *interthinking* (Mercer 2000).

There has been a great deal of research interest in children's collaborative working, learning and problem solving, though much of the research has not been carried out in school. The issue has been researched in diverse ways – for example, through large-scale surveys of life in classrooms; experiments in which pairs or groups of children work on specially designed problem-solving tasks; and detailed analyses of talk between pairs or groups of children working on curriculum-based tasks in school. We will now consider each of these in turn.

Perhaps one of the first messages to emerge from work *surveying* classroom activity is that, at least in British primary schools, truly collaborative activity rarely happens. This was the alarming conclusion of a large-scale research project carried out in the 1970s called ORACLE (Galton, Simon and Croll 1980). The ORACLE team of researchers, observing everyday practice in a large number of British primary schools, found that just because several children were sitting together at a table (as was common) this did not mean that they were collaborating. Typically, children at any table would simply be working, in parallel, on individual tasks. While they might well have talked as they worked, and while they might possibly have talked to each other about their work, the activities they engaged in did not encourage or require them to talk and work together. This problem of children working *in* groups but rarely *as* groups has also been underscored in a number of more recent studies, some of which have shown that even when children are set joint tasks their interactions are rarely productive (Galton, Hargreaves, Comber, Wall and Pell 1999; Blatchford and Kutnick 2003; Alexander 2005). This tells us something important about the nature of everyday educational practice and leads to the conclusion that much everyday classroom-based talk among children may be of limited educational value.

Much of the early collaborative learning research consisted of *experimental studies* of peer interaction, which were designed to establish whether working and solving problems collaboratively was more effective than working alone. Typically, children would be given the same task, but allocated either to working collaboratively or working alone, and their performance on the task assessed. Reviewing such studies, Slavin (1980) noted that collaborative learning was often judged to increase students' academic achievement, self-esteem and motivation. These sorts of investigations gave rise to research in which independent variables, such as group size (e.g. Fuchs and Fuchs 2000), group composition (e.g. Barbieri and Light 1992; Howe 1997; Webb 1989) and nature of the task (e.g. Cohen 1994; Light and Littleton 1999; Underwood and Underwood 1999) were manipulated and the effects assessed. (See Wilkinson and Fung 2002 for a review of work in this field.) However, because such variables interact with each other in complex ways, it has been virtually impossible to isolate the conditions for effective collaboration. Researchers thus started to focus less on establishing parameters for effective collaboration and more on ways in which factors such as task design or group composition influence the processes of collaborative interaction (Dillenbourg, Baker, Blaye and O'Malley 1995; Littleton 1999).

Some experimental studies of collaborative interaction have focused on how children talk together when they are working on a problem or task. They have handled the data of recorded talk by reducing it to predefined coded categories, which in turn lend themselves to treatment by statistical analyses. In particular, correlational techniques have been used to establish whether there is an association between features of learners' talk and on-task success or subsequent learning gain. For example, Azmitia and Montgomery (1993) found that the quality of children's dialogue is a significant predictor of their successful problem solving. Studying children engaged in joint computer-based problem-solving tasks, Barbieri and Light (1992) found that the amount of talk about planning, negotiation and the co-construction of knowledge by partners correlated significantly with successful problem solving by pairs, and to successful learning outcomes in subsequent related tasks by individuals. Similar analytic techniques used by Underwood and Underwood (1999) demonstrated that for pairs of children working on a computer-based problem-solving activity, those who were most observed to offer opinions, analyse the situation in words and express agreement and understanding achieved the best outcomes.

Regarding effects on individuals, a series of experimental, and observational, studies by Howe and colleagues (this volume) have shown that conceptual understanding in science is enhanced by children's discussion of ideas during group work. They found that some features of dialogue are particularly associated with solving complex problems, such as requiring that partners should try to achieve consensus in their discussion (Howe and Tolmie 2003). Reviewing their own and other research (mainly school-based), they conclude that the most productive interaction seems to involve pupils proposing ideas and explaining their reasoning to each other (Howe, Tolmie, Thurston, Topping, Christie, Livingstone, Jessiman and Donaldson 2007). Moreover, the expression of contrasting opinions during group work was the single most important predictor of learning gain. They also found that the positive effects of group work are often delayed (Howe, Tolmie and Rodgers 1992) and this seems to be because dialogue primes children to make good use of subsequent experiences (Howe, McWilliam and Cross 2005). Howe *et al.* (2007) also found that group work seemed most productive when teachers did not intervene, but left pupils to work through problems without intervention. Barnes and Todd (1977, *see also* 1995; Barnes 2008) also draw attention to how teachers can inadvertently undermine group collaboration, a point further underscored by Hertz-Lazarowitz (1992).

Overall, then, the experimental evidence supports the view that focused, sustained discussion among children not only helps them solve problems but promotes the learning of the individuals involved. This conclusion may seem like common sense: but if it is so obviously true, one is led back to the question of why high-quality peer discussion has not been directly promoted and facilitated in formal education.

In the 1970s Barnes and Todd undertook one of the most important early studies of how children talk while working together in school. It involved secondary-age children, but the insights that research provided have informed much other research since, including that focused on the primary years. Barnes and Todd (1995: 127) suggested that pupils are more likely to engage in open, extended discussion and argument when they are talking with their peers outside the visible control of their teacher and that this kind of talk enabled them to take a more active and independent ownership of knowledge:

> Our point is that to place the responsibility in the learners' hands changes the nature of that learning by requiring them to negotiate their own criteria of relevance and truth. If schooling is to prepare young people for responsible adult life, such learning has an important place in the repertoire of social relationships which teachers have at their disposal.

Based on their detailed observations, Barnes and Todd suggest that classroom discussion has to meet certain requirements for explicitness that would not normally be required in everyday conversation. One of their key ideas was the concept of Exploratory Talk, in which a speaker articulates half-formed thoughts so that they can be tested out in the telling, and so that others can hear them, and comment. In that kind of talk, knowledge is made publicly accountable, relevant information is shared effectively, opinions are clearly explained and explanations examined critically. They also argued that the successful pursuit of educational activity depends on learners a) sharing the same ideas about what is relevant to the discussion and b) having a joint conception of what is trying to be achieved by it. These points have been supported by other research based in primary schools (e.g. Bennett and Dunne 1992; Galton and Williamson 1992; Mercer and Littleton 2007).

The significance of Exploratory Talk

In the Spoken Language and New Technology (SLANT) project in the early 1990s researchers observed the talk of children aged 8–11 years when they worked together in small groups at the computer in classroom settings (as described in Wegerif and Scrimshaw 1997). Classroom talk was recorded in ten primary school classrooms across five counties in South East England. Detailed analysis of the children's joint sessions of work suggested that most of the interactions recorded were not task-focused, productive or equitable. In some pairs or groups one child so completely dominated the discussion that the other group members either withdrew from the activity, becoming increasingly quiet and subdued, or else they participated marginally, for example, as the passive scribe of a dominant child's ideas. In other groups the children seemed to ignore each other, taking turns at the computer, each pursuing their own particular ideas when 'their turn' came round. Some groups' talk involved them in unproductive, often highly competitive, disagreements. From time to time these disagreements escalated, with the children becoming increasingly irritated with each other and engaging in vehement personal criticism. On the other hand, much group talk was relatively brief, somewhat cursory and bland. Particularly when groups of friends worked together, the discussions were uncritical, involving only superficial consideration and acceptance of each other's ideas. These observations resonated with those of the other research projects, detailed earlier, that indicated that although grouping children was a common organizational strategy, talk of any educational value was rarely to be heard. That said, very occasionally there was evidence of a distinctive kind of interaction that was qualitatively different and more educationally productive. Here the children engaged in discussions in which they shared relevant ideas and helped each other to understand problems. They were mutually supportive and were constructively critical of each others' ideas, with challenges and counter-challenges being justified and alternative ideas and hypotheses being offered. There was more of the kind of interaction, which Barnes and Todd (1977) called Exploratory Talk.

On the basis of the analysis of the SLANT data, the researchers devised a three-part typology of talk, designed to characterize the different ways in which children in the project classrooms talked together (Fisher 1993; Mercer 1995). In this typology, the concept of Exploratory Talk differs from the original usage by Barnes and Todd by being less focused on individuals sorting out their thoughts and more on collaborating partners thinking together – what we would term 'interthinking' (Mercer 2000):

- *Disputational Talk*, which is characterized by disagreement and individualized decision-making. There are few attempts to pool resources, to offer constructive criticism or make suggestions. Disputational talk also has some characteristic discourse features – short exchanges consisting of assertions and challenges or counter assertions ('Yes, it is', 'No it's not!').
- *Cumulative Talk*, in which speakers build positively but uncritically on what the others have said. Partners use talk to construct 'common knowledge' by accumulation. Cumulative discourse is characterized by repetitions, confirmations and elaborations.
- *Exploratory Talk*, in which partners engage critically but constructively with each other's ideas. Statements and suggestions are offered for joint consideration. These may be challenged and counter-challenged, but challenges are justified and alternative hypotheses are offered. Partners all actively participate, and opinions are sought and considered before decisions are jointly made. Compared with the other two types, in Exploratory Talk knowledge is made more publicly accountable and reasoning is more visible in the talk.

(Mercer and Littleton 2007: 58–9)

The reader might like to test the application of the typology by considering each of the following short examples of discussions, Excerpts 1–3 below (to which we will also provide a commentary). In all three of the transcripts below, the participants are primary school children who are working at the computer. They are all engaged in the joint task of making up a conversation between two cartoon characters portrayed on a computer screen, and also have to decide what the characters are thinking as they speak. They then type the words into the relevant 'speech' and 'thought' bubbles. (Whenever it seemed to the researchers that the children were speaking the voices of the characters, the words have been placed in inverted commas.)

Excerpt 1: Jo and Carol

CAROL: Just write in the next letter. 'Did you have a nice English lesson.'

JO: You've got to get it on there. Yes that's you. Let's just have a look at that. 'Hi, Alan did you have a nice English lesson. Yes thank you, Yeah. Yes thank you it was fine.'

CAROL: You've got to let me get some in sometimes.

JO: You're typing.

CAROL: Well you can do some, go on.

JO: 'Yes thank you.'

CAROL: [*unintelligible.*]

JO: You're typing. 'Yes thank you' 'I did, yeah, yes, thank you I did.'

CAROL: You can spell that.

JO: Why don't *you* do it?

CAROL: No, because *you* should.

Excerpt 2: Sally and Emma

SALLY: Yeah. What if she says erm erm 'All right, yeah.' No, just put 'Yeah all right.' No, no.

EMMA: No. 'Well I suppose I could.'

SALLY: 'spare 15p.' Yeah?

EMMA: Yeah.

SALLY: 'I suppose.'

EMMA: 'I suppose I could spare 50p.'

SALLY: '50?'

EMMA: Yeah. 'Spare 50 pence.'

SALLY: '50 pence.'

EMMA: '50 pence.' And Angela says 'That isn't enough I want to buy something else.'

SALLY: Yeah, no no. 'I want a drink as well you know I want some coke as well'.

EMMA: 'That isn't enough for bubble gum and some coke.'

SALLY: Yeah, yeah.

Excerpt 3: Tina, George and Sophie

GEORGE: We've got to decide.

TINA: We've got to decide together.

GEORGE: Shall we right, right, just go round like take

TINA: No, go round. You say what you think, and she says.

GEORGE: I think she should be saying 'Did you steal my money from me?'

TINA: Your go

SOPHIE: I think we should put 'I thought that my money's gone missing and I thought it was you'

GEORGE: 'I think it was you'.

SOPHIE: Which one?

TINA: Now what was it I was going to say, Um, um.

GEORGE: No because she's *thinking*, so we need to do a thought. So we could write her saying.

SOPHIE: 'My money's gone missing so'.

TINA: I was going to say if we're doing the one where she's saying, this is *saying* not thinking.

SOPHIE: 'My money's gone do you know where it is?'

TINA: No, on the saying one she could say

GEORGE   You should be saying.

TINA: Like she could be thinking to say to Robert, she could be saying 'Do you know where's my money?' 'Do you know anything about my money going missing?'

GEORGE: Yeah, what, yeah that's good. When she's thinking I think she should be thinking 'Oh my money's gone missing and its definitely Robert.'

TINA: Yeah.

SOPHIE: No 'cos she's *saying* it to him isn't she?

TINA: No she's *thinking* at the moment.

GEORGE: No she's *thinking*.

TINA: *That's* the speech bubble.

The talk in Excerpt 1 has characteristics of Disputational Talk. Both participants take an active part, but there is little evidence of joint, collaborative engagement with the task. Much of the interaction consists of commands and assertions. The episode ends with a direct question and answer, but even this exchange has an unproductive, disputational quality. Excerpt 2 has obvious features of Cumulative Talk. There is no dispute, and both participants contribute ideas that are accepted. We can see repetitions, confirmation and elaborations. The interaction is co-operative, but there is no critical consideration of ideas. Excerpt 3 has some characteristics of Exploratory Talk. It begins with Tina and George making explicit reference to their task as requiring joint decision-making, and they attempt to organize the interaction so that everyone's ideas are heard. They then pursue a discussion of what is appropriate content for the character's 'thought' and 'speech' bubbles in which differing opinions are offered and visibly supported by some reasoning (for example 'No, because she's *thinking*, so we need to do a thought.', '... if we're doing the one where she's saying, this is *saying* not thinking.'). However, their reasoning is focused only on this procedural issue: they do not discuss explicitly or critically the proposed content of the character's thoughts and words. Were the space available to include longer examples, we could show that their later discussion also has some 'cumulative' features.

It is important to emphasize that the three-part typology described and exemplified above is not only meant to be descriptive: it has an evaluative dimension, reflecting a concern with educational effectiveness. Talk of a mainly 'disputational' type, for example, was very rarely associated with processes of joint reasoning and knowledge construction. While there may be a lot of interaction between children, the reasoning involved was mainly individualized and tacit. Furthermore, the kind of communicative relationship developed through disputation was defensive and overtly competitive, with information and ideas being flaunted or withheld rather than shared. It was common for this type of talk to comprise tit-for-tat 'Yes it is', 'No it isn't' patterns of assertion and counter-assertion. Disputational argument of this kind has little in common with the kind of reasoned argument that is represented by Exploratory Talk. Children engaged in a disputational type of talk are not, however, orientated to the pursuit of reasoned argument, they are being 'argumentative' in the negative sense of squabbling and bickering.

In contrast with Disputational Talk, Cumulative Talk characterizes dialogue in which ideas and information are shared and joint decisions are made: but there is little in the way of challenge or the constructive conflict of ideas in the process of constructing knowledge. Cumulative Talk represents talk that seems to operate more on implicit concerns with solidarity and trust, hence the recourse to a constant repetition and confirmation of partners' ideas and proposals.

Exploratory Talk represents a joint, co-ordinated form of co-reasoning in language, with speakers sharing knowledge, challenging ideas, evaluating evidence and considering options in a reasoned and equitable way. The children present their ideas as clearly and as explicitly as necessary for them to become shared and jointly analysed and evaluated. Possible explanations are compared and joint decisions reached. By incorporating both constructive conflict and the open sharing of ideas, Exploratory Talk constitutes the more visible pursuit of rational consensus through conversation. Exploratory Talk foregrounds reasoning. Its ground rules require that the views of all participants are sought and considered, that proposals are explicitly stated and evaluated, and that explicit agreement precedes decisions and actions. It is aimed at the achievement of consensus. Exploratory Talk, by incorporating both conflicting perspectives and the open sharing of ideas, represents the more visible pursuit of rational consensus through conversations. It is a speech situation in which everyone is free to express their views and in which the most reasonable views gain acceptance.

The purpose of this three-part analytic typology is quite circumscribed: to focus attention on the extent that talk partners use language to think together when pursuing joint problem-solving and other learning activities. It is not designed to deal with many other important ways that the forms of talk reflect a variety of purposes used, such as the maintenance of social identities, expression of power and solidarity, emotional ties among speakers and so on (as studied extensively by socio-linguists, social psychologists and other researchers). The three types of talk were not devised to be used as the basis for a coding scheme (of the kind used in systematic observation research). Rather, the typology offers a way of exploring the functional variation of talk as a means for pursuing collaborative activity. In an initial consideration of the data, it helps an analyst perceive the extent to which participants in a joint activity are at any stage behaving collaboratively or competitively and whether they are engaging in critical reflection or in the mutual acceptance of ideas. It has also proved useful for helping teachers and others involved in educational practice gain insights into the functional variety of children's talk. Other educational researchers have independently come up with very similar characterizations of intellectually stimulating, collaborative and productive classroom talk – though usually with secondary school students. In the US, Anderson and colleagues (Anderson, Chinn, Waggoner and Nguyen 1998; Chinn and Anderson 1998) have identified the kind of talk they call 'Collaborative Reasoning' (CR). On the basis of data they obtained through their own interventional studies they say that, during CR discussions, the quality of children's reasoning is high and they display higher levels of thinking than in usual classroom discussions. 'In the course of CR discussions, children actively collaborate on the construction of arguments in complex networks of reasons and supporting evidence' (Kim, Anderson, Nguyen-Jahiel and Archodidou 2007). It should be noted, however, that the source of such talk in their studies was *teacher-led* discussion with groups of children. There are also strong links between the concept of Exploratory Talk (as we have defined it) and what some educational researchers have called 'accountable talk' (Resnick 1999; Michaels and O'Connor 2002).

Drawing on their own extended work, as well as that of several other cognitive scientists, philosophers and discourse analysts, Keefer, Zeitz and Resnick (2000) also tried to identify the characteristics of the most productive classroom discussion when the subject matter is literature. They define a set of four types of informal dialogue, which we summarize as follows:

1   *Critical discussion*, which has the main goal of achieving shared understanding through accommodating divergent viewpoints and reconciling differences of opinion.
2   *Explanatory enquiry*, which starts from a position of lack of knowledge with the main goal of overcoming and identifying correct knowledge, using cumulative discursive steps.
3   *Eristic discussion*, in which initial conflict and antagonism among participants is acted out through rhetorical attacks and defences of participants' own positions, and which may achieve some 'provisional accommodation'.
4   *Consensus dialogue*, which is discussion among speakers whose opinions are in agreement.

There are some obvious connections between eristic discussion and Disputational Talk; consensus dialogue and Cumulative Talk. It would seem that Exploratory Talk subsumes characteristics of both critical discussion and explanatory enquiry, though given the emphasis we have placed on group members achieving some kind of agreed conclusion to their joint enquiry, it is perhaps closer to the latter. Keefer *et al.* also make reference to 'discursive norms', essentially invoking what we have called 'ground rules'. In relation to the particular curriculum focus of their research, they argue that 'critical discussion is the most appropriate dialogue type for a discussion focused on literary content' (2000: 58) and so they go on to use that dialogue type as a model for an evaluation of the discussions of groups of children, aged around 9 years old, in a school in the US as they were talking about literature. Their evaluative analysis was based on the view that

> ... a productive discussion ... should include some progress in the participants' understanding of the original question or issue being debated (e.g., participants ought to show greater interest in the development of ideas and issues than they do in the presentation and defense of their own positions). Furthermore, we believe that participants in discussions having these qualities might be more prepared to change their views – in other words, to seriously listen to (and even construct) arguments that run counter to views that they might initially hold.
>
> (2000: 60)

We can see more clearly here some strong similarities between this notion of a 'critical discussion' and Exploratory Talk. Keefer *et al.*'s analysis also examined the extent to which the relevant literary content was directly invoked and discussed by the groups. They concluded that the most productive groups were those in which the talk included a high proportion of literary content and in which the talk most resembled 'critical discussion'. They conclude by commenting on 'the challenge of helping teachers to lead discussions that are appropriate to the content and goals of the dialogue, scaffolding children to reason within the constraints of the dialogue rules and to initiate shifts in context when the content or the course of argumentation might warrant it' (2000: 79).

From our consideration of the research above, we can conclude that evidence supports the view that working and talking together can provide a powerful support for children's learning. However, the evidence also shows that much of the talk in collaborative activity in classrooms is 'disputational' or 'cumulative' rather than 'exploratory'. One reason may be that many children do not have much experience or skill in generating talk of an 'exploratory' kind. It has been found that the amount and quality of talk between parents and young children at home varies considerably (for example, Wells 1986: Hart and Risley 1995): in some homes, rational debates, logical deductions, extended narrative accounts and detailed explanations may seldom be heard. Without guidance, instruction and encouragement from a teacher, many children may not gain access to some very useful ways of using language for reasoning and working collaboratively, because those 'ways with words' are simply not a common feature of the language of their out-of-school communities.

It also seems that teachers may not be aware of children's lack of understanding and skill in using talk for learning; or at least, they assume that children will know exactly what to do when a teacher asks them to 'discuss' a topic, or 'talk and work together' to carry out a talk or solve a problem. Children are left to somehow work out what is required and what constitutes a good, effective discussion, but they rarely succeed in doing so. Throughout the primary years, children are able to use language effectively as a tool for thinking together, but many may not know how to, or at the least do not recognize that is what is expected of them.

As demonstrated some years ago now (Edwards and Mercer 1987), the norms or ground rules for generating particular functional ways of using language in primary school – spoken or written – are rarely made explicit. It is often simply assumed that children will pick these sorts of things up as they go along. But while picking up the ground rules and 'fitting' in a superficial way with the norms of classroom life may be relatively easy, this may conceal children's lack of understanding about what they are expected to do in educational activities and why they should do so. The distinction between structures for classroom management (for example, lining up in pairs or sitting rather than kneeling on chairs) and structures that support learning (for example, listening to a partner or asking a question) may not be apparent to children. Even when the aim of talk is made explicit 'Talk together to decide'; 'Discuss this in your groups' – there may be no real understanding of how to talk together or for what purpose. Many children may not appreciate the significance and educational importance of their talk with one another. They frequently assume that the implicit ground rules in play in the classroom are such that teachers want 'right answers', rather than discussion.

Back in the 1980s, researchers such as Wells (1986) commented that the normative environment for talk in most primary classrooms was not compatible with children's active and extended engagement in using language to construct knowledge. This characterization of the classroom environment for talk is also one that emerges from more recent work by Alexander (2005: 10), which has indicated that classroom discourse is 'overwhelmingly monologic' in form because, as the orchestrators of classroom discourse, teachers typically only offer children opportunities for making brief responses to their questions:

> ... if we are not careful, classrooms may be places where teachers rather than children do most of the talking; where supposedly open questions are really closed; where instead of thinking through a problem children devote their energies to trying to spot the correct answer, where supposed equality of discussion is subverted by ... the 'unequal communicative rights' of a kind of talk which remains stubbornly unlike the kind of talk that takes place anywhere else. Clearly if classroom talk is to make a meaningful contribution to children's learning and understanding it must move beyond the acting out of such cognitively restricting rituals.

Interventional studies on talk and collaborative activity in primary schools

In recent years we have, together with colleagues, undertaken a series of classroom-based research projects explicitly designed to improve the quality of children's collaborative activity. More specifically, we have worked closely with teachers to try to increase the use of Exploratory Talk by children in their classroom activities, and then to evaluate the effects on the quality of children's talk, problem solving, reasoning and learning. Children aged between 6 and 13 years have been involved, but we will here concentrate on the research with the age group 8–11, which has been the most substantial. This was pursued by designing a programme of planned intervention focused on the use of talk that integrated teacher-led whole-class dialogue and group activity. Its main aim was to ensure children would enter collaborative activities with a shared conception of how they could talk and think together effectively.

The programme consisted of a set of 12 *Thinking Together* lessons created by researchers working with teachers (as included in Dawes, Mercer and Wegerif 2003; Dawes and Sams 2004; Dawes 2008). The programme was then, in collaboration with teachers, implemented with children aged 8–11 years in primary schools, and evaluated using a quasi-experimental method in which children in the experimental or 'target' schools (those who followed the programme) were matched with children of the same age in other local 'control' schools with similar catchments (who pursued their normal curriculum activities). This method permitted a systematic evaluation of the programme while ensuring the normal contextual factors of school life were still in play.

At the start of the intervention, each participating teacher received a basic training in the approach and was introduced to the *Thinking Together* lessons. The first five core lessons provided teachers with activities for collectively negotiating and establishing with their classes a set of 'ground rules' that embody the essential qualities of Exploratory Talk (serving to open up and maintain an 'intersubjective space' in which alternative solutions to problems are generated and allowed to develop and compete as ideas without threatening either group solidarity or individual identity). That is, these lessons were mainly aimed to develop children's understanding and use of Exploratory Talk. The complete programme included lessons that related to specific curriculum subjects and consists of both teacher-led sessions and group activities (some of which use specially designed computer-based tasks based on curriculum topics). In order to evaluate changes in the quality of children's talk, we video-recorded groups of children carrying out activities. This was done in both the target classes and in the control classes.

As mentioned above, the research was designed to test the effects that the intervention had on children's ways of talking, on their curriculum learning and on their individual reasoning skills. To assess effects on reasoning, the Raven's Progressive Matrices test was used. This is a test that has been commonly used as a general measure of non-verbal reasoning (Raven, Court and Raven 1995). Both target and control sets of children were given this test before the target classes began the experimental programme, and then again after the series of lessons had been completed. Using two sets of the Raven's test items, we were able to assess the children's thinking both collectively (as they did the test in groups) and individually (when they did the other version of the test alone). This research (described in Wegerif, Mercer and Dawes 1999; Mercer, Dawes, Wegerif and Sams 2004; Wegerif and Dawes 2004; Mercer and Littleton 2007) has produced three main findings. First, a qualitative and quantitative analysis of the children's talk showed that children in target classes came to use significantly more Exploratory Talk than those in control classes. Second, by examining the recorded talk of the groups in conjunction with their scores on the Raven's test, we found that groups who used more Exploratory Talk tended to solve the Raven's problems more successfully. Thus, when we compared groups in target classes who had failed on specific problems in the pre-lessons test with their successes in the post-lessons test, we could see how the 'visible reasoning' of exploratory talk in the transcripts had enabled them to do so. We will discuss the third finding shortly. But first, to illustrate our first two findings, there are two excerpts from the talk of children (aged 10 and 11) in the same target group. They are doing one of the Raven's problems, which requires them to choose which of a numbered set of shapes will logically complete a series of such shapes (hence the children's remarks 'It's 2' and so on). Excerpt 4 was recorded before they did the series of lessons, while Excerpt 5 was recorded after they had done so.

Excerpt 4: Graham, Suzie and Tess doing Raven's test item D9 (before the Thinking Together *lessons)*

TESS: It's that
GRAHAM: It's that, 2
TESS: 2 is there
GRAHAM: It's 2
TESS: 2 is there Graham
GRAHAM: It's 2
TESS: 2 is there
GRAHAM: What number do you want then?
TESS: It's that because there ain't two of them

GRAHAM: It's number 2, look one, two
TESS: I can count, are we all in agree on it? (*Suzie rings number 2 – an incorrect choice – on the answer sheet*)
SUZIE: No
GRAHAM: Oh, after she's circled it!

Excerpt 5: Graham, Suzie and Tess doing Raven's test item D9 (after the Thinking Together *lessons*)

SUZIE: D9 now, that's a bit complicated it's got to be
GRAHAM: A line like that, a line like that and it ain't got a line with that
TESS: It's got to be that one
GRAHAM: It's going to be that don't you think? Because look all the rest have got a line like that and like that, I think it's going to be that because …
TESS: I think it's number 6
SUZIE: No I think it's number 1
GRAHAM: Wait no, we've got number 6, wait stop, do you agree that it's number 1? Because look that one there is blank, that one there has got them, that one there has to be number 1, because that is the one like that. Yes. Do you agree? (*Tess nods in agreement*)
SUZIE: D9 number 1 (*Suzie writes '1', which is the correct answer*)

In Excerpt 4, the talk is not 'exploratory' but more aptly described as 'disputational'. Cycles of assertion and counter assertion, forming sequences of short utterances that rarely include explicit reasoning, are typical of disputational talk. We can see that Tess does offer a reason – a good reason – for her view, but Graham ignores it and she seems to give up in the face of his stubbornness. Suzie has taken the role of writer and she says little. At the end, having ringed the answer Graham wanted, she disagrees with it. It is not the right answer; but they all move on to the next problem anyway.

Excerpt 5 illustrates some of the ways that the talk of the same children changed after doing the programme of *Thinking Together* lessons and how this helped them to solve the problem. The children's language clearly shows characteristics of Exploratory Talk. Graham responds to opposition from Tess by giving an elaborated explanation of why he thinks 'number 1' is the correct choice. This clear articulation of reasons leads the group to agree on the right answer. Such explanations involve a series of linked clauses and so lead to longer utterances. All three children are now more equally involved in the discussion. They make more effective rhetorical use of language for expressing their opinions and persuading others of their value. Compared with their earlier attempt, language is being used more effectively by the group as a tool for thinking together about the task they are engaged in.

The third main finding was that the before-and-after comparisons of children's *collective* performance on the Raven's test confirmed that the *Thinking Together* lessons were changing the quality of children's joint reasoning. But the results also showed that the target children improved their *individual* Raven's scores much more than the control children. It seemed, therefore, that the target children learned more effective strategies for using language to think collectively (and so become better at collaborative working) and that, as a result of taking part in the group experience of explicit, rational, collaborative problem solving, their *individual* reasoning capabilities had also improved. (It should be noted that the target children had no more or less experience or training in doing the Raven's test, together or alone, than the control children.). However, it is not clear what the target children learned from their experience that made the difference. It may be that some gained from having new, successful problem-solving strategies explained to them by their partners, while others may have benefited from having to justify and make explicit their own reasons. But a more radical and intriguing possibility is that children may have improved their reasoning skills by internalizing or appropriating the ground rules of Exploratory Talk, so that they become able to carry on a kind of silent rational dialogue with themselves. That is, the *Thinking Together* lessons may have helped them become more able to generate the kind of rational thinking that depends on the explicit, dispassionate consideration of evidence and competing options. That interpretation is consistent with the claims of Vygotsky (1978, as discussed earlier) about the link between social activity and the development of children's thinking. Such compelling evidence in respect of improved reasoning skills and educational attainment also negates the claims made by some researchers (e.g. Lambirth 2006) that the 'ground rules' associated with Exploratory Talk have no intrinsic value as a basis for collaborative activity.

Summary

Evidence has shown that, under certain conditions, interaction with peers helps children's learning and development. They can develop important communicative skills through interaction, which again they would not learn through only taking part in conversations with adults. But, paradoxically, observational studies have shown that collaboration in classrooms is often unproductive and inequitable. Some studies have suggested that the quality of collaboration can be improved if attention is given to developing an atmosphere of trust and mutual respect (see also Kutnick and Colwell, this volume). Others have shown that the quality of interaction is significantly improved if children are a) helped to become more aware of how they use language as a tool for thinking together and b) taught some specific strategies for carrying on 'exploratory', productive discussions. That is, it seems that although collaborative interactions and discussions are potentially very valuable for children's learning and development, that potential may only be realized if children are given structured guidance by their teachers on how to make the most of the opportunities that classroom activities offer.

References

Alexander, R. (2005) *Towards Dialogic Teaching:rethinking classroom talk*, Cambridge: Dialogos.

Anderson, R. C., Chinn, C., Waggoner, M. and Nguyen, K. (1998) 'Intellectually-stimulating story discussions', in J. Osborn and F. Lehr (eds) *Literacy for All: issues in teaching and learning*, New York: Guildford Press.

Azmitia, M. and Montgomery, R. (1993) 'Friendship, transactive dialogues and the development of scientific reasoning', *Social Development*, 2:202–21.

Barbieri, M. and Light, P. (1992) 'Interaction, gender and performance on a computer-based task', *Learning and Instruction*, 2:199–213.

Barnes, D. (2008) 'Exploratory Talk for learning', in N. Mercer and S. Hodgkinson, (eds) *Exploring Talk in School*, London: Sage.

Barnes, D. and Todd, F. (1977) *Communication and Learning in Small Groups*, London: Routledge and Kegan Paul.

Barnes, D. and Todd, F. (1995) *Communication and Learning Revisited*, Portsmouth, NH: Heinemann.

Barron, B. (2000) 'Achieving co-ordination in collaborative problem-solving groups', *Journal of the Learning Sciences*, 9:403–36.

Bennett, N. and Dunne, E. (1992) *Managing Classroom Groups*, London: Simon and Schuster.

Blatchford, P. and Kutnick, P. (2003) 'Developing groupwork in everyday classrooms', Special issue of the *International Journal of Educational Research*, 39.

Chinn, C. F. and Anderson, R. (1998) 'The structure of discussions that promote reasoning', *Teachers College Record*, 100:315–68.

Cohen, E. G. (1994) 'Restructuring the classroom: conditions for productive small groups', *Review of Educational Research*, 64:1–35.

Daniels, H. (2001) *Vygotsky and Pedagogy*, London: RoutledgeFalmer.

Dawes, L. (2008) *The Essential Speaking and Listening: talk for learning at Key Stage 2*, London: Routledge.

Dawes, L. and Sams, C. (2004) *Talk Box: speaking and listening activities for learning at Key Stage 1*, London: David Fulton.

Dawes, L., Mercer, N. and Wegerif, R. (2003) *Thinking Together: a programme of activities for developing thinking skills at KS2*, Birmingham: Questions.

Dillenbourg, P. (1999) *Collaborative Learning: cognitive and computational approaches*, Oxford: Pergamon.

Dillenbourg, P., Baker, M., Blaye, A. and O'Malley, C. (1995) 'The evolution of research on collaborative learning', in H. Spada and P. Reiman (eds) *Learning in Humans and Machines: towards an interdisciplinary learning science*, Oxford: Elsevier.

Edwards, D, and Mercer, N. (1987) *Common Knowledge: the development of understanding in the classroom*, London: Methuen/Routledge.

Fisher, E. (1993) 'Distinctive features of pupil-pupil talk and their relationship to learning', *Language and Education*, 7:239–58.

Fisher, R. and Larkin, S. (2008) 'Pedagogy or ideological struggle? An examination of pupils' and teachers' expectations for talk in the classroom', *Language and Education*, 22:1–16.

Fuchs, L. S. and Fuchs, D. (2000) 'Effects of workgroup structure and size on student productivity during collaborative work on complex tasks', *Elementary School Journal*, 100:183–212.

Galton, M. and Williamson, J. (1992) *Group Work in the Primary Classroom*, London: Routledge.

Galton, M., Hargreaves, L., Comber, C., Wall, D. and Pell, A. (1999) *Inside the Primary Classroom: 20 years on*, London: Routledge.

Galton, M., Simon, B. and Croll, P. (1980) *Inside the Primary Classroom (the ORACLE Project)*, London: Routledge and Kegan Paul.

Hart, B. and Risley, T. R. (1995) *Meaningful Differences in the Everyday Experience of Young American Children*, New York: Brookes.

Hertz-Lazarowitz, R. (1992) 'Understanding interactive behaviours: looking at six mirrors of the classroom', in R. Hertz-Lazarowitz and N. Miller (eds) *Interaction in Cooperative*

Groups: the theoretical anatomy of group learning, Cambridge: Cambridge University Press.

Howe, C. (1997) *Gender and Classroom Interaction: a research review*, Edinburgh: Scottish Council for Research in Education.

Howe, C., Tolmie, A., Thurston, A., Topping, K., Christie, D., Livingston, K., Jessiman, E. and Donaldson, C. (2007) 'Group work in elementary science: towards organisational principles for supporting pupil learning', *Learning and Instruction*, 17:549–63.

Howe, C. J. and Tolmie, A. (2003) 'Group work in primary school science: discussion, consensus and guidance from expert', *International Journal of Educational Research*, 39:51–72.

Howe, C. J., McWilliam, D. and Cross, G. (2005). 'Chance favours only the prepared mind: incubation and the delayed effects of peer collaboration', *British Journal of Psychology*, 96:67–93.

Howe, C. J., Tolmie, A. and Rodgers, C. (1992) 'The acquisition of conceptual knowledge by primary school children: group interaction and the understanding of motion down an inclined plane', *British Journal of Developmental Psychology*, 10:113–30.

Keefer, M., Zeitz, C. and Resnick, L. (2000) 'Judging the quality of peer-led student dialogues', *Cognition and Instruction*, 18:53–81.

Kim, I.-H., Anderson, R., Nguyen-Jahiel, K. and Archodidou, A. (2007) 'Discourse patterns during children's online discussions', *Journal of the Learning Sciences*, 16:333–70.

Lambirth, A. (2006) 'Challenging the laws of talk: ground rules, social reproduction and the curriculum', *The Curriculum Journal*, 17:59–71.

Light, P. and Littleton, K. (1999) *Social Processes in Children's Learning*, Cambridge: Cambridge University Press.

Littleton, K. (1999) 'Productivity through interaction: an overview', in K. Littleton and P. Light (eds) *Learning with Computers: analyzing productive interaction*, London: Routledge.

Mercer, N. (1995) *The Guided Construction of Knowledge: talk among teachers and learners*, Clevedon: Multilingual Matters.

Mercer, N. (2000) *Words and Minds: how we use language to think together*, London: Routledge.

Mercer, N. (2008) 'Talk and the development of reasoning and understanding', *Human Development*, 51:90–100.

Mercer, N. and Littleton, K. (2007) *Dialogue and the Development of Children's Thinking: a sociocultural approach*, London: Routledge.

Mercer, N., Dawes, R., Wegerif, R., and Sams, C. (2004) 'Reasoning as a scientist: ways of helping children to use language to learn science', *British Educational Research Journal*, 30:367–85.

Michaels, S. and O'Connor, M. C. (2002) *Accountable Talk: classroom conversation that works* [CD-ROM]: University of Pittsburgh.

Nystrand, M. (1986) *The Structure of Written Communication: studies of reciprocity between writers and readers*, London: Academic Press.

Raven, J., Court, J. and Raven, J. C. (1995) *Manual for Raven's Progressive Matrices and Vocabulary Scales*, Oxford: Oxford Psychologists Press.

Resnick, L. B. (1999) 'Making America smarter', *Education Week Century Series*, 18:38–40.

Rogoff, B. (1990) *Apprenticeship in Thinking: cognitive development in social context*, Oxford: Oxford University Press.

Ryder, J. and Campbell, L. (1989) 'Groupsense: when groupwork does not add up to "groupwork"', *Pastoral Care in Education*, 7:22–30.

Slavin, R. E. (1980) 'Co-operative learning', *Review of Educational Research*, 50:315–42.

Underwood, J. and Underwood, G. (1999) 'Task effects in co-operative and collaborative learning with computers', in K. Littleton and P. Light (eds) *Learning with Computers: analysing productive interaction*, London: Routledge.

Vygotsky, L. S. (1962) *Thought and Language*, Cambridge, MA: MIT Press.

Vygotsky, L. S. (1978) *Mind in Society*, Cambridge, MA: Harvard University Press.

Webb, N. M. (1989) 'Peer interaction and learning in small groups', *International Journal of Educational Research*, 13:21–39.

Wegerif, R. and Dawes, L. (2004) *Thinking and Learning with ICT: raising achievement in primary classrooms*, London: Routledge.

Wegerif, R. and Scrimshaw, P. (eds) (1997) *Computers and Talk in the Primary Classroom*, Clevedon: Multilingual Matters.

Wegerif, R., Mercer, N. and Dawes, L. (1999) 'From social interaction to individual reasoning: an empirical investigation of a possible socio-cultural model of cognitive development', *Learning and Instruction*, 9:493–516.

Wells, G. (1986) *The Meaning Makers*, London: Hodder and Stoughton.

Wells, G. (1999) *Dialogic Inquiry: towards a socio-cultural practice and theory of education*, Cambridge: Cambridge University Press.

Wells, G. and Claxton, G. (2002) (eds) *Learning for Life in the 21st Century*, Oxford: Blackwell.

Wertsch, J. V. (1991) 'A sociocultural approach to socially shared cognition', in L. B. Resnick, J. M. Levine and S. D. Teasley (eds) *Perspectives on Socially Shared Cognition*, Washington: American Psychological Association.

Wilkinson, I. and Fung, I. (2002) 'Small group composition and peer effects', *International Journal of Educational Research*, 37: 425–47.

Chapter 14

Teaching and learning disciplinary knowledge

Developing the dialogic space for an answer when there isn't even a question

Phil Scott, Jaume Ametller, University of Leeds, Eduardo Mortimer, Universidade Federal de Minas Gerais and Jonathan Emberton, Calder High School, Mytholmroyd

Introduction

One of the key characteristics of scientific knowledge is its provisional nature. In other words, no matter the extent to which the community of scientists takes a certain idea to be a 'fact', based on tens of years of agreement with empirical measurement and countless successful predictions, there is always the possibility that what is taken to be the case might ultimately fall from grace. Having said this, much of science, and certainly much of what is currently taught in school constitutes a robust body of knowledge, with some of it dating back to the eighteenth century and earlier. For example, Newtonian mechanics was first published in the *Principia* in 1687 and the calculations that took Neil Armstrong and his crew to the surface of the Moon and back in 1969, some 300 years later, were based solidly on Newton's work. In this sense large tracts of scientific knowledge are both stable and reliable.

This 'authoritative' nature of scientific knowledge raises an interesting challenge for all of those involved in *teaching* science and this becomes increasingly apparent when meaningful learning is taken to involve a *dialogic* process. Here the word 'dialogic' is used to signal the bringing together of different ideas in a process of personal sense-making. For example, a student might try to make sense of what the teacher is saying about Newton's first law of motion ('no resultant force is required for steady motion') in terms of their existing everyday understandings ('a steady push is needed to keep something going with a steady speed'). In this example the dialogic meaning-making process is consequent upon major challenges and if the student gets to the point of saying or thinking, 'This just doesn't make sense!' they'd be making some progress towards developing a meaningful understanding of Newton's first law. Volosinov describes this dialogic meaning-making process as follows:

> For each word of the utterance that we are in the process of understanding, we ... lay down a set of our own answering words. The greater their number and weight,

the deeper and more substantial our understanding will be ... understanding strives to match the speaker's word with a counter word.

(Voloshinov 1986: 102)

Voloshinov goes on to say that 'Meaning is like an electric spark that occurs only when two different terminals are hooked together' (Voloshinov: 102–3). Taking this electrical analogy one step further, problems can arise in teaching and learning situations when the teacher short-circuits the dialogic meaning-making process by addressing the authoritative epistemology of science through an authoritative pedagogical approach. Thus the science teacher might argue that 'students need to be *told* the facts' and in doing so offers few opportunities for students to bring together different points of view, working with words and counter words.

In this chapter we present a case study of a teacher teaching his class about one aspect of the topic 'forces'. The aim of the study is to describe and analyse the ways in which the teacher interacts with his students to support them in developing a meaningful understanding of this area of disciplinary knowledge. The study is part of an ongoing research programme into teacher–student interactions in the context of teaching and learning scientific conceptual knowledge (see, for example, Mortimer and Scott 2003; Scott, Mortimer and Aguiar 2006; Scott and Ametller 2007; Scott, Ametller, Dawes, Kleine Staarman and Mercer 2007).

In analysing the teaching, we draw upon various aspects of theory. Firstly we refer to the analytical framework presented by Mortimer and Scott (2003) and in particular to the concept of 'communicative approach' (Mortimer and Scott 2003: 33). The communicative approach provides a perspective on *how* the teacher works with students to develop ideas in the classroom. It focuses on questions such as whether or not the teacher interacts with students (teacher and students taking turns in the classroom talk), and also on whether the teacher is open to the students' ideas as the lessons proceed. The communicative approach is defined by characterizing the talk between teacher and students along each of two dimensions *interactive-non interactive* and *dialogic-authoritative*. An interactive approach sees both teacher and students taking turns in the classroom talk, while a non-interactive approach typically involves the teacher in presenting ideas. The teacher takes a dialogic approach if they are open to students' ideas, while an authoritative approach sees the teacher focusing solely on the scientific point of view. The two dimensions give rise to four classes of communicative approach: *interactive/authoritative*; *non-interactive/authoritative*; *interactive/dialogic*; *non-interactive/dialogic*.

In addition we draw upon Wegerif's concept of 'dialogic space', which he introduces in his book, *Dialogic Education and Technology: expanding the space of learning* (Wegerif 2007). Here Wegerif takes a Bakhtinian perspective in stating that 'dialogic space opens up when two or more perspectives are held together in tension' (4). He further argues that 'meaning arises out of, and depends upon, an original "creative difference" or "opening" that could be thought of as the opening of a dialogue' (26). In other words, Wegerif (as with Voloshinov) sees recognizing and dealing with differences in perspectives, or gaps between views held together in the tension of a dialogue (281), as being fundamental to the act of meaning-making. Wegerif goes one step further in arguing that 'the dialogic relation of holding two or more perspectives together in tension at the same time always opens up an unbounded space of potential perspectives'. Creating a dialogic space is therefore central to a pedagogy 'for thinking, creativity and learning to learn' and it is important 'to treat dialogue not only as a means to the end of knowledge construction, but also as an end in itself' (8).

While agreeing with Wegerif about the possible dual outcomes of a dialogically based pedagogy, we should emphasize that in this study our principal interest lies, not in the development of general thinking skills, but in the meaningful learning of disciplinary knowledge. In this sense, we are exploring the other side of the pedagogical coin to Wegerif.

In the following sections, we first of all present a description of one part of a teaching-and-learning sequence on forces, outlining the key interactions between teacher and students. This is followed by an analysis of the sequence, which is framed in terms of the changes in the communicative approaches taken and the ways in which the teacher interacts with the students to support the development of a dialogic space. The analysis leads to a discussion of the possible value of such a perspective for thinking more generally about teaching and learning scientific conceptual knowledge.

The case: two kinds of arrows

The setting for this case is a large state comprehensive school in the North of England. The lessons involved Jonathan the science teacher working with a mixed-ability Year 7 class (aged 11–12 years) of 24 students. Jonathan is a highly experienced (over 20 years) teacher whose expert abilities are recognized through his 'advanced skills teacher' status. He is unusual among his peers in being able to sustain the kind of dialogic discourse that is of central interest to this study.

The science topic under consideration in the lessons was that of 'forces', with a total of five 1-hour periods being spent on an introduction to a range of forces: pushes, pulls, friction, the normal force, gravity. The actual teaching sequence was developed co-operatively between the teacher and two of the researchers with attention being given to the purposeful use of different communicative approaches (see Scott, Leach, Hind and Lewis 2006). In the sequence presented here the focus is on how forces can be represented with force arrows (or vectors). This arrow representation is a notation agreed upon by scientists as part of the language of physics, and given its 'convention-based' nature this topic would seem to offer little opportunity for dialogic exploration. In fact, at first glance the force-arrow notation appears to be an excellent candidate for the teacher just 'telling the facts'.

Episode 1: Who's that, Paula?

We join the class as they are sat in their places in the science teaching laboratory. The teacher shows a big projected photograph of one of the girls on the whiteboard and asks: 'Who's that, Paula?'

In the previous lesson Jonathan had organized an activity in which the students were challenged to 'have a go at bashing gravity!' This involved student volunteers hanging by their hands from the beam at the front of the room for as long as possible in a bid to overcome the pull of gravity. The competition produced a scene of great excitement, with students desperate to have a go at 'bashing gravity'. As the students struggled to hang on, Jonathan kept up a running commentary: 'Can you feel the pull of gravity?'; 'Strong stuff this gravity!'; 'Can you feel the Earth pulling down on you?' In this way the ontologically challenging idea of the Earth pulling from a distance was brought to life through activity and talk in the laboratory: this was a memorable event for the students.

The photograph on the whiteboard shows Paula, the 'champion gravity basher' hanging from the beam. Jonathan now builds on this activity:

1. TEACHER: We'll try to put some *arrows* onto there to show what was going on with Paula in terms of forces. Now I'm *not* going to do it myself, I'm going to ask you to have a little chat with each other cos I know that some of you at junior school … have already started to think a bit about arrows and I know that some of you have got an idea about which way the forces are going, cos we did a lot of pointing on Wednesday. And I want you just to have a quick chat … about if you could put some arrows on there to show the forces on Paula as she's hanging from here [raises his arms up to the beam] where would you put them? And then we'll get a few people out to come and draw them in and we're gonna get them to tell us *why* they put them there. OK! Two minutes.

The students immediately start talking in their groups and after about 5 minutes Jonathan stops the class and invites them to sit around his table at the front of the room. The teacher starts by stating a 'rule' for the class:

2. TEACHER: The only rule here everybody, as well as listening obviously, is to compare. That's a real rule here. Compare what they're doing and the words they're using [with your own ideas].

Two of the students, Levi and Jed, volunteer to show what 'was going on with Paula in terms of forces' and use a red pen to draw arrows on, and to annotate, the photograph of Paula on the whiteboard. As they do this Jonathan stands well clear and he and the rest of the class watch intently. As soon as the students start drawing in their arrows, other students spontaneously put up their hands to offer comment.

Levi draws in an arrow and adds the word 'tension'. Jed draws a line and adds the word 'gravity'. The teacher asks Jed, 'Are you gonna put an arrow head on there, or …?'. Jed adds an arrow head pointing upwards and the photograph appears as follows (Figure 14.1).

Comment

This episode sets the scene for what is to follow, with the teacher stepping back and the students taking the lead in drawing out their ideas on the whiteboard. Furthermore Jonathan's direction to the students, that 'the only rule … is to compare' points clearly to the dialogic approach he is trying to establish.

The first two inscriptions, from Levi and Jed, show significant differences from the conventional scientific point of view, which is hardly surprising. The scientific view involves two forces acting on Paula: the pull (or tension) in her arms acting upwards on her body; the pull of gravity acting downwards on her body. These two forces can be represented by two arrows (or force vectors), one acting up through Paula's arms and one acting down on Paula's body. The students, though, use the arrows to point to a *location* (in this case the location of the tension and gravity), which is one of the conventional uses of arrows. A second use of arrows is to signify *action* of some sort, they are the verbs of the visual grammar (Kress and van Leeuwen 1998). This action-focused convention links to the scientific use of arrows to signify forces. By initially not placing an arrowhead Jed opts to use a line and not an arrow, hence neither indicating the exact location of the gravity force nor its action upon the suspended student.

Episode 2: Any comments?

Jonathan thanks Levi and Jed, praising their efforts: 'They're using good words aren't they? Tension … gravity.' He then asks the class for comments. One of the girls, Alex, leads off:

1. TEACHER: Any comments? Alex.
2. ALEX: They felt tension down their sides as well
3. TEACHER: So it's interesting Alex is talking about *where* she knows that Paula and Zoe [another 'Gravity Basher'] *felt* the tension and they *felt* it in their arms and you're saying they also felt it down their sides. Let's hear some other ideas.

Figure 14.1 Levi and Jed's annotations.

Another one of the girls has her hand up:

4. TEACHER: Holly what have you got to say?
5. HOLLY: Gravity pulls down so the arrow pulls down
6. TEACHER: so you've looked at the *direction* that the gravity is going. Now you would make a change there and move it. What, the other way? [teacher pointing downwards on the photograph]
7. HOLLY: yeah.
8. TEACHER: And why do you say that?
9. HOLLY: cos gravity is pulling her down
10. TEACHER: to where? Where's it pulling her?
11. HOLLY: to the Earth
12. TEACHER: Ok. So you'd make a change there

Comment

In responding to Alex's comment, Jonathan clarifies how the students are initially talking about the forces acting on Paula: 'Alex is talking about *where* she knows Paula and Zoe felt the tension.'

Holly's comment builds on what the students already know about gravity: that it acts downwards. Hence the student is proposing a change in direction that would match the scientific view of the action of gravity upon the student, but at this point no changes are made on the whiteboard. Jonathan now starts to erase the first arrows to let someone else have a go: 'thanks that's a brilliant effort guys [Levi and Jed], brilliant effort!'

Episode 3: Just kind of join in thinking even if you're not saying anything!

Another group of three students, led by Paula, now have a go. They add three arrows: gravity acting down on the body; tension in the arms; upthrust acting up. As the teacher and class watch the arrows being added, Jonathan says:

1. TEACHER: I wonder if you're looking at this and thinking, 'Yeah, we've got that! Or if you're thinking, 'Oh, I'm not sure about that', or thinking, 'Oh I wish I'd done it this way'. Just kind of join in thinking even if you're not saying anything.

As Paula's team finish, Jonathan comments: 'That's absolutely fantastic … we've got a record of that, we've got the camera … so don't worry about the fact that I'm rubbing stuff off.' Josie and her group now come to the front:

1. TEACHER: Come on then Josie, let's see what's she's got to say. Remember to face your audience Josie and tell them as you're doing it. Nathan! Have you got ants in your pants?

Josie starts drawing out her ideas on the board and provides an accompanying commentary:

1. JOSIE: Well, gravity is pulling down
2. TEACHER: Yeah. She's saying gravity is pulling it down.
3. JOSIE: Em, you've got tension like … she's got tension like all there [Josie draws in 3 arrows pointing to the arms]
4. TEACHER: in the arms … ok …
5. JOSIE: And she's sort of got, I'm not sure what the word for this is, but she's got like a force in her arms keeping her up [Josie holds her arms up in the air].

At this point, Josie hesitates and Jonathan comes in:

6. TEACHER: Well we used a word … it was hanging down from that beam over there on top of George's head and it was in the rope. What word was that?
7. JOSIE: Haaa!! Tension?
8. TEACHER: It was tension, wasn't it? So where will you put that then?
9. JOSIE: In her hand …

And Josie draws in a further arrow to indicate tension in Paula's hand (Figure 14.2). As Josie draws in her arrow, Jonathan questions her:

10. TEACHER: Go on then … is that the direction it goes? Is that what you're trying to show or …?
11. JOSIE: No it's showing *where* it is.
12. TEACHER: This is interesting … you've talked Josie about a tension in her arms keeping her up there. Is there anything else you want to add?

Comment

Josie starts with gravity: 'Well, gravity is pulling down.' The matter-of-fact way in which Josie refers to gravity suggests that she (and probably most of the class) now take this to be 'obvious': the gravity arrow points downwards clearly referring to the action of pulling on the suspended student.

Josie goes on to mark the tension in Paula's arm with three bold arrows, but then hesitates: 'but she's got like a force in her arms keeping her up'. The teacher makes a link to the previous lesson where the idea of the tension force was introduced in relation to a rope suspending a very big load: 'the tension in the rope keeps the load up'. Between Josie and the teacher, they decide that there must also be a tension force here keeping the load, which is Paula, up. Josie decides to position this tension in Paula's hand. At this point, Josie appears to be bringing together two ideas relating to the word tension: the feeling of tension (or aching) Paula experienced in her arm and the tension force in her hand that holds her up.

Finally Jonathan asks Josie about her arrow: '… is that the direction it goes? Is that what you're trying to show or . . ?' Josie's response is clear: 'No it's showing *where* it is.' At this point, Josie is displaying different ontological understandings of force. She represents gravity in terms of an action, a force pulling down, while she refers to tension as both something felt in the arm (an ache) and a force in the hand keeping Paula up. Here she uses an arrow, on the one hand, to represent the force of gravity and, on the other, to point to where the ache is felt and the tension (force) is located.

Episode 4: I've listened to three groups so far

At this point there is a clear shift in approach from Jonathan as he offers a review:

1. TEACHER: *Now*, I've listened to 3 groups so far and I think I'm making sense of what you're getting and what you're not getting … None of these diagrams explain to me why Paula wasn't falling off the beam … I know she did eventually and gravity beat her. But for 31 seconds she beat gravity. And at the moment there's nothing on this diagram that tells me that that force *down* [pointing to the gravity arrow] is being matched by something going somewhere else … Now the way everybody's drawn their arrows so far, they're using an arrow as a way of showing *where* the force is here [pointing to the three tension arrows] and here [pointing to the gravity arrow], they're doing it *right* they're showing *which way* the force goes and *how big* it is …

Figure 14.2 Josie's annotations.

Comment

Jonathan first of all draws attention to the fact that (from a scientific point of view) if the arrows are as placed in Figure 14.2, then Paula would fall off the beam. There is a gravity force acting down but no forces shown acting upwards. He then distinguishes between the two ways in which the arrows are being used and finishes by explicitly stating that the students are 'doing it right' with the gravity arrow.

As we have seen before, the interplay between verbal and visual language is being used in the ongoing dialogue to define both the concepts of gravity and tension as forces and the graphical convention (based on arrows) to represent them. To do the latter Jonathan does not directly introduce the scientific convention. Rather he takes advantage of the everyday meaning of visual representations in general and arrows in particular and, links these to the children's developing understanding of force to move towards the scientific vector notation.

Episode 5: We should be able to put a tension arrow in here

Jonathan now turns the class's attention to the tension arrow:

1. TEACHER: Now we should be able to put a tension arrow on here … in the right place. What do you think Holly?

At this point Holly has her hand up as she offers to add the tension arrow. Holly draws in the arrow as follows (Figure 14.3).

2. TEACHER: Now then, this is very interesting. Tell us what you've done.
3. HOLLY: Because she's pulling the tension in her arms is moving up her arms …
4. TEACHER: Yeah, you can feel it can't you. Still a bit of work to do on this. I reckon we've got the right direction. We haven't quite got the right place. And we haven't quite got that that matches that …

Comment

This part of the teaching sequence thus comes to a close with the force arrows being used in a way that is consistent with a scientific point of view. As Jonathan intimates, however, there is 'still a bit of work to do'.

Analysis: creating a dialogic space and moving to the scientific point of view

Having provided an overview of what happened in the case, we now turn our attention to analysing how the teacher worked with the students to develop a dialogic space where various views about the representation of forces were articulated and compared and how this led to the scientific convention of force vectors. The analysis is conceptualized in terms of four overlapping phases, which are mapped onto the episodes set out in the previous section.

Phase 1: Engaging the students: an invitation to participate [Episode 1]

At the start of this short teaching sequence, the teacher had the instructional aim of introducing the students to the scientific representation of forces, a goal the students, at that point, had neither any stake nor interest in. The first pedagogical challenge therefore involved engaging the students intellectually and emotionally in the context of the problem (Mortimer and Scott 2003).

The teacher addressed this challenge by first making a temporal link to the previous lesson, displaying the large photograph of Paula and asking: 'Who's that, Paula?' This was an arresting moment for the class: 'Hey! Look it's Paula!' The teacher thus built upon the memorable shared experience of the gravity-bashing competition and personalized the way into the problem for this group of students, grabbing their attention and prompting them to wonder about what was to happen next. The teacher then focused attention on the specific problem at hand and invited the students to participate:

1. TEACHER: We'll try to put some *arrows* onto there to show what was going on with Paula in terms of forces. Now I'm *not* going to do it myself …

The invitation is carefully worded: 'We'll try … to show what was going on … in terms of forces', so that the students might respond in whatever terms they saw fit. This is

Figure 14.3 Holly's annotations.

rather different to, for example, asking: 'Does anyone know how forces are represented in physics?' The teacher thus opened the way for students to draw upon their 'everyday' ideas of how arrows might be used, with the onus on them and their thinking: 'Now I'm *not* going to do it myself ...' Furthermore, the use of the words, 'We'll try' signalled that this might well involve thinking-in-progress rather than finished ideas.

Phase 2: Opening up and shaping the dialogic space [Episodes 2 and 3]

Throughout this phase the students took the lead in setting out their ideas on the whiteboard with the teacher symbolically handing over the red pen to each group as they came forward. In fact *all* of the inscriptions on the board were made by students. During this activity, the teacher interacted with the students in a distinctive way asking for ideas and prompting students to elaborate upon what they were saying. Mortimer and Scott (2003) refer to this as an *interactive/dialogic* communicative approach, where the teacher is open to a range of views (rather than just focusing on the accepted scientific account).

Alongside supporting the students in opening up the dialogic space ('Just kind of join in thinking even if you're not saying anything!') the teacher also made a number of interventions to begin to *shape* that space. Thus, in Episode 2 (3), the teacher commented: 'So it's interesting, Alex is talking about *where* she knows Paula and Zoe felt the tension.' In this way the teacher explicitly drew attention to how these students initially were talking about the forces: in terms of their location or *where* they were acting.

In addition to comments made by the teacher, there was also evidence, during this phase, of the bringing together or interanimation (Bakhtin 1981) of student ideas. Thus Alex commented on the first drawing by Levi and Jed, suggesting the need for 'tension down their sides as well' and Holly challenged the direction of Jed's upward pointing gravity arrow.

In response to Holly's comment about gravity, the teacher made another shaping move, emphasizing the directionality underlying Holly's suggestion: 'So you've looked at the *direction* that the gravity is going.' In this way he started to bring shape to the dialogic space by foreshadowing the two distinct emergent ways in which the arrows were being used: arrows to indicate *where* the force was acting; arrows to indicate the *direction* of the force. In the first case the arrows were being used in an everyday way as a location-labelling device (the force acts here). In the second, the arrow was being used in a way closer to that of a scientific force vector signifying an action (although it is clear that Holly did not have force vectors in mind when she made her comment).

When Josie added an arrow to show tension 'in her hand', the teacher focused once more on the *direction/location* issue, asking: 'Is that the direction it goes?' Josie's response was clear: 'No it shows *where* it is.' Once again the student's use of an arrow as a labelling device was clearly articulated and made explicit in the dialogic space.

Phase 3: Juxtaposition of ideas [Episode 4]

The student annotated photograph (Figure 14.2) beautifully captures the two different ways in which the arrows were being used by the students. The tension arrows label where forces are acting, while the gravity arrow shows the direction of the gravity force. These different ways reflect the difference between everyday and scientific social languages (Mortimer and Scott 2003: 13), not in relation to verbal concepts but here in terms of symbolic representations.

At the start of Episode 4, a *turning point* (Scott and Ametller 2007) was reached in the development of the dialogic space, such that the teacher enacted a transition from the dialogic collection of ideas to foregrounding and clarifying the authoritative scientific account. This turning point takes us back to the opening comments in this chapter about the authoritative nature of scientific knowledge. In teaching scientific disciplinary knowledge it is not sufficient simply to develop a dialogic space encompassing various accounts of phenomena: collecting students' points of view. It is the responsibility of the teacher to support this kind of dialogic engagement by students and then to identify and to make intelligible and plausible the scientific point of view.

In this case, the teacher negotiated the turning point to introduce the scientific point of view through two steps. He first of all set out a logical argument asking where the upward force was on Paula to match the downward pull of gravity. He then used a *non-interactive dialogic* communicative approach (Mortimer and Scott 2003) to highlight the two uses of arrows, emphasizing that with the gravity arrow the students were 'doing it right':

> 'Now the way everybody's drawn their arrows so far, they're using an arrow as a way of showing *where* the force is here and here, they're doing it *right* they're showing *which way* the force goes and *how big* it is …'

Returning to the title of this piece, the students were now faced with a *question* about a problem whose genesis they had participated in and for which they could provide an *answer*: 'Now we should be able to put a tension arrow on here … in the right place. What do you think Holly?'

Phase 4: Resolution [Episode 5]

Resolution of the question was achieved as Holly drew in the upward tension arrow (Figure 14.3), such that the gravity force was balanced by the tension force and the arrow depicted the direction (and size) of the tension force. This representation provided an authoritative statement of the scientific point of view. As the teacher commented, there was a 'still a bit of work to do on this' and this was manifested in subsequent lessons through applying and talking through these new ideas about force arrows in similar and then less familiar contexts.

Discussion

In the analysis set out above, the opening up of a dialogic space and movement towards the scientific point of view is conceptualized in terms of four phases:

1 Engaging the students: an invitation to participate
2 Opening up and shaping the dialogic space

3   Juxtaposition of ideas
4   Resolution

The staging of the sequence sees a shift from dialogic communicative approaches in the first two phases to more authoritative approaches in the latter two.

From a pedagogical point of view, there are a number of questions that might be asked in reflecting on the teaching approach taken here. Why not just tell the students? Why not just explain how to represent forces scientifically with arrows? Why bother asking the students what they think, when they can't possibly get the 'right answer'? There are at least two kinds of responses to such questions.

First there is a problem in relation to the kind of learning likely to follow from 'just telling'. Thus the science teacher might start the lesson with the all too familiar opening gambit: 'Today we are going to do force vectors.' This fully-focused-on-the-outcome approach has minimal potential for making the links between ideas that underpin meaningful learning. In striking contrast, through the subtle process of developing the dialogic space, Jonathan was able to get the students in his class to a point where they recognized a real intellectual tension between ideas relating to the differing usages of the arrow symbol. Using the terms introduced earlier, this intellectual tension, or 'creative difference' (Wegerif 2007) provided a driving force for subsequent meaning-making. Through this dialogic process involving the interanimation of ideas, we would argue that an understanding of the scientific concept of force vectors runs deeper and becomes more meaningful as students come to understand not only what they *are* but also what they *are not*.

A separate but related argument concerns the engagement and motivation of the students. Our experience with the kind of teaching outlined in this case is that the act of asking students what they think can be effective in drawing them into a problem and therefore be personally motivating. In this case the subject matter for the lessons was that of representing forces. This is not a topic that has obvious 'relevance' for young people, but by engaging the students in the development of the dialogic space, Jonathan was able to invoke a form of intellectual relevance for the students that led to their sustained engagement.

Another feature of the pedagogy concerns the role of the technology employed: in this case the interactive whiteboard. Throughout the sequence, the students were seated around the front table facing, and in close proximity to, the whiteboard. As pairs of students drafted their ideas onto the board, and talked through their thinking, the symbols and words became the focus of attention for the whole class. In this way the whiteboard provided a shared visual display of developing ideas and a shared focus for dialogic interaction about those ideas. It was interesting to note how often students working at the board were spontaneously interrupted by comments from others in the class. The whiteboard provided the facility for making explicit ideas-in-the-making, which were available to comment from others in the class. This approach is in stark contrast to much science teaching where the pedagogical focus is on the apparatus and activities themselves, and what is to be *done* by the students, rather than on the talk that might be prompted by those activities.

Underpinning all of the interactions and activities described in this sequence are the skills of the teacher and his ability to work with children in this way. Such a performance may appear daunting to less experienced teachers who might aspire to this level of expertise. A fundamental point to remember, however, is that the teaching and learning scenario set out and analysed in this chapter is unlikely to be idiosyncratic. In other words, if another teacher with a different class was to try out this teaching approach, then it is highly likely it would develop along similar lines. The interpretation of arrows as location-labelling symbols is part of our everyday social language and will almost certainly appear during teaching if the opportunity is given. In this respect, it can be argued that teaching 'routines' such as the example outlined in this chapter are things that can be appraised and put to use by other teachers with their classes, with some foresight about what is likely to happen. Wegerif (2007) argues along similar lines when he suggests that 'Dialogic learning cannot be designed for directly but it can be designed for indirectly by opening the kind of spaces that support it'. Nevertheless, the skills involved both in getting to know the 'intellectual terrain' for a particular piece of teaching (encompassing both everyday and scientific views and the relationship between them) and being able to work with children through the various pedagogical phases outlined above are not to be underestimated.

In this chapter, a short science teaching sequence has been conceptualized in terms of opening and shaping a dialogic space, through different communicative approaches. This perspective has its attractions, particularly for those topic areas where there are significant differences between everyday and scientific views and there is the potential to develop the teaching and learning through exploring those differences. Of course, if the differences between everyday and scientific views are small (as is often the case), the science seems like 'common sense' and more straightforward both to learn and to teach. In such cases (maybe in learning about the bones of the body, for example) it would make less sense to spend time in trying to open up a dialogic space because the intellectual tensions between ideas simply would not be forthcoming. Teachers commonly (and rightly) worry about the time they have available to teach lengthy curricula. One way of addressing this problem is to become more systematic in apportioning time according to the learning demand (Leach and Scott 2002) of specific topics. It's where the learning demands are high that time is well spent in opening up and exploring dialogic spaces. Furthermore, it is reasonable to suggest that the dialogic space might be opened up through a whole range of teaching strategies involving the teacher to a greater or lesser extent. The example given in this case sees the teacher in a relatively central role; it is not difficult to imagine alternative approaches involving more independent activity by the students.

Wegerif (2007: 285) states that 'the evidence is clear that learning through dialogue can enhance the learning of curriculum content knowledge, especially when that "content" is not factual information but subject specific forms of higher order thinking, such as problem solving in mathematics, investigative and experimental methods in science and writing argumentative texts in English' . We are keen to argue through this case that 'dialogic methods' are also fundamentally important in teaching and learning scientific conceptual knowledge, and more generally disciplinary knowledge. Referring to such knowledge as 'factual information' that can be contrasted with 'higher order thinking' gives the impression that it is simply 'stuff to be absorbed' in a non-problematic manner. In the context of science teaching and learning this, more often than not, is far from the case and student learning would certainly benefit from dialogic engagement with ideas. Furthermore, we believe that such approaches, involving the dialogic treatment of disciplinary knowledge, can contribute to the other side of the pedagogical coin in supporting the development of more general thinking skills.

1.TEACHER: I wonder if you're looking at this and thinking, 'Yeah, we've got that! Or if you're thinking, 'Oh, I'm not sure about that', or thinking, 'Oh I wish I'd done it this way'. Just … join in thinking even if you're not saying anything. [Lesson 2]

References

Bakhtin, M. M. (1981) *The Dialogic Imagination* (ed. M. Holquist, trans. C. Emerson and M. Holquist), Austin: University of Texas Press.

Kress, G. and van Leeuwen, T. (1996) *Reading Images: the grammar of visual design*, London: Routledge

Leach, J. and Scott, P. (2002) 'Designing and evaluating science teaching sequences: an approach drawing upon the concept of learning demand and a social constructivist perspective on learning', *Studies in Science Education*, 38:115–42.

Mortimer, E. F. and Scott, P. H. (2003) *Meaning Making in Secondary Science Classrooms*, Buckingham: Open University Press.

Scott, P. and Ametller, J. (2007) 'Teaching science in a meaningful way: striking a balance between "opening up" and "closing down" classroom talk', *School Science Review*, 88:77–83.

Scott, P., Ametller, J., Dawes, L., Kleine Staarman, J., Mercer, N. (2007) 'An investigation of dialogic teaching in science classrooms', paper presented at *NARST 2007*, New Orleans.

Scott, P., Leach, J., Hind, A. and Lewis, J. (2006) 'Designing research evidence-informed teaching sequences', in R. Millar, J. Leach, J. Osborne and M. Ratcliffe (eds) *Improving Subject Teaching: lessons from research in science education*, London: Routledge.

Scott, P., Mortimer, E. and Aguiar, O. (2006) 'The tension between authoritative and dialogic discourse: a fundamental characteristic of meaning making interactions in high school science lessons', *Science Education*, 90:605–31.

Voloshinov, V. N. (1986) *Marxism and the Philosophy of Language*, Cambridge, MA: Harvard University Press.

Wegerif, R. (2007) '*Dialogic Education and Technology: expanding the space of learning*, New York: Springer.

Chapter 15

Dialogue and teaching thinking with technology

Opening, expanding and deepening the 'inter-face'

Rupert Wegerif
University of Exeter

Introduction

In a book about productive educational dialogues it is appropriate to reflect upon the relationship between dialogue and thinking. The concept of education, as opposed to say indoctrination or vocational training, implies more than just the acquisition of knowledge, it also implies some growth in the intellectual freedom of the learner (Biesta 2006). For me the ideal of teaching thinking or of teaching *for* thinking in education implies a central concern with expanding the degrees of intellectual freedom of the learner: this means the freedom to be able to question what is taught and the freedom to participate in the creation of new knowledge. Therefore, it could be argued that dialogues that do not promote the development of thinking should not be called educational at all. Of course teaching for knowledge content and teaching for thinking do not need to be mutually exclusive goals, but there are often choices about how teaching is done that may influence the extent to which what is learnt will liberate or enslave. I want to claim that the most educationally productive dialogues are those that teach thinking in the sense of liberating students to be able to think for themselves, regardless of what else they may also learn.

In this chapter I explore the relationship between dialogue, technology and teaching thinking and argue for the value of a dialogic approach to educational design. In the first half of the chapter I prepare a dialogic theoretical foundation for educational design through a very brief history of metaphors for thinking: thinking as face-to-face dialogue, thinking as mechanism and thinking as tool use, each with different implications for the role of dialogues and the role of educational technology. In the second half of the chapter I interact this theory with practice to put forward and illustrate a provisional framework for educational designs that have the aim of thinking through inducting students into dialogue across difference.

Unlike some of the other authors in this volume I do not think that 'dialogic' fits easily with Vygotskian theory in a broad 'socio-cultural' paradigm. To help make the case for the distinctive contribution of dialogic I begin with a return to the father of dialogic education, Socrates, to see if there is still something new to be learnt from his account of the relationship between dialogue, thinking and technology.

Metaphor 1: Thinking as face-to-face dialogue

At the dawn of the Western tradition of philosophy, that is to say at the beginning of the spread of the new technology of writing into Europe, Plato, somewhat ironically perhaps, wrote down for posterity a complaint about the negative consequences of writing made by his teacher, Socrates. In this critique of writing Socrates initially sounds very like a conservative older man objecting to new skills simply because they will drive out the skills that he learnt when he was a boy. In particular he objects that writing will have a bad effect on memory since people will no longer have to learn things for themselves, so that they can recite them from memory but will merely acquire a superficial appearance of learning by looking things up in books. However, on closer inspection, Socrates' critique of writing is more interesting than this. His objection to writing appears to stem from a view of thinking as essentially tied to the context of face-to-face dialogue such that writing words down to carry beyond the context in which they are spoken will destroy living thought, leaving only a kind of shadow or 'ghost' of thought.

In his dialogue *Phaedrus*, Plato reports Socrates as telling a story about what Thamos, the god of Egypt, said when the god 'Theuth' offered men the gift of writing:

> ... you give your disciples not truth, but only the semblance of truth; they will be hearers of many things and will have learned nothing; they will appear to be omniscient and will generally know nothing; they will be tiresome company, having the show of wisdom without the reality.
>
> (Plato trans. B. Jowett, 2006)

Socrates then expands on why writing encourages this superficiality and irresponsibility in his further dialogue with Phaedrus.

SOCRATES: I cannot help feeling, Phaedrus, that writing is unfortunately like painting; for the creations of the painter have the attitude of life, and yet if you ask them a question they preserve a solemn silence. And the same may be said of speeches. You would imagine that they had intelligence, but if you want to know anything and put a question to one of them, the speaker always gives one unvarying answer. And when they have been once written down they are tumbled about anywhere among those who may or may not understand them, and know not to whom they should reply, to whom not: and, if they are maltreated or abused, they have no parent to protect them; and they cannot protect or defend themselves.

PHAEDRUS: That again is most true.

SOCRATES: Is there not another kind of word or speech far better than this, and having far greater power – a son of the same family, but lawfully begotten?

PHAEDRUS: Whom do you mean, and what is his origin?

SOCRATES: I mean an intelligent word graven in the soul of the learner, which can defend itself, and knows when to speak and when to be silent.

PHAEDRUS: You mean the living word of knowledge which has a soul, and of which the written word is properly no more than an image?

Socrates concedes, a little later, that it might be a noble amusement for a man growing older and losing his faculties to write down some of his dialogues so that he can recall them when he is no longer capable of real thinking, but he continues:

> nobler by far is the serious pursuit of the dialectician, who, finding a congenial soul, by the help of science sows and plants therein words which are able to help themselves and him who planted them, and are not unfruitful, but have in them a seed which others brought up in different soils render immortal, making the possessors of it happy to the utmost extent of human happiness.

Socrates contrasts these fruitful living words with written words that are like seeds planted on flagstones in the heat of sun, dead seeds incapable of new growth. For Socrates then it seems that words live and have meaning only in the context of relationships in which they give birth to new words and new understandings. On this dialogic metaphor for thinking, thinking and teaching thinking cannot be separated since to think in a dialogue is both to teach thinking and to learn thinking. Socrates appears to be defining here the essential educational relationship, a relationship in which new learning happens through the open-ended discussion of ideas.

Socrates saw his dialogues as educational but it is not obvious that he saw them as 'productive' in the superficial sense of generating knowledge. Socrates is famous for claiming that he knew more than all his contemporaries only because he knew that he did not know whereas they all thought that they did know. His model of productive educational dialogue could be described as moving his students from a starting point of superficial knowledge to an end point of profound ignorance. The educational productivity of such dialogues lies not in constructing knowledge but in expanding awareness and developing in students a capacity to question and to be able to think for themselves.

Metaphor 2: Thinking as computation

According to Toulmin (1990) the assumption that the primary location of thinking is face-to-face dialogue continued in the humanist revival of classical learning that preceded the Enlightenment. Montaigne, writing in the sixteenth century (Montaigne 1595) addressed the reader as 'tu' and often began his pithiest observations with the phrase 'entre nous', implying a context of two friends chatting together perhaps over the garden fence or over a glass of wine in the tavern. It is hard to imagine Montaigne doubting the existence of others but, in 1642, after seeing dancing marionettes on display in Paris, Descartes could argue that he could not be sure of the presence of other minds since the appearance of intelligence in others might be the result of clever clockwork mechanisms (Descartes 1996). In the seventeenth and eighteenth century the image of clockwork came to be used routinely for the workings of the mind (Pasanek 2008). Clockwork is even used as a metaphor for the soul in Alexander Pope's 1737 *An Essay on Man* (Pope 1737). The association of clockwork with thinking was greatly helped by the construction of clockwork calculating machines first by Blaise Pascal (1642), then by Leibnitz (1673) and later by Charles Babbage (1822). Babbage linked his machine to the working of thought and proposed the thesis: 'That the *whole of development and operations of analysis* are now capable of being executed by machinery' (emphasis in original, as cited by Gandy 1995: 54).

This thesis was taken up independently in the early twentieth century by Alan Turing whose idea, on paper, of a Universal Turing Machine is now widely credited as the first computer. While Turing's paper idea was later implemented using valves and wires in the first electronic computers, in principle it could have been implemented using clockwork or any other mechanism capable of storing and processing information.

Whereas the metaphor of the mind as 'like clockwork' remained fanciful, the logically similar metaphor of thinking as like electronic computation has been very influential in the science of psychology and so in the literature and practice of teaching thinking.

The significance of this change of underlying metaphor can be illustrated by unpacking the popular term 'metacognition' (Flavell 1979). If thinking (cognition) is part of dialogue and relationship then it is always already reflective and it is not obvious what extra value comes with the term 'metacognition' unless this means having dialogues about dialogue or reflecting on reflection. The term seems useful to Flavell and others because they are thinking of thinking as like a computer programme or algorithmic process, which one can reflect back upon just as programmes written in high-level language can monitor programmes written in machine code in computer systems. Indeed in the artificial intelligence research community, metacognition is a term applied interchangeably to feedback loops in computer systems and to humans monitoring their own thinking (Anderson 1983). So when people refer to educational dialogues as helping to promote 'metacognition' as they often do (see Wegerif 2003), they are probably assuming an essentially non-dialogic or monologic picture of thinking as a mechanical operation of the kind that could be performed by an electronic computer or a well-constructed clockwork calculating machine.

Metaphor 3: Thinking as cultural tool use

The computer metaphor of mind implies that good thinking everywhere is pretty much the same in following certain abstract logical laws or general problem-solving patterns. This has been challenged by those who point out that thinking never occurs in the abstract but always in a situation where the thinking is mediated by cultural tools and practices. Learning to think then, on the cultural tool use metaphor, is not to be understood as a general 'cognitive development' but as always about learning to use specific tools in specific contexts (Rogoff, Gauvain and Ellis 1991; Wertsch and Kazak in press) Anne Edwards gives an illustration of this when she points out that the way in which young children solve arithmetic problems reveals the cultural tools that they are using, which may be external tools involving pencil and paper or mental strategies (Edwards 2005). Technology, here, has the role of mediating thinking to make new and better kinds of thinking possible. As Perkins puts it, the thinker becomes 'person plus' as in 'person plus tools' (Perkins 1993).

This socio-cultural approach is often associated with the critique of the aspiration to teach thinking in general precisely because the concept of thinking in general no longer makes sense on this model (e.g. Hennessey, McCormick and Murphy 1993). However, the aspiration to teach thinking in general can be salvaged in the form of teaching learners how to use cultural tools that can be applied across a range of contexts.

Particular 'educated' ways of talking together, including 'Exploratory Talk', defined through social ground rules such as shaping responses to each other in dialogues, questioning claims, giving reasons and so on, have been offered as a 'cultural tool' effective in supporting thinking in many contexts (Littleton and Mercer this volume; Wegerif, Mercer and Dawes 1999). For the 'Exploratory Talk' approach to teaching thinking the 'cultural tool' is an oral 'genre' or way of using words. In this sense the 'Socratic dialogue' approach with which I began this chapter could also be re-interpreted as a cultural tool to be taught and learnt. Working with Neil Mercer, Lyn Dawes, Karen Littleton and others, I helped develop and propose this socio-cultural approach to teaching thinking through teaching ways of talking (see Wegerif and Dawes 2004). Now, however, I no longer think that the metaphor of learning to use cultural tools that the socio-cultural approach relies upon can understand the creative kind of thinking we learn through engaging in dialogue. I think we need a new metaphor that captures something of what Socrates was saying about the primacy of the dialogic relationship but develops this original dialogic account of thinking in a way that can account for the role of technology in mediating dialogue.

Metaphor 4: Thinking as dialogue across difference

For Lévinas, as for Buber before him, a person is a response of an 'I' to a 'thou' in a relationship (Lévinas 1978; Buber 1958). Reasoning, on this dialogic view, is seen in the ethical context of an original responsibility for the other. Lévinas argues that 'the face of the other' is a sign that means something in a way that cannot be reduced to a relation of equivalence with any other signs. He refers to the meaning of this 'sign' as 'la signifiance même de le signification' ('The very signifyingness of signification', Lévinas 1978, p. 158; Lévinas 1989: 90) by which he means that responsibility in the face of the other is the context of meaning, rather than a content of meaning. His warrant for this claim is based upon a detailed phenomenology of the experience of the face of the other, showing that the face of the other is not completely reducible to being just another thing in my world related to other things, or a sign related to other signs, but that there is an appeal in the face of the other that always outstrips my capacity to understand the other and to control the other.

Both Bakhtin, another major influence on contemporary dialogic theory, and Lévinas follow Socrates in contrasting living words with dead words where living words are 'internal' to a dialogic relation and carry infinite potential for making new meaning while dead words are external to the dialogue and have become sedimented into things with a fixed meaning (e.g. Bakhtin 1981: 276; Lévinas, 1978: 239). However, whereas Socrates appears to identify these living words with the warm breath of face-to-face speech ('breath' is a translation of the Greek word 'pneuma', which can also be translated as 'spirit'), in my reading at least, both Bakhtin and Lévinas locate the source of meaning not in the words themselves so much as in the particular kind of difference that characterizes dialogic relations. The point that meaning requires difference is summed up best by an often repeated claim from Voloshinov, a close collaborator of Bakhtin in the 1920s: 'meaning is like an electric spark that occurs only when two different terminals are hooked together' (Voloshinov 1986: 102–3).

It is this focus on the dialogic relation as a kind of difference rather than a kind of identity that most clearly distinguishes the new metaphor of thinking as dialogue across difference from Socrates' original version of thinking as face-to-face dialogue. Understanding dialogue as more like a spark across difference than like a tool in a social context makes it possible to understand the positive role of technology in educational dialogues. Bakhtin, for example, went beyond the face-to-face to explore dialogue between texts, arguing that it is the difference between texts that opens up 'bottomless' depths of 'contextual meaning' and leads to sparks of 'inter-illumination' (Bakhtin 1986: 162). He gives the example of how for him reading the texts of ancient Greece, like *Phaedrus* with which I started this chapter, gave him an extra perspective from which to see his situation in twentieth-century Russia in a way that opens up the possibilities of thought in general (Bakhtin 1986: 7). Lévinas directly relates this valuing of difference to new technology. He takes on Heidegger's criticism of modern technology as enframing our thoughts and alienating us from 'being'; claiming, by contrast, that Heidegger's mystical association of being with place leads directly to the horrors of Nazism and that it is the role of technology to liberate us from this perpetual warfare by taking us out of our home space and bringing us into relationship with others. He writes in an article in praise of the achievement of Gagarin that:

> Technology wrenches us out of the Heideggerian world and the superstitions regarding *place*. From this point on, an opportunity appears to us: to perceive men outside the situation in which they are placed, and let the human face shine in all its nudity. Socrates prefers the town in which one meets people to the countryside and the trees.
>
> (Lévinas 1990: 233)

It is hard to connect this ethical vision of relating to people 'outside the situation in which they are placed' to socio-cultural theory. Lévinas stressed the infinity implicit in the dialogic difference. What makes each person truly unique and, in his language, a 'singularity', is precisely what makes us all the same, that we resist all attempts to be located and situated. This speaks to Lévinas of the infinity of an outside of any meaning system and it is this transcendence and infinity of the 'naked face of the other' that calls us out and gives us a direction. Bakhtin, from within a very different tradition of thought, appears to articulate a point of view with some similarities. He points out that 'In order to understand, it is immensely important for the person who understands to be located outside the object of his or her creative understanding – in time, in space, in culture' (Bakhtin 1986: 7) He was dismayed by the narrow frame of reference within which most people 'fuss about' and writes that we need to think always in the 'great time' that unites all cultures (1986: 167). He echoes the infinity that Lévinas refers to when he claims that the meaning of any utterance is found in the whole dialogue but that this whole dialogue has no end (1986: 170). His notion of 'great time' was of the place of meeting between all voices from every time and place. Teaching thinking on the dialogic model stimulated by Bakhtin is then about drawing students from narrow concerns to the more universal thinking of 'great time'. In a similar, if distinct, way, an approach to teaching thinking inspired by Lévinas would take us beyond all the place-bound identities we are attached to and all the systems of thought that we build to contain and control otherness towards a more open, honest, generous and creative response to the challenge of the radical otherness that shines through the face of each individual other.

How 'dialogic space' relates to the ZPD

Vygotsky's well-known 'zone of proximal development' or ZPD has been seen by many as bringing dialogic relations into educational theory. In the ZPD the teacher has to engage with the perspective of the student and vice-versa in order to connect the development of ideas in the student to pre-existing culture. The dialogic relation, which is well characterized as atunement to the atunement of the other (Rommetveit 1992), is certainly implicit in the idea of the ZPD but it is invoked as a temporary tool or scaffold to help in a direction of individual development known in advance. Mercer suggested we turn this ZPD into a more open and multidirectional 'intermental development zone' (IDZ) where 'interthinking' can occur between peers without the assumption of a teacher leading a learner (Mercer 2000). This is clearly a move in a more dialogic direction, but the notion of 'dialogic space' goes further again in that it is not primarily conceptualized as a 'mediating means' supporting cognitive develop-ment but as an end in itself. The point of education is not to use dialogue to achieve something other than dialogue, as notions such as ZPD and IDZ imply, but to enter more deeply and fully into dialogue.

The origins of the metaphor of dialogue across difference in classroom research

The metaphor of dialogue across difference might sound a bit abstract and philosophi-cal when presented through the ideas of Bakhtin, a literary theorist, and Lévinas, an existential phenomenologist, but another important source for this metaphor is situated in classroom research. The idea that teaching and learning thinking could be translated as movement into dialogic space emerged for me most clearly out of trying to under-stand what was happening as children learned to solve problems better when working together in small groups in the context of a research programme exploring the impact of teaching Exploratory Talk on the solving of reasoning tests (see Littleton and Mercer this volume for more on this work and also Wegerif 2005). Groups that became more successful at thinking together after teaching the ground rules of Exploratory Talk shifted away from initial fixed identity positions, where either individuals identified with a self-image and sought to win the argument (which we called 'disputational talk'), or they identified with a harmonious group image and resisted any kind of questioning or criticism (which we called 'cumulative talk'), towards something new, which I could only describe as identifying with the space of dialogue itself (Wegerif and Mercer 1997). After watching many video recordings of groups shifting from either disputational or cumulative talk to what we called 'Exploratory Talk' and thereby becoming better at solving reasoning test problems together I became convinced that the important shift that I was seeing was less about explicit reasoning, a feature of both Douglas Barnes and Neil Mercer's definitions of Exploratory Talk, than about an improved quality of their group relationship. This is partially confirmed by a study in Mexico, which suggests that teaching and learning the ground rules of Exploratory Talk can improve the quality of creative tasks such as writing a joint text without producing indicators of explicit reasoning (Rojas-Drummond *et al.* 2006). The more dialogic relationship in groups thinking better together could be seen best not through the use of logical connectors such as 'because' and 'therefore' (such language may be task-specific), but in the increasing prevalence of admissions of uncertainty, asking for advice and individuals changing their minds in the face of evidence.

I used the phrase 'identifying with the space of dialogue itself' writing with Neil Mercer in 1997, by which I meant at the time an answer to the question: What standpoint are we taking when we find ourselves forced, despite our best interests and our intentions, to recognize that we are wrong in a dialogue and to change our position? Using the cultural tools represented by the language of explicit reasoning does not help us understand this kind of identity.

I noticed that the more successful children and groups in the research programme were becoming more able to remain with the silent pauses in the dialogue characterized by uncertainty, multiplicity and open-endedness. These silences were crucial for shared problem solving as they almost invariably preceded a leap into a new solution to a problem that the groups had originally found difficult, but such silences were not easy to measure using coding schemes since the characterization of a silence as 'dialogic silence' as opposed to say 'shocked silence' or 'bored silence' requires the intuition of a participant in the dialogue. In order to understand further the nature and significance of these moments of pregnant silence it became necessary to address the philosophical question of the nature of 'dialogic space'. The 'I' identity of disputational talk and the 'we' identity of cumulative talk are easy to grasp as social identities of the kind dealt with routinely by social identity researchers (e.g. Haslam, Jetten, Posmes and Haslam 2009). The problem is that dialogic space is not a kind of 'thing' than one can identify with but more like a kind of relationship or a kind of 'difference', and not simply the easy kind of difference that one can see between two things but a 'constitutive difference' that helps bring the things apparently in relation into being in the first place. This constitutive role of dialogue was expressed by Bakhtin in a neat one-liner: 'the ancient Greeks did not know the most important thing about themselves, that they were '*ancient* Greeks'" (Bakhtin 1986: 6).

Although dialogues are always situated in history and culture it is also true that it is within dialogues that we interpret and give meaning to our history and our culture. The concept of 'dialogic space' gains its generative power from being an inside-out/ outside-in kind of concept (Wegerif 2007). Viewed externally each dialogic space is situated and is different from all the others, experienced internally each dialogic space opens onto the same infinite potential for new meaning.

The key switch in learning to think, as Nietzsche argued, is to shift from being a passive recipient of meaning to becoming an active creator of meaning. This may be experienced as an increase in freedom but also as in increase in responsibility. It is a movement from identification with dead images, the products of previous dialogues, to identification with, and engagement in, the dialogic process of creating meaning through "inter-illumination" (Bakthin 1981). Identifying with dialogic space implies the apparent oxymoron of identifying with difference because it is the difference between voices that enables meaning to flow and new ideas to emerge. However, despite this conceptual impossibility, it is in practice quite possible for students to become more comfortable dwelling in a space of uncertainty, multiplicity and potential: in so far as they do, they could plausibly be described as becoming more 'dialogic'.

A dialogic foundation for the design of educational technology

In 1986 Winograd and Flores published a little book that inspired me: Understanding Computers and Cognition: A New Foundation for Design (Winograd and Flores 1986). In this book they applied Heidegger's early account of situated cognition to challenge the abstract rationalism that then dominated cognitive science. I was impressed that they did this in the form of a new way of thinking about the design of computer applications that would be more use to people because it is based on a better analysis of what being human in the world is really like. In a similar spirit I would like to propose dialogue across difference as a foundation for design.

In a dialogic account of thinking the aim is not always to replace false representations with true ones so much as to augment understanding with new perspectives. In the rationalist tradition, represented here by the thinking as computation metaphor, there is a strong understanding of the vertical development of thinking from context-bound thinking towards universality through abstraction but little acknowledgement of the horizontal dimension of different kinds of thinking embedded in different ways of being. In the socio-cultural tradition, represented here by the thinking as cultural tool use metaphor, there is a strong understanding of the horizontal dimension of awareness of the variety of different kinds of thinking but no effective way to account for verticality. A model of learning to think as appropriating cultural tools and participating in cultural practices offers no way to say which tools or which practices are better in general, only in relation to a particular task already shaped by a community. This issue of verticality is important for education, which is inevitably about values and directions as well as processes. The metaphor of teaching and learning thinking as drawing students into spaces of dialogue across difference offers a vertical direction for the development of thinking without losing a sense of the horizontal. The direction of travel from narrow and local identifications that block dialogue towards increasing openness and engagement in universal dialogue is different from rationalism as it does not presuppose any overarching universal logical structures. The only universal presupposed, 'dialogic space', refers to the context of thinking rather than any specific content of thinking. It is also different from rationalism because the teaching of thinking, on this metaphor, does not just mean changing minds but also changing the world. If one side of dialogic space is transcendent and infinite the other side is embedded in the world. The task of teaching thinking by opening, deepening and widening spaces of dialogue involves changing cultural practices and social structures.

Towards a framework for the design of educational technology that can teach thinking as dialogue across difference

Converting the theoretical foundation for design argued for above into educational activities requires an intermediate framework for design consisting of flexible design principles, exemplars and key questions to ask. Below I put forward a provisional framework for design based on: 1) conceptual analysis of the components of an account of teaching and learning thinking understood as movement into dialogue across difference and 2) an assessment of what has worked in already tried-and-tested educational designs to promote creative dialogic thinking.

Conceptually this model of teaching thinking assumes that thinking is limited by closed identities and monologic or systemic practices so the first aim must be to open dialogic spaces understood as spaces of internal freedom within the external constraints of a situation and the next aim is to improve the educational quality of these spaces, drawing participants more completely into dialogue through deepening and widening these spaces.

1. Opening dialogic spaces

There are ways of using ICT in education that close down dialogic space and ways that open this up. Tutorial software used individually closes down dialogue when the same sort of questions and tasks given to a group will open up dialogic spaces within the curriculum. Simulations that encourage fast and furious engagement will close down dialogue when the same interfaces with a prompt for talking that interrupts the action will open up dialogic spaces (Wegerif, Littleton and Jones 2003).

A singular affordance of new media technologies is the possibility of supporting new dialogic spaces anywhere and everywhere, from interactive blogs under exhibits in museums to texted exchanges between pupils in different classrooms. But the technological support alone does not make a dialogic space.

One of the key findings from my own research with Neil Mercer, Lyn Dawes, Karen Littleton and others on collaborative learning around computers in classrooms is that for effective shared thinking it is not enough just to place people in groups – they need to be prepared for working together in groups beforehand (e.g. Wegerif and Dawes 2004). While in this chapter I have questioned the interpretation of how and why the ground rules of Exploratory Talk promote improved group thinking I have no doubt that they do so. I think that ground rules, such as asking open questions and listening with respect to others, open up a creative dialogic space. Like the *Thinking Together* approach described by Littleton and Mercer (this volume), *Philosophy for Children* also seems effective as a method of teaching for engagement in dialogic thinking (see Hardman and Delafield this volume). In one EC-funded study, 'Philosophy Hotel', similar *Philosophy for Children* pedagogy was extended successfully to internet-mediated philosophy discussions in different classrooms in several European countries (a study by Steve Williams and Richard Athlone described in Wegerif 2007: 267). The same principle that effective shared thinking needs to be positively taught emerges from reviews of collaborative learning in online environments (De Laat 2006: 163).

2. Widening dialogic spaces

Baker, Quignard, Lund and Séjourné (2003: 11) distinguish between deepening and broadening a space of debate:

Students broaden their understanding of a space of debate when they are better acquainted with societal and epistemological points of view, their associated
arguments and value systems; they deepen it when they are able to go deeper
into argument chains, to elaborate upon the meaning of arguments, and to better
understand the notions involved.

While the idea of dialogic space is broader than that of a space of debate, since it is
not concerned only with explicit argumentation, the distinction between broadening
and deepening remains useful. Broadening or expanding means roughly increasing the
degree of difference between perspectives in a dialogue while maintaining the dialogic
relationship. Broadening can be done through the use of the Internet to engage in real
dialogues about global issues. An illustration of this is the Oxfam website where video
stories from across the world are exchanged and discussed (http://tv.oneworld.net). In
practice this does not support much real dialogue, since everyone tends to agree that
it is all the fault of America and/or global capitalism, but when used with a dialogic
pedagogical approach, as described above, the same technology could be a powerful
means for so doing. Broadening in the classroom can be done through structured
WebQuest-type activities where an issue is posed and learners are sent to different
websites to explore it and to question the people behind different viewpoints.

3. Deepening dialogic space

Deepening refers to increasing the degree of reflection on assumptions and grounds.
With the right pedagogy the broadening potential of internet dialogues also becomes
a deepening as students are led to reflect on the assumptions that they carry with them
into dialogues.

Talk in face-to-face dialogues exists only momentarily and only for those immediately present. Technologies that support drawing and writing can thus be thought of
as a way of deepening dialogues, by turning transitory talk and thoughts into external
objects that are available to learners for discussion and shared reflection (Goody 1977).
Computer documents can offer a kind of halfway stage between the evanescence of talk
and the permanence of written texts. Harry McMahon and Bill O'Neill, the origina-
tors of Bubble Dialogue software, use the term 'slow-throwness' to refer to the way
their tool can externalize the thoughts and feelings of the participants and also support reflection and the possibility of returning and retrospectively changing dialogues
(McMahon and O'Neill 1993; Bubble Dialogue II, developed by Wegerif and Barrett,
is available free from http://www.dialogbox.org.uk/intro.htm).

Often deepening follows from widening, where exposure to other ways of seeing
things can lead one to question one's own framing assumptions. In this sense deepening is a form of 'deconstruction' insofar as this means consciously exploring the key
distinctions that frame constructions of meaning in order to become aware of how
things might be otherwise.

A specific form of deepening is to reflect on the process of dialogue and shared
enquiry in order to become more aware of it and to refine it. Awareness tools to support collaborative learning online showing who is talking to whom and how much
and what sort of things they are saying could serve this function. The most powerful

example I have seen is the filming of groups of children talking together and then showing this to them to support a discussion on what sort of behaviours are helpful and which are not.

4. Teach content through induction into fields of dialogue

Interactivity makes it easy for software to simulate multiple points of view in a dialogue, thus allowing learners to be inducted into a field of dialogue rather than into fixed 'truths'. Any content can be taught through engagement in dialogue between alternative points of view. In this way the student learns not only the current consensus view on a topic but also how to justify it and how to question it and so is inducted into knowledge as shared enquiry rather than as authoritative and final. The forum design whereby multiple voices speak on a topic and then a group of learners discuss what they think is easy to implement. What students learn from this is how to negotiate for themselves a position in a field of dialogue. The term 'field of dialogue' here mediates between the completely open concept of dialogic space and more circumscribed curriculum areas. A good example of a field of dialogue might be the range of views on global warming or on capital punishment.

From a dialogic perspective the Internet is not so much a 'tool of tools' but a cacophony of voices offering countless opportunities for dialogic engagement with multiple perspectives on every topic. While these perspectives are mediated by technology, signs for the voices of the other, faces, voices, avatars, videos and so on are not best understood on the model of tools but as stand-ins for the face of the other or 'epiphantic' signs that lead one to the voice of another person (Leimann 2002). The issue for design is how to use these different ways of mediating the presence of the other to support dialogue across difference that issues in reflection and learning. WebQuests offer one way of scaffolding dialogic encounters between voices. Email links between geographically distant groups are another. Dialogues via avatars in 3D virtual worlds are a further way (see Ligorio and Pugliese 2004).

An example of broadening dialogic space

Computer mediated dialogues generally expand the 'space' of dialogue by spatializing time so that many can 'talk' in parallel and their different voices can be represented by spatial differences in an interface. In web forums or email in-boxes this different way of doing dialogue is represented in a kind of play-script with one utterance after another listed in a temporal sequence prefaced by the name of the participant. This linear list is a metaphor for the progression of moments in time, the line below being the utterance after the line above. Even this arrangement makes it easy to lose the context of the argument. The 'dialogue maps' of more map-like graphical dialogue environments like Digalo are made up of boxes of different shapes and colours representing different types of contribution and links between them, which can also be given a meaning. Digalo has mainly been used synchronously with boxes appearing and disappearing and being moved around and linked in real-time but the end result is not a temporal arrangement but a spatial arrangement (see Figure 15.1).

Figure 15.1 illustrates the potential for spatial arrangements of ideas looking at the

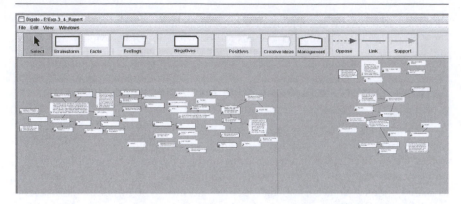

Figure 15.1 Illustration of a Digalo map using the Six Hats technique.

patterning of messages rather than the content of messages. This is a map created by a group of university students using Edward de Bono's Six Hats technique to encourage them to look at an issue in a range of different ways. The dialogic process of exploring an issue through various perspectives, all of which are valid and none of which are ever simply 'overcome' in a 'synthesis', is well supported by the spatial representation of Digalo and its flexibility. Moving shapes around on the map supports reflection on the relationships between different perspectives.

Through combining a content analysis of the 'maps' for the emergence of new perspectives with critical event recall, we have explored the extent to which this tool affords creative reflection on multiple perspectives and so could be seen as a tool that supports that widening of dialogues (Wegerif, McLaren, Chamrada, Scheuer, Mansour and Mikšátko 2009). The development of dialogic reasoning is often signalled through the expression of openness of other points of view, through changes of mind and through inclusion of multiple voices in one 'utterance'. The evidence of the combination of discourse analysis, including a coding of the emergence of new perspectives with interviews eliciting the first-person experience of students generating new perspectives, confirms that their awareness of the multiple strands in the map around a topic helped to stimulate students to produce new ideas that they themselves experienced as 'unexpected' (see Figure 15.2).

ICT and dialogue between media

Meaning can be explored using a variety of media. According to the dialogue across difference perspective I have outlined above, dialogues are not simply an exchange of words. They consist of a relationship between voices or perspectives motivating a flow of meaning. This flow of meaning is focused and articulated by signs and communications technologies but is not reducible to those signs or technologies. Exploring the dialogue between meanings in different modes has the potential to broaden dialogues, by giving access to new kinds of perspectives and to deepen dialogues, by encouraging one mode to reflect on another. For example, asking students to reflect on musical representations of different arguments can give access to the emotions that are often implicit behind

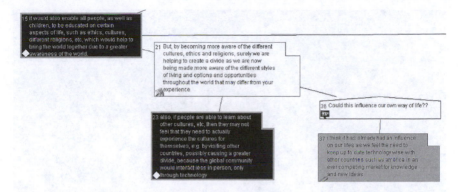

Figure 15.2 A cluster of shapes around the emergence of a new perspective.

neutral-seeming words in texts and so broaden and deepen the dialogic space.

This can be illustrated through a recent project in a Devon school where the use of ICT was central. This was a creative workshop combining together music composition, dance movement and art work using light to produce a response to an initial poem entitled 'Light Shifts'. The multimodal result, presented in a PowerPoint presentation, is a powerful expression of multimedia dialogue effectively evoking that 'dialogic space' between and around different media that enables meaning to transgress and to transfer. Figure 15.3 gives an edited version, still combining light and text, but to this you have to add in imagination, movement, music, and voice (see Cunliffe 2008).

Blogging as an example of induction into and creation of dialogic space

The problem with neo-Vygotskian accounts of how we learn to think is that they focus on the tools within the dialogue rather than the space of dialogue itself. Some have argued, in this neo-Vygotskian way, that writing provides a kind of cognitive technology for mediated thinking, especially through tools like tables and lists that make abstract formal thinking possible (e.g. Goody 1977). Walter Ong makes a different point when he describes how the initial custom of reading texts aloud in groups was gradually replaced by silent individual reading. This habit, combined with the sense of closure in printed texts, as if thought could become a thing, supported the development of a sense of a fixed inner self separate from the interplay of communal life. This was con-ceptualized as a new 'inner space' from which individuals had the freedom to reflect critically on the culture around them (Ong 1982). This kind of sense of an inner space of freedom that one carries around with one is the very model of the 'autonomous self' that education systems still aim to produce (Biesta 2006).

Ong's careful and persuasive case offers a model for relating technologies to the development of embodied higher order thinking. On the whole, in the contexts of its use, electronic text is more immediately dialogic and communal than print technol-ogy. Yet, as writing, it continues, unlike oral dialogue, to endure over time and so it has the potential to support the disembedding of ideas from their contingent contexts

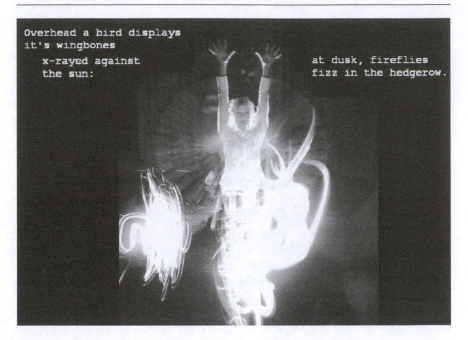

Figure 15.3 Edited still from 'Light Shifts', a multimodal PowerPoint presentation.

that Ong attributes to writing. If electronic writing does support the kind of 'inner space' of reflection away from the contingencies of time and physical context that Ong refers to, then this inner space is no longer the inert individualized space generated by earlier writing-and-reading practices but a collective and dialogic 'inner space'. Ong's account of the way in which communicative practices associated with literacy led to the creation and deepening of individual inner space is applicable to analysing the impact of new communicative technologies not as tools that are internalized but as new kinds of dialogic spaces that become part of the lifeworld of participants. The practice of blogging, for instance, can be a participation in a process of collective reflection. Events seem different when they are seen not only through one's own eyes but also through the eyes of the potential audience for one's blog. One course at Exeter University is assessed entirely through mutually visible multimedia blogs in a Facebook-like web 2.0 environment and this has proved effective in creating a motivating shared reflective space. The majority of students report that seeing the views of others helps them to think and reflect and create new ideas.

Discussion and conclusion

I began this chapter with Socrates partly in order to offer a challenge to the socio-cultural assumption that thinking is situated and mediated by cultural tools. We live in a very different society to that of Socrates and the cultural tools available to us, such as the Internet, are enormously more sophisticated than those available to him. If the socio-cultural hypothesis were true surely this gulf would make more of a difference than it does. In fact, despite the 'cultural tools mediate thinking' theory, Socrates' voice can still speak to us as freshly as the voice of any of our contemporaries, more freshly than most I would say. In what space exactly then is my dialogue with Socrates situated? And are the nature and limits of the dialogue you are having with me now really determined in advance by culture and history? Or is that just something that people choose to believe to avoid the potential discomfort of an encounter with the unexpected?

In the first half of this chapter I tried to make it clear that dialogic theory offers an alternative vision of education that is as different from socio-cultural theory as it is from rationalism. Dialogic theorists like Bakhtin and Lévinas can offer education a different vision of the vertical development of thinking – a movement into the space of dialogue itself characterized by leaving behind narrow attachments and identities and becoming more open to otherness, where otherness is understood as that which does not fit into existing structures of thought and prejudices. This dialogic verticality is different from the verticality of the rationalists because it is a movement from identity into difference. At the end of the journey there are no universal structures of reason, only uncertainty, multiplicity and possibility.

In the second half of the chapter I proposed this theoretical perspective as a foundation for the design of education with technology and tentatively put forward a framework for educational design based on unpacking the conceptual implications of the theory and on examples of activities that seemed to have worked in promoting movement into dialogic space. There remains a considerable gulf between the high level of theory offered and details of educational practice. The concepts of opening, deepening and widening dialogic space are perhaps too broad to distinguish usefully between different educational designs. Some guiding principles do emerge, however, such as the value of teaching content through drawing students into fields of dialogue and the importance of combining the use of technology with face-to-face pedagogies that actively teach the skills and social ground rules required for engagement in dialogue across difference. One key to future work in this area will be finding effective ways to assess the development of dialogic capabilities and dispositions in individuals and groups so that it is possible to distinguish approaches that work to develop these from those that merely look as if they ought to. Another study that is called for to test the framework would be an ethnographic investigation into the impact of blogging on styles of thinking in individuals and communities.

Although it remains weak on the details this framework offers a new way of understanding the role of the Internet in teaching thinking. As well as the external relationships of voices situated in dispersed places and times, dialogue, it is claimed, offers the potential for internal relationships between voices. In mediating multiple voices in dialogue with each other the Internet should be understood on the model of this internal dialogic space more than on the model of an external structure. The signs of the Internet are perhaps best understood as stand-ins for the 'face of the other', described by Lévinas as a kind of sign that signifies not content but a context for meaning. This context for meaning is dialogue with others and with otherness in general. While the Internet is not itself dialogic space it appears to make possible the partial external realization of what has always been the internal intuition of dialogue: the ideal of all voices from all cultures and all times in dialogue together. Teaching thinking with the Internet, understood as opening, widening and deepening dialogic space, is a practical proposal for how education could participate most productively in the creation of a more peaceful and more creative future.

References

Anderson, J. R. (1983) *The Architecture of Cognition*, Cambridge, MA: Harvard University Press.

Baker, M. J., Quignard, M., Lund, K. and Séjourné, A. (2003) 'Computer-supported collaborative learning in the space of debate', in B. Wasson, S. Ludvigsen and U. Hoppe (eds) *Designing for Change in Networked Learning Environments: proceedings of the International Conference on Computer Support for Collaborative Learning*, Dordrecht, The Netherlands: Kluwer, pp11–20.

Bakhtin, M. M. (1981) 'Discourse in the novel', in M. M. Bakhtin, *The Dialogic Imagination: four essays by M. M. Bakhtin*, Austin, TX: University of Texas Press.

Bakhtin, M. M. (1986) *Speech Genres and Other Late Essays*, Austin, TX: University of Texas Press.

Biesta, G. (2006) *Beyond Learning: democratic education for a human future*, Boulder, CO: Paradigm Press.

Buber, M. (1958) *I and Thou* (2nd edn, trans. R. Gregory Smith), Edinburgh: T. and T. Clark.

Cunliffe, L. (2008) 'A case study: how interdisciplinary teaching using information and communication technology and supported by a creative partner impacted on creativity in an extra-curricular school activity', *International Journal of Education through Art*, 4:91–105.

De Laat, M. (2006) *Networked Learning*, Apeldoorn: Politieacademie.

Descartes, R. (1996) *Meditations on First Philosophy*. Available online at: http://www.philosophyarchive.com/person.php?era=1600-1699&philosopher=Descartes (accessed 1 August 2008).

Edwards, A. (2005) 'Let's get beyond community and practice: the many meanings of learning by participating', *The Curriculum Journal*, 16:49–65.

Flavell, J. H. (1979) 'Metacognition', *American Psychologist*, 34:906–11.

Gandy, R. (1995) 'The confluence of ideas in 1936', in R. Herken (ed.) *The Universal Turing Machine: a half-century survey*, New York: Springer.

Goody, J. (1977) *The Domestication of the Savage Mind*, Cambridge: Cambridge University Press.

Haslam, A., Jetten, J., Posmes, T. and Haslam, C. (2009) 'Social identity, health and well-being: an emerging agenda for applied psychology', *Applied Psychology: an International Review*, 58:1–23.

Hennessy, S., McCormick, R. and Murphy, P. (1993) 'The myth of general problem-solving capability: design and technology as an example', *The Curriculum Journal*, 4:74–89.

Leimann, M. (2002) 'Toward semiotic dialogism: the role of sign mediation in the dialogical self', *Theory and Psychology*, 12:221–35.

Lévinas, E. (1978) *Autrement qu'être ou au-dela de l'essence*, Paris: Livre de Poche.

Lévinas, E. (1989) 'Substitution' (trans. A. Lingis), in S. Hand (ed.) *The Lévinas Reader*, Oxford: Blackwell.

Lévinas, E. (1990) 'Heidegger, Gagarin and us', in *Difficult Freedom: essays on Judaism* (trans. S. Hand), Baltimore: Johns Hopkins Press.

Ligorio, M. and Pugliese, A. C. (2004) 'Self-positioning in a text-based virtual environment',

Identity: an international journal of theory and research, 4:337–353.

McMahon, H and O'Neill, W. (1993) 'Computer-mediated zones of engagement in learning', in T. Duffy, J. Lowyk and D. Jonassen (eds) *Designing Environments for Constructive Learning*, Berlin: Springer.

Mercer, N. (2000) *Words and Minds: how we use language to think together*, London: Routledge.

Montaigne, M. (1595) *Les Essais*. Available online at: http://www.lib.uchicago.edu/efts/ARTFL/projects/montaigne/ (accessed 1 August 2008).

Ong, W. J. (1982) *Orality and Literacy: the technologizing of the word*, Methuen: London.

Pasanek, B. (2008) *The Mind is a Metaphor*. Available online at: http://mind.textdriven.com/ (accessed 1 August 2008).

Perkins, D. (1993) 'Person plus: a distributed view of thinking and learning', in G. Salomon (ed.) *Distributed Cognitions: psychological and educational considerations*, Cambridge: Cambridge University Press.

Plato (2006) *Phaedrus* (trans. B. Jowett). Available online at: http://ebooks.adelaide.edu.au/p/plato/p71phs/ (accessed 1 August 2008).

Pope, A. (1737) *An Essay on Man*. Available online at: http://www.gutenberg.org/etext/2428 (accessed 1 August 2008).

Rogoff, B., Gauvain, G. and Ellis, C. (1991) 'Development viewed in its cultural context', in P. Light, S. Sheldon and M. Woodhead (eds) *Learning to Think*, London: Routledge.

Rojas-Drummond, S. Fernandez, M., Mazon, N. and Wegerif, R. (2006) 'Collaborative talk and creativity', *Teaching Thinking and Creativity*, 1:84–94.

Rommetveit, R. (1992) 'Outlines of a dialogically based social-cognitive approach to human cognition and communication', in A. Wold (ed.) *The Dialogical Alternative: towards a theory of language and mind*, Oslo: Scandanavian Press.

Toulmin, S. (1990) *Cosmopolis: the hidden agenda of modernity*, New York: Free Press.

Voloshinov, V. (1986) *Marxism and the Philosophy of Language*, Cambridge, MA: Harvard University Press.

Wegerif, R. (2003) *Thinking Skills, Technology and Learning: a review of the literature*, Bristol: NESTA FutureLab.

Wegerif, R (2007) *Dialogic Education and Technology: expanding the space of learning*, New York and Berlin: Springer.

Wegerif, R. (2005) 'Reason and creativity in classroom dialogues', *Language and Education*, 19:223–38.

Wegerif, R. and Dawes, L. (2004) *Thinking and Learning with ICT: raising achievement in primary classrooms*, London: Routledge.

Wegerif, R. and Mercer, N. (1997) 'A dialogical framework for researching peer talk', in R. Wegerif and P. Scrimshaw (eds) *Computers and Talk in the Primary Classroom*, Clevedon: Multilingual Matters.

Wegerif, R., Littleton, K. and Jones, A. (2003) 'Stand alone computers supporting learning dialogues in primary classrooms', *International Journal of Educational Research*, 39:851–860.

Wegerif, R., McLaren, B. M., Chamrada, M., Scheuer, O., Mansour, N. and Mikšátko, J. (2009) 'Recognizing creative thinking in graphical e-discussions using artificial intelligence graph-matching techniques', paper presented at the 8th International Conference on Computer Supported Collaborative Learning (CSCL-09), 8–13 June, University of the Aegean, Rhodes, Greece.

Wegerif, R., Mercer, N. and Dawes, L. (1999) 'From social interaction to individual reasoning: an empirical investigation of a possible socio-cultural model of cognitive development', *Learning and Instruction*, 9:493–516.

Wertsch, J. V. and Kazak, S. (in press) 'Saying more than you know in instructional settings', in T. Koschmann (ed.) *Theorizing Learning Practice*, Mahwah, NJ: Lawrence Erlbaum.

Winograd, T. and Flores, F. (1986) *Understanding Computers and Cognition: a new foundation for design*, Norwood, NJ: Ablex Publishing Corporation.

Chapter 16

Collaborative learning of computer science concepts

R. Keith Sawyer and Kenneth J. Goldman
Washington University in St. Louis

Introduction

This chapter reports on a study of conversation between pairs of undergraduate college students as they were engaged in collaborative programming activities as part of a college course for non-computer science majors. The goal of the course was not for students to learn a specific programming language; rather, it was for students to develop a deeper conceptual understanding of the central ideas of computer science. Toward this end, a special computer-based learning environment was developed that allowed students to program by visually manipulating screen icons, rather than typing text that conformed to the syntax of a particular programming language. This learning environment is called JPie, which is short for Java Programmer's Interactive Environment.

This study extends our understanding of educational dialogues by applying methods and theories to a new learning context, computer science, and by helping us understand the role played by external, mediating artefacts (the JPie computer application) in scaffolding educational dialogues.

Over 20 years of educational research has consistently demonstrated that collaboration helps students learn (e.g. Bossert 1988–9; Johnson and Johnson 1992; Kumpulainen and Mutanan 2000; Slavin 1990, 1992; Webb and Palincsar 1996). Collaboration in structured, in-class formats has been shown to increase students' knowledge in a wide range of subjects, including computer programming (Webb, Ender and Lewis 1986).

In explaining how collaboration benefits learning, researchers from a wide range of theoretical perspectives have hypothesized that conversation mediates between the group and individual learning (Fisher 1993; Johnson and Johnson 1992; Kumpulainen and Mutanan 2000; Mercer 1996; Vygotsky 1978; Webb 1991, 1995; Webb and Palincsar 1996). In the 1980s, this consensus led education researchers to begin to use interaction analysis to study educational dialogues. Researchers who study collaborative learning have focused on three aspects of dialogue that could contribute to learning. First, providing and receiving explanations are both thought to contribute to children's learning (Bargh and Schul 1980; Fuchs, Fuchs, Hamlett, Phillips, Karns and Dutka 1997; Swing and Peterson 1982; Vedder 1985; Webb 1984, 1991, 1992). Second, researchers working within a Piagetian socio-cognitive framework have emphasized the mediating role played by conflict and controversy (Bearison, Magzamen and Filardo 1986; Doise and Mugny 1984; Perret-Clermont, 1980). Third, researchers working within a Vygotskian or socio-cultural framework have emphasized how participants build on each other's ideas to jointly construct a new understanding that none of the participants had prior to the encounter (Forman 1992; Forman and Cazden 1985; Palincsar 1998).

Of these three, the socio-cultural tradition has focused the most closely on educational dialogues (Durán and Szymanski 1995; Forman 1992; Gee and Green 1998; Hicks 1995; Palincsar 1998; Wells and Chang-Wells 1992). Much of this research has combined Piaget's emphasis on cognitive conflict with Vygotsky's emphasis on social interaction, to develop a view that knowledge is co-constructed in social settings (Kelly, Crawford and Green 2001; Musatti 1993; Tudge and Rogoff 1989; Verba 1994), and that meanings are socially constructed through discursive interaction (Wells and Chang-Wells 1992). An emphasis on the processes of group interaction, rather than educational outcomes, has been a defining feature of the socio-cultural tradition.

These three traditions have reached a consensus that dialogue is the mediating mechanism whereby collaboration contributes to learning. This is why education researchers have increasingly studied the discourse processes of collaboration – the turn-by-turn interaction patterns that occur among students in a group. Recent studies have examined the discourse processes of collaboration in science (van Boxtel, van der Linden and Kanselaar 2000; Finkel 1996; Green and Kelly, 1997; Kelly and Crawford 1997; Kelly, Crawford and Green 2001; mathematics (Cobb 1995; Cobb, Gravemeijer,Yackel, McClain and Whitenack 1997; Saxe and Bermudez 1996; Sfard and Kieran 2001; Sfard and McClain 2002) and literacy education (Nystrand, Gamoran, Kachur and Prendergast 1997).

In this chapter, we draw on a theoretical framework that emphasizes processes of *emergence* in educational dialogues. Emergence is a concept that has been explored most deeply in the study of complex systems, and only recently applied to dialogue (see Sawyer 2003b, 2005). Emergence refers to a process whereby system-level patterns and regularities result from complex interactions among system components. Emergence is generally said to occur when the system-level patterns could not have been predicted given a full and complete knowledge of the system's components and their relations. Thus, emergence results in something new that was not present in the components themselves; these new higher-level patterns are said to *emerge* from interaction among the system's components, and are called *emergent phenomena*. In simple systems, higher-level phenomena are relatively predictable given the configuration of the system's components, and the best way to explain the higher-level phenomena is to reduce it to explanation of the components and their interactions. In complex systems, in contrast, emergent phenomena are difficult to reductively explain.

The central claim of constructivism – that learning occurs when learners construct their own understandings – implies that this new knowledge emerges from the learner's active engagement with objects and others. This concept of cognitive emergence was central to Piaget's theory of how schemas emerge in development (Sawyer 2003a). Several educational researchers, working broadly within a constructivist framework, have noted that collaborative discourse results in the emergence of new insights and representations (Cobb *et al.* 1997; Sawyer 2003b; Saxe 2002; Saxe and Bermudez 1996). For example, Scardamalia and Bereiter (2006) describe such educational dialogues as 'knowledge building' to emphasize that new knowledge is created by dialogue between learners and teachers. In emergent, knowledge-building dialogues, the process and outcome cannot be known in advance. These dialogues are therefore fundamentally improvisational (Sawyer 2003b). Emergent dialogues demonstrate the following four characteristics:

1 The activity has an unpredictable outcome, rather than a scripted, known endpoint.
2 There is moment-to-moment contingency: each person's action depends on the one just before.
3 The interactional effect of any given action can be changed by the subsequent actions of other participants.
4 The process is collaborative, with each participant contributing equally.

These processes of emergence are discursive, distributed processes. Our approach in this chapter is thus influenced by researchers who study distributed cognition; we argue that knowledge and intelligence reside not only in people's heads, but are distributed across situated social practices that involve multiple participants in complex social systems. In the distributed cognition perspective, mind is considered to be 'social, cultural, and embedded in the world' (Gee 2000: 195). Likewise, our focus is on discourse and communication as externally visible group knowledge (cf. Middleton and Edwards 1990; Sfard 2002). In order to reveal the mechanisms by which educational dialogues contribute to learning, we use the methods of *interaction analysis* (Sawyer 2006a) to closely analyse the processual, turn-by-turn dynamics of collaborative dialogue.

Teaching the big ideas of computer science

One of the central emphases of learning sciences research is how to design learning environments that result in deeper conceptual understanding (Sawyer 2006b). Traditional 'instructionist' classrooms tend to emphasize lower-level forms of learning, such as memorizing facts and procedures (cf. Bloom 1956). This study originated when the second author, a computer science professor, observed a similar contrast in the teaching of beginning computer programming. Students in introductory programming courses often spend almost all of their time learning the detailed text syntax of one specific programming language, or other mechanics of that language. Consequently, they rarely master the deep, fundamental concepts that underlie computer systems.

This may not be a problem for computer science majors, who go on to take additional courses and eventually acquire a deeper conceptual understanding. But it is a problem for non-computer science majors, because the details of syntax are only marginally related to the concepts we want them to learn. It is not important for non-majors to learn any one particular programming language; rather, it would be more useful for them to learn via a *concepts first* curriculum in which virtually all class time could be devoted to discussions about algorithms and software design in terms of high-level abstractions. The desired learning outcome would be a deeper understanding of the core concepts involved in computer application and development. This would provide non-majors with an understanding that would help them in many spheres of life – a better understanding of the computer systems they interact with every day, a better appreciation of the potential of computer technology for solving problems in new ways, and a better foundation for interacting with computing professionals to help bring about change.

Object-oriented programming (OOP) is the dominant software development paradigm in use today; the core concepts underlying today's software applications are object-oriented concepts. Object-oriented approaches are particularly popular for developing web-based applications. Consequently, the goal of the college course we analyse in this chapter was for students to master the core concepts of OOP.

A brief discussion of object-oriented concepts will be helpful in understanding the dialogues we analyse below. In object-oriented languages, programmers begin by breaking down the overall task into progressively smaller modules called *objects*. An object is a computational unit; it contains data and procedures that can be executed using this data. Objects are grouped into categories called 'classes'. Classes are roughly comparable to concepts, and are hierarchically nested, just as concepts are. For example, the concept ANIMAL has subordinate concepts DOG and CAT. A computer application's classes are organized into a *class hierarchy*.

A common assignment given to introductory programming students is to create classes that represent the accounts at a bank. ACCOUNT is the most general class; it contains more specific types of accounts, called *subclasses*, such as CHECKING ACCOUNT and SAVINGS ACCOUNT. The ACCOUNT class has procedures attached to it that accomplish common tasks, like *deposit* and *withdraw*. In object-oriented languages, these procedures are referred to as *methods*. In the class hierarchy, all descendant classes *inherit* the methods of the parent class. This saves the programmer work, because the instructions to deposit and withdraw only need to be specified one time. For example, if the program asks an instance of the CHECKING ACCOUNT or the SAVINGS ACCOUNT class to deposit or withdraw funds, the method that was defined for the parent class ACCOUNT will be used, unless a more specific method is defined in the subclass, as described in the following paragraph.

Suppose we want to create a new kind of class, IRA (INDIVIDUAL RETIREMENT ACCOUNT), which must handle depositing and withdrawing in a special way, different from other bank accounts. In an object-oriented language, the way this is done is to *extend* the ACCOUNT class to create a more specialized subclass, called IRA, in the class hierarchy. And for this subclass, the programmer *overrides* the deposit and withdraw methods by writing IRA-specific methods that work differently. Because of this design, an object of type ACCOUNT could behave differently when asked to 'deposit' or 'withdraw', depending on which subclass the object was. This feature is referred to as *polymorphism*. Polymorphism is desirable because it allows the rest of the bank's computer programs to ignore which type of account they are interacting with; the accounts themselves are responsible for handling a given request (to deposit funds, for example) in an appropriate manner. The knowledge about, and responsibility for, handling an object appropriately is *encapsulated* in the object.

This example briefly introduces some of the most important big ideas of object-oriented programming: objects, encapsulation, class hierarchies, extending classes into subclasses, inheritance of methods, overriding and polymorphism. Nothing in the above summary is specific to a particular programming language, and nothing depends on learning the details of any one programming language.

Our goal was to create a learning environment that was targeted at supporting students in learning and working with these big ideas, rather than focusing on the detailed syntax of a specific programming language. Toward this end, Goldman (2004) created JPie, a *visual language* that allows software to be constructed by direct manipulation of graphic objects on the screen – for example, dragging an icon from one window to another. In text-based programming, programmers work with files of characters. Inexperienced programmers often become distracted by the textual syntax used to describe these abstractions. When a program fails to work properly, it is often due to a mistyped colon or semicolon, or some comparable textual error, and these errors can be difficult to diagnose or 'debug'. And the process of diagnosing such textual errors does not result in any deeper conceptual understanding of how to program. Visual programming, on the other hand, provides on-screen icons that represent computational abstractions, like classes and methods, that the programmer can manipulate to build an application. And it is impossible for the programmer to make simple errors like misplacing a parenthesis or semicolon. The primary motivation for creating JPie was to elevate the level of discourse in program construction so that the abstractions themselves become the manipulated units, rather than the lines of program code that describe them. Elevating the unit of discourse allows the learner to think and work directly in terms of abstractions, and frees the learner from the process of translating those abstractions into a textual code that describes them. If the programmer makes an error, it will be an error involving the level of abstraction, and working through this sort of error is likely to result in deeper understanding of important concepts and abstractions.

Collaborative programming

As computers began to be introduced into K-12 classrooms in the 1980s, observational studies revealed that most classroom computer use involved pairs or groups of students (Cummings 1985; Jackson, Fletcher and Messer 1986). Several studies have suggested that children perform better, and learn better, when working together at a computer compared to working alone (Blaye, Light, Joiner and Sheldon 1991). Barbieri and Light's 'King and Crown' study (1992) found that with 11-year-olds, verbal measures of the amount of knowledge co-construction related to successful problem solving and to individual learning outcomes. In a follow-up study with college students, Blaye and Light (1995) found that pairs accomplished substantially more than solitary programmers. A later study with a 'Honeybears' task, incorporating pre-test and post-test performance measures, did not find a post-test learning benefit for students who solved adventure game problems in pairs, compared with students who played the game alone – even though the pairs accomplished more, especially pairs that had similar pre-test scores (Light and Littleton 1999).

Outside of educational contexts, there have been several studies that suggest pair programming is superior to solitary programming. In professional software development, it has become increasingly common for two programmers to work together at the same computer (although occasionally each programmer has his or her own workstation and they work side by side). One person types and uses the mouse, while the other person actively observes, looks for technical and strategic defects, refers to printed documentation, writes down implications for other later tasks, and thinks of alternatives. The person doing the typing and focusing on the details of the coding is known as the *driver* and the person who is guiding is known as the *navigator*. The partners switch roles periodically, typically every 30 minutes.

The first study of pair programming showed that it reduced development time and increased software quality (Constantine 1995), and this finding has been replicated (Coplien 1995; Nosek 1998). Pairs finish the task 40 per cent to 50 per cent faster, and with substantially fewer errors. Even though pairs finish faster, they are slightly less productive because two individuals were working at the same time; even so, the reduction is rather small – on the order of 15 per cent – and in exchange, the benefit is that the programs generated by pairs have fewer errors, thus saving the cost associated with later testing and debugging (Williams, Kessler, Cunningham and Jeffries 2000). Other benefits are that pair programmers report much higher job satisfaction and greater confidence in their solutions, and often generate more readable programs, which are easier to modify in future revisions.

We have found only one study of a pair of programmers that transcribed and analysed the dialogue between the two programmers (Flor and Hutchins 1991). That study analysed a pair of experienced programmers who were adding new functionality to an existing software package. They each worked at their own computer workstation, side by side. Most characteristics of their conversation reflected their high level of expertise; for example, Flor and Hutchins (1991) reported that the most prominent aspect of their dialogue was how to re-use existing software components, and to modify them to satisfy the new requirements as quickly as possible. Because they shared knowledge about this existing software, and they shared clear goals about the outcome of the task, their communication was extremely efficient (1991: 54).

The research cited above on the general benefits of collaborative learning and educational dialogues suggest that collaborative programming might be an effective learning technique. The research on pair programming provides additional reason to believe that pair programming in a learning setting would result in more effective outcomes: for example, because pairs finish each programming task faster, student learning pairs could potentially end up covering more material during the semester than they would working alone, if the curriculum were structured to allow pairs who finish faster to go beyond the basic lab.

The course

The course, Computer Science 123 (CS 123), was centred on 14 participatory activities, the execution of which would result in the mastery of the core concepts of OOP. Nine of these activities involved collaborative programming:

- *Clock*. Students create a computer program that displays the date and time on the screen. *Big ideas*: the difference between a model and a view; the difference between a class and an instance; how to create and call methods; how to create new instances of a class.
- *Fractions*. Students create an educational program that helps middle school students understand fractions. The user of the program inputs a numerator and a

denominator, and then a pie chart is displayed on the screen visually representing the fraction. *Big ideas*: working with mathematical expressions and algorithm design; learning about sequential and conditional execution.

- *Animated Characters.* Students create a simple videogame with multiple animated characters, and implement some simple rules about how the characters interact (for example, changing direction if they bump into each other). *Big ideas*: polymorphism; inheritance; method overriding.

- *Pong.* Students design the classic simple videogame, with a paddle at the bottom of the screen that bounces a ball off of the top of the screen. *Big ideas*: multiple threads and concurrent computation.

- *Dining Philosophers.* A classic programming task to help students understand resource sharing. Five philosophers sit at a table eating. There is one chopstick between each pair of philosophers (a total of five chopsticks). To eat, a philosopher must pick up two chopsticks; thus, no two neighbouring philosophers can eat simultaneously. Students have to think of a technique that will prevent any one philosopher from starving. *Big ideas*: understand resource sharing in concurrent threads; understand how to use locking to control potential conflicts; and understand how *deadlock* can occur in a system.

- *Color Gradient and 15 Puzzle.* Students create an electronic version of the class puzzle with 15 tiles in a 4×4 grid, with the tiles numbers 1 through 15. Students then colour each of the 15 tiles with a gradient, so that the colour continuously changes from the left to the right side of the tile. *Big ideas*: algorithm design; iteration and loops; understanding multiple co-ordinate systems on a graphics display.

- *Persian Recursion.* Students create a program that designs a complex symmetric multi-coloured image that resembles a Persian rug (Burns 1997). *Big ideas*: how recursion can be used to solve problems by reducing them into smaller instances of the same problem.

- *Dictionary.* Students develop a computer-based dictionary that will allow users to enter a word and its definition, and to later look up those definitions. *Big ideas*: using data structures to store information.

- *Internet Chat.* Students develop a simple version of online chat. By the end of the lab, different pairs of students are able to talk to each other using the lab's computer network. *Big ideas*: distributed computing, where processes on different computers can talk to each other, specifically by sending messages over a reliable stream.

The visual nature of JPie makes it possible for non-majors to complete this broad range of fairly advanced tasks in one semester. These activities are more advanced than the typical computer science majors attain in their first semester course; many of these concepts are not addressed in the computer science major until the second semester.

Research setting

We videotaped classes during the Spring 2005 semester of CS 123, 'Introduction to Computer Science Concepts', a class with no prerequisites offered by the Department of Computer Science but open to all students at the university. Class met twice each week, for 1 ½ hours each time. All students granted informed consent and agreed to participate in the research project. There were eight students in the class, resulting in four pairs:

M = Mitch	D = Dorothy
C = Carrie	R = Rich
S = Sam	K = Katie
J = Jon	S = Stefan

The students remained in the same pairs over the course of the semester. During each class, the professor and two graduate teaching assistants were available to respond to students' queries. Classes began with brief comments by the professor about assignments due or homework being returned.

Of the 26 classes, we videotaped every other class, resulting in 13 sessions for analysis. Prior to each class, one pair was chosen at random to be videotaped. A directional microphone was placed on a tabletop microphone stand approximately 18 inches in height, immediately next to the computer monitor, and roughly level with the two students' heads. This resulted in good audio quality with very little background noise from the rest of the class. A digital video camera was placed on a tripod a few feet behind the students, so that both of the students, the computer screen, and the keyboard, mouse, and lab notes were all within the camera frame.

All videotape data was downloaded to a desktop computer and stored on a remote hard drive optimized for digital video storage. Dialogue was transcribed directly from the video files, using Transana, a software package designed to support transcription and analysis of digital video data (http://www.transana.org).

Results

Pair dynamics

Some of the dialogue we observed corresponded to the types of dialogue reported to be found in professional programming pairs – the navigator observed technical and strategic defects, noting connections with what had been done before or what was to come, and had the responsibility of reading the written lab instructions.

Excerpt 1

J (Jon) and S (Stefan) doing the Pong lab, 21-3-05. Lines 7–16. S has the mouse and the keyboard.

7 J: Wait, go back to behaviours for a sec
8   We changed the until, right?
9   Until

10 Go back to ballmotion.
11 What is that?
12 That's the problem.
13 (pause)
14 S: Yeah
15 J: Until the score is …
16 something.

Excerpt 2

28-2-05. Pong lab. Lines 58–68. S (Sam) is the navigator and K (Katie) is the driver.

58 S: Okay. So now,
59 Type in,
60 (K starts to type)
61 four ninety
62 (K types)
63 S: Okay (reads, mouses)
64 (K reading, S mouses, coordinating with no talking, because they are both reading the lab)
65 S: What should we name it?
66 K: Um, score?
67 S: Sure. (K types it)
68 (S mousing, not much talk)

Excerpt 3

28-2-05, later. Lines 84–7. S (Sam) is doing most of the work; K (Katie) is observing and checking that work.

84 K: Wait, you skipped something.
85 S: What'd I skip?
86 K: We need to make a property connection from score to text
87 (Silence as S does it)

However, in the majority of the dialogue, our pairs exhibited a new pattern not observed in professional programming pairs: one person typed at the keyboard while the other person manipulated the mouse. The person manipulating the mouse had substantially greater control over the work than the person typing at the keyboard, due to the visual, graphic nature of the JPie interface. Unlike traditional computer programming, the JPie user only rarely has to type at the keyboard. Essentially the only opportunity to type at the keyboard is to enter the name for an object that has just been created with cursor manipulations. As a result, the person manipulating the mouse had greater control over JPie than the person typing at the keyboard. So in most cases, the 'driver' role was associated with the person holding the mouse.

Excerpt 4

D (Dorothy) and M (Mitch), Animated Characters lab. 16-2-05. Lines 34–45. M is sitting on the right, holding the mouse; D is sitting on the left, typing at the keyboard. M is reading a step in the lab instructions, which reads 'Declare a method called "initialize". In its method body, call the inherited method "setImage"'. Italics indicate the words are being read from the lab.

34 M: *declare the method.*
35 So this needs to be called, initialize now.
36 (pause)
37 D: (types) Is that right?
38 M: Yeah.
39 D: Wow.
40 M: *In the method body, call the inherited method set image, and provide as a parameter*
41 D: (points at screen looking, as M scrolls through the methods with the mouse, searching for it)
42 Ohp
43 M: This thing's really,
44 (he drags the method)
45 *provide as a parameter the string*

In line 2, M, as the driver, instructs D to type the word 'initialize' as the name of the method. In line 4, D types the word and M looks at the screen to confirm that she has typed it correctly. But note that in line 8, M uses the mouse to scroll through the method list in search of the method 'setImage' and then he uses the mouse to drag the method into the proper window on the screen.

With one student in control of the mouse and the other in control of the keyboard, the driver role could be somewhat fluid, with the keyboard student occasionally 'driving' the mouse student as well as vice-versa. Note how fluid the driver role alternates in Exerpt 5.

Excerpt 5

2-2-05. R (Rich) and C (Carrie) are working on the Fractions lab. Lines 148–59. C is at the keyboard and R holds the mouse.

148 C: OK.
149 Then click there.
150 (he is dragging icons)
151 (silence)
152 C: Oh we forgot to add (points), [] (eye glance)
153 You have to do [min]
154 R Now, what we wanna do,
155 is we wanna set

156 we wanna set whole part, to that, plus sign
157 (R does a few mouse movements, then motions for C to type at the keyboard.)
158 C: (As she reaches to type the '+' sign on the number pad) It's on your side
159 R: So [] use that little guy (pointing to the regular keyboard). That guy [is fine]

C 'drives' R at line 2, and then R drives C at line 10. The fluidity of the driver role in this pair is evident when C jokingly protests (in line 158) that although she has been the typist, the number pad (at the right side of the keyboard) is closer to R (because the mouse is just to the right side of the keyboard). The students constantly negotiate their participation roles, and they share elements of the driver and navigator roles in creative, emergent ways. This results in a more improvisational style of interaction than if rigid roles had been assigned and enforced, increasing the likelihood of collaborative emergence in these pairs.

Scaffolding constructivist learning

The JPie design team had frequent discussions about the best way to structure the labs. The labs were quite detailed, providing step-by-step instructions about exactly what was the next required activity. This type of lab is common in computer science classrooms, especially in courses for non-majors. When a new concept or technique is first being introduced, fairly detailed step-by-step instructions are provided. In later labs, concepts and techniques that have already been covered are no longer specified in detail – an example of the 'fading' of support that is associated with effective scaffolding. The first six steps from the Animated Characters lab, reproduced below, demonstrate the balance of scaffolding and fading. For example, in step 3, students were expected to know how to declare a method, call a method, and pass a parameter. In a later lab, they might not be told this at all, but just be told at a high level what needed to be done to initialize the object. In contrast, step 5, which introduces the idea of a constructor for the first time, gives 'click by click' instructions.

1 Open JPie and select the Sprite class in the 'sprites' package. Then choose 'extend Sprite' from the File menu and create a subclass called 'MovingSprite', also within the 'sprites' package.
2 Look at the methods summary to see all of the inherited methods.
3 Declare a method called 'initialize'. In its method body, call the inherited method 'setImage' and provide as a parameter the string h:/myclasses/sprites/planet. gif.
4 Also within the initialize method, call the inherited method 'setName' and pass in a desired name for this sprite, such as 'planet'.
5 Click on the 'Constructor' tab in JPie, and open the provided constructor. A **constructor** is like an ordinary method, except that it is only called once on each instance, when that instance is created. In the body of the constructor, call your initialize method so that the image will be set when the MovingSprite as created.
6 Create an instance of MovingSprite. A new window should pop up and your sprite should show up on it. If you put the cursor over the sprite, its class and name

should pop. Since all of your sprites will show up in the same window, this popup text will help you identify them.

After completing these six steps, the JPie screen will display the sprite image that is in the file 'planet.gif' (as specified in step 3). The sprite does not yet move; subsequent steps in the lab instruct the students how to program the sprite so that it moves around the screen.

The labs were designed to scaffold the learning pairs; occasionally, click-by-click instructions were necessary because there was a large gap between the students' pre-existing knowledge and the desired end state. Although the labs provided detailed steps of action, they did not specify every mouse movement and every keyboard command. Through the course of the semester, the labs provided progressively less detail about how to accomplish the task described in a lab step, resulting in the 'fading' (Collins 2006) associated with effective scaffolding.

Although the labs are relatively structured, we believe that they represent an appropriate level of scaffolding to aid learners in developing a deeper conceptual understanding of computer programming. For example, we observed that the students had substantial difficulty understanding the logic behind each step in the labs, and they often had difficulty executing the lab's instructions. Recall step 3 from the above example: 'Declare a method called "initialize". In its method body, call the inherited method "setImage" and provide as a parameter the string h:/myclasses/sprites/planet.gif.' In Excerpt 6 below, two students become confused about whether the string specifying the gif file is supposed to be a parameter for the 'setImage' method, or the 'initialize' method. D has attempted to type in the file name as the parameter for 'initialize', and when that did not work, she called over a teaching assistant.

Excerpt 6

16-2-05. Animated Characters lab. Lines 87–103. D (Dorothy) and M (Mitch) have reached an impasse; JPie is not letting them enter the filename as the parameter to 'initialize,' so they call over a teaching assistant (TA).

87 TA: [] call the inherited method setimage
88 So did you call setimage?
89 M: Yeah
90 TA: OK, then you can put the string in there
91 M: We can pass that back in there
92 TA: Well why do you even need the parameter?
93 M: Cause it says make it a parameter.
94 TA: Not to initialize.
95 It's the parameter to set image, not to initialize.
96 M: So maybe
97 TA: Oh, I see what you're doing.
98 (gets up to point)
99 Yeah, this is a parameter of your new method, initialize.
100 So if someone else is gonna call initialize they would pass that, that value (pointing), right?

101 M: Right, so we just need it [ ]

102 TA: What we're talking about here is, the parameter that you pass TO set image, when you're calling set image. Does that make sense?

103 The new method you're creating doesn't need to have a parameter. Because you're just going to call it with no, parameters.

The teaching assistant realizes at line 97 that the students have incorrectly tried to pass the string parameter to the 'initialize' method, when the 'initialize' method does not take any parameters. The students make this mistake even though the lab instruction is unambiguous in specifying that the parameter should be passed to 'setImage'. The fact that students frequently had difficulties of this type suggests that the labs were not providing so much detail as to prevent constructivist learning from occurring.

Thinking out loud

Perhaps the most significant difference between learning alone versus collaborative learning is that collaboration forces each learner to vocalize their own unfolding understandings. Externalizing developing understandings contributes to learning (Sawyer 2006b), and we frequently observed students voicing thoughts at various stages of formulation – explaining an unfolding thought to their partner, suggesting a path of action, or inquiring about something not fully understood.

This pattern varied with the driver or the navigator. The navigator – the person reading from the lab and occasionally typing at the keyboard – was much more likely to voice developing conceptual understanding than the driver (who was usually the person manipulating the mouse). Some drivers did voice aloud while they were typing and/or manipulating the mouse, but others worked silently, not keeping the navigators apprised of what they were doing. We hypothesize that learning would be least effective in those pairs where thinking out loud did not occur.

Excerpt 7 presents the trajectory of M and D working on the Colour Gradient lab. They are attempting to design an algorithm to program a two-dimensional colour gradient in a square on the screen that is 40 pixels by 40 pixels. The key concept is that two loops must be nested; one loop iterates through the x-dimension pixels, and the other iterates through the y-dimension pixels. The colour of the pixel changes based on the x and y values of the pixel, so inside both loops, two local variables – one for the x value of the pixel and the other for the y value – must be used to set the pixel's colour. M is at the keyboard; D has the mouse and thus is playing more of the driver role. Here is the first discussion (lines 144–51):

Excerpt 7

28-3-05. Colour Gradient lab. Lines 144–151. M (Mitch) and D (Dorothy).

144 D No, no.

145 It starts at zero and goes to 39.

146 Cause its forty pixels across and the first one is zero.

147 M Right.

148 So its zero to thirty nine.
149 So its while y is less than, what, less than or equal to thirty= less than forty (writing on his notepad)
150 Then it's gonna do the
151 Then it'll do all the x

M then recalls the instructor's comments about this lab (159–61):

159 M =cause this is what I remember him talking about,
160 this is what he was talking about last class,
161 like it's gonna start at zero, so you're gonna go, y is gonna be zero, and it's gonna go through and fill in every x (motioning in air with his hands) at y equals zero=

And then (169–72):

169 M =so that's what I'm saying is,
170 do you get what I'm saying? With,
171 we do something where it holds y at zero and then does all the, like fill in all the x's, and then we go increment y, up one? So,
172 D I should have paid attention in my web development class, cause we did this?

M seems to understand more than D, but he doesn't understand fully yet:

193 M Cause here's what I'm wondering. For each one, x is gonna go, when y is zero x is gonna go all the way from zero to 39, so how do we reset it back to zero for the next when y equals one. Cause we wanna start at zero again.

The dialogue context requires M to explain to D why he thinks she is wrong; he is able to do this, even though his understanding is incomplete. Although M's conceptual understanding is more developed than D's, D nonetheless has a partial understanding, and is occasionally able to challenge M's misconceptions. The dialogue context thus provides an opportunity for both D and M to develop their understandings.

The team then realizes that the key is to use a local variable inside the loops (201–7):

201 M I wonder if that'll
202 I wonder if it being a local variable
203 Like it you do, once you get out of the small loop with the x, if once y jumps up again and you go back into it, does it, cause it's a local does it start back
204 D I think so, yeah because it changes the one
205 M I think, yeah.
206 D So then it'll go through all of them with a one. (motioning vertically)
207 And then it'll go through all of them with a two, (another vertical motion), and then it'll go through all of them with a three (another motion)

But D still doesn't understand that the two loops must be nested, and M tries to explain (346–50):

346 M Cause we need two, we're gonna have two,
347   we're not just gonna have one. (pointing at lab)
348   We're gonna have one for i,
349   one for x,
350   and one for y.

D becomes frustrated and M takes over the mouse and becomes the driver. When he nests the two loops (421–2):

421 D Why'd you put another while?
422 M Relax.

Then while watching and listening, D figures it out (481–2):

481 D Okay.
482   I see what you're doing.

By line 482, both M and D have constructed a preliminary understanding of the concept of nested loops. The above extended dialogue demonstrates how their collaborative dialogue contributed to the emergence of this understanding.

The preliminary understanding at line 482 is correct, but is incomplete. Later, in discussion with the TA, the pair learns that there are two ways to do a loop: one with the WHILE command, and one with the FOR command. The pair has been using WHILE, but the FOR command is preferable because it increments the local variable automatically (697–703).

697 TA Yeah, you could do it with a while loop.
698   But it's gonna be easier with for, which is (points)
699 D   Should it be in the same method as this, also?
700 TA Cause then you don't have to increment it yourself.
701 D   So like for x, zero to forty (pointing)
702 M   See I was just gonna do it with while and then type in y plus 1 or x plus 1. It's the same right?
703 TA Yeah, it's the same.

Lines 697 through 703 demonstrate that the students have developed a rich conceptual understanding of nested loops – because they are able to immediately transfer that understanding and extend it to quickly grasp the variation that the TA has suggested. Collaborative dialogue, guided by the scaffolding of the lab and the JPie interface, enabled the students to construct a much deeper understanding than if they had simply memorized information from a textbook, or followed step-by-step instructions.

Learning through external representations

In JPie, program entities are represented on the screen visually. Relationships between entities are also represented visually – for example, a loop that is nested inside another loop actually appears *inside* the outer loop object on the screen. If a variable is assigned to a value, this is represented with an arrow from the value icon to the variable icon.

The visual representation of JPie supports a natural aspect of collaborative learning – learning through external representations. A wide range of research has demonstrated that external representations – such as graphs, figures, maps, and text, either on paper or on a computer screen – can enhance the educational benefits of collaborative conversation (Cobb 1995, 2002; Crawford, Sandoval, Bienkowski and Hurst 2002; Kelly and Crawford 1997; Kelly, Crawford and Green 2001; Lehrer and Schauble 2000; Michalchik, Schank, Rosenquist, Kreikmeier and Kozma 2002; Saxe 2002; Saxe and Bermudez 1996; Sfard and McClain 2002; Suthers and Hundhausen 2002). This line of educational research draws on a recent tradition of studying collaboration in the workplace, particularly in groups whose interaction is mediated by technological artefacts like oscilloscopes, radar screens, or computer displays (Engeström and Middleton 1996; Hutchins 1997), and on studies of scientific laboratory practice, where external representations such as whiteboard scribbles or lab notebooks have a strong impact on discourse (Lynch and Woolgar 1990; Ochs, Gonzales and Jacoby 1996).

Pairs frequently gesture at the screen, identifying the referents of their talk while they talk. This can be done with textual programming as well, but would be much more difficult, because in text programs, complex relationships are often represented by very short pieces of text, and thus more difficult to point at accurately.

Excerpt 8

21-3-05. Lines 49–66. S (Stefan) and J (Jon) are doing the Pong lab. They have reached the point where they can play an early version of their game. S has the mouse and the keyboard and is playing the game. J is observing and offering advice. The game score is supposed to start at 10, and decrement by one each time the player fails to hit the ball. The player loses when the score drops to zero.

49 J: No, you don't have to do that,
50 just go to instances (points to the 'instances' tab on the screen)
51 (S plays)
52 OH, wait a second.
53 Go back to,
54 I just thought of something weird.
55 Go back to instances. (points again)
56 S: Okay. (S clicks on instances tab to bring up instances window)
57 J: (pointing to the 'score' window) the score right now is negative four.
58 We need it to reset to ten.
59 (S works)
60 Yeah.
61 Okay, that's what happened.

62 We, we need the score to automatically reset to ten.
63 Here,
64 Go back to behaviours (points at the 'behaviors' tab)
65 S: (S adds an instruction to reset) Let's see what happens
66 (S plays)

J is able to reinforce his verbal suggestions by using the conceptual space represented on the JPie screen. Significant programming objects and concepts, such as 'Instances' and 'Behaviors', each have their own display windows on the screen. J realizes that there is a problem with the score for the game; he notices that it is not resetting to ten at the beginning of a new game. To demonstrate this to S, J instructs S to look at the score's value, by clicking on the tab that brings up the Instance window (lines 50 and 55). When S does that (line 56), it is then apparent that the score has not been reset, because it has decremented below zero. At line 64, J points to the 'Behaviors' window to suggest to S that the behaviour needs to automatically reset the score when a new game starts.

Excerpt 9

31-1-05. Lines 18–23. D (Dorothy) and M (Mitch) are doing the Clock lab. D has the mouse and M has the keyboard.

18 D: I tried dragging
19 M: Try that [pointing]
20 M: Try dragging that [pointing] into there [pointing].
21 D: Oh that's a variable. Oh, yeah, we should be able to do that.
22 D: [reads from screen] or the method must be=
23 M: =let's try [pointing], go up here, let's delete this [points] and create a new instance.

In JPie, many programming tasks are accomplished by dragging one icon over to another icon. For example, to assign a value to a variable, one clicks on the value and drags it over to the icon representing the variable. To create a method that is called with an argument of a particular type, a variable of that type is dragged over the icon representing the method. In this way, students can communicate about complex computer science concepts simply by gesturing how the objects should be manipulated. This provides an important scaffold, because these same students are not yet capable of communicating these same concepts in the technical language that a computer scientist would. The visual nature of the JPie programming environment allows learners to externally represent their conceptual understanding, and to communicate those understandings with each other, long before they are capable of discussing those same concepts verbally. If the two learners had been programming together using a text-based programming language, the dialogues above would have required the students to have mastered relatively advanced technical terms – to have mastered, essentially, an entire manner of speaking about programming.

There are many ways that the visual interface scaffolds effective learning conversations.

As seen in Excerpt 8, the visual interface groups similar concepts together visually; instances are together, behaviours are together. As students work in JPie, the conceptual structure of OOP is implicitly reinforced, long before students are able to verbally discuss that conceptual structure.

Conclusion

In this chapter, we have analysed educational dialogues in a computer science classroom, using a theoretical framework (collaborative emergence) and a method (interaction analysis) that have been broadly applied to educational dialogues in a range of content areas. We believe this study is of interest not only to computer science educators, but to scholars of educational dialogues in general, for three reasons.

First, we have demonstrated an example of a more generally desirable transformation: shifting from a type of learning that results in lower-level learning (memorization) to a type of learning that results in deeper conceptual understanding. Learning scientists have emphasized the importance of deeper conceptual understanding, and have argued that traditional or 'instructionist' teaching methods are limited to the transmission of lower-level knowledge (Sawyer 2006b). Educators today are faced with the challenge of teaching deeper conceptual understanding, rather than simply memorization of relatively low-level information. This has proven to be a particular challenge for science, technology, engineering, and mathematics (STEM) educators – because the great majority of students lose interest in such subjects at the early stages of low-level information mastery, and never reach a later stage where they might begin to master deeper concepts.

Students in introductory programming courses often spend most of their time on details of programming language syntax that are only marginally related to the deeper conceptual understanding we want them to acquire. A visual programming interface like JPie allowed us to develop a *concepts first* curriculum; virtually all class time was devoted to discussions about algorithms and software design in terms of high-level programming abstractions that are made tangible by the environment.

These same problems are faced by many technical departments in colleges and universities, and are pressing issues among middle school mathematics and science educators as well. How can instructors effectively communicating deep intellectual content in introductory courses? How can STEM educators recruit a diverse population into the field, and reach out to students in other disciplines who could benefit from a deeper understanding of STEM concepts?

Second, the JPie programming environment provides an example of how visual scaffolds, when designed so as to result in dialogue about core concepts (rather than syntax details), can result in such conversation. We have demonstrated that educational dialogues focus more intensely on core concepts if the scaffolds in the environment facilitate such dialogue. And these dialogues result in exchanges of explanations and justifications that foster learning.

Third, these transcripts demonstrate a more general point: that understanding educational dialogues requires a rather sophisticated understanding of the learning content. These dialogues cannot be understood (nor analysed) without incorporating the core computer science concepts we intend the students to learn. This is why it was necessary for us to introduce the chapter with a brief summary of these concepts, which are likely to be unfamiliar to most readers. But this point is not limited to computer science; any interaction analysis requires deep conceptual understanding of the desired learning outcomes. The majority of such analyses should probably be published in content-targeted outlets, i.e. mathematics education or science education journals.

We hypothesize that a concepts-first curriculum supports a broader range of learning styles than the traditional computer programming course, making it more likely to attract and retain students from under-represented groups, particularly women. By raising the level of abstraction and eliminating the edit-compile-execute cycle, JPie helps students understand the big picture without the distraction of irrelevant syntactic details. And because JPie makes it possible for students to develop relatively sophisticated interactive applications, students achieve early success and build confidence.

Our experience with CS 123 demonstrates that JPie indeed makes it possible to provide non-computer science majors with a basic understanding of how computer applications work. JPie may be accessible enough for even younger students to use: the research team has conducted several workshops to help secondary school teachers learn how to use JPie with their students. Most freshmen entering college know that some knowledge of computer science may be beneficial to them in their career. However, they usually have little or no exposure to computer science, and often have misconceptions about the field, so they may be hesitant to try. Compounding the problem, introductory computer science courses often have a reputation as being extremely difficult. JPie makes the software development process more accessible, and can help make computer science attractive to a wider range of students. Having students use JPie in collaborative teams enhances these benefits.

References

Barbieri, M. S. and Light, P. (1992) 'Interaction, gender and performance on a computer based problem solving task', *Learning and Instruction*, 2:199–214.

Bargh, J. A. and Schul, Y. (1980) 'On the cognitive benefits of teaching', *Journal of Educational Psychology*, 72:593–604.

Bearison, D. J., Magzamen, S. and Filardo, E. K. (1986) 'Socio-cognitive conflict and cognitive growth in young children', *Merrill-Palmer Quarterly*, 32:51–72.

Blaye, A. and Light, P. (1995) 'The influence of peer interaction on planning and information handling strategies', in C. O'Malley (ed.) *Computer Supported Collaborative Learning*, Berlin: Springer.

Blaye, A., Light, P., Joiner, R. and Sheldon, S. (1991) 'Collaboration as a facilitator of planning and problem solving', *British Journal of Developmental Psychology*, 9:471–83.

Bloom, B. S. (1956) *Taxonomy of Educational Objectives, Handbook I: the cognitive domain*, New York: David McKay Co.

Bossert, S. T. (1988–9) 'Cooperative activities in the classroom', *Review of Research in Education*, 15:225–52.

Burns, A. M. (1997) 'Persian recursion', *Mathematics Magazine*, 7:196–9.

Cobb, P. (1995) 'Mathematical learning and small-group interaction: four case studies', in P. Cobb and H. Bauersfeld (eds) *The Emergence of Mathematical Meaning: interaction in classroom cultures*, Hillsdale, NJ: Lawrence Erlbaum.

Cobb, P. (2002) 'Reasoning with tools and inscriptions', *Journal of the Learning Sciences*, 11:187–215.

Cobb, P., Gravemeijer, K., Yackel, E., McClain, K. and Whitenack, J. (1997) 'Mathematizing and symbolizing: the emergence of chains of signification in one first-grade classroom', in D. Kirshner and J. A. Whitson (eds) *Situated Cognition: social, semiotic, and psychological perspectives*, Mahwah, NJ: Lawrence Erlbaum.

Collins, A. (2006) 'Cognitive apprenticeship', in R. K. Sawyer (ed.) *Cambridge Handbook of the Learning Sciences*, New York: Cambridge University Press.

Constantine, L. L. (1995) *Constantine on Peopleware*, Englewood Cliffs, NJ: Yourdon Press.

Coplien, J. O. (1995) 'A development process generative pattern language', in J. O. Coplien and D. C. Schmidt (eds) *Pattern Languages of Program Design*, Reading, MA: Addison-Wesley.

Crawford, V., Sandoval, W. A., Bienkowski, M. and Hurst, K. (2002) 'Understanding how phenomenological and discursive representations mediate collaborative learning', paper presented at the Annual Meeting of the American Educational Research Association, New Orleans, April.

Cummings, R. (1985) 'Small group discussions and the microcomputer', *Journal of Computer Assisted Learning*, 1:149–58.

Doise, W. and Mugny, G. (1984) *The Social Development of the Intellect*, New York: Pergamon Press.

Durán, R. P. and Szymanski, M. H. (1995) 'Cooperative learning interaction and construction of activity', *Discourse Processes*, 19:149–64.

Engeström, Y. and Middleton, D. (eds) (1996) *Cognition and Communication at Work*, New York: Cambridge University Press.

Finkel, E. A. (1996) 'Making sense of genetics: students' knowledge use during problem solving in a high school genetics class', *Journal of Research in Science Teaching*, 33:345–68.

Fisher, E. (1993) Distinctive features of pupil-pupil classroom talk and their relationship to learning: how discursive exploration might be encouraged', *Language and Education*, 7:239–57.

Flor, N. V. and Hutchins, E. W. (1991) 'Analyzing distributed cognition in software teams: a case study of team programming during perfective software maintenance', in J. Koenemann-Belliveau, T. G. Moher and S. P. Robertson (eds) *Empirical Studies of Programmers: Fourth Workshop*, Norwood, NJ: Lawrence Erlbaum.

Forman, E. A. (1992) 'Discourse, intersubjectivity, and the development of peer collaboration: a Vygotskian approach', in L. T. Winegar and J. Valsiner (eds) *Children's Development Within Social Context. Volume 1: metatheory and theory*, Mahwah, NJ: Lawrence Erlbaum.

Forman, E. A. and Cazden, C. B. (1985) 'Exploring Vygotskian perspectives in education: the cognitive value of peer interaction', in J. V. Wertsch (ed.) *Culture, Communication, and Cognition: Vygotskian perspectives*, New York: Cambridge University Press.

Fuchs, L. S., Fuchs, D., Hamlett, C. L., Phillips, N. B., Karns, K. and Dutka, S. (1997) 'Enhancing students' helping behavior during peer-mediated instruction with conceptual mathematical explanations', *The Elementary School Journal*, 97(3): 223–49.

Gee, J. P. (2000) 'Discourse and sociocultural studies in reading', in M. L. Kamil, P. B. Mosenthal, P. D. Pearson, and R. Barr (eds.) *Handbook of Reading Research, Vol. 3* Mahwah, NJ: Erlbaum, pp. 195–207.

Gee, J. P. and Green, J. L. (1998) 'Discourse analysis, learning, and social practice: a methodological study', *Review of Educational Research*, 23:119–69.

Goldman, K. J. (2004) 'An interactive environment for beginning Java programmers', *Science of Computer Programming*, 53:3–24.

Green, J. and Kelly, G. (eds) (1997) *Special Issue of Journal of Classroom Interaction on 'Discourse in Science Classrooms'*, 32, Houston, TX: University of Houston.

Hicks, D. (1995) 'Discourse, learning, and teaching', *Review of Research in Education*, 21:49–95.

Hutchins, E. (1997) 'Mediation and automatization', in M. Cole, Y. Engeström and O. Vasquez (eds) *Mind, Culture, and Activity: seminal papers from the laboratory of comparative human cognition*, New York: Cambridge University Press.

Jackson, A., Fletcher, B. and Messer, D. (1986) 'A survey of microcomputer use and provision in primary schools', *Journal of Computer Assisted Learning*, 2:45–55.

Johnson, D. W. and Johnson, R. T. (1992) 'Positive interdependence: key to effective cooperation', in R. Hertz-Lazarowitz and N. Miller (eds) *Interaction in Cooperative Groups: the theoretical anatomy of group learning*, New York: Cambridge University Press.

Kelly, G., Crawford, T. and Green, J. (2001) 'Common task and uncommon knowledge: dissenting voices in the discursive construction of physics across small laboratory groups', *Linguistics and Education*, 12:135–74.

Kelly, G. J. and Crawford, T. (1997) 'An ethnographic investigation of the discourse processes of school science', *Science Education*, 81:533–59.

Kumpulainen, K. and Mutanan, M. (2000) 'Mapping the dynamics of peer group interaction: a method of analysis of socially shared learning processes', in H. Cowie and G. van der Aalsvoort (eds) *Social Interaction in Learning and Instruction: the meaning of discourse for the construction of knowledge*, New York: Elsevier Science.

Lehrer, R. and Schauble, L. (2000) 'Modeling in mathematics and science', in R. Glaser (ed.) *Educational Design and Cognitive Science*, Mahwah, NJ: Lawrence Erlbaum.

Light, P. and Littleton, K. (1999) *Social Processes in Children's Learning*, Cambridge: Cambridge University Press.

Lynch, M. and Woolgar, S. (eds) (1990). *Representation in Scientific Practice*, Cambridge, MA: MIT Press.

Mercer, N. (1996) 'The quality of talk in children's collaborative activity in the classroom', *Learning and Instruction*, 6:359–77.

Michalchik, V., Schank, P., Rosenquist, A., Kreikmeier, P. and Kozma, R. (2002) 'Visual representations in the collaborative learning of chemistry', paper presented at the Annual Meeting of the American Educational Research Association, New Orleans, April.

Middleton, D. and Edwards, D. (1990) 'Collective remembering', in D. Middleton and D. Edwards (eds) *Collective Remembering*, Newbury Park, CA: Sage.

Musatti, T. (1993) 'Meaning between peers: the meaning of the peer', *Cognition and Instruction*, 11:241–50.

Nosek, J. T. (1998) 'The case for collaborative programming', *Communications of the ACM*, 41:105–8.

Nystrand, M., Gamoran, A., Kachur, R. and Prendergast, C. (1997) *Opening Dialogue: understanding the dynamics of language and learning in the English classroom*, New York: Teachers College Press.

Ochs, E., Gonzales, P. and Jacoby, S. (1996) '"When I come down I'm in the domain state': grammar and graphic representation in the interpretive activity of physicists', in E. Ochs, E. A. Schegloff and S. A. Thompson (eds) *Interaction and Grammar*, New York: Cambridge University Press.

Palincsar, A. S. (1998) 'Social constructivist perspectives on teaching and learning', in J. T. Spence, J. M. Darley and D. J. Foss (eds) *Annual Review of Psychology*, 49, Palo Alto, CA: Annual Reviews, pp. 345–75.

Perret-Clermont, A.-N. (1980) *Social Interaction and Cognitive Development in Children*, New York: Academic Press.

Sawyer, R. K. (2003a) 'Emergence in creativity and development', in R. K. Sawyer, V. John-Steiner, S. Moran, R. Sternberg, D. H. Feldman, M. Csikszentmihalyi and J. Nakamura (eds) *Creativity and Development*, New York: Oxford University Press.

Sawyer, R. K. (2003b) *Group Creativity: music, theater, collaboration*, Mahwah, NJ: Lawrence Erlbaum.

Sawyer, R. K. (2005). *Social Emergence: societies as complex systems*, New York: Cambridge University Press.

Sawyer, R. K. (2006a) 'Analyzing collaborative discourse', in R. K. Sawyer (ed.) *Cambridge Handbook of the Learning Sciences*, New York: Cambridge University Press.

Sawyer, R. K. (2006b) 'The new science of learning', in R. K. Sawyer (ed.) *Cambridge Handbook of the Learning Sciences*, New York: Cambridge University Press.

Saxe, G. B. (2002) 'Form and function in children's mathematical representations: a cultural-developmental framework', paper presented at the Annual Meeting of the American Educational Research Association, New Orleans, April.

Saxe, G. B. and Bermudez, T. (1996) 'Emergent mathematical environments in children's games', in L. P. Steffe, P. Nesher, P. Cobb, G. A. Goldin and B. Greer (eds) *Theories of Mathematical Learning*, Mahwah, NJ: Lawrence Erlbaum.

Scardamalia, M. and Bereiter, C. (2006) 'Knowledge building', in R. K. Sawyer (ed.) *Cambridge Handbook of the Learning Sciences*, New York: Cambridge University Press.

Sfard, A. (2002) 'The interplay of intimations and implementations: generating new discourse with new symbolic tools', *Journal of the Learning Sciences*, 11:319–57.

Sfard, A. and Kieran, C. (2001) 'Cognition as communication: rethinking learning-by-talking through multi-faceted analysis of students' mathematical interactions', *Mind, Culture, and Activity*, 8:42–76.

Sfard, A. and McClain, K. (eds) (2002) 'Analyzing tools: perspectives on the role of designed artifacts in mathematics learning', Special issue of *The Journal of the Learning Sciences*, 11.

Slavin, R. E. (1990) *Cooperative Learning: theory, research, and practice*, Boston: Allyn and Bacon.

Slavin, R. E. (1992) 'When and why does cooperative learning increase achievement? theoretical and empirical perspectives', in R. Hertz-Lazarowitz and N. Miller (eds) *Interaction in Cooperative Groups: the theoretical anatomy of group learning*, New York: Cambridge University Press.

Suthers, D. D. and Hundhausen, C. D. (2002) 'Influence of representations on students' elaborations during collaborative learning', paper presented at the Annual Meeting of the American Educational Research Association, New Orleans, April.

Swing, S. R. and Peterson, P. L. (1982) 'The relationship of student ability and small-group interaction to student achievement', *American Educational Research Journal*, 19:259–74.

Tudge, J. and Rogoff, B. (1989) 'Peer influences on cognitive development: Piagetian and Vygotskian perspectives', in M. Bornstein and J. Bruner (eds) *Interaction in Cognitive Development*, Hillsdale, NJ: Lawrence Erlbaum.

van Boxtel, C., van der Linden, J. and Kanselaar, G. (2000) 'Deep processing in a collaborative learning environment', in H. Cowie and G. van der Aalsvoort (eds) *Social Interaction in Learning and Instruction: the meaning of discourse for the construction of knowledge*, New York: Elsevier Science.

Vedder, P. (1985) *Cooperative Learning: a study on processes and effects of cooperation between primary school children*, Groningen, The Netherlands: Rijksuniversiteit Groningen.

Verba, M. (1994) 'The beginnings of collaboration in peer interaction', *Human Development*, 37:125–39.

Vygotsky, L. S. (1978) *Mind in Society* (trans. A. Kozulin), Cambridge, MA: Harvard University Press.

Webb, N. M. (1984) 'Stability of small group interaction and achievement over time', *Journal of Educational Psychology* 76:211–224.

Webb, N. M. (1991) 'Task-related verbal interaction and mathematics learning in small groups', *Journal for Research in Mathematics Education*, 22:366–89.

Webb, N. M. (1992) 'Testing a theoretical model of student interaction and learning in small groups', in R. Hertz-Lazarowitz and N. Miller (eds.) *Interaction in Cooperative Groups: the theoretical anatomy of group learning*, New York: Cambridge University Press, pp. 102–119.

Webb, N. M. (1995) 'Group collaboration in assessment: multiple objectives, processes, and outcomes', *Educational Evaluation and Policy Analysis*, 17:239–61.

Webb, N. M. and Palincsar, A. S. (1996) 'Group processes in the classroom', in D. C. Berliner and R. C. Calfee (eds) *Handbook of Educational Psychology*, New York: Simon and Schuster Macmillan.

Webb, N. M., Ender, P. and Lewis, S. (1986) 'Problem-solving strategies and group processes in small groups learning computer programming', *American Educational Research Journal*, 23:243–61.

Wells, G. and Chang-Wells, G. L. (1992) *Constructing Knowledge Together: classrooms as centers of inquiry and literacy*, Portsmouth, NH: Heinemann.

Williams, L., Kessler, R. R., Cunningham, W. and Jeffries, R. (2000) 'Strengthening the case for pair programming', *IEEE Software*, 17:19–25.

JPie technical overview

This brief appendix illustrates the visual representations of programming abstractions, discusses how those representations are manipulated, and describes user feedback and consistency checking. Additional support for properties and events in user interface construction, streamlined support for periodic threads, exception handling, and debugging are also described briefly.

When the system starts, the programmer is provided with a 'Packages and Classes' window containing 1) a tree representation of all the packages and classes in the Java API, as well as the programmer's own classes and 2) a place for the programmer to create short-cut panels in which to organize frequently used classes into categories. From this window, one can open classes for editing and create new classes that extend other classes or implement interfaces.

Each class is opened in a separate window. For example, Figure 16.1 shows the class window for a 'ShapePanel' class that has been defined to extend Java's 'JPanel' class. The main panel of the class window is organized using tabs for the various aspects of a class. This is designed to manage screen space, improve navigation, and keep the programmer focused. The tabs include 'Data' (instance variables), 'View' (graphical appearance, layout, and property connections), 'Events' (listeners to the view components), 'Constructors', 'Methods' (shown), 'Behaviors' (periodic tasks that run as separate threads), and 'Instances' (a selectable list of instances of this class). Selecting an instance in the instances panel shows the defined view in accordance with the state of that instance. The left side of the window provides convenient lists of the variables and methods of the class (including those that are inherited, in a different colour).

Direct manipulation operates in terms of spatial semantic contexts. For example, the panel associated with each tab provides a spatial semantic context in which items can be declared and manipulated. Dragging a type into the Data pane declares a variable of that type (and automatically defines associated 'get' and 'set' methods), whereas dragging that same type into the Methods pane declares a method with that return type. Similarly, dragging an inherited method into the Methods pane creates a method to override the inherited one.

The *capsule* is the principal visual unit. Capsules are used to represent variable declarations, variable accesses, properties, methods, method calls, constructors, constructor calls, and can also contain constants and expressions. Each capsule has a label (typically used to display a textual identifier), an icon (to indicate the type of the variable or property, or the return type of a method), and a colour (to indicate the scope of declaration). Providing all of this information at a glance saves the programmer from having to remember the parameter type or return type of a method, or if a variable is local or an instance variable. Capsules are used by direct manipulation (selection or drag-and-drop), so the identifiers on capsules have no semantic significance and serve only as documentation. The system maintains consistency of identifiers. For example, if a method is renamed, the labels on all of its method calls are updated accordingly.

Some capsules, such as methods and constructors, can be expanded in order to look inside and define their functionality. Opening a capsule exposes additional spatial semantic contexts. For example, within methods there are separate places in which to declare formal parameters, to declare local variables, to create statements within the method's body, and to provide a return expression if the return type is not void. Thus, with a simple drag-and-drop gesture, one can intuitively declare a variable, complete with its type and scope.

Capsules are chained together to form statements and expressions. The indentation on the left provides a place for attaching the target expression, whereas the bump on the right provides an opportunity for extending the chain. The bump, which also indicates type of the expression at that point in the chain, is intended to serve the functionality of the dot ('.') notation in textual programming. Nested boxes provide an intuitive visual representation of scope and the order of execution. All execution, including assignment, occurs left to right, respecting the indicated nesting. This avoids any possible confusion about order of operations, and provides a convenient way to move statements among scopes. In addition, the capsules for method and constructor calls provide special spatial semantic contexts, called *slots*, in which actual parameters can be specified. A calculator-like interface is provided to build up statements and expressions.

Figure 16.1 illustrates the visual representation of variables, methods and formal parameters, method calls and actual parameters, casting, assignment, and modifiers. Overriding the paint method in this subclass of JPanel was simply accomplished by dragging the inherited method (from the left) into the methods panel. Upon declaration, the method *takes immediate effect*, even for objects that have already been instantiated and whose paint method is called polymorphically. Note that the 'for each' construct is provided to simplify iteration over a collection, but the programmer also could have used an iterator in conjunction with a while loop.

The user interface prevents the formation of syntactically incorrect statements and expressions. For example, a variable can only be dropped into a scope with access to that variable. However, it is necessarily the case that type mismatches and incomplete expressions can be formed along the way to completing a statement. When this occurs, the offending expression is immediately outlined in red, and placing the mouse over the red border provides pop-up text with a description of the error. For example, each slot in a method call knows its expected type and will highlight itself whenever its contained expression's type is not compatible. References to deleted variables and methods are greyed out.

Programmers can create threads in the conventional way, by creating a subclass of the 'Thread' class and calling its start method. In addition, we provide the Behaviors pane to streamline the definition of threads that carry our periodic tasks within objects of the class. For example, instances of an 'animation' class might have a behaviour to

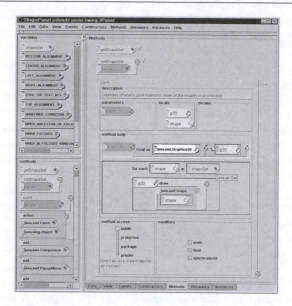

Figure 16.1 The class window for the ShapePanel class.

periodically change the image in the animation. Each behaviour looks like a method with a void return type. However, there are additional contexts in which to specify a rate expression and a termination condition.

Together, the View and Events panes support user interface construction. Within the View pane, one can drop component classes onto a panel and manipulate their sizes and positions. (In addition, there are automatic layout options.) Selecting a component allows the programmer to see the properties of that component and to connect those properties to the properties (instance variables) of the class or to properties of other components in the view. This is done by chaining together capsules representing those properties. In addition, the initial value of a component property can be specified within an expanded view of the property's capsule.

Within the Events pane, components of a view can be selected in order to create event handlers to process user input. Each event handler is a listener method in the Java event model. The programmer demonstrates the user event to listen for (mouse click, mouse entered, etc.) by performing the event on the selected component, and then selecting from a list of recorded events. At that point, the event handler method turns into the appropriate listener method and the programmer can edit the body of the method just as for any other method of the class. The listener is automatically added to the component by the system, so that when the event occurs in the view of any instance of the class it triggers execution of the event handler within that instance.

The system provides a thread-oriented debugger that uses the same visual representation. Programmers can set breakpoints on method calls, constructor calls, and expressions. When a breakpoint is reached within execution of a thread, the debugger window pops up, showing the call stack as a series of tabbed panes. The debugger highlights, within the current stack frame, the expression that is about to execute. The programmer can control the execution speed and watch the execution unfold, or can single-step through the execution expression by expression. In addition to breakpoints, any consistency errors (type mismatches or incomplete expressions) cause the debugger to appear when execution of the offending expression is attempted. The programmer is then given the opportunity to complete or correct the expression and resume execution. Similarly, the debugger supports on-the-fly exception handling; when an exception occurs that is not explicitly caught or thrown by a method, the debugger pops up and provides the programmer with the opportunity to catch (or throw) the exception and resume execution. In addition, the debugger provides support for detecting common logic errors before they become fatal errors. This includes dynamically adjustable stack bounding to detect infinite recursion, dynamically adjustable loop bounding to detect infinite loops, and deadlock detection. In the case of deadlock, a separate window appears with a visualization of the wait-for graph. The programmer can then click on threads involved in the deadlock in order to bring up debugging windows for them, and optionally terminate them to break the deadlock.

Index

Note: references in *italic* indicate a table or a figure

DATE DUE

GAYLORD   PRINTED IN U.S.A.